GEOGRAPHIES FOR ADVANCED STUDY

EDITED BY PROFESSOR S. H. BEAVER, M.A., F.R.G.S.

THE SOVIET UNION

GEOGRAPHIES FOR ADVANCED STUDY

Edited by Professor S. H. Beaver, M.A., F.R.G.S.

THE SOVIET UNION AND ITS NEIGHBOURS

THE
SOVIET UNION
THE LAND AND ITS PEOPLE

GEORGES JORRÉ
Late Professor in the University of Toulouse

WITH AN INTRODUCTION BY
A. PERPILLOU
Professor of Geography at the Sorbonne

TRANSLATED AND REVISED BY
E. D. LABORDE
Sometime Assistant Master in Harrow School

John Wiley & Sons Inc
New York, N.Y.

Published throughout the world except the United States by
Longmans, Green & Co Ltd

Second Edition © Longmans, Green & Co Ltd, 1961
First published 1950
Second Impression 1952
Third Impression by photolithography 1955
Fourth Impression by photolithography 1957
Second Edition 1961
Second Impression 1961
Third Impression 1963

NOTE

The original edition of this work was published by Editions
S.E.F.I., Paris; copyright in the English language in the Berne
Convention countries by Longmans, Green & Co Ltd, London.

Made and Printed in Great Britain by
Butler & Tanner Ltd, Frome and London

TRANSLATOR'S FOREWORD

No apology is needed in offering to the public a book which gives information about the Soviet Union, especially when the author is as highly qualified to write on the subject as was M. Jorré. The present version is, moreover, a second edition rather than a mere translation, for the author has kindly brought the whole book up-to-date, and has added long sections on the considerable areas of Europe which have been added to the Soviet Union as a result of the recent war.

The place-names have been a difficulty. A large number of such names in the Soviet Union have been changed, sometimes twice and even three times, in the past thirty years; and it has been no easy matter to keep pace with the variations. A further complication has arisen from the recent official decision to adopt the American system of transliteration of Russian characters. Official practice has been followed here, but it has been thought best to retain such familiar forms as Tiflis instead of the—to an English tongue—unpronounceable Tbilisi.

It has been considered unnecessary to include the bibliography of the original because the translation into English of French versions of Russian authorities would be unhelpful, and it was thought that in any case the relatively few English-speaking readers who could make use of those authorities would prefer to turn to the original. When once the Russian portion of the bibliography had been omitted, there seemed little point in keeping the rest.

References will be found in the Index to the pages on which an explanation is given of the meanings of Russian geographical terms occurring in the text.

The translator's thanks are due to M. Jorré for his kindness and care in revising the translation and for his unfailing agreeableness and good humour which made our correspondence a pleasure.

E. D. L.

HARROW-ON-THE-HILL

REVISER'S FOREWORD

After years of success this best of all existing descriptions of the Soviet Union had necessarily become out-of-date. It is not always easy to get clear-cut information of Russia. As a rule facts have to be picked up here and there from announcements or reports of ministerial speeches printed in *Pravda*. Appeal to official sources is met with delay and evasion. But in 1957 the Soviet Union issued for the first time a statistical abstract in which many tables gave absolute figures instead of the percentages generally used, and an official English translation of this was published by Lawrence & Wishart of London. This was followed in 1958 by a publication in English entitled *The Soviet Union in Facts and Figures*, which brought a good many of the statistical tables up to 1956. Later figures have been culled from *Pravda*.

Monsieur Jorré's death early in 1957 prevented his undertaking the revision of the book himself, but the aim of the present edition has been to preserve the author's treatment as far as possible and to make all changes and additions in his manner. In Part I there was little to change, except the description of the *merzlota*, which seemed inadequate in the previous editions. As might be expected, Part III with its picture of the Soviet economic system has had to be transformed; and Part IV has also undergone considerable revision owing to the writings of Berg and other Soviet geographers and the general increase in knowledge of the territories of the Soviet Union.

E. D. L.

1960

CONTENTS

Part III

THE ECONOMIC SYSTEM

Part IV

MAIN NATURAL REGIONS OF THE SOVIET UNION

MAPS AND DIAGRAMS

ACKNOWLEDGMENT

Figs. 2, 3, 12, 19, 20, 23, and 28 are based on maps in *Soviet Russia in Maps,* by permission of Messrs. George Philip & Son, Ltd.

PHOTOGRAPHS

*(All photographs not otherwise acknowledged are re-
produced by permission of the Society for Cultural
Relations with the U.S.S.R.)*

INTRODUCTION

The people of this country, whatever their condition or education, have never appreciated better than during the last few years how much and how closely political events and international problems depend on geographical factors. Of course, it would be risky to simplify the facts too much and to believe that geography furnishes the key to strategy and diplomacy, that it alone reveals the secrets of economic competition, territorial deals, and even the ideological sympathies and antipathies among nations. It would be asking too much of the mere study of geographical facts to expect to find in them an explanation of the conduct of human societies in the past or in the future. Man's reactions remain essentially unforeseeable, and, whether a nation adapts itself to geographical circumstances or not, it remains, when all is said and done, the arbiter of its choice and of its fate, be this fortunate or tragic.

But unquestionably, a knowledge of the environment in which a civilisation has grown up, of the latter's evolution and present conditions, of its current needs and aspirations, allows one to reach a better understanding of the part it plays in the modern world, because human actions always touch on some aspect of geography.

This was indeed vaguely suspected by all those who during the course of the six years of war bent over maps of Africa, the Pacific, and eastern Europe one after another—even when these were on a small scale—with the rather trustful feeling that a better acquaintance with geography would permit them to foresee the *dénouement* of the drama. Clearly, it is by a study of the environment and the geographical circumstances that one must seek that basis of sure information, that mass of directly verifiable facts, which enables one to throw light upon, if not explain completely, the great events of the past and of the modern world. If geography renounces its ambition to explain everything, it can at least describe and compare, bring out analogies hidden under the complexity of facts, and make the unknown better known. When all is said and done, is this not in every branch of learning the limit to the processes of the scientific mind, whose characteristic function is not so much to explain as to reach successive provisional approximations?

On approaching the study of the Soviet Union the reader experiences the same feeling of bewilderment as when he undertakes the study of America. It is difficult for him at once to form an exact picture of that vast world. An examination of the map itself distorts perspectives and detracts from the prime geographical fact, the enormous size of the Soviet Union. No doubt it may seem commonplace to stress the gigantic proportions of the Soviet world and yet that is in fact the fundamental characteristic which the geographer should set out in strong relief. The Soviet Union is twice as big as China, huge though the latter is, two and a half times the size of Brazil, nearly three times the size of the United States, and seventy times as big as the British Isles. It marches with Norway and Afghanistan, Romania and Alaska, from which last it is barely separated by the 30-mile-wide Bering Strait. It also marches with Poland and China, and with Persia and the ice-bound Arctic. The great distances between these places on the map of the world is certainly a matter for astonishment.

Let us try to get a more concrete idea of the Soviet Union. We see that from east to west it stretches 6000 miles, or one-fourth of the circumference of the earth. From north to south it covers more than 3700 miles, for in the south it touches lat. 35° N. and in the north it goes beyond lat. 80° N. Its area is greater than that of the whole of North America. Of course, it would scarcely cover more than three-fifths of the British Empire, but the latter, to quote Allix, presents the very image of dispersion, whilst the Soviet Union forms a single continuous territory. With its 8,199,000 square miles the Union was —even within its 1939 frontiers—the largest state in the world and had one-sixth of the dry land beneath its flag. Today its area covers about 8,357,000 square miles.

Do we really realise that when—by the sun, if not by clock time— it is midday in Moscow and very little after 11 a.m. on the Russo-Polish frontier, it is past 7 p.m. in Vladivostok, 8 o'clock in Petropavlovsk, 9 o'clock in the upper Anadyr valley, and 10 p.m. on the shores of Bering Strait? That is, there is a difference of 11 hours between the extreme meridians of the Union, whilst between London and Tokyo the difference is only 9 hours and 20 minutes.

In the immensity of the Soviet Union the natural divisions are on a different scale from that of our little Western Europe. The same scenery monotonously occurs again and again over vast areas. There is none of that juxtaposition of basins of sedimentary rocks, ancient Hercynian blocks, and young mountain ranges, which is characteristic of the west and divides it into separate compartments. Nor is there that marvellous variety of geological outcrops which in an area as restricted as, say, that of France offers an extraordinary diversity of agricultural possibilities and encourages the cultivation of innumerable different crops. In the Soviet Union the lofty mountains are pushed out to the eastern and southern perimeter, so that from the Baltic to the banks of the Yenisey there are vast expanses of low plain or of ancient plateaus of small elevation, between which no high mountain ranges impose any barrier. No high relief divides Russian territory, no noteworthy obstacle cuts off the European from the Asiatic portion of the Union. Almost everywhere one sees the same rocks, the same soils, which afford the same agricultural possibilities —and those only—over vast expanses of country.

The climate introduces another element of uniformity in the already general monotony. A trip to the Soviet Union leaves a disconcerting impression on us Western Europeans, accustomed as we are to a change of climate with a change of place, to pass in a few hours in winter from the sunny shores of the Riviera to the snow-clad Alps or the misty coasts of the Atlantic, to travel in an equally short time in summer from the *garrigues* of Languedoc scorched by the Dog Star to the green forests of the Île de France and the verdant, rain-drenched pastures of Ireland. In winter, particularly, the mantle of snow covers the Arctic tundra in the north and the Black Sea steppes in the south, leaving out only a narrow fringe on the Crimean coast which is sheltered by a little mountain range and contains Russia's seaside resorts.

The exact significance of this hard, monotonous climate commonly escapes us because here too we are victims of our maps and our systems of projection which mislead us as to the precise situation of the territories of the Soviet Union. Ask if Moscow is much farther north than London, and you will scarcely find anyone who can tell you that Moscow, the heart of Russia, is 250 miles and Leningrad 500 miles farther north than London. Many people, furthermore, would be surprised on being told that Leningrad is north of Orkney, Stalingrad very nearly in the same latitude as Paris, and Yalta, the most southerly town in Russia, in the latitude of Bordeaux. So, after having stressed the vast size of the Soviet Union, it is not superfluous to insist also on its very northern position.

Maps showing relief, climate, or vegetation display the same colouring over immeasurable spaces, and travellers all vie with each other in stressing the boredom they have felt at beholding the same scenery repeated indefinitely. From this it seems possible to deduce an extreme simplicity of geographical features, and on the whole this impression is not far wrong. In this respect, even to the west of the Urals the Soviet Union is infinitely more Asiatic than European.

Especially is it so because of its extraordinarily continental character. In this it is in contrast with central and western Europe, which is usually much indented and obstinately turned towards the Atlantic. In the south an enormous mountain barrier, huge depressions alternating with colossal plateaus, and gigantic ranges separate it from the open ocean. In the south-west the Caspian is a lake and the Black Sea almost as completely shut in. On the west the Soviet outlet to the Baltic has never been more than a narrow 'window'. In the east the Seas of Japan, Okhotsk, and Bering are frozen over for months in the year, as are the White and Arctic Seas in the north. Fundamentally, the Soviet Union is imprisoned in the continent.

This fact does not tend to facilitate its relations with other countries. Intercourse with foreign lands was as a rule possible for the frontier provinces, but, owing to the vast area of the territory, the interior regions would have achieved such contact only at the cost of endless, exhausting, ruinous, and often very perilous voyages through boundless forests and across almost uninhabited, ice-bound lands, arid steppes, or terrible deserts. How could they help being driven to retire within themselves? Is it astonishing that the Russian state should have led a life apart for so long, cut off in a way from the advantages of universal experience, and that up to the nineteenth century its contribution to civilisation in general should have been insignificant?

Their position on the outer edge of the world explains to a great extent the backwardness of the Russian people in the paths of modern culture, the slowness with which the political unification of the diverse populations constituting this enormous empire has been achieved, and, lastly, the necessity for the Soviet world to make a prodigious effort if it was to raise itself to the level of other nations.

Once we are acquainted with the exact position and form of this immense area peopled by Russians, we shall no longer be astonished that its great monotony should for long ages have favoured the continuance of a simple type of agriculture based on the cultivation of cereals, practising rudimentary crop-rotation, and leaving the land fallow for lengths of time depending on the quantity of manure available to the peasant. We shall no longer be surprised at seeing that, in this country of extensive cultivation in which arable areas extend as far as the eye can see and in which much land must be sown in order to reap large quantities of grain, agrarian systems inconceivable in our own country have been set up and mechanical methods of cultivation have been developed, without which an up-to-date use of the soil would have been impossible.

Just as no common measure exists between the topography of the Soviet Union and that familiar to us, so there is scarcely any greater resemblance between the unequally developed masses of humanity in the U.S.S.R. and the peoples in our western states. No common measure is observable between the *moujik*, who for centuries has been reduced to the status of mere labour and almost to that of a beast of burden, and our farmers, who for centuries have been owners or lease-holders of the land they till. And, lastly, there is no common measure between the masses of Soviet industrial hands, who but yesterday were still bound to the plough, and our own working-people, who have inherited a long tradition of craftsmanship and for whom the factory is only a development of the workshop.

Once this basic peculiarity of the country and its people has been understood, many facts become clearer and assume their real meaning. The experiment with the *kolkhoz*, for instance, which is so foreign to our way of thinking, seems less strange in a country where for centuries agriculture has willy-nilly existed under a communal system which our old farming classes had thrown off since the Middle Ages in favour of free individual holdings. How can anyone, who knows that for more than three hundred years the majority of *moujiks* have owned none of the land beyond their *izby* and the few acres of their *dvors*, be surprised—all things considered—at the ease with which they have accepted the communism of the *kolkhoz*? And when large masses of humanity were demanding provisions in increasing quantities, how can one be surprised at the attempts to industrialise agriculture in a country where the fields are not marked off from each other, are badly cultivated, and kept fallow for long periods?

In reading the following chapters we shall be stirred by the wholesale transfers of peasants to Siberia and by the removal of whole populations from one province to another. But the facts should be viewed in their proper surroundings. Of course, some of these displacements, notably the one which followed the elimination of the *kulaks*, were real deportations. But organised migration had often also been in answer to the aspirations of the peasants themselves. Instability is the congenital vice of the Russian peasant. In all ages complaints have been made of his errant disposition, and serfdom was, after all, only a means of binding a truant labourer to the soil. The lack of stability is doubtless explained by the fact that the peasant had little interest in land which he did not own; but it is certainly also explained in part by the very structure of the country in which the wanderer found everywhere the exact equivalent of the district he had left. The uniformity of the land surface indubitably favours instability in the rural population.

To try to paint within the narrow limits of a single book a faithful picture of so vast a country might seem something of a venture, since to all the problems mentioned above are obviously to be added others of more topical interest.

For thirty years this division of the world has been in the throes of evolution. Of course, the political revolutions which have forged the Soviet Union out of the Russia of old have made a greater impression on men's minds than has the economic transformation. Yet the latter is of ampler dimensions and has a more important future. Russia, which at the beginning of this century was with her dependencies a strictly agricultural country, has covered herself with clusters of industrial establishments. Such a transformation postulates a new social and economic structure, a new distribution of population, and a different outlook on life and work. Even though Russia had known nothing of the Communist system beyond the upheaval of her traditional economy, she would have brought into her archaic and obsolete institutions a change as deep and as brutal as the one we have witnessed. In the eyes of a geographer it matters little whether the political revolution preceded or followed the great change. The two phenomena are indissolubly bound together and react inexorably upon one another.

This in many ways imposing evolution is, moreover, actually taking place at the present moment, and it is very difficult to know what the Soviet Union will be like in the future, for the war and the peace that followed have introduced new factors. Here is an instance. Since the Soviet Union was a continental state cut off from the sea and pushed away even from the Baltic by the establishment of the Baltic States, it made no serious effort to acquire a merchant navy of dimensions corresponding to its own size. In 1939 it still bought most of its ships in England and even Japan. Its foreign commerce was largely carried on under alien flags. But now, fresh possibilities appear. In recent years the Soviet Union has recovered a wider frontage on the Baltic than it had formerly had. It again possesses Riga, but it also holds Königsberg, which it did not have before. Who can say what advantages a state which has become a great worker in metals will derive in future from this contact with the sea? It remains to be seen. For the moment the Soviet Union is concentrating on the reconstruction of its devastated areas and on the absorption of its new acquisitions into the political and economic framework of its federation.

A. Perpillou

Part I

THE PHYSICAL SETTING

CHAPTER 1

STRUCTURE AND MAIN FEATURES OF RELIEF

The Soviet Union has often been likened to an amphitheatre facing the Arctic Sea and bounded on the east, south-east, south, and south-west by a high rim of mountains. An examination of its relief does in fact show a framework of high ground running half-way round the periphery of an immense plain. This peculiar arrangement requires some explanation.

The main feature of the structure is clearly a foundation of very ancient rocks extending under nearly the whole country. As a rule it does not appear at the surface, but there are outcrops in Karelia, where it indicates the presence of the Fennoscandian Shield; in the valleys of the Ukraine, notably that of the lower Dnepr; on the Donets plateau and in north-eastern Russia, where it reappears in the tops of the Timanski Hills between the Urals and Cheshskaya Bay; and then much farther eastward in central Siberia, where it forms the plateaus of the 'Siberian Shield' between the Yenisey and middle Lena. There is no doubt that these various strata are continuous underground, for, even apart from the occurrence of small, isolated outcrops, numerous borings (for instance, near Minsk, Pskov, Voronezh, and especially to the south of Ufa) have revealed the presence of these basement rocks quite near the surface.

The basement rocks have, of course, not remained stable or horizontal in the process of geological ages. The Huronian and Caledonian foldings affected them considerably, and the warping which resulted from these movements acted as end-buffers to later orogenic pressure; for example, the Ufa plateau, on which the Urals were later moulded; or else they checked the invasion of the sea, as when the Ukrainian and Voronezh plateaus arrested the advance of the Donets Sea in the Carboniferous era. But important traces have been left, especially by the folding which took place in Hercynian times. The

2

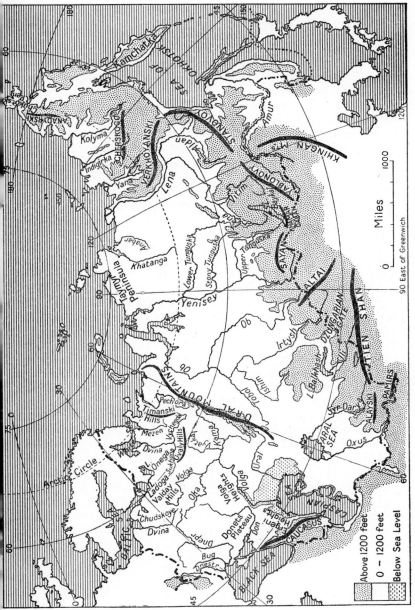

FIG. 1. RELIEF OF THE SOVIET UNION.

3

Valday plateau, Volga Heights, various north–south undulations, the Urals, the Altai and Sayan Mountains, the ranges in Transbaykalia, and the Khingan Mountains are all due to it.

This seems to have been the last fold movement which affected the whole of the Soviet Union, for the great Alpine upheaval disturbed its fringes only. The principal fact in the geological history of the country, especially its European portion, was the frequent alternation of marine transgression and regression. It was easy for the sea to advance over or retreat from a region almost all of which is, and nearly always has been, low lying. Since the beginning of the Primary epoch the north-west and south-east of Russia seem to have been the only parts which have constantly remained, the one above, the other beneath the sea. Everywhere else the sea has been continually receding or advancing, invading or evacuating basins, some of which run north-and-south, others east-and-west. This explains the variety of age and character in the deposits and, hence, the variegation of the geological map.

Broadly speaking, the rocks become more and more recent towards the south. Thus, Cambrian and Silurian clays and sands are found near Lake Ladoga; Devonian marls, sandstones, and limestones extend from the shores of the Baltic right up to the White Sea and to Smolensk; Carboniferous rocks outcrop from the Valday Hills to the headwaters of the Don; the Permian stretches along the Urals; Triassic limestones, sandstone, marls, and clays cover vast areas in the basins of the Mezen, Sukhona, Dvina, upper Volga, Vetluga, and Vyatka, reaching as far as the neighbourhood of Kuybyshev and Chkalov; and Jurassic sediments occupy the basins of the Pechora and Vychegda and form patches in the districts around Kalinin, Moscow, and Ryazan, and even Kuybyshev and Chkalov.

South of a sinuous line joining the southern Urals with south Sweden the outcrops of these beds become very rare. Primary rocks, for instance, outcrops near Voronezh and in the south of the middle and lower Donets valley; and Jurassic beds appear south of Orel and to the west of Saratov. In general, the surface rocks consist of far younger sedimentaries; e.g. the Cretaceous strata of the upper Desna and Oskol valleys and the basins of the Donets, Khoper, and middle Don; and the Tertiary beds occurring throughout southern Russia and visible especially in the Dnepr and lower Don basins, central Crimea, the plateau of the middle Volga, the Ergeni Heights, and the western portion of the Manych depression.

In Siberia there is less variety. Whilst in the west Jurassic beds cover large areas near the Arctic Sea, the rest is mainly an expanse of Lower Tertiary from which the sea retreated after the Oligocene at the time of the final separation of the Aralo-Caspian basin from the ocean. In the east the plateaus lying between the Yenisey and the middle Lena, as well as the districts around the Anabar and Khatanga rivers have a mantle of Cambrian and Silurian beds over their gneisses, crystalline schists, and granites, whilst between these two ancient masses sedimentaries of Secondary origin, mainly of the Trias, bear witness to a great invasion of the sea.

The sedimentary beds deposited at such times on the sea bottom were originally horizontal. Roughly speaking, they may be said to have remained so. A close examination, however, would show that they have sagged slightly and that here and there the Russo-Siberian 'platform' is marked by gentle undulations. The Ergeni Heights to the north of the Caspian depression are the most conspicuous of these ridges; but there are others, like the one through which the Oka cuts at Kasimov, another which the Don pierces before reaching the apex of the bend where it nears the Volga, and a third which runs from Kirov to Nikolayevski, a distance of some 450 miles. It seems clear that the Russian 'platform' really consists of a series of immensely long anticlinal and synclinal folds; but in actual fact this feature has only an insignificant effect on the relief.

The Alpine folding has, of course, been far more important. This is due not so much to the area of the regions affected by the movement, which has in fact touched only the periphery of the Russian 'platform', as to the height of the mountains to which it has given rise, some of them ancient, worn, and rejuvenated ranges, like the Altai, and other chains newly formed in Tertiary times. According to Wegener's theory, it is probable that the convergence of the ancient rigid crustal block of Gondwanaland in the south and central Siberia in the north has violently compressed and folded the beds lying between them; that these beds, spurting out as it were towards the north, spread out thither in sheets of rock-waste, whilst under the influence of the thrust ancient Primary relief was revived and old dissected mountains elevated anew. In any case, vigorous folds caused by a thrust from the south were moulded against old, resistant blocks. In this way mountain ranges, some of which were of great height and many of which have remained well-preserved, have been formed from the Carpathians to eastern Siberia. Such is the origin of Kamchatka, the Cherski, Verkhoyanski, Stanovoy, Yablonovy, Sayan, Altai Mountains, the Tien Shan, and Za-alayski Mountains, the Pamir plateau, the north Persian ranges, the Caucasus, and, lastly, the Crimean Hills. Naturally, this formidable orogenic upheaval did not fail to provoke violent movements in the adjacent regions and even in some cases at very great distances. It certainly cannot be regarded as responsible for every individual dislocation, fault, or subsidence occurring at the intersecting points of the tectonic features of the Russian 'platform'; but it is a fact that central and eastern Siberia have been particularly affected by recent shocks, fractures, uplifts, and subsidences, of which the Baykal trench is proof, especially as the orogenic impulse seems to have originated in the region of Irkutsk. It is noticed that today the seismic belts still border on the Alpine zones or are mingled with them. Earthquakes occur especially in the Crimea, Caucasia, central Asia, and Baykalia. On the whole, it seems clear that the Russian 'platform' is neither as rigid nor as stable as it is commonly thought to be.

Furthermore, its movements did not end with the Tertiary era. The Quaternary witnessed an essential episode in the genesis of the existing structure of the territory of the Soviet Union, viz. the ice ages. The history of these in the Union is far from being known. However, it may be assumed that there were at any rate in European Russia four ice ages contemporary with those in the Alps and somewhat analogous to those which, originating likewise in Scandinavia, invaded north-western Europe and the northern part of central Europe. Their greatest extension is seen in the western areas, which had the greatest rainfall. In the drier east the area affected was much smaller. Its limits correspond to a sinuous line which begins at the headwaters of the Vistula, traces a great curve to the south as far as the bend of the Dnepr, where it turns north, the ice not having been able to cover the hills 1200 ft. high to the south of Kaluga and Tula. The line then thrusts a second lobe southwards to the middle Don, turns again north to avoid the high ground on the right bank of the Volga, and runs towards the northern Urals, reaching them in lat. 64° N. Thus, it is roughly defined as passing through Kiev, Tula, Voronezh, and Gorky, and includes the greater part of the basin of the Dnepr and a large fraction of those of the Don and Oka.

It was long thought that meagre precipitation had rescued Siberia from widespread invasion by the ice-cap. The northern Urals, it was agreed, had sent out a glacier-tongue beyond the Ob, but it was said that the great western plains as a whole had not been touched; and that, though there were morainic deposits and indeed, under protecting layers of clay and sand, fossil ice in the lower Yenisey valley and on the peninsula of Taymyr not to mention the New Siberian Islands, eastern Siberia had not experienced glaciation in Quaternary times. This is quite wrong. It may be that the region was never covered by a continuous ice-cap, but certain it is that the plateau of Vitim, Khamar-Daban, the Yablonovy, the Cherski range, the Verkhoyanski and Kolymski Mountains, and the Chukotski peninsula contain erratic blocks, striated rocks, moraines, U-shaped valleys, and rock-barriers. Hence, ice-caps had formed on the various mountain ranges at least. It is still a matter of controversy whether there were only two ice ages or three or even four in these regions; but the occurrence of such periods in the past can no longer be denied. Indeed, according to a recent work (1937), the whole of Siberia, except certain central sectors where no trace of drift has been found, was buried under ice in Quaternary times.

In the belt affected almost all the soil has been due to ice action. Whether actually formed by ice or by fluvio-glacial action, it is composed of boulder clay between beds of sand. The thickness of these formations varies greatly, as do also the number and size of the pebbles, which swarm in some places, but are very rare in others. The materials have to a great extent been sorted out by the action of melt-water, which has transported them to a greater or lesser distance according to their weight. Coarse and fine gravel, sand, and loess, which have been affected by the wind, are today found well beyond the limits of the ice-cap, so that the effects of the ice are not confined to the belt invaded by it.

Nevertheless, glacial soils are not the only Quaternary soils in the Soviet Union. Marine, lacustrine, fluvial, æolian, and vegetable formations cover vast spaces not only in central Asia, where the Aralo-Caspian Sea has almost entirely dried up in recent times, but also in western Siberia and especially in Russia, where they form the regions of the lower valley of the Ural, the left bank of the lower and middle Volga, the Ponto-Caspian depression to the north of the Caucasus and the shores of the Black Sea, not to mention the southern part of White Russia and the district of Gomel. These formations complete the structure of the territory of the Soviet Union.

The complexity of this geological history is rather badly reflected in the extreme simplicity of the existing relief which, when reduced to its chief features, presents two main divisions, viz. the Russo-Siberian platform and the surrounding belt of mountains.

The term 'Russo-Siberian platform' is convenient, but not very exact, for it seems to ignore the vast plains of central Asia and, besides, the relief is far from being everywhere that of a strictly horizontal platform. The series of plains and plateaus which constitute it are certainly not very high above sea level, as a rule less than 1000 ft., rarely more, and never reaching 1300 ft., except near the Carpathians, on the Valday and Donets plateaus, and on the right bank of the Volga. The sources of the rivers are not much above sea level, that of the Dnepr being at a height of 830 ft. and that of the Volga at one of 730 ft. Their water partings are ill defined, the one between the Oka and Don valleys, for instance, being only 583 ft. above sea level. Nevertheless, railway construction has many a time been confronted with appreciable gradients, deep and narrow river valleys, and ravines, and has clearly shown that, though in the eyes of a traveller Russia, western Siberia, and Turkistan are endless plains, their flatness is far from being complete.

A vast arid basin as a whole, Turkistan is a country of dunes in the centre and south. Northwards in Kazakstan it frequently presents a hilly landscape. On the other hand, the relief of central Siberia is one of eroded and faulted plateaus. Very much flatter, western Siberia, whose hills do not rise above 400 ft., is one of the best examples of the plain in existence. In Russia, on the contrary, besides the Uvaly Hills (1070 ft.) which separate the basins of the Dvina and Pechora from the Volga-Kama-Vyatka system, there is a succession of plains from east to west as follows: the valleys of the lower Kama and of the middle and lower Volga; the Volga plateau, on which the Dzhyguly Hills (870 miles long and with a southern extension in the Ergeni Heights) reach an elevation of 1000 ft. above the river near Saratov; the valleys of the upper Oka and upper Volga, which are extended southwards by the valleys of the Don and its left-bank feeders; the plateau of central Russia, with an average height of at least 575 ft. and prolonged northwards by the Valday plateau (1050 ft.), north-westwards by the plateau of Minsk (1225 ft.), and southwards by the heights of the Donets, some of whose hills exceed 1180 ft.; the broad, but shallow, valley of the Dnepr and its feeders; and, lastly, the plateau of Podolia (650 ft.), in which the Bug and the Dnestr have carved fairly deep valleys.

The generally low elevation of the Russo-Siberian platform would suffice to arouse suspicion that its relief is one of denudation. This suspicion is strengthened by the fact that the land-surface extends over many geological strata whose outcrops are bevelled; that the highest ground is also that in which the rivers rise; and that in every Russian valley there is a contrast between the steep right bank and the low, easily flooded left bank, which suggests that the action of running water has played a preponderant part in shaping the relief. The plateaus, across which portages used formerly to be made, seem from their flatness to represent the remains of a continuous surface which, after the retreat of the ice-cap, has been carved by the rivers into the broad valleys now existing.

The relief has little connexion at any point with the structure, since it has been shaped mainly by erosion. In past ages denudation almost effaced the ancient folds; and after the retreat of the ice-cap the uplift of the areas relieved of an enormous weight caused a resumption of activity. The same process was repeated in central and eastern Siberia and was assisted by wholesale uplifting. Today, erosion continues to carve the orographical details, but its agents vary according to the district. The action of running water is seen nearly everywhere, except in a few very dry parts of the Aralo-

Caspian basin; so, too, is the disintegration of the surface by the alternation of heat and cold. But whilst in the southern districts, especially in Turkistan, the wind plays a leading part, in the north, and particularly in Siberia, the action of frost has had great influence and its effects are seen in cracked and rotten rocks, eroded heights surrounded by screes, pebble-strewn expanses, and reticulated surfaces, not to speak of river-banks corraded by the break-up of ice. Hence, there is a real contrast in detail between the topography of the north and that of the south.

The north, which has experienced the invasions of the ice-cap, has a relatively varied relief, with humps, hollows, little valleys known locally as *prapotoki*, which run parallel to the old front of the ice-cap and are analogous to the *pradoliny* in Poland and the *Urstromtäler* in Germany, and little morainic hills which by obstructing the drainage have caused the formation of some great lakes—Ladoga, Onega, Pskov, Chudskoye (Peipus), and Ilmen—and of innumerable swamps. 'The district in which the head waters of the Volga fall from one level to the next is an example of this succession of woods, hills, meadows, lakes, and marshes. There rises and falls of a hundred feet occur within short distances' (Camena d'Almeida).

The south is as a rule far more monotonous. In the Black Earth country and the Pontic depression, Podolia and the Ukraine do indeed have a few terraces here and there, but the only normal feature of the relief in the Black Earth country is the *ovrag*, or ravine, where the tooth of erosion has gashed the surface.

There is nothing to break the uniformity of the steppes, except some ancient *tumuli*, which are known locally as *korgany* and *moghily*, and some little basins formed by erosion and known as *bliuda*, or saucers. It is true that farther east the Aralo-Caspian depression has a far more varied and irregular appearance. This is due especially to its æolian morphology which evinces itself not only in the sand deserts, but also in the steppes of Kazakstan.

In spite of these minor irregularities, the Russo-Siberian platform is none the less characterised by remarkable flatness. In this respect it is in contrast with the mountain barriers of the periphery. These are only 'the northern slopes of the great folded masses of Asia' (Gibert) and form mighty arcs arranged concentrically to the Siberian 'shield'.

This old Archæan landmass is known to have remained stable between the Yenisey and Lena, but in the south and east it has been vigorously uplifted, folded, dislocated, and dotted with volcanoes in parts, so that eastern Siberia is a very broken country and consists of a complexity of horsts, rift valleys, terraces, and mountains. Some of the last mentioned are glaciated (e.g. those in Kamchatka which rise to 15,800 ft., the Anadyrski, Kolymski, Cherski, Verkhoyanski, Stanovoy, Yablonovy, and Sayan Mountains) and contain a curious mixture of old forms giving evidence of erosion over a long period in their gently sloping ridges and wide and often marshy-bottomed valleys, and young features, like jagged crest-lines, gorges, waterfalls, and rapids, which are due to recent uplift.

Farther west are the Altai (14,825 ft.), whose bold, picturesque configuration is comparable with that of the Swiss Alps. More recent than the ranges in the east and north-east, the Altai are less easy to cross, and the route into Mongolia skirts it on the south through the rift known as the Dzungarian Gate. Beyond this gate begin the great mountains of central Asia, which are still more recent and lofty, with dizzy peaks, deep valleys, and huge glaciers. They are the Tien Shan (22,500 ft.), the monstrously high Alayski (24,600 ft.), and the gigantic Pamir, 'the Roof of the World'. The ranges in the north of Persia are slightly lower, but scarcely easier to cross than those just mentioned. Then, after the lofty plateau of Armenia to the south and separated from it by the Caucasian trench, comes the majestic bulwark of the Caucasus (18,500 ft.), which contains some fifteen peaks higher than Mont Blanc and is crossed by very few passes. But farther west the orogenic force which elevated these mountains weakens. The Tauric range in the Crimea rises to only 5000 ft. above sea level. Yet it is undoubtedly a trace of the former connexion between the Caucasus and the Balkans.

In short, though the Russo-Siberian platform opens wide on to central Europe on the south-west and west as well as on to the Arctic Sea in the north, it is bounded throughout the length of Siberia and central Asia by an enormous barrier of recent or rejuvenated forms, which is nearly, if not quite, continuous and has been termed a 'great natural rampart'. This fact is all the more serious because the Soviet Union is very badly off for coastline.

CHAPTER 2

COASTLINE

The most striking physical feature of the territory of the Soviet Union is the shortness of its coastline relatively to its area, viz. 9940 miles (exclusive of the Caspian coasts) compared with 8,336,510 square miles. This is in contrast with France, which has 2000 miles of coastline to 213,000 square miles of surface, and Great Britain with 7110 miles to 89,000 square miles. Furthermore, it would be no exaggeration to say that on a large-scale map the Soviet coast appears to consist of a series of nearly straight lines. There is a great dearth of features. The inlets do not penetrate deeply, the peninsulas do not jut out far, and the islands are few and small. The Sea of Azov, the Crimean peninsula, the Gulf of Finland, the Kolski peninsula, the White Sea, the Kanin peninsula, Novaya Zemlya, the stocky Taymyr peninsula, the New Siberian Islands, the Chukotski peninsula, the Gulf of Anadyr, Kamchatka, the Sea of Okhotsk, and Sakhalin complete the list of features of any size. There are certainly many other indentations, but they are small, at least relatively to the area of the country. The absence of really deep-penetrating inlets is another aspect of the general monotony of the relief.

This relatively short coastline is, moreover, usually low and marshy. It follows from the flatness of the land surface and the ease with which extensive marine transgressions can take place that the seas are shallow and the coasts flat. There are few good anchorages, very few safe harbours deeply indented in high ground and capable of accommodating modern vessels. On the contrary, the coastline is choked with sand and gravel terraces owing to the uplift of the land surface consequent on the retreat of the ice-cap, and behind them morainic banks have given rise to the formation of many lakes and marshes. Elsewhere sandspits built up by currents have more or less completely sealed the mouths of the valleys which, if entered by the sea, might have provided excellent ports.

Lastly, the Soviet coasts are handicapped nearly everywhere by the climate. Not only are they for the greater part of their length adjacent to cold, poor, and almost uninhabited areas and thus are of little use to the inhabited inland regions, but, moreover, their waters are frozen over for long months not merely in the Arctic, but even in the Pacific, Baltic, and indeed the Black Sea. In the last case freezing is not general and lasts only a short time; but the sea is almost landlocked, and another power holds the exit. Wherever the seas of the Soviet Union are not blocked by ice, they are obstructed by the relief or political factors. This does not mean, however, that the value of the coastline is everywhere nil.

The only coasts in central Asia are those of the Caspian. This body of water, which was formerly connected with the Black Sea, has undergone many variations in level since the ice ages. Today, it is certainly drying up gradually but continuously, and it is of no great depth, at least in its northern part. Hence, its coasts are generally flat and unserviceable. Furthermore they border on poor steppe or desert. But, as Gibert says, the Caspian 'has at any rate played the immense part of opening up to the Russians the horizons of central Asia'.

The Caucasus, which looks out on to the Caspian on the east, faces the Black Sea on the west. This sea, whose very complex geological history must have had no fewer than nine phases, during some of which it was connected with the ocean whilst in others it was lacustrine, is an excellent example of a residual sea. It once formed part of a Mediterranean lying farther north than the existing sea of that name; it has been completely landlocked; and finally, in prehistoric times it resumed a slender connexion with the existing Mediterranean. This eventful past explains the variety of its coastal scenery and its differences in depth. A large part of its southern half has a depth of more than 1000 fathoms, but near the shores of Russia, where a continental shelf continues the land-relief beneath the water, the depth is less than 100 fathoms. The Russian coast is very varied here. On the west a positive movement of the sea has drowned the lower ends of the valleys, forming drowned valleys or *limans*, which are barred by sandspits and are being slowly transformed into deltas. This low coast is succeeded along the south of the Crimea by a line of high cliffs worn in hard rocks and containing useful sheltered bays like that of Sevastopol.

Farther east the Sea of Azov, which has an area of 14,500 square miles and a maximum depth of 45 ft., is being gradually silted up by sandy deposits brought down by the Don, and islands like Biryuchi are in process of developing into peninsulas. But the coasts, being formed of sand or clay, show little resistance to the attacks of waves driven by the furious winds that blow for several days on end, and their outline is constantly being modified. There are some places where the invasion of the sea has drowned between 50 and 150 acres in the space of five years. To the west of the Don, on the other hand, north-east winds build long spits. Still farther on, beyond the Strait of Kerch, stretches a low *haff* coast. Away in the east the coast rises near Novorossisk, and its steep slopes, though interrupted for a time by the alluvial plain of Colchis, reappear towards Batum, where the cliffs are being steadily eroded by the sea.[1] In fine, the coast has estuaries and a few favourable bays which have been made into busy ports; but it has serious drawbacks, including that of being ice-bound nearly every year in the region of the *limans* and of opening on to a sea whose outlet is a strait not under Russian control.

Apart from the Black Sea coasts, Russo-Siberia as a whole has a gateway on the Baltic and an immense frontage on the Arctic Sea and Pacific Ocean. The Baltic coast, which before the re-annexation of the Baltic States was only 134 miles in length, has been modelled by glacial action, but it should not be thought for that reason to be like the coast of Norway. Since the bottom of the Bay of Kronshtadt bristles with humps and has many deep pockets, its extreme shallowness, often less than 80 ft., makes its numerous shoals and reefs a danger to navigation; and the frequent occurrence of fogs does not lessen the difficulties. To complete the inhospitality of this gulf, sediments from the Neva and Narva have choked the coast, and the calmness of the water, together with its low salinity, helps the rigorous winters to block it with ice for about 160 days. A modern port on the Baltic was an absolute necessity to the Leningrad district and to Russia as a whole. The construction of one has been possible, but only at the cost of great labour.

In truth, Russia could not do without Riga, and that is one of the main reasons why she has reoccupied her former Baltic provinces. Not that their coastline is without drawbacks. The rocky northern coast of Estonia is edged with cliffs or fringed with shoals and reefs; whilst the west coast in Latvia and Lithuania has low shores smoothed by a current which closes its *haffs* and straightens it out. Yet besides Riga, there are some good harbours, like those of Tallin and Liepaya. But taken all round, the Baltic coast is unsatisfactory.

The Arctic coasts are still less useful. The Murmanski area is an exception, however. Its numerous fjords are so many harbours, and it enjoys an abnormally mild climate because the warm waters of the North Atlantic Drift wash its shores, prevent the freezing over of its inlets, and drive away northwards the margin of the frozen seas. It

[1] At the mouth of the Medzhina the coast receded 270 yds. between 1880 and 1926.

S.U.—B

is the only place in which the Soviet Union has access to an open sea which is always free from ice. Far less favoured, the White Sea is regularly ice-bound from October to April. This is due to its very continental position, to the calmness of its water, to its low salinity which is caused by the large amount of freshwater brought down by the Dvina, Onega, and other rivers, and, lastly, to the fact that its western portion alone is reached by a warm current. Furthermore, it is very foggy and its entrance has dangerous shoals. Its great importance to navigation depends on the fact that its backland must at all costs have an outlet to the sea. Similarly, in the eastern portion of the Barents Sea the coast is flat and marshy, and its water is liable to be frozen over, because the last branches of the warm current pass much farther to the north.

To the east of Novaya Zemlya and Vaygach Island conditions are worse still, and the greater part of the Kara Sea is always ice-bound. The coast of Siberia, however, as far eastwards as the Yenisey becomes ice-free in summer. Farther east the break-up of the ice is sometimes far from complete, especially in the dangerous Chukchee Sea, and is as late as the freezing-up is early. Some parts of the Arctic coastal waters of the Soviet Union are in the grip of ice for five months and others for six, eight, or ten months—sometimes for the whole year. In other ways too the coast is horrible. So low is it that between the Lena and the Kolyma the shoreline cannot be identified in winter under the ice which covers sea and land alike, and during the summer in the Yana district north winds at times drive the waves some 40 miles inland. The coast is therefore swampy, with no natural harbours and only a wretched anchorage here and there. The estuaries alone are of interest to modern shipping, but they can be used for only a few weeks in the year.

One might be tempted to think of the Pacific coast as distinctly better, and, in truth, it is more irregular and generally higher. Bering Strait, named after the Russian explorer Vitus Bering, is 55 miles wide at its narrowest point and less than 35 fathoms deep. Asia is here separated from North America by an artificial line passing between Great Diomede Island (Russia) and Little Diomede Island (United States), the distance between the two islands being about three miles. Along the coast of the Sikhote Alin, at any rate in the north, there are safe harbours like De-Kastri Bay, and still farther north the lower Amur is a magnificent waterway into a moderately productive backland. Unfortunately, the delta of this river is a labyrinth impeded by sandbanks, and here again too many stretches of the coast are choked with ill-drained silt. Okhotsk, at the upper end of the *liman* of the Okhota, is a very mediocre port. To the almost general drawback of fog is added the freezing-over of the sea. The harbour of Nikolayevsk is ice-bound for six months in the year and that of Vladivostok in the latitude of Marseille for three and a half months. In fact, the Bering and Okhotsk Seas are polar in character, and even the Sea of Japan is very cold.

To sum up, the coasts of the Soviet Union are nearly everywhere badly endowed by Nature, and the seas, which are generally cold, scarcely penetrate the land. This has serious effects on the climate, which is, moreover, greatly influenced by the arrangement of the surface relief.

CHAPTER 3

CLIMATE AND SEASONS

The massive character and flatness of the Soviet territory give rise
to two fundamental climatic features. The first is the astonishing
uniformity of the climate. Of course, local shades of difference can
be noticed even on the Russo-Siberian platform, for areas of moderately high ground have a colder climate than their lower surroundings, whilst certain well-sheltered valleys, like those of the Oka, upper
Volga, and Dnestr, enjoy relatively mild temperatures. But these
differences are of minor importance. Camena d'Almeida has stressed
the contrast between the enormous area of the country and the slight
differences in the statistics relating to the various meteorological
phenomena; and Woeikof has said that 'in winter it is possible to
travel by sleigh from Archangel to Astrakhan, and in summer the
peasant works in shirtsleeves near Leningrad as in the Crimea'. The
same climate prevails over vast areas, and, though, in spite of all,
there exist in the Soviet Union several climatic belts, these pass into
one another by an imperceptible transition, as if the various climates
gradually fused into each other and amalgamated.

The second characteristic is the markedly continental nature of
the climate, a feature which is due to the extraordinary weakness of
the influence of the sea. A scanty rainfall with a summer maximum,
strong winds, very marked temperature ranges, and a spring and
autumn much reduced in length to add to the summer and winter:
such are the normal conditions in the Soviet lands. It is significant
that at Stavanger in Norway the growing period of plants begins as
early as it does in the Crimea or on the Syr Darya, both of which are
much farther south; and that the Russian Far East, though it has
a maritime situation and is in the latitude of Stavanger, is between

[1] The mean annual temperature is 17·6° F. in the Strait of Yugor, but 50° F.
on the Black Sea.

16

a month and a half and two months behind, whilst Kamchatka is three months behind.

There are indeed three exceptionally favoured regions:

Firstly, THE RUSSIAN FAR EAST, particularly the basin of the Amur, where the differences in the pressure systems on land and sea cause a system of seasonal winds that blow in summer from the sea on to the land and in winter from the land on to the sea. Here, as in the whole of eastern Asia, there prevails a typical monsoon climate. It is a rigorous one, with mean January temperatures of 8° F. at Vladivostok and −3° F. at Voroshilov, and with 243 days of frost at Tigil in Kamchatka and 110 at Vladivostok. But it is moist too, Vladivostok having a rainfall of 30 ins., Olga one of 31 ins., and Petropavlovsk one of 47 ins. And the abundance of snow, especially on the shores of the Sea of Okhotsk and in eastern Kamchatka, the cold and cheerless spring, the bright mild autumn, and above all the wet summer, when it sometimes rains for twenty days on end, endow it with very special characteristics.

Secondly, TRANSCAUCASIA, where the valleys, which, as it is, are situated in a fairly southerly latitude, are enclosed between the Caucasus and the Armenian heights and so are well sheltered from the cold north winds. Though the summers are very hot, the winters are proportionately mild. The rainfall is heavy, at any rate on the plain of Colchis in the west; but the maximum is in winter, and the summers are, on the other hand, remarkably dry. The climate is in fact sub-tropical.

Thirdly, THE SOUTH COAST OF THE CRIMEA, which, being also protected by a screen of mountains from the icy north winds, has mild and fairly wet winters and very sunny, very dry summers. It enjoys a Mediterranean climate.

But these exceptions concern only minute fractions of Soviet territory. The rest is subject to a continental climate, if ever there was one. In winter the presence over central and eastern Siberia of a pronounced high-pressure system, which extends as far as central and southern Russia, but is replaced in summer by a no less marked low-pressure system, explains the icy blasts which blow over the Soviet Union in winter and the parching winds of summer. Furthermore, these winds blow unchecked by the presence of mountains. No barrier exists between Siberia, Turkistan, and Russia, for the Urals are too low and do not extend far enough southwards to act as one. From the Siberian high-pressure system in winter issue masses of cold air with nothing to stop them spreading, just as in summer blasts of hot air are freely sucked in towards the low-pressure system of central Asia. The west is certainly the point from which it is least easy for the winds to come. When in summer low pressure prevails

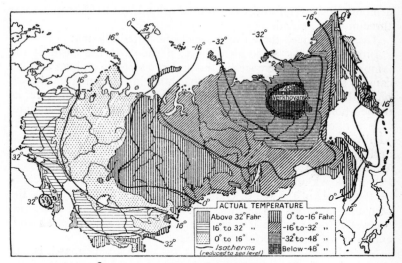

FIG. 2. DISTRIBUTION OF TEMPERATURE IN WINTER.

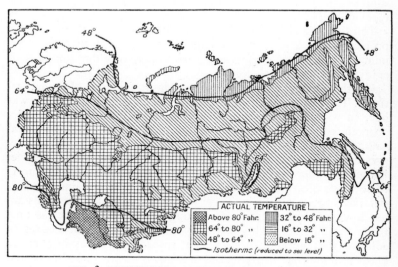

FIG. 3. DISTRIBUTION OF TEMPERATURE IN SUMMER.

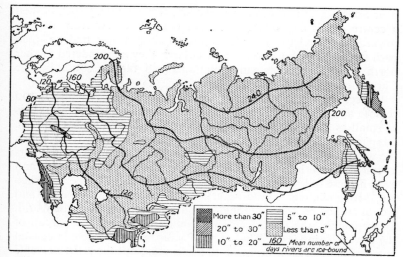

FIG. 4. DISTRIBUTION OF RAINFALL IN WINTER.

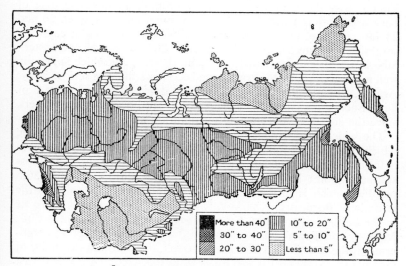

FIG. 5. DISTRIBUTION OF RAINFALL IN SUMMER.

19

over Soviet Asia and even over Russia, the Atlantic, which is then a centre of high pressure, sends out currents of air from the sea towards the Soviet Union; but, though these winds find an open path through north Germany and Poland, they are hindered farther north by the Scandinavian mountains and farther south by the Carpathians.

Hence, the rainfall is scanty on the whole. The Atlantic is too remote and the Baltic is a poor source of water vapour, since it is as small as it is shallow. The same is true of the Black Sea and the Caspian, which are hardly more than immense lakes from which the winds cannot derive much moisture. In the east and south, Turkistan and Siberia are sheltered by enormous mountain ranges, and even if these did not exist, the adjacent countries of Chinese Turkistan, Mongolia, etc., would nevertheless be remote from the sea and would still be reckoned amongst the most arid regions in the world. Consequently, the influence of the Indian Ocean on the rainfall of the Soviet Union is nil. That of the Pacific is considerable in coastal areas, which get an average of 40 ins. a year; but the relief prevents it from being felt inland. As for the Arctic Sea, it is too cold to allow of much evaporation and it sends few clouds over the continent. Besides, even if moist winds could blow over the Soviet Union from all sides, the absence of high relief which might cause condensation over the inland areas would make them lose much of their value. That is why the Union has a scanty rainfall. Though the west of Russia is favoured with an annual precipitation of between 20 and 24 ins., yet the amount quickly diminishes towards the east and south-east. Western Siberia has scarcely 20 ins., central and eastern Siberia get little more than 16 ins., and the drought which is already well marked in south-eastern Russia becomes still more serious in the Aralo-Caspian region, where the rainfall does not exceed some 6 or 8 ins. Such figures mean that the region is semi-desert or even desert, since the summers are hot and evaporation active.

The widespread drought partly controls the temperature system, which, however, is influenced also by the position of the Union in a far more northerly latitude than is usually thought. The most southerly point in Soviet territory (in Turkistan) is on the 36th parallel, which is in the latitude of Gibraltar. Sevastopol is in the latitude of Bordeaux; Kharkov, which from the map appears to be in the latitude of southern France, is in fact in that of Land's End; Moscow and Tomsk on the 56th parallel in that of Glasgow; Leningrad on the 60th in that of Cape Farewell, the southern extremity of Greenland; Archangel is 120 miles from the Arctic Circle, and vast stretches of Siberia and Russia too are north of the 70th parallel. Corresponding positions could be found only in Greenland and the islands of the Canadian Arctic. Altogether, therefore, the Soviet Union is a high latitude state. Hence, it is understandable that its winters should be very long and very severe. Continuous frost lasts for three or four months in the west and south of Russia, five months in the centre and east, eight months in the neighbourhood of the White Sea, nine or ten months in the extreme north of Siberia; and the temperature minima are of the order of −40° F. or −60° F. The cold becomes more and more severe towards the north and east, but

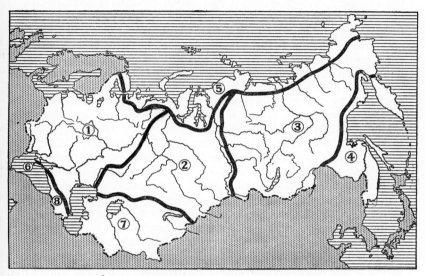

FIG. 6. MAIN CLIMATIC REGIONS OF THE SOVIET UNION.

1. Russian climate (definitely continental).
2. Western Siberian (still more continental).
3. Central Siberian (dry and extreme).
4. Far Eastern (monsoonal; rough, but moist).
5. Arctic.
6. Mediterranean.
7. Central Asiatic (desert and semi-desert).
8. Transcaucasian (warm, moist sub-tropical).

even in relatively low latitudes it is rigorous. On the other hand, the summers are hot everywhere. Temperatures higher than 86° F. have been recorded north of the Arctic Circle. Moscow has a July mean but little less than that of Lyon; Chkalov one nearly as high as that of Toulouse; and Irkutsk one equal to that of Lille; and south-eastern Russia, like Turkistan, suffers from broiling heat. Thus, the extreme seasons are strongly marked. The intermediate seasons, on the other hand, are of short duration. The last cold days of winter are quickly followed by hot summer temperatures, just as frost and snow soon succeed the fine days of summer. The suddenness of the changes of temperature is no less striking than the range, and this extreme nature of the Soviet climate emphasises once again its continental character.

Nowhere else are the factors mentioned above so well marked as in Siberia. Its very northerly position gives it long winters with very short days and short summers with very long days. Its relief shelters it from the influence of the Atlantic and Pacific, but leaves it open to the influence of the Arctic Sea. Lastly, in the east and south-east the existence of high plateaus and actual mountains considerably increases the cold. Hence, Siberia presents the very type of cold continental climate. In winter, high barometric pressures of 30·5, 30·6, and often of 30·7 ins. in January, centring over eastern Siberia, make the country a source of freezing winds. In summer, on the other hand, when the pressure falls to 29·9 or 29·7 ins., the same region becomes a centre of attraction for the more or less moist air of the neighbouring regions. So precipitation occurs mainly in summer. Winter, however, has its share; but though snow remains on the ground for months and thus constitutes one of the most typical features of the landscape, it is not deep, especially in eastern Siberia, where certain districts are perforce ignorant of the use of the sleigh. All things considered, the country as a whole is rather dry. On account of this the temperature goes to great extremes. The expression 'Siberian cold' is a by-word, and indeed Verkhoyansk, at an elevation of 160 ft. above sea level, has earned the name of 'cold pole' owing to its having experienced a temperature of −94·6° F. Furthermore, the title is disputed by Oymyakon, which has in fact experienced −90° F. and perhaps −115·8° F. and normally has a more severe winter than Verkhoyansk. On the other hand, the Siberian summer is really hot. On the tundra the ground sometimes seems burning hot to those walking over it, and Verkhoyansk has recorded a temperature as high as 100° F., which is not exceeded in Trinidad, in spite of the latter's almost equatorial position. The annual range, which as a rule is of the order of 140° F. or 160° F., may at times reach and even exceed 180° F. No more extreme climate is known on the globe.

Of the four seasons winter evidently contributes most to determining the character of the climate. Its majestic serenity strikes the European almost as much as its severity.[1] The constant high pressures and low temperatures cause a stillness in the air which makes the terrible cold endurable, and a dryness which gives a wonderful clearness to the sky. At sunrise on the snow-mantled steppe 'the sky assumes soft, blending tints, the light is wholly diffused over every

---

[1] And its length, which causes the rivers to be frozen over for five months at east, in many places for six, and in some for more than eight.

object. . . . There are no deep shadows, nothing but tinges and transparency . . . shades so delicate that the eye cannot leave them' (J. Legras). The thin snow cover, as well no doubt as the intensity of the cold, explains the extensiveness of the phenomenon of *merzlota* ('permafrost'), that is, permanently frozen rock beneath the surface. It occurs in the Soviet Union in more than 3½ million square miles, or 47 per cent. of the territory. It is most pronounced in Siberia to the north of a line which cuts the lower Ob at Berezovo and the Yenisey at Turukhansk, turns south round Lake Baykal and includes Transbaykalia and all the Far East, except the valleys of the Seya, Bureya, and Ussuri, nearly all of Primorsk and Kamchatka, and all of Sakhalin. It is found in a belt in which the temperature is

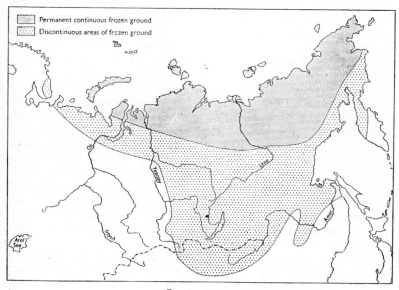

FIG. 7. THE MERZLOTA.

below 32° F. for half the year and in hardly any part of which the thermometer registers 68° F. for more than a fortnight. In this belt the ground thaws only on the surface to a depth which varies with the vegetation: 6 ft. 6 ins. in coniferous forests, 3 ft. in marshy areas, 18 ins. in peat bogs. Below this is a layer of permanently frozen rock which also varies in thickness from place to place. This is the *merzlota* proper. The depth of the layer is 60 ft. at Olekminsk, between 70 and 100 ft. in the Aldan valley, and between 270 and

670 ft. in the Yakutsk region. It is nearly everywhere separated from the active surface layer by a layer of unfrozen rock.

Throughout the belt the *merzlota* acts as a real agent of erosion. The expansion of water below the surface as it freezes causes humps and cracks, the pressure of the surface ice causes underground water to rise to the surface, where it floods wide areas and freezes to form *naledy*. Thaw leads to solifluction and landslides, the instability of the ground causes the destruction of roads, damage to bridges, and subsidence of large buildings. Rock in the *merzlota* is so hard that it makes mining difficult. Its presence affects the seasonal volume of rivers and renders difficult the supply of water for domestic purposes.

Winter is scarcely over before April. The rivers are set free in an impressive break-up of the ice, which is generally accompanied by terrible floods. The snow melts, and highways, which shortly before were streets of towns like Tomsk, are turned into indescribably evil-smelling sloughs and streams of brown mud into which horses sink past their fetlocks, carriages become stuck fast, staggering drunkards are in danger of being engulfed, and cows have been seen to disappear. Then comes a spring which would be delightful but for the too frequent returns of cold weather and which is anyhow extremely short. Summer follows abruptly, is very pronounced, generally as hot as in France, and sometimes scorching; but on the whole is not very pleasant owing to its whirling clouds of dust, its thunder- and hailstorms, and its myriads of mosquitoes which are fierce enough to have discouraged colonisation in some places. However, the season does not last long. By August the north and east may have night frosts and slight falls of snow, and the trees begin to shed their leaves. These are the first signs of an autumn which is as short as the spring. At the end of September bits of ice begin to drift down some of the rivers, and a few weeks later winter is back again, frigid and silent.

But a country as immense as Siberia cannot fail to offer some variety of climate, and, in addition to the Pacific region, at least three main divisions are to be recognised.

Eastern Siberia is particularly dry. Khabarovsk has a rainfall of only 22·2 ins., Bulun 8, Khatanga 9, Yakutsk 7. The days on which snow falls are few: 45 at Khabarovsk and 9 at Blagoveshchensk, whilst certain districts have none in some years. Transbaykalia has between 100 and 140 perfectly clear days, which is as many as or more than are had by Naples or Athens. However, the country east of the Yablonovy Mountains is damp, a fact reflected in the appearance of broad-leaved trees among the conifers. Eastern Siberia is also particularly cold. In it are the two 'cold poles'. Khabarovsk has a mean annual temperature of 33·6° F., a January mean of −9·6° F.,

and a July mean of 68·4° F.; Verkhoyansk has a January mean of
−60° F., and vast regions in the Upper Amur, Transbaykalia, and
Yakutia have mean annual temperatures of less than 32° F. Hence,
the ground seldom thaws completely. On the other hand, the July
isotherm for 68° F. goes farther north in Yakutia than anywhere
else, which shows the exceptional amplitude of the annual range of
temperature. But it should be noticed that in these almost snowless
parts spring and autumn are longer and more pleasant than elsewhere.

Central Siberia is similarly very cold, except near Lake Baykal,
evaporation from which perceptibly moderates the variations in temperature, makes the summers cooler, and prolongs the autumn.
Whilst Yeniseisk has snow on 87 days in the year, Irkutsk has it on
only 27, and even then the snow cover is so thin in this region that
on the outskirts of Krasnoyarsk cattle are sometimes put out to
graze in winter. All the same, it is very cold: Irkutsk has a January mean of −40° F. But its summers are as warm as those in
Portugal.

Finally, western Siberia has very severe winters. Surgut has experienced a temperature of −58·5° F., and a similar temperature has been
recorded even in the south. But the January mean for the region as
a whole is only −4° F. (14·6° F. at Surgut), and the ground does
not freeze very deeply or for very long. All the same, Tomsk has
snow falling on 121 days, and the snow, which is often brought by
raging storms, is deep enough to be blown by the wind into lines
of regular parallel dunes. However, summer, which is as warm here
as in the east of France, is also the wettest season and has heavy
rainstorms; but the total annual precipitation is again scanty, with
17·5 ins. at Tyumen, 17·4 at Surgut, 17·3 at Ishim, 16 at Tobolsk,
and only 15·1 at Novosibirsk, 12·4 at Omsk, 12·5 at Kurgan, 10
at Salekhard, and 9·8 at Kainsk. But the rainfall is on the whole
higher here than in the central and eastern regions, and Tomsk
has only 38 absolutely cloudless days in the year, for the influence
of the Atlantic, though much weakened, is at times perceptible
here.

This influence is found also in Russia, where it is rather stronger,
but still weak, for the Carpathians, Caucasus, and Balkan Mountains
hinder the penetration of winds from the Mediterranean, just as the
Scandinavian Mountains check that of the winds off the Atlantic.
The climatic factors are the same as in Siberia: a high latitude
position, no mountain screen to stop the Arctic winds, and no
serious barrier to shut out those from Asia. Compared with that of
Europe, the climate of Russia is undoubtedly continental, and as a
whole it is remarkably uniform. Nevertheless, the contrast between

the enormous windbreak formed by the Alps, Bohemian Mountains, the Carpathians, and the Balkan Mountains on the one hand and the Baltic depression and the North German Plain on the other causes the north-west to be affected, though weakly, by the influence of the sea, whilst the eastern and southern regions are sheltered from it.

In fact, the greater part of Russia—east, south, and centre—is invaded in winter by the Siberian high-pressure system, and its dry, cold winds come from Asia. The north-west, on the other hand, being a centre of fairly low pressure, receives moist and relatively mild west winds. Similarly, in summer, whilst the north and north-west and centre have a prevailing wind from the sea, southern and eastern Russia have prevailing hot, dry winds from the continent.

This division of the country between a prevailing continental influence and the weak influence of the sea is reflected in the distribution of rainfall. The number of fine days, though fewer than one would think, steadily increases towards the south-east. There are 39 at Leningrad, 59 at Kiev, and 91 at Astrakhan. The same is true of days not definitely wet, of which there are not quite 180 at Petrozavodsk or Smolensk, 196 in Moscow, 225 at Kazan, and 291 at Yalta. Also, in the same way, the total yearly precipitation, which is modest on the whole, diminishes from north-west to south-east. It is 21·3 ins. at Pskov, 21 in Moscow, 18·7 at Penza, 14·9 at Saratov, 13·5 at Chkalov, and 6·4 at Astrakhan. The same is true of the depth of the snow cover, which is clearly less than in Poland or Germany, but very appreciable nevertheless in the region of the great lakes, in White Russia, and even in the centre; but it is certainly thinner in the Black Sea area and the lower Volga, where the winds sweep it about at will. Anyhow, though snow lies on the ground in Russia for months, it is not very deep, because winter is the driest season with 18 per cent. of the annual precipitation at Kuybyshev, 17 per cent in Moscow, 15 per cent. at Poltava, and 13 per cent. at Ufa.[1] Very heavy showers, interspersed with longish periods of drought which are sometimes disastrous, as in 1921 in the districts of the middle and lower Volga, make the summer the rainiest season, if not the dampest. It gets 40 per cent. of the total precipitation at Kaluga, 39 per cent. at Ufa, 36 per cent. in Moscow, 35 per cent. at Kuybyshev, and 29 per cent. at Odessa.

In summer the influence of latitude on the temperature is very perceptible. Whilst the north remains relatively cool and Archangel has a mean of 59° F., the south is hot, Odessa for instance having a

[1] In Russia the snow is generally dry and quickly hardens. This is what makes possible the use of *valenki*, or felt boots, which form an ideal footwear in very cold weather.

mean of 72° F.; or even very hot, as at Astrakhan, where the mean is 77° F. In winter this climatic factor is less important. Certainly, Odessa has only 90 days of frost, whilst Leningrad has 150 and Yugor 240; and it is true that the temperature minimum at Astrakhan is −25° F. as against −53° F. at Archangel. But distance from the sea contributes more to a reduction of temperature than does distance from the Equator. The north-west–south-east direction of the winter isotherms proves this. At Leningrad the January mean is 18° F., in Moscow 11° F., at Ulyanovsk 7° F., and at Chkalov 4° F. The increase of summer warmth towards the east-south-east is more gradual than that of winter cold; thus, Leningrad has a July mean of 64° F., Kalinin 64·5° F., Moscow 66° F., Penza 67° F., Kuybyshev 70° F., and Chkalov 82° F. Hence, winter temperatures play a predominant part in determining the annual means. It is a striking fact that the difference between the January and July means rises from 45° F. at Leningrad to 51° F. at Kalinin, 53° F. at Moscow, 58° F. at Tambov, and 66° F. at Uralsk, and that the range at Kiev is 46° F., at Kursk 53° F., at Voronezh 55° F., and at Chkalov 67° F., though these places are on almost exactly the same parallel of latitude. Altogether, winter in the north-west is less severe, has less snow, and above all is shorter than that in the east and south; whilst summer in the east and south is warmer, drier, and above all longer than in the north-west. The division of Russia into climatic regions is determined by the length of the extreme seasons far more than by their heat or severe cold. Besides, in spite of the shades of difference and slow gradations, 'there are moments when Russia is almost all over just like itself' (Camena d'Almeida), and the play of the seasons throughout the country can be studied without much trouble.

The severity of the winters was well known even in ancient times, and Herodotus placed Scythia on the edge of the inhabited world. In modern times the thermometer has registered −44° F. in Moscow, −49° F. at Perm, −35° F. at Tambov, −42° F. at Kursk, −40° F. at Chkalov, −41° F. at Voroshilovgrad, and −19° F. at Odessa on the shores of the Black Sea. True, these are exceptional minima. But the duration of cold weather is no less remarkable than its severity. For six and a half months at least, and for seven or eight in certain parts, the far north has a mean temperature not above 32° F. Five or six months of frost must be expected at Leningrad, Gorky, Kazan, and Chkalov; four or five in Pskov, Moscow, Tula, Orel, Kuybyshev, and Chapayev; three or four in Kiev and nearly the whole of the Ukraine, in Rostov, and at Astrakhan; and between one and three at Odessa, Kherson, and the northern Crimea. But though it is very long and hard, the Russian winter lacks the majestic settled conditions of the Siberian season. Like the latter, it has terrible snowstorms, or *burany*, which are fatal to man and beast alike;[1] but it also has cold snaps which are as violent as they are sudden. At Chkalov the temperature once fell from 38° F. to −22° F. in twenty minutes; and, above all, temporary thaws, known as *otepely*, often occur during the first weeks at any rate. These make the ground sodden, free the streams from ice for a while, and cause disastrous floods, especially in the Leningrad region. It was an *otepel* that made the crossing of the Berezina disastrous to the French army in 1812. Anyhow, though winter brings nearly all work to a standstill, imposes an unhealthy confinement on the peasants, and forces many of them, at any rate in the poorer regions in the north, to economise in effort and hence to eat as little as possible, thus practising a kind of hibernation (*leika*) after the manner of bears and marmots, yet it offers certain advantages, for it creates reserves of water in the form of snow for agriculture, it is the season for hunting, and also for minor domestic industries, especially in the central districts, and it facilitates transport by allowing sledges to travel over the compact snow and on the ice, which is strong enough at times to bear tip-carts and in Leningrad even trams.

Spring-time, which is greatly encroached on by winter and summer, does not begin before April or even May. It is the period of the break-up of ice on the rivers in the north, of floods, and of the melting of the snow, which swells the streams, but also thoroughly saturates the ground, liquefies the soil, makes the roads into gutters, and all Russia into an epic of mud. This *rasputitsa* (= traffic stoppage) makes overland transport impossible for a time, just as the break-up of the river ice stops transport by water. Spring is also the wonderful time of reawakening of plant life and of the resumption of rural occupations; and, as soon as the snow has melted, traffic on the rivers comes to life in a flash.

Spring is short, especially in the south, east, and south-east, where it hardly lasts for one or two months before the full heat of summer comes on. The far north is somewhat of an exception. There summer comes gradually and is rather cool in some years. But the centre, east, and south have high temperatures,[2] and, as this is the season of clear skies, evaporation is intense. Although summer is as a rule the wettest season, the volume of the streams diminishes greatly, many lakes dry up, the surface of phreatic bodies of water sinks, and dust- and sand-storms sweep down at times from the east,

---

[1] An excellent description of a *buran* will be found in Pushkin's *The Captain's Daughter*, Ch. 2, an English translation of which has been published in Everyman's Library.

[2] 97° F. recorded in Leningrad, 99·5° F. in Moscow, 100° F. at Perm, 102° F. at Kuybyshev, 103° F. at Kherson, and 106° F. at Astrakhan.

severely damaging the crops by tearing them up, withering, or burying them. Fortunately, such storms are rare. Thunderstorms are far more frequent,[1] and though severe hailstorms are exceptional, the same cannot be said of the fierce deluges of rain which cut gullies in the surface of the steppes and in recent years have caused many a railway accident by damaging the tracks. In Russia the summer has been regarded as the time when most deaths occur, for the winds from central Asia bring the germs of many diseases, and epidemics work havoc among the swarms of migratory agricultural labourers, who are overworked and crowded together without regard to hygiene, and among the workpeople who are exhausted by heavy toil which must be finished in a few weeks and by lack of sleep. In the northern half of the country at any rate, the very brief summer nights—the famous 'white nights'—exact a heavy toll for the enchanting sunset colours which, in the opinion of de Maistre and many others, made the charm of the 'evenings in St. Petersburg'.[2] In spite of its feverish activity, summer is the 'good season', when the parks, gardens, and *galianiya* (promenades) in the towns are full of gay crowds, and when until recently the great fairs, rural markets, and pilgrimages were at their zenith. It used to be, and is once more becoming, the time for holidays in the country, sea-bathing, and spells at watering-places in the Caucasus. It is above all the food-gathering season, when man endeavours to accumulate the greatest possible amount of food and provisions in view of the long winter period of forced inaction.

Winter comes early. Even at the end of September the temperature has become strangely cool. Week by week the midday sun seems to decline more quickly and the days to shorten at a faster pace. By the beginning of October tiny snowflakes often swirl about the sky in Moscow. Gradually, the showers become thicker and more frequent; but the snow-cover does not lie yet, and *otepely* bring on *rasputitsy* scarcely less muddy than those in spring. Finally, about mid-November or early December autumn gives place to winter. It does not last two months in Russia as a whole, and most of the regions scarcely notice its occurrence.

So the climate of Russia seems to be merely a weakened form of that of Siberia. But it becomes milder from east to west, and it deteriorates towards aridity from north-west to south-east. And the tendency to drought, which is evident even in south-eastern Russia, is still more pronounced farther east. In this respect the region of the

[1] Perhaps no other writer has so felicitously described them as I. S. Turganev has done in *Tales of a Hunter*.

[2] Joseph de Maistre (1754–1821), who represented the King of Sardinia at St. Petersburg, expressed his own political ideas in a work entitled *Soirées de Saint-Pétersbourg*.

lower Volga marks the transition between the climate of Russia and that of Russian Turkistan.

In the northern part of Further Russia, that is, broadly, in Kazakstan, the prevailing climate is still drier and more extreme. Precipitation rarely attains 10 ins. (Turgay has just under that figure), and its distribution is capricious and varies from year to year. As a rule, the minimum is recorded in February and March in the north and in July in the south, whilst the maximum occurs in May or June. Although terrible *burany* are occasionally known, the snow-cover is very thin, 4 ins. at most. Spring, like autumn, is almost non-existent. A severe winter, with January mean temperatures of between 3° F. and 10° F. and minima which may reach —40° F., is abruptly followed by a broiling summer, which has July means of between 85° F. and 90° F. and which seem dry owing to the intensity of the evaporation.

The climate of the regions situated farther south, that is, the Aralo-Caspian lands, is even more difficult. In winter cold winds blow from the north-east, in summer north-westerlies prevail. The latter are moister than the former, but the characteristic feature of this climate is scanty rainfall. Although near the mountains the total rises a little and Tashkent gets 13 ins. a year, the region as a whole has a mean annual rainfall which ranges between 3 and 8 ins. according to the place. These are poor figures; and half of this rain falls in spring, from March to May according to the more or less southern position. The rest falls at the end of autumn and especially in winter. Summer is practically dry, and it sometimes happens in the centre and even more in the south that for several years on end not a drop of rain falls in July, August, or September. In any case, though 'nebulosity is relatively high in winter, summer is almost cloudless' and 'generally speaking Soviet central Asia is the land of the sun' (Berg). This dryness explains the great range of temperature, not only diurnal (which in September is 29° F. at Tashkent, 34° F. on the Hungersteppe, and 108° F. in summer at Repetek), but also annual. The lower course of the Syr Darya has a mean January temperature of 10° F., but its July mean varies between 79° F. and 100° F.

So these countries have very severe winters, except in southern Turkmenistan, where the season is mild, Repetek having a January mean of 45° F. Snow falls, but not heavily, on 18 days in the year at Leninabad, 37 at Tashkent, and 70 at Kazalinsk. The Aral Sea freezes over for four or five months and sometimes has icefloes up to about the 15th of May. In latitude 35° N. a temperature of —22° F. at Tashkent and at Kushka one of 27° F. is caused by waves of cold air from the north. Spring, which is moderately rainy, is short. By mid-May the temperature becomes high, and summer begins. The extreme dryness of the air helps to make these high temperatures endurable. At 1 p.m. in July Kazalinsk normally registers 90° F., Tashkent 92° F., Margelan 93° F., and the Hungersteppe 96° F.; and the mean for this month in Turkmenistan is at least 86° F. A temperature of 122° F. has been recorded at Termez on the Oxus, and everyone knows that eggs can be cooked in the sand in Turkistan, where the thermometer registers 158° F. at Tashkent and 174° F. at Repetek. Finally, autumn is very fine and sunny, except in the second half; but it is very short. By the end of October it is freezing even in the south. On the whole, this brilliant, dry climate of extremes is well and truly of desert type, and the Aralo-Caspian lands are certainly to be termed deserts. But in spite of what has been said, the attribute in the term 'cold desert' should be denied to them, since, though their winters are severe, their summers are blazing hot. They are deserts of middle and normally temperate latitudes. Their climatic features are due to geographical, not cosmic, factors and are somewhat accidental. They are determined not by their position in latitude, but by their continental situation and by the arrangement of the relief of the land.

To sum up, the climate of the Soviet Union is as a whole very severe. Apart from Turkistan, it may be compared with that of Canada, and in fact the distribution of vegetation belts is nearly the same in both countries. But to understand this latter fact, it is not enough to consider the temperature and rainfall: the nature of the soils, which is partly the work of the climate, must also be examined.

CHAPTER 4

TYPES OF SOIL

Owing to the absence of relief and the consequent difficulty of determining the limits of the natural regions, the soil soon attracted the attention of scientists, who have studied it carefully in Russia, Siberia, and, in recent times, even in Turkistan. Pedology is to a high degree, a Russian science.

There occur in the U.S.S.R. soils which are by way of being exceptions. Thus, certain arid steppes have shifting sands; the southern shores of the Crimea have very peculiar marly soils; in the great forest belt the river-banks display long strips of sand or fine alluvium which are flooded every spring; and in some places the northern regions have pebbly morainic soils. But such details are negligible in a general sketch. It is essential to remember that, as Sibirtsev points out, there are in the U.S.S.R. two great soil-regions, viz. the north, which has been covered by glacial deposits from bottom- and end-moraines and by fluvio-glacial rock-waste; and the south, which is the domain of æolian deposits and is overlaid by a thick mantle of fine, light, yellowish earth that looks very much like loess. During a period after the last ice age, when a steppe climate prevailed, the wind probably transported a great deal of glacial waste in the form of dust and laid it down in the south, where it formed the silty layer which is there seen. Finally, it should be noted that the huge basin of the old Aralo-Caspian inland sea has only recently become dry land.

Glacial and æolian deposits and dry marine sediments have all been refashioned and more or less transformed by the action of heat, cold, frost, water, and snow, by the wind, by the vegetation, by burrowing animals, including man, and perhaps even more by micro-organisms. That is how the soil has been formed. A map of the distribution of its various types shows divisions which are markedly different from those of the geological map. The zonal arrangement is fairly clear in Siberia, but is even more definite in Russia. It runs from north-west to south-east, rather than from north to south, a fact which is enough to suggest the leading part played by the climate in its genesis.

In the extreme north, where very severe cold lasts for long months, stretch the soils of the tundras. Their most striking characteristic is that they are permanently frozen below a certain depth. Hence, vegetation is practically absent, and burrowing animals cannot break them up. Nor can organic matter crumble or become buried so as to mingle with the minerals of the subsoil. It merely rots where it lies, and the originally sandy or clayey earth changes into an acid, blackish soil which has been described by de Martonne as 'a kind of heath-mould or half-formed humus'. The shallow peat bogs, which are far less common than is usually thought, except on the southern fringe, must have had a similar origin. On the whole, the soil is execrable. Besides, the *merzlota* chills it and often makes it marshy by checking the percolation of water. All the same, the tundras contain vast expanses of dry ground; and all the more so because their surface, far from being regularly flat, is much broken. In some parts there are damp hollows or marshes with great peat humps; in others there are rises caused perhaps by a bulging of the ground owing to the upward pressure of the ice underneath; and elsewhere there are just pebbly knolls where the rock is almost bare, forming what Sibirtsev calls a 'skeleton surface'.

Farther south prevail the *podzols*, so named from their ashen appearance (*pod* (Russ.) = under; *zola* = ash). This type of soil is, when dry, powdery and whitish, or rather, greyish. When damp, it has the appearance of plastic clay. Wherever the winters are long and relatively moist and the summers moderately hot, leaching takes place in the upper layers, and the mineral elements (bases, oxides of alumina and of iron) are carried downwards together with particles of silt. Finally, a greyish layer of almost pure silica slightly mixed with clay forms on the surface. Below it is a dirty white layer, and still farther down, under a bed of yellowish-brown clay, is often found an impermeable ferruginous seam, or 'hard pan', similar to the *alios* of the Landes of France. This explains the presence of a number of swamps in this belt. But even where there are no swamps, the podzol is a poor soil, much impoverished by incessant leaching. No natural improvement can be expected in it, because, since its usual cover of vegetable matter, 10 to 13 ins. deep, is not well aerated, organic matter cannot be destroyed and mixed with the soil by the plentiful fauna. Podzol is typical of north-western Russia. The process of 'podzolisation' is hindered by low temperatures in the north and by lack of moisture in the south. In Siberia the podzol has deteriorated in many parts, having been alkalinised in some places and mingled in others with carbonated clay or peat. Anyhow, it affords but poor physical conditions for tillage, a fact all the more serious as it covers large tracts—two-fifths of Russia alone. Actually, it is mostly forested.

The transition from the podzols to the black earth area is not abrupt, but is marked by a narrow, irregular belt of grey soils. In many places where the black-coloured humus combines with the red oxide of iron, it becomes brown. Though its abundance of acid organic matter differentiates it from the black earth, its humus content gives it some relation to the latter type. Indeed, the transitional soils are probably black earth which has deteriorated through the leaching of its carbonates and other salts or oxides and by the thinning out of the humus layer. Their appearance varies considerably with local climate as well as with the nature of the parent rock; but as a rule the top layer, which has a lumpy structure, is surfaced with decayed vegetable matter. Below this is a grey humus which becomes yellowish deeper down. Underneath it a 'podzolised' layer rests on the parent rock. The seam of 'hard pan' is absent, and this fact, together with the relative abundance of humus, gives the grey soils a distinct superiority over the podzols, although, like the latter, it is mainly given up to forest growth.

But their value is not to be compared with that of the BLACK EARTH, the Russian *chernoziom*. Formed in a fairly temperate climate which has tolerably frequent rains, but in sufficiently moderate warmth for evaporation not to take place too quickly, the black earth has two horizons: the top layer, which is between 20 and 40 ins. deep and has a very peculiar granular structure in the upper part, is of a blackish colour which tends to chocolate brown in the south and south-east. This colouring is due to its great humus content. Under this compost there is a yellowy-brown layer with numerous concretions of carbonate of lime. 'The essential condition in the formation of black earth is the presence of a large quantity of carbonate of lime in the parent rock,' says Berg; 'without lime there can be no black earth', says Tanfiliev.

But it would appear, too, that the area must be treeless, since the roots of trees would favour oxidation, and that it should have now, or formerly have had, a continuous cover of grass. It is the decomposition of the grass during millennia that has imparted a black colour to the surface layer. When all is said and done, it seems that the presence of *chernoziom* is related less to the nature of the underlying rock than to the climate. However, it has been established that 'loess best favours the formation of black earth' (Berg), and some writers consider *chernoziom* to be loess on a foundation of clay or marl. It is found also on alluvium and indeed on calcareous rocks, such as chalk. Clayey subsoils have been observed to carry a thinner layer of *chernoziom* than sandy subsoils. In the former case its depth hardly exceeds 20 ins.; in the latter it reaches 30 or even 40. But the proportion of humus in the soil is by no means a function of this depth. In the Ukraine, where the *chernoziom* reaches its greatest depth, as well too as its maximum extension, the proportion of humus is between 6 and 10 per cent.; whilst in the region east of the Volga, where the black earth belt is much narrower, and in Siberia, where it finally ends in isolated patches, the depth of the *chernoziom* is far less, but the humus content rises to 15 per cent. and sometimes more. In any case, this type of soil is wonderfully fertile and is by far the best in the U.S.S.R.

In the *chernoziom* belt, however, and more particularly in its depressions, alkaline soils are no rare occurrence. According to Berg, *solonchaki* 'are soils slightly impregnated with soluble salts (potassium, magnesia, or lime, or a mixture of these)'. Damp and leaching cause most of the soluble salts and particles of alluvium to be carried downwards. The soil thus newly formed is called *soloniets* and is friable and rich in potassium. Since the *solontsy* have little stability, they turn into *solody* with very little humus, if there is an increase in the humidity.

These alkaline areas are, nevertheless, far commoner in the more southerly regions stretching from the Crimean steppe to beyond the lower Volga and then into Kazakstan and the extreme south of western Siberia. They give soils of a dark chestnut colour, which differ noticeably from *chernoziom*. Since they have been formed in drier, warmer regions where evaporation is more intense and rapid and the primæval plant cover was far less dense, they have at their bases very numerous concretions of carbonate of lime which tend to constitute a continuous layer. But their total depth does not exceed 2 ft. and their humus content is never more than between 3 and 4·5 per cent. This means that they are far inferior to the black earth areas, and all the more so because saline depressions are fairly numerous in the alkaline belt.

Still farther south-east up to a line which follows the northern shores of the Caspian and the northern escarpment of the Ust-Urt plateau, and passes a little north of the Aral Sea and Lake Balkhash, lies a still drier region with soils of a light chestnut colour. Above the level at which *solonchaki* occurs, these have a carbonated layer rather like that of the *soloniets* type, then a humiferous layer, at most 14 or 16 ins. deep, in which the humus of the rich upper part is of the order of 1 to 3 per cent. This lack of humus is caused by drought, which in its turn results in poverty of vegetation and insufficient leaching of the minerals. Hence, the parent rock is much more important here than in less-arid regions. Unfortunately, these light-chestnut soils tend to become more and more saline towards the south-east, especially on clayey ground.

Still farther south the desert belt begins. Consequently, the action of water and vegetation has been slight in the formation of the soil, the evolution of which is not very far advanced. Brown in colour—distinctly so on top, but lower down becoming much paler and even tending to grey—the soils in the northern part consist of '*solonietsised*' clays which have a pebbly surface and an increasingly large proportion of salts in their composition, are rather poor in carbonate of lime and very poor in humus, this component reaching its maximum of 1 per cent. in the upper layers. Sometimes there is shifting sand, and consequently in such areas soil cannot form. Here and there, however, the surface layers become somewhat modified by the action of woody vegetation which, says Berg, 'enriches the soil with salts and finely granulated earth at the expense of the gritty material and other products of a more active disintegration of the minerals contained in the sand'. Here *solonchaki* are hardly found, except in valleys and places where the ground water can rise to the surface to evaporate; and *solontsy* are rare.

Finally, at the foot of the mountains of central Asia stretches, luckily for this region, a belt of loess covered by a typical grey earth which, from the chemical and mechanical points of view, differs little from loess properly so-called. Its æolian origin is very doubtful. The soil is of a dirty grey-brown colour, 30 or 40 ins. deep, and poor in humus, but very rich in carbonate of lime, which forms 10 or 15 per cent. of the composition of the upper layers and 25 per cent. lower down. When well watered, it is of remarkable fertility. The only drawback is that, when ground water rises to the surface, it tends to form *solonchaki* here and there.

Thus, there are very varied soils in the U.S.S.R. To pause for a moment to study them was right, for, whilst their origin is explained by geology and by the effects of climate and vegetation, they react in turn very vigorously on the last mentioned; and the zonal distribution of soils is as much responsible as climatic differences for the distribution of vegetation-types and so of the fauna.

CHAPTER 5

VEGETABLE AND ANIMAL LIFE

Climatic, edaphic, and vegetative phenomena are inseparately bound together; but their existing relations do not adequately explain the distribution of vegetation in the Soviet Union, and the effects of the Quaternary ice ages must also be taken into consideration. Russian flora is poor in species because it was destroyed over an immense area by the ice-cap and until recently was unable to recover its ground by spreading out from the unglaciated uplands of the Volga, Donets, and central Russia.

The distribution of animals naturally depends on that of vegetation. Whilst man has modified the latter by clearing away the forest in some places and cultivating the steppe in others, he has had an even greater influence on the fauna. Witness the growing scarcity of the sable and fur-bearing animals in general; the complete disappearance since about 1870 of the equine known as the *tarpan*, or wild horse; the almost total destruction of the musk rat, the saiga antelope, and the beaver, which, to judge from place-names, was widely distributed at one time. Of course, the distribution of animals is less rigid than that of plants. Thus, the wolf, fox, hare, and crow are found throughout Russia and Siberia, the lizard ventures as far north as the mouth of the Dvina and the viper into the Murmanski peninsula. On the other hand, reindeer spend the winter as far south as the north-east of the Tatar Republic of Kazan. In spite of this, it is no exaggeration to say that, broadly speaking, the tundra, forest, and steppe all have their distinct animal associations and that the map showing the distribution of fauna in the Soviet Union is closely related to the climatic and vegetation charts.

Just as in the climatic map there are regions that form exceptions, so it is with the vegetation map; and the exceptional regions are the same in both. This clearly proves that botanical peculiarities are essentially caused by the climate rather than by the soil.

Rather mild winters with a more or less sun-dried limestone scenery give quite a Mediterranean appearance to the south coast of the Crimea, and an examination of the vegetation confirms this impression. There is no pause in plant growth, and spring blossoms follow immediately on the last blooms of autumn. Although, owing to the definitely northern latitude, there is no *maquis*, yet the native flora is Mediterranean in character, and many Mediterranean, Japanese, and Chinese species have been acclimatised without difficulty. Evergreens like the ruscus, pimento, cistus, and ivy (*Hedera helix*) are numerous, and the lower slopes of the hills are wooded with juniper, pubescent oak, and terebinth, with nettle-tree among the undergrowth. Still lower down grow the laurel, cherry-bay, magnolia, myrtle, various palms, the cork oak, cypress, oleander, Judas-tree, black pine, box, and arbutus, not to mention a number of Mediterranean fruit-trees. Whilst the pelican is found in the Sivach lagoon and the jay, tit, goldfinch, and chaffinch come to winter on the coast, the presence of the 'mountain lizard' and the white-breasted swift is further evidence of the Mediterranean character of the region, which is exceptional for Russia.

Exceptional, too, is the vegetation in the Transcaucasian valleys. In the west Colchis has, by reason of its warm, damp climate, a luxuriant vegetation, and an extraordinary abundance of lianas and climbing plants (sarsaparilla, hops, bindweed, milk-vine, epiphyte ferns, Colchis ivy, and wild vine) cling to its evergreens (Pontic rhododendrons, holly, ruscus, and box), to its arbutus bushes and blue brambles that grow near the coast, to its dense alder- and willow-brakes on the marshes, and to its copses of oak, hornbeam, pear-trees, and *zelkovas*; whilst vast expanses are covered with ferns that grow to man's height in summer, not to speak of the dog roses. hazel bushes, low chestnut-trees, pomegranate bushes, and Pontic azaleas that form the undergrowth.

In the west the Talysh valley has similar characteristics. Evergreens are rarer, but climbing plants are abundant, and the ironwood, a native of Persia, grows in thick clumps. The fauna, with its pheasants, Caspian gulls, sultan hens, zebus, porcupines, panthers, and tigers, is far more peculiar than that of Colchis, in which only the native pheasant calls for mention.

The lower portion of the Amur basin from Blagoveshchensk downwards, and perhaps the whole of the Soviet Far East, must also be set apart as exceptional. In the Zeya-Bureya depression lies a steppe thickly covered with reed bent-grass and comose feather grass and frequented by the bustard and a rodent called the gopher; and here and there resinous species (forest pine and spruce) form woods but hardly large forests. The predominant type is the forest of broad-leaved trees with the Manchurian oak, white and black birch, elm, wild cherry, maple, and spindle-tree. On the banks of large rivers the balsam poplar, Manchurian ash and walnut, and Amur linden grow in forests which are liable to be flooded, have a luxuriant under-growth, and are carpeted with Amur creeper. Though not so plentiful as in Transcaucasia, climbing plants hold an important place, especially in the districts near the Ussuri. These latter are characterised by the frequency of southern species; for example, the cork-tree and Amur lilac. The same is true of the fauna. Besides the lemming, the miniver, sable, wild boar, and stag, there are the Manchurian tiger, the leopard, Amur wild cat, Japanese spotted deer, Japanese crane, Japanese red-legged ibis, the cuckoo of southern China, and the Indian oriole. Hence, in its fauna and flora as well as in its monsoon climate this region bears sure evidence of the warm, damp influence of the south.

Lastly, a special place must be reserved for the high mountain areas of the Caucasus, Pamir, Tien Shan, and Altai. As they are situated in very different latitudes and as the climatic, orographical, and edaphic conditions are not very similar, it is difficult to formu-late a botanical and zoological table which will apply to them all. But at any rate we may provisionally note that a series of different zones of vegetation occur at different heights: first, more or less arid steppe, then grassland with arborescent plants, followed in turn by a generally undeveloped woodland of broad-leaved species, coniferous forest, sub-alpine pasture, alpine pasture, mountain tundra, and, lastly, bare rock.

All these exceptional regions occupy only a tiny fraction of the Soviet Union, and nearly the whole of the territory is divided between four main vegetation-types: tundra, forest, steppe, and desert.

Several hundred miles in width, the tundra is marked in Siberia and Russia alike by its monotonous and slightly undulating relief, its vast horizons, and especially by the absence of trees owing to the severity of the winter, the violence of the winds, the shortness of the growing period, the dryness of the climate, the shallow penetration of roots owing to the *merzlota*, and, above all perhaps, the coldness of the soil, which by depriving the roots of the necessary moisture prevents them from enduring the evaporation that occurs in the hot season.

The woody vegetation consists of small bushes and tiny creeping shrubs growing where the soil thaws for a little time. They include the black birch, marsh andromeda, dwarf willow, whortleberry, and the still smaller sedge, crowberry, bilberry, and juniper. Nearly every-where else there are more or less peaty bogs or else vast expanses covered with a dirty yellow moss or dull white reindeer-lichen. These

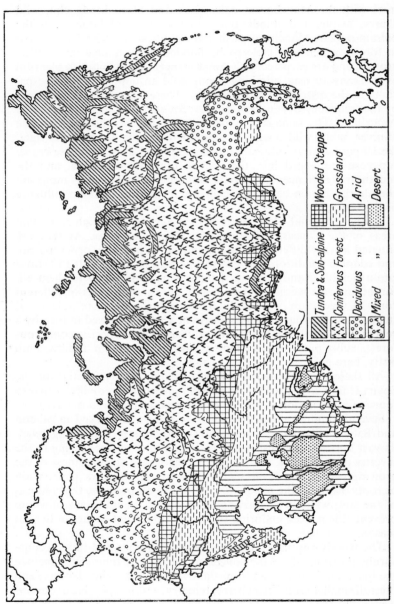

FIG. 8. VEGETATION BELTS.

Tundra & Sub-alpine
Coniferous Forest
Deciduous ,,
Mixed ,,
Wooded Steppe
Grassland
Arid ,,
Desert

are interrupted at intervals by bare patches which, when of clay, are known as 'speckled tundra', and when rocky, as 'pebbly tundra'. Here and there are patches of grass brightened for a fleeting moment by vividly coloured polar flowers, some of the commonest of which are the forget-me-not, buttercup, and saxifrage. On the whole, the landscape is extremely depressing in the dim light of a low sun, and the flora is remarkably poor.

Though the fauna is also of recent development, it is a little more plentiful. Cold-blooded animals are almost completely absent, and there are no reptiles or amphibians, very few worms or land molluscs. Insects are rare, with the exception of butterflies and swarms of mosquitoes in summer. On the other hand, there are many birds, especially semi-aquatic species, among which are the ptarmigan, snow owl, willow grouse, swan, goose, wild duck, and gull; and also a good number of rodents, such as the lemming, Arctic hare, shrew, and *rat à sabots*, which are pursued by the carnivorous snow polecat, sable, wolf, blue fox, and glutton. Special mention must be made of the reindeer. The wild species has almost disappeared in Europe, but the domesticated species plays an essential part in the life of these regions. Both species live on lichens and mosses. They spend the winter on the fringes of the forests and in summer try to escape from the clouds of mosquitoes by fleeing to the coast.

The tundra and forest intermingle in a transitional zone of forest-tundra of varying breadth, which advances very far north in Siberia. In it islands of open woodland composed of spruce and Siberian larch, birch, and in some places poplar or willow—all equally low, poor, stunted, and often dying—form dark patches on the mossy, swampy surface. This transitional zone is from the zoological point of view a meeting-place of the fauna of the tundra and of the forest.

Gradually, the trees become more numerous and more robust, and the expanses of tundra in their turn shrink to islands in the forest. Then the islands become smaller by degrees until they disappear, and the forest belt begins. This belt corresponds broadly to the podzol zone and is situated in climates with moderately warm, moist summers, and long severe winters which are fairly dry in eastern Siberia, but relatively snowy in Russia and western Siberia. It covers nearly half the territory of the Soviet Union. Its northern limit leaves outside it a good half of the Kolski peninsula, skirts the White Sea, cuts across the base of the Kanin peninsula, passes to the south of the middle Vychegda, crosses the Pechora at Pustozersk in lat. 67° 30′ N., goes over the Urals, and follows the Arctic Circle for a time until it reaches the mouth of the Taz. Then it crosses the Yenisey in the latitude of Khantayka, runs along the plateau of central Siberia in lat. 70° N., passes Nizhne Kolymsk and the upper basin of the

Anadyr, and reaches the Bay of Korfa in Kamchatka. Its southern boundary runs more or less through Zhitomir, Kiev, Kaluga, Ryazan, Gorky, Kazan, the mouth of the Vyatka, and the confluence of the Kama and Belaya to Ufa. Then it goes round the Urals and passes through Nizhni Tagil, Irbit, Tyumen, Ishim, Kolyvan, and Tomsk. After this it turns south in eastern Siberia to reach the mountains. It is the world's largest forest.

In dealing with the origin of the various species, a distinction might be drawn between the east, where truly Siberian species predominate even in eastern Russia, and the west, where the influence of Fennoscandian deposits is great and into which the Hercynian Forest of central Europe extends in some degree. But it is better to recognise two main divisions: the *tayga*, or forest, which is essentially composed of conifers; and the mixed forest, in which deciduous trees are largely mingled with the conifers. The mixed type prevails in Europe south of a line through Leningrad, Kostroma, Kirov, and Sverdlovsk. It is absent in Siberia, where, as in northern Russia, only *tayga* is found.

The Siberian word *tayga*, properly speaking, denotes damp, spongy forests which have many peat bogs and marshes; but its use has been extended to cover all forests in which the predominant species are spruce, fir, larch, pine, and cedar. Here and there in it, however, are found clumps of birch, aspen, or alder, which generally appear to have taken the place of conifers that have been destroyed. Soviet scientists distinguish four types of spruce forests as well as of pine forest (or *bors*). They are, first, the type that grows on well-drained or sandy ground carpeted with green moss; secondly, the type distinguished by a long species of moss and found on highly podzolised soil with a tendency to marshiness; thirdly, the type which occurs on swampy plains and is marked by sphagnum; and, lastly, the type found at the bottoms of little valleys and carpeted with grass. In western Siberia a north-to-south series of sub-zones is recognised, first, of larch and spruce, then of cedar and marsh, and, lastly, of marsh and *urmany*, or extremely dense and almost impenetrable thickets of fir, 'into which one must have ventured in order to know fear'. In spite of these differences in detail, the *tayga* may be described as a monotonous, dark, and mournfully silent forest with trees that grow close together, but are rarely fine specimens, the biggest having a girth of little more than 3 ft. Even in Russia there are great expanses of virgin forest. In Siberia the *tayga* is of a poorer kind than in Russia, because it suffers from the dry, severe climate as well as from gigantic fires which are so frequent that the distant smell of burning wood at once reminds many travellers of the country.

Whilst the area covered by the *tayga* corresponds roughly to that of the podzol properly so called, the mixed forest grows on grey soils and 'is marked by the presence of both the peduncular oak and the spruce' (Berg); but, together with the pine and fir—not to mention the walnut thickets under the shade of the oak groves—it also includes the aspen, hornbeam, linden, ash, alder, elm, maple, sycamore, and, above all, birch, the national tree of the Russians, which being resistant to cold advances very far north. The predominance of broad-leaved species increases southwards until at last conifers disappear. Hence, the peculiar appearance of this type of forest, which is brighter, clearer, and more cheerful than the *tayga*. But its composition is not hard-and-fast, and there is a tendency for the more shade-giving species to replace those which give less. In central Russia the mixed forest has already been cut up into more or less vast sections and loses ground every day to man's attacks.

For that matter, it does not form a continuous mantle even in the north, for it is interrupted in some places by swamps overgrown with rushes, reeds, or mosses, or else turned into peat bogs whose neighbourhood makes the adjacent pinewoods into an unhealthy and inhospitable *mshara*; in other places by deforestation which is particularly common in the Baltic areas, where the *liady* have been abandoned owing to the exhaustion of the soil and are slowly being forested once more; and in yet other places by natural glades called *polya*, which generally occur on patches of steppe soil and have been enlarged by human agency. The presence of game was not the least of the advantages that attracted man to these glades.

The forest has infinitely more game than the tundra, especially of course in the parts seldom visited by the hunter. This means that not so much of its fauna has been killed off in Siberia as in Russia, and in the *tayga* as in the mixed forest, large animals are noticeably fewer. However, the bear, a magnificent beast with prodigious strength, is still fairly common in Siberia and even in the north and north-west of Russia. The same is true of the wolf and the fox. The glutton, lynx, elk, and roebuck are hunted too. The sable, marten, beech-marten, and badger survive even in Russia, in spite of being hunted, and squirrels, polecats, and hares, both grey and white, are still numerous. To some 150 species of mammals are to be added more than 200 species of birds, among others the capercaillie, ptarmigan, grouse, hazel-hen, partridge, and woodcock, to say nothing of the three-toed woodpecker, red bunting, wax-wing, hawfinch, nutcracker, white-winged crossbill, or of the green woodpecker, roller, goldfinch, and willow-warbler, which are found on the fringes of the forest-steppe.

Just as there is a woodland-tundra, so there is, usually on grey soils, a woodland-steppe marking the transition from forest proper to steppe.[1] Its southern boundary runs approximately through An-anyev, Kremenchug, Poltava, Borisoglebsk, Saratov, Sterlitamak, Troitsk, Barnaul, and the foothills of the Altai. Beyond that, wood-land-steppe exists only in patches in central and eastern Siberia. To some extent it is the result of felling, but it is especially due to the greater dryness of the climate. In Russia the predominant species is the oak, together with the ash, lime, maple, elm, beech in places, and, above all, the aspen; in Siberia it is the birch. Pinewoods are sometimes seen on sandy soil. But between the wooded areas are large treeless spaces, some natural and others not, where steppe plants, like the *kovils* (feathergrass) and fescues, are to be seen in large numbers. Similarly, the fauna is a mixture of forest species (wolf, fox, roebuck, elk, squirrel, and capercaillie) with steppe spe-cies (marmot, jerboa, gopher, and steppe eagle). But intensive hunt-ing has terribly impoverished the fauna. Its individuals are becoming rare, and a number of species have quite disappeared, as the aurochs and wild horse have done, or like the bear, maral stag, and beaver, which have nearly gone. In the same way the original steppe vegeta-tion has nearly all been destroyed by agriculture.

This is true not only in woodland-steppe, but also in the steppe proper, which comprises all the rest of the Union, except the Aralo-Caspian deserts. The chief characteristic of the steppe is its bareness. Its moderately thick carpet of herbaceous plants is practically treeless, except on river-banks which are liable to flooding. It has often been said in the past that the steppe was formerly wooded and that the nomads destroyed the trees; and this opinion still has a few sup-porters. But it is probably wrong. In the first place, although the limits of the forest and steppe belts do not coincide exactly with those of the podzols and loess, it seems to be accepted that forest and *chernoziom* do not go well together, for black earth deteriorates in contact with trees. Similarly, saline subsoils are unfavourable to forest growth. But the chief obstacle to forest growth in the steppe belt is the climate, for there is not enough rain for tree life in summer, added to which is the intense evaporation in the hot weather owing to the dryness of the air and the strength of the winds.

In the Black Earth region nearly the whole steppe is cultivated and bears little resemblance to the scene evoked by Gogol's poetic enthu-siasm in *Taras Bulba*.[2] But at any rate a few remnants enable us to guess what it was once like. With a far denser mantle of vegetation

---

[1] It is important to notice that the northern half of the belt called 'steppe' by the Russians was in fact a sort of prairie like that in Canada. The term is often used to mean poor steppe such as exists in the south of Russia and central Asia. In this book the word 'steppe' will be given as wide a meaning as is usual among Russian scientists.

[2] There is a translation in Everyman's Library.

The Black Earth country. Harvest in the Ukraine

onion towers in Kiev and the bridges over the Dnepr showing the high right and low left bank usual in Russia

The Cathedral of St. Sophia, Novgorod, built 1045–1052

than exists on the Argentine *pampas*, it was above all an association of grasses, though dicotyledons were not rare. The narrow leaves of the grasses like the narrow-bladed *kovil*, the villous *kovil*, and the fescue are well adapted to a dry climate. But with the grasses are associated little bush-like trees; e.g. the wild plum, locust-tree, and dwarf almond; plants with bulbs or tubers to protect them from drought, such as the iris, hyacinth, and tulip; and hardy herbaceous plants like the anemone and clematis. At least, this is the case in the north on the *chernoziom* proper, where herbaceous Ranunculaceæ, Cruciferæ, Papilionatæ, and Umbelliferæ grow in large numbers. Thanks to them, the steppe is flecked with myriads of spots of colour. Steppe tulip, iris, pheasant's eye, dark red peonies, and blue sage bloom one after the other, hastening to complete their cycle of growth. But this wonderful sight does not last long. By the end of June the steppe turns greyish; in August it looks scorched; and only the grasses are now seen, especially the *kovils*, whose straight, bare stems cover the country in autumn with what looks like the bristles of a giant brush.

In the south-south-east on the northern shores of the Black Sea in the valley of the lower Dnepr, the northern Crimea, the middle Don, Trans-Volga, and, lastly, the northern part of Kazakstan and the Siberian steppes of Kalunda and Minusinsk, the same vegetation does not appear. On the chestnut soils that occur here, a few hardy bulbous plants and little shrubs may still be found, but the predominance of grasses, *kovil*, thyrsus, and sheep fescue especially, is overwhelming. Here and there, when the soil is slightly saline, are a few halophytes. Of course, everything is scorched in summer, except the meadows in the *bliuda* and the copses of willow, oak, black poplar, elm, and maple, which stretch out along damp valley bottoms and are overgrown with hawthorn and wild vine.

Like the original steppe flora, the original steppe fauna is becoming rarer. There remain none of the equines which were once characteristic of the country: Prjvalski's horse, the tarpan, and the kiang; no saiga antelopes, stags, wild boars, or beavers, scarcely any roebuck, only a few bustards, and far fewer wild bees, though butterflies in their myriads still haunt the flowers among the grass. But birds are very numerous (grey partridges, larks, pipits, buntings, quails, pelicans, herons, ducks, curlews, etc.), and there are also birds of passage, including the gull, wild goose, starling, peewit, bullfinch, hoopoe, and nightingale. Although birds of prey, especially the steppe eagle, make life hard for them, the incredible abundance of warrens and mole-hills which make so many holes or mounds on the ground as at times to interfere seriously with the movement of horses, bears witness to the number and activity of burrowing animals and rodents.

Siberia and Russia both swarm with rats, hares, hamsters, bobacs, lemmings, polecats, moles, jerboas, and above all with susliks, whose amazing fertility laughs at the most scientific means of extermination and inflicts damage on the crops equal to that sometimes done by flights of locusts in the southern Ukraine during dry and scorching summers.

Still farther towards the south-east the dryness of the climate increases and the soil becomes poorer and more saline. This is the grey steppe, marked not only by *kovil* grasses, but also by artemisia much mixed with grass. The lower valleys of the Volga and Ural are exceptional, with their reed- and willow-brakes and poplar copses which once harboured hosts of pheasants, egrets, and ibises, but now serve as refuges for moorhens and wild duck. Elsewhere there are only bushes and creepers, brightened in spring by a few short-lived annuals, like the tulip, buttercup, and rhubarb. On saline soils, which increase towards the south-east, the vegetation is even poorer and is halophilous, being composed mainly of goosefoot, white and black wormwood, and tamarisk. This is the White Steppe, with its lichens and algæ, a semi-desert region whose fauna includes the saiga antelope, fox, lark, and, above all, the hamster and suslik.

Finally, as the drought increases, we reach the desert. Wormwood and goosefoot grow in its northern portion, where wide expanses are covered with *boyalysh* bushes, 12 to 18 ins. high, and *byurgun*, 4 to 6 ins. tall, as well as by various species of wormwood growing 4 or 8 to the square yard. The uniformly insufficient distribution of rainfall does not allow the usual blooming of brightly coloured flowers in spring and thus prevents the appearance of any seasonal differences. Only a purely xerophilous flora can adapt itself to the continuously precarious conditions. Farther south the problem for the vegetation is not merely to adapt iself to the drought, but also to struggle against the invasion of sand. Hence, many bushes have only tiny leaves or thorns. Some, like the shrublike goosefoot and sand astragal, drop their branches; others, like milk parsley and sand carex, the calligonum *juzgun*, and acacia, as well as wormwood, couch-grass, brome-grass, or viviparous meadow-grass, develop long roots which fix the shifting sand. But the most peculiar plant is the saxaul which, once the sand has been fixed, quickly ousts the plants that fixed it. The white species grows on sand and has quite small leaves; the black species prefers slightly saline, clayey soil and is completely devoid of foliage. From 12 to 20 ft. high, of wood so hard that an axe can hardly cut it, and of startling weirdness of shape, it forms little forests, or rather scrub, obstructed by an extraordinary litter of dead branches. Lastly, on the loess plains among the foothills in spring there is a sudden flowering of short-lived plants,

mainly meadow-grass and sedges which then form a continuous carpet dotted with stars of Bethlehem, speedwell, poppies, and geran-
iums. But by the middle of May these have all been withered away
by the sun, and only dreary euphorbias, assafœtida, wormwood,
and goosefoot are to be seen. The valleys which are liable to flooding
stand out alone on account of their green grass.

Of course, the desert has a fauna which is very peculiar because of
its protective mimicry as well as owing to its adaptation to the great
heat, drought, and the nature of the soil. The suslik, ground hare,
rat-mole, and *zapode* are plentiful, but saiga antelopes and *jeiran*
antelopes, wild sheep, wild asses, a fair number of birds, many lizards
and tortoises, and, above all, numbers of snakes are seen. Lastly, a
multitude of aquatic birds, the hare, the jackal, the reed-cat, wild
boar, and its enemy the tiger, live in the reed-brakes in the valleys
which are liable to inundation.

To sum up, there are in the Soviet Union, apart from the icy
wastes of the tundra which until recently were of no interest except
to small communities of Hyperboreans, two main vegetation-types:
the forest and the more or less dry steppe. Owing to the splendour
of its spring flowers, the steppe has counted for much in the formation
of Russian artistic feeling. The monotony and unsettling immensity
of its horizons, which tempt one to travel, has certainly had some
influence in forming the ever-restless and unstable Russian mind and
has greatly contributed to the rise of Russian economic power.
Lastly, it has played an immense part in Russian history. At first
this part was negative, for the steppe was the path of the dreaded
invasions and, even after the victory of Kulikovo had brought back
freedom in 1380, it was long called *dikoye polye*, 'the field of fear'.
Its positive action came later when its conquest made the prince of
Moscow a very great monarch, a 'tsar' indeed and heir to the Basileus
of Byzantium. But certainly, the part it has played in Russian life
has been much less important than that of the forest.

The forest is indeed a great benefactor to man, whom it attracts
and who thrives in its glades. There he finds game, furs, room for his
fields and stock, bark for tanning, and wood to build his house, to
warm himself, and to make his furniture and agricultural implements.
Even today the Russian woodcutter shows an unrivalled ingenuity
and skill in his use of wood. Ordinary utensils, real objects of art,
rough *izby*, the villas of rich merchants, the ramparts and towers of
olden days, and churches—'there is nothing', says Camena d'Almeida,
'that the Russian has not been able to make out of wood from his
forests.' The same writer has forcefully pointed out how great a
place the forest has had in the history of this people, how when the
old 'Russia of Kiev' tottered and then fell under the blows of the

nomads of the steppes, the Russians took refuge in the forest glades. The centre of the new state was Moscow, a town situated in an open space in the forest; and the value to the defence of those *zaseki*, or forest retreats strengthened with *abattis* of trees on the woodland-steppe, is well known. 'The forest assured the safety of Russia and preserved her from lasting servitude,' and in it began the reconquest. 'The Muscovite state might be defined as a forest state with all its peculiarities.'

What decided the course to be followed by the natural routes across these infinitely vast spaces? It might be said that the steppe had no need of natural routes, since one could gallop about it at will. But what routes passed through the forests? This is where the important part played by the rivers comes in.

CHAPTER 6

RIVERS

There is obviously no need to discuss the Caucasian rivers—the Kura, Araks (Araxes), Terek, and Kuban—which for a great part of their courses are rushing torrents; the rivers of the Kola peninsula and Karelia, which rush headlong down over rapids and falls and in some cases never freeze; or even the rivers of central Asia which, though at the start well fed by the snow and glaciers of the mountains, are extremely attenuated by intense evaporation during their passage across the desert and disappear in the sand without being able to reach the sea. The Syr Darya and Oxus alone struggle through to the Aral and can be used to some small extent for transport. Both these types of river are exceptional in the Soviet Union, the former owing to the steepness of the gradient and the latter because of the desert climate prevailing in the basins. The Amur river system may also be said to be exceptional, since it depends on a monsoon climate and thus has a régime unlike any other in the whole of the Soviet Union. What is said here, therefore, is intended to apply mainly to the rivers in Russia and Siberia.

These show certain differences among themselves. Thus, the period of freezing-up is not the same in all of them, nor is their absolute or relative volume; floods occur earlier and are not so great in some as in others; and gradients do not have the same uniformity in all cases. But these are minor details, and, as M. Pardé has shown, the fundamental likenesses are far more important. This is easily understood when we consider the monotony of the relief and the sameness of the climate.

Most of these rivers have immense basins. The Volga drains 563,000 square miles; the Dnepr 197,109; the Don 166,037; the Kama 202,322; the Dvina 139,772; the Pechora 123,555; the Neva 108,883; and the Oka 94,597 square miles. As for the Ob, Yenisey, Amur, or Lena, any one of their basins would contain the British Isles seven

49

or eight times. There is also a likeness in the great length of the rivers. Although the Neva, which is merely the waste-pipe of Lake Ladoga, is only 47 miles long, the modest Pechora is 1034 miles, the Don 1124, the Kama 1170, the Dnepr 1328, the Ural 1477, the Volga about 2000, the Yenisey 2492, the Lena 2508, the Amur 2690, and the Ob-Irtysh 3114! A further resemblance lies in the gentleness of their gradients, that of the Volga being 1 in 1000, the Dnepr 1 in 1250, the Don 1 in 1430, and the Amur 1 in 9000 from Pokrovka to the mouth, whilst that of the quiet Seine averages 1 in 167 on its whole course and 1 in 834 downstream from Paris.

The Ob is only 300 ft. above sea level 1200 miles from the Arctic Sea, and at an elevation of 500 ft. the Yenisey still has 1200 miles to travel. This means that another characteristic common to all the rivers is an extremely slow current, normally less than 20 ins. per second. Even at the height of its flood the Volga scarcely attains a rate of $4\frac{1}{2}$ ft. per second. They all suffer from a lengthy freeze-up, which lasts three months at Astrakhan, Rostov-on-Don, and Kiev; three and a half to four months on the Neva, the middle and upper Don, and upper Dnepr; four and a half to five months on the Oka and upper and middle Volga; five and a half months on the Kama; more than six months on the Pechora; nearly seven months on the lower courses of the Siberian rivers, and indeed in cold years ten months at the mouths of the Yenisey and Lena.

Most of them, especially those in Russia, have a rather peculiar form, resembling a very wide-mouthed funnel with a narrow neck. The Volga affords a particularly clear example of this characteristic, the cause of which is to be found in the retreat of seas which were once far more extensive than now, when the Black and Caspian Seas had advanced northwards and the Arctic Sea towards the south. In many instances this retreat greatly lengthened the courses of the rivers, that of the Volga, for example, being increased nearly threefold.

The rivers have another feature in common. Though their rates of discharge are relatively small, their absolute rates are as a rule quite moderate and in some cases even large. Thus, whilst the Don has an average annual rate of 918 cu. yds. per second at Kalach, the southern Bug has one of only 119 (i.e. less than the Doubs or Ain); and though the Donets 'is shamefully weak' (Pardé), the Dnepr on the other hand has an average rate of 14,832 cu. yds. per second, the Pechora one of 5241, the Dvina 4539, the Kama 5366, the Ural 527, and the Volga 10,202 at Kuybyshev, 10,921 at Saratov, and 11,157 at Stalingrad. The Siberian rivers flow more slowly on the whole. Recent Soviet publications give the mean annual rate as 591 cu. ft. per second in the Ob, 819 in the Yenisey, 518 in the Amur, 737 in the Lena, and only 62 in the Oxus and 20 in the Syr Darya.

These enormous rates of discharge explain the widening of the valleys. The Volga has a width of 550 yds. at Rybinsk and at least 1100 or 1600 yds. in its middle and lower courses; the Oka measures 700 yds. from bank to bank at Gorky; the Kama 760 below Perm; the Dnepr 1100 at Kiev; the Yenisey $2\frac{1}{2}$ miles on the upstream side of the gorge at Yeniseisk and 30 miles in its estuary which, like that of the Ob, is really much like an arm of the sea. The lower Amur, where the river is braided, opens out to six miles for much of its course.

These figures are poor, however, considering the great size of the basins. This is not surprising in view of the moderate rainfall. The Russo-Siberian rivers are but poorly fed; and they would cut a paltry figure if during much of the year evaporation was not greatly reduced owing to the low temperatures. The fairly general impermeability of the rocks, not in the Black Earth country, but in the regions mantled in glacial deposits, assists the run-off, but leads to a great decrease in the volume of the rivers in the dry months.

The lowest level of the water does not occur in summer. The rivers become very low then, but their want of water is mitigated by heavy rainstorms. It is in winter, and particularly in February, that the volume is least. That of the upper Volga falls in this season to 1131 cu. yds. per second, that of the middle Volga to 1504, and that of the lower Dnepr to 327. The Don has been known to fall as low as 55 cu. yds. and the Bug to 6·5 cu. yds.! These low volumes are due to the arrest of the water by frost, an agent which is of prime importance in the north-west, where, on the upper Volga, for example, only 30 per cent. of the annual precipitation is in the form of rain. In eastern Siberia the small streams freeze to the bottom, an occurrence which causes difficulties in water supply. But in spring the reverse process releases melt-water to cause the highest volume for the year. True, a period of high water occurs in the warm season, right at the beginning of summer, when the heaviest showers fall, and also in autumn when warm rains accompany *otepely*; but these are both moderate and not to be compared with the floods due to melt-water in spring. There is an increase from west to east in the regular occurrence and dimensions of these floods, which begin in April in the west, in May in the east, and as late as June in the north. Very slow in spreading, they attain enormous proportions, thanks to the concentration of the tributary rivers, especially when copious spring rains follow on heavy falls of snow. At this time the Svir increases its rate of discharge to 1831 cu. yds. per second, the Neva to 6017, the Don to 17,657, the Oka to 26,160, the Dnepr to 30,083, the Kama to 41,855, and the Volga to 82,401 cu. yds. per second at Saratov, where the river has been known to rise $52\frac{1}{2}$ ft. It is therefore

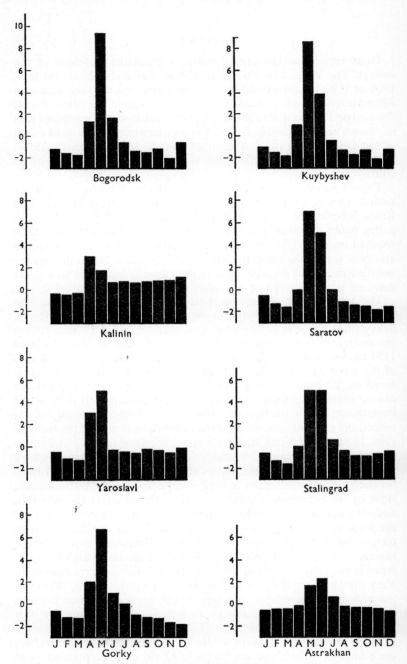

FIG. 9. MEAN MONTHLY VARIATIONS OF THE VOLGA AT DIFFERENT POINTS
ON ITS COURSE.

The figures show feet above and below the normal depth.

52

not surprising that the spring floods represent 58 per cent. of the annual discharge of the Dnepr and 75 per cent. of that of the Don, or that, as Pardé says, they form the most striking feature of the seasonal variations.

'In short,' concludes this writer, 'there are many more features of similarity between the Don and the Pechora or the Niemen and the Kama than between the Seine and the Garonne or the Rhone and the Loire. If a few minor dissimilarities are neglected, the river régimes in the vast plains of Russia appear uniformly subjected to the same despotic, pitiless, and monotonous regularity.' Yet it is not impossible to draw a distinction between the rivers of the north and those of the south.

The northern rivers have been greatly affected by the invasion of the ice-cap, which blocked a number of the streams and compelled them to flow along its front for varying distances. This explains the importance of the *prapotoki* in the existing relief. The ice-cap more than once diverted rivers and caused captures, as it did in the case of the Luchesa, a tributary of the Dnepr, which was diverted into the western Dvina a little downstream of Vitebsk. On the other hand, moraines have greatly retarded the evolution of the gradient profiles of the rivers. After a very long, flat reach across the plain often comes a passage through a moraine, where there is constriction aggravated by rapids and falls. Above Rzhev the upper Volga has 32 rapids in 60 miles. The Kivach Falls on the Suna, which flows into Lake Onega, are 23 ft. high; the Ghirvas Falls 33 ft., and the Poor Falls 59 ft. There is no river in the north-west whose longitudinal profile does not show irregularities of this kind. But the northern river system has other peculiar features. Owing to greater precipitation in winter, they have a higher coefficient of nivosity than their southern counterparts. Their discharge benefits not only from weaker evaporation, but also from the presence of the *merzlota*, which checks the percolation of water. Siberia, and especially the Lena basin, shows this with particular clearness. Finally, because of their south-to-north direction, they become ice-free in their upper courses sooner than lower down, and the break-up of the ice, which is a phenomenon of terrific and awe-inspiring violence, causes floods which are often catastrophic and which spread out to 15 miles on either side of the river.

As the southern rivers flow through unglaciated country, they run in a more definite direction, viz. roughly north-to-south, and their longitudinal profiles are far less subject to irregularities. The famous falls of the Dnepr are an exception due to the fact that in corrading its bed the river has met crystalline rock through which it has had difficulty in cutting. The contrast between the height of their right banks, and the low, flat left banks is greater than in the northern rivers. It was by noticing this that Baer formulated his famous law of asymmetrical valleys. Frost paralyses their life for a shorter time than it does those flowing into the Baltic or Arctic Seas, and as their lower courses are freed from ice first the break-up in spring is far less dangerous. Lastly, in spite of the disadvantages of the Black Sea, the southern rivers, with the exception of the Volga, certainly have outlets which are definitely superior to those in the north. In the Amur and its feeders floods occur very suddenly after heavy rain in summer and often do great damage. In 1872 the water rose 50 ft. at Poshkova in the middle course of the river.

Anyhow, both groups of rivers have played a leading part in the life of the Russian people, first because of the incredible amount of fish in them, which has often compensated for the short-comings of the harvests; secondly, owing to their navigability, even though this lasts for only a short period in the year. Linked together as it were by the *voloki*, or portages, which are so low as to be crossed without difficulty, they have constituted an admirable network of communications. The radial character of the chief rivers in European Russia was a main factor in the growth of the principality of Moscow.

For the steppe peoples they have been important routes towards the forest; for the forest-dwellers they have been natural ways into the steppe; and the service rendered by them to the merchants of the riverside towns in their trade with Byzantium is well known. Great river routes, like that along the Dvina and Volga or the one along the Dvina and Dnepr, by which the Varangians reached Greece, led from the Baltic to the Black Sea or Caspian. The importance of the part played in the Russian penetration into Siberia by the navigation of the Ob, Irtysh, Yenisey, Angara, Lena, or Amur can never be forgotten. In fact, the conquest of Russia and in large measure that of Siberia moved along the rivers where there was good alluvial soil, more moisture than elsewhere, food to be got by fishing, and above all a convenient means of moving about. Lastly, it must be noticed that the existence of a high right bank, usually sheltered from the worst floods, though not from landslides due to undercutting by erosion, has favoured the growth of towns in Siberia as in Russia. Krasnoyarsk, for instance, means 'red cliff'. Most of the large Russo-Siberian towns are situated on rivers; for example, Pskov on the Velikaya, Novgorod on the Volkhov, Smolensk, Kiev, and Dnepropetrovsk on the Dnepr, Kaluga and Ryazan on the Oka, Kalinin, Yaroslavl, Kostroma, Gorky, Kazan, Ulyanovsk, Kuybyshev, Saratov, Stalingrad, and Astrakhan on the Volga, Omsk on the Irtysh, Novosibirsk on the Ob, Tomsk on the Tom, Krasnoyarsk on the Yenisey, Irkutsk on the Angara, Yakutsk on the Lena, Blago-veshchensk and Khabarovsk on the Amur.

Thus, in spite of their numerous drawbacks, the Russo-Siberian rivers have rendered immense service to man. The 'strength of the Russians', wrote A. Allix, 'came from the alliance of river and forest.' It has been said that the hesitations of Russian policy, influenced at one time by the Baltic and White Seas, that is, by the West, and at other times by the Black Sea and Caspian, that is, by Asia and the Near East, have merely reflected the dual character of the Russian river system, which leads towards both these groups of seas. This is certainly an exaggeration. What is certain is that the Soviet Union is lamentably poor in coastline and that at a time when over-land journeys could only be made on foot or on horseback, the immense distances might almost have precluded the country from all appreciable progress, if the waterways had not provided communica-tion betwen the different regions. 'The history of Russia', says G. de Korff, 'began on the rivers. . . . For nearly ten centuries the water-ways were the chief guides of the destinies of the country and of the men who ruled it.' Besides having been an essential means of colonis-ing, first, Russia itself and then Siberia, they have greatly aided in the formation of the Russian State and Empire.

Part II

EXPANSION OF THE RUSSIAN WORLD FROM EARLY TIMES

CHAPTER 7

FORMATION OF THE RUSSIAN NATION AND STATE

The Soviet empire is colossal not only in area, but also in the number of its inhabitants. The census of January 1959 credited it with 208,826,000. By January 1960 this figure had risen to 212,486,000. This enormous swarm of humanity is certainly not quite half as much as the population of China and is greatly inferior in number to that of India. But the Soviet Union contains 45 million persons more than the United States; more than twice as many people as there are in Japan; and nearly four times as many as there are in Great Britain and Northern Ireland. This means that it has one of the largest populations in the world. There would be no great exaggeration in saying that out of every ten human beings in the world one is a Soviet citizen. But though this figure has an enormous absolute value, its relative value is small, for 200,000,000 inhabitants on an area of 8,648,000 square miles gives a mean density of only 23 per square mile; this is far greater than the density in Canada (3 per square mile) or Australia (2 per square mile), but very much less than in the United Kingdom (509), Japan (400), Italy, (343), Germany (347 in 1939), China proper (231), Poland (233), France (197), and even the United States (44).

There are in the Soviet Union, as P. George has pointed out, immense expanses of ice-ridden and, as a rule, useless surface, not to mention gigantic areas of virgin forest. Except where population has been attracted through the presence of immediately utilisable resources, these expanses should in all fairness be deducted from the totals on which the density is calculated. If cultivated areas were alone taken into account, the Soviet Union would be found to have a density of 112 persons to the square mile as against 91 in the United States. Be that as it may, the Soviet Union is certainly sparsely peopled and could hold a far larger population than it does in many parts of its territory.

58

Not everywhere, however. Thanks to its industries, the Moscow district, for instance, has nearly 259 persons to the square mile. The fertile Black Earth in the Ukraine has 150 or 180, and many of the districts near the Volga have about 130. But these are exceptional figures. In Siberia, outside industrial areas, the density rarely exceeds 25 or 40 even in the south-west, and it is far less in the centre and south-east. Although in restricted areas the oases of Turkistan and Transcaucasia have a fairly dense population which varies, according to the place, from 65 to 150 persons to the square mile, the Russo-Siberian forests, the Caspian steppes, and more especially the tundras and Aralo-Caspian deserts, are almost uninhabited. On the whole, the density decreases from west to east, and it is remarkable to see how similar regions with equal or at any rate perfectly comparable natural conditions have a greater population in Europe than in Asia.

The inequality that exists between east and west is due to human as well as natural conditions and is partly the work of history. The west has been and still is the great reservoir of man power; in the east have been and still are great expanses whose emptiness has exercised an irresistible attraction. The colonising thrust, which will apparently continue until the settlement of the Soviet Union has reached equilibrium, has come and still comes from Russia, that is, from the region longest occupied by a settled people. The movement, which is one of the great facts of contemporary history, is the work of the Russians, who certainly rank among the peoples with the most prodigious power of increase. In three centuries and a half, remarks Camena d'Almeida, Russia has poured out beyond the frontiers reached by Ivan the Terrible 35 million of her offspring, whilst four hundred years were needed before 85 million whites of western and central European origin could be found in America.[1]

The beginnings of the Russian people were, however, very modest. Neither the extent of their original domains nor their standard of civilisation seemed to destine them to surpass their neighbours; and in order to impose their authority at long last on the latter, they had to endure severe trials and undergo bitter struggles.

Whilst in the steppe region peoples from Asia (Scythians, Huns, Bulgars, Magyars, Pechenegs, and Romanians) succeeded each other rapidly, certain elements trying to settle, but the main body leading the life of pastoral or pillaging nomads, the forest region was occupied by two ethnic groups. One consisted of the Finns, whose numerous tribes lived a settled life there, whilst their racial brethren on the tundra led a nomadic life. The other consisted of the Slavs who

---

[1] It should be remembered, however, that between 1820 and 1956 nearly 41 million Europeans were admitted to the United States.

dwelt in the forest belt in the south-west around the headwaters of the Dnepr, western Dvina, and Nemen. These people were divided into a host of branches: Slavs of the Ilmen (Novgorod, Pskov), Kriviches (Smolensk), Polochans (Polotsk), Vyatiches (upper Oka), Severians (Chernigov), Polians (Kiev), etc.; but gradually these tribes all became known as Russians. Those in the south, who had settled on the middle Dnepr, tilled the steppe and had their centre at Kiev. They were the Little Russians. Those in the north, the Great Russians, were much influenced by Scandinavians (the Varangians) and as early as the ninth century had organised themselves into powerful states, like that of Novgorod; and gradually in the course of the following centuries settlers from Novgorod easily ousted the Finns from the whole of northern Russia. The Kriviches, who met with stiffer resistance, advanced along the line of moraines from Smolensk to Moscow and by degrees occupied the territory between the Oka and Volga with the future Moscow as their centre. Lastly, the Severians and Vyatiches, on their part, moved forward along the ridge-line of the woodland-steppe between the Seym and the Don.

During this time there was being formed round Kiev a little Russian state which soon opened commercial relations with Byzantium. Varangians escorted the caravans on the way to Constantinople to protect them from robbers. On its part, Byzantium tried to convert these tribes, who several times made vain attacks on her. In 989, Vladimir, prince of Kiev, was baptised and imposed Orthodox Christianity on his subjects. Henceforth, through the instrumentality of the Greek colonies on the Black Sea coast, Byzantium was destined to be the instructress of the Russian people, both when the Little Russians were united under a single authority, as they were under Vladimir, and when they formed independent states. This 'Russia' which was focused on Kiev and was the first to be known to history, had to suffer greatly from the attacks of nomads, and this fact, together with social instability, set in motion two main streams of emigration, one towards Volhynia and Galicia, the other towards the Oka and upper Volga, where it powerfully reinforced the Great Russians in their struggle with the Finns. In the thirteenth century there was a collapse. In 1237 a wave of invasion more terrible than all previous ones, namely that of the Tatars, broke over Russia and even over central Europe. Kiev was taken in 1240, and the Russian domain was dismembered. Whilst the greater part of Little Russia came under the rule of the Poles and Lithuanians, the plains in the south and south-east formed a Russia that was Asiatic and Mohammedan. The Great Russians alone kept alight a spark of their national life and maintained a semi-autonomy under the overlordship of the Tatar khans.

The attacks of the Tatar horsemen could never advance very far into this group, protected as it was by the fortified towns of Vladimir, Rostov, Moscow, etc., which were interconnected by roads lined with *abattis* of trees. And the movement of liberation started from these Muscovite clearings. About a hundred years after the victory of Kulikovo (1380), which put an end to the Tatar hopes of domination, the prince of Moscow shook off the Khan's yoke and assumed the title of Tsar. In 1552, the khanate of Kazan was occupied and in 1557 that of Astrakhan. 'The Tsars who *restored* the Russian land' began the conquest of the steppes, on which Great Russian colonisation, protected by fortified lines, followed on the heels of bands of freebooters, known as Cossacks, who were later organised as frontier guards and settlers in regions into which the Russians were expanding; whilst in the opposite direction the subjection of the north country was completed and the penetration of Siberia begun by Yermak and the fur-traders. In spite of some alarms, like the inroad of the Kalmucks in 1630 and the momentary loss of Moscow in 1633 during the last great rising of the Tatars of the south, progress continued at a faster rate in the seventeenth century. In 1654 the Ukraine, which was henceforth to be threatened less and less by a waning Poland, was again brought under the imperial crown, the advance across the southern steppes continued, and that into Siberia became far more rapid. In 1689, the Treaty of Nerchinsk sanctioned the establishment of the Russians on the Pacific at a time when they had not yet reached the Baltic.

It was, however, necessary for them to reach this sea—and the Black Sea too, for by snapping the Byzantine link, the Turks had long since shut Russia out of the Mediterranean and had almost wholly cut off her contact with Europe. Although Peter the Great was but for a time master of Azov, he opened a window on the Baltic for his empire. Under his successors Russian settlement on the steppe, reinforced at times by foreigners, notably Germans, expanded as much by emigration as by natural increase, and the raids of the nomads became impossible. The Cossacks of the Don were subdued and their territories incorporated in the empire. In 1774, Catherine II wrested from Turkey the Black Sea provinces, whose last Tatar khans submitted in 1783. Thus, the forest and steppe regions were finally joined together, political union being strengthened by an economic bond due to the natural needs of these two zones for each other's very different, but complementary products.

The first moves towards the Caucasus began soon after, whilst the Caspian opened to the Tsars the way into central Asia. And in fact the nineteenth century witnessed a tremendous Russian advance eastwards, an advance which was particularly intense when the Balkan setbacks in 1856 and 1878 induced the Government to seek compensation elsewhere. Hence, the occupation of Siberia as far as the borders of Manchuria was completed by Muraviov; in spite of fierce resistance by the natives, which was symbolised by the great name of Shamil, 'the Caucasian Hereward the Wake', the conquest of the Caucasus and even a strip of Armenia was carried out; the subjugation of Turkistan was accomplished by Annenkov and Skobelev; and that of Afghanistan would certainly have followed but for British opposition. By about 1900 the formation of the most gigantic, compact empire that history has known had been achieved.

The process should not be termed 'colonial conquest', for such a phrase would be inaccurate. It was rather a groping forward, step by step, and, *mutatis mutandis*, something like the 'westward march' in the United States. Nevertheless, in the time of the Tsars Siberia, Caucasia, and Turkistan were in fact regarded as colonies, of which Russia was the metropolitan land. They were used as commercial outlets for Russian industry, and it was their business to supply that industry with raw materials, such as cotton from central Asia, which was transported to the textile region near Moscow.

They also served as outlets for emigration, which was as considerable as it was necessary. Certain districts of Russia were, in fact, overpopulated, seeing the inadequacy of their resources. As soon as serfdom was abolished, these regions had recourse to a temporary emigration which towards the end of tsarist rule was entered upon mainly to secure employment in industry in the northern regions and in agriculture in the south. On the average, the yearly recorded departures amounted to 150,000 in the 'government' of Kaluga, 300,000 in that of Nizhne Novgorod (now Gorky), 250,000 in that of Tver (now Kalinin), 100,000 in that of Yaroslavl, 300,000 in that of Ryazan, 230,000 (68,000 of whom were women) in that of Tula, 200,000 in that of Tambov, 150,000 in that of Penza and the same number for Orel, and 400,000 in that of Kostroma, whose whole male population above the age of twelve used to go to work in the towns during the winter and whose north-western portion was therefore called 'the kingdom of women'. This 'government' mainly furnished carpenters, stone-masons, and tanners; that of Tver coachmen, porters, and domestics; that of Nizhne Novgorod sawyers, brick-makers, and boat-builders; and that of Ryazan and Tula coachmen, carters, and stove-setters. But as this temporary emigration was an inadequate remedy for overpopulation, it was accompanied by a parallel movement of permanent emigration which was often encouraged by the central Government and which was directed towards districts of Russia which were underpopulated and potentially rich. A number of *moujiks*, however, moved to the towns as factory workers. The need to get industrial labour from rural districts is known to have been the chief motive which led Alexander II to abolish serfdom. Besides, the settlement of Russians in the middle and lower valleys of the Volga was one of the aims of the mid-nineteenth century. After 1861, an enormous stream of freed peasants swept into the Black Earth country in search of a less restricted life less over-weighted with feudal survivals and above all a less exiguous plot of ground to till.

There was also emigration abroad. In the last years of the nineteenth century many Russians left for America. On the eve of the first world war they formed a good fifth of the immigrants into the United States and were no fewer than 100,000 in Canada. But permanent emigration, which was the result of both an exuberant birth-rate and a bad agrarian system by which the share of each peasant was continually being reduced and the Russian village prevented from keeping all its children, was mainly to the *Okrainy* (literally 'the extremities', i.e. the areas conquered in Asia). At first the tsarist Government regarded these vast displacements of people with some displeasure, and the great landowners, who were thereby losing cheap labour, sought to persuade it that this emigration was a danger to the State. But the Government was not long in being convinced that this was not so, for the empire would be strengthened by peopling Asia with Russians; and in addition the crisis of 1905 made it try to lessen the danger of revolution by removing agitators from Russia and by guaranteeing to them land taken from other people than the nobles.

Then a Russian emigration to the Caucasus began, but was rather small. The tardily conquered districts of this region, which were largely mountainous, remote, and difficult of access, attracted few European colonists. They received, however, some Moldavians, about 90,000 Greeks, and about 50,000 Württembergers, the first of whom arrived as early as 1817. Village names like Alexandershilf, Alexandersdorf, Ekaterinfeld, Elisavettal, Marienfeld, Petersdorf, and Freudental, which occur in the Tiflis district, attest their German origin. But more important, by 1914 nearly four million Russians, together with a few thousand Estonians, had already come to settle in the Caucasus. They were mostly descendants of Cossacks and *raskolniki*.[1] But the mountainous country was uncongenial to these plainsmen, who also lived in fear of the warlike tribes close by; and it has therefore been almost wholly neglected. Transcaucasia, which was more fertile, would certainly have been more congenial, but its

---

[1] A theologico-political party which clung to the old Russian church ritual and social and political customs. It was formed in the seventeenth century, and its members were known as 'Old Believers'.

warm, damp climate did not suit them, and furthermore the native population was densest there. Consequently, Russians have settled in large numbers only in the western half of Ciscaucasia, that is to say, the steppes of the Kuban, which were somewhat similar to those of southern Russia; and where nearly all of the emigrants are to be found. That is why, racially speaking, Caucasia as a whole has been little affected by Russian influence.

There has also been a large migration of Russians into central Asia. It was no easy matter. Not that the climate was a hindrance, for the summer heat is very great, but dry; and the cold of winter tests the human constitution. Nor was the malaria problem insoluble. But a native population swarmed in the fertile oases which the Russians themselves wanted. And the natives were not weak and ignorant tribesmen, but rather tough and relatively civilised Mohammedans. To expropriate them as a body might have been dangerous and was contrary to the ideas of a Government which protected the native states of Bukhara and Khiva and respected their local customs. Hence, there were few places available. Besides, the country is not very like Russia, and the almost universal need for irrigation repelled most of the colonists. There were some, however; but the first comers had many disappointments. They were mainly Cossacks. Those in Khiva were intractable 'Old Believers' with a low standard of living; those in Semireshye ('Seven Rivers') were idle and drunken and distinguished themselves mainly by their brutal treatment of the natives, whom they 'russified' less than they themselves became 'kirghizised'. Consequently, the Government thought it well to suspend this disorderly colonisation as a whole and to plan the settlement of the country methodically.

Appreciable results were obtained. On oases formed on loess in Transcaspia there grew up agricultural Russian villages which as early as 1891 contained more than 7000 colonists. A number of settlements were also made along the Zeravshan and on the Oxus, around Khiva, in fertile Ferghana, and around Margelan, as well as in the province of Syr Darya between Tashkent and Chimkent, where in 1906 a thousand, and in 1909 five thousand, colonists were engaged in stock-rearing and in large-scale production of cereals, whilst towns like Tashkent, Margelan, Kokand, Andizhan, Leninabad, and Samarkand also received their share of Russian immigrants. In Turkistan proper there were in 1914 altogether 171 Russian villages and 73,500 Russians. But these still represented only 8·7 per cent. of the total population of Transcaspia; 3·2 per cent. in the Syr Darya districts; 1·4 in the province of Samarkand; and 0·6 in Ferghana.

On the other hand, colonisation was very great in the northern provinces. On the Kirghiz steppes at about the same date Russians formed 7·7 per cent. of the population of the province of Turgay; 9·9 of that of Semipalatinsk; 11·8 per cent. in Semireshye, where the soil and climate are rather like those in southern Russia and irrigation is not indispensable. This territory received large numbers of Russian peasants, especially after the famine of 1890 and again after the Russo-Japanese War and the agrarian crisis. In 1908 alone 7600 arrived, 25 per cent. of whom settled in the province of Uralsk, 33 per cent. in that of Akmolinsk, where in 1908 they totalled 140,000. Land hunger explains the volume of this stream of settlers; but it was also due to the fact that labour was attracted by the wages offered, which were higher than those paid in Russia. There is no doubt that, just as the opening of the Trans-Siberian Railway hastened colonisation in the province of Akmolinsk, the building of the Trans-Aralian gave rise to villages often of considerable size along its course, like Ak-Bulak, 72 miles from Chkalov, which in about 1910 contained something like a thousand houses.

But the colonising movement in central Asia is not to be compared with the one which occurred in Siberia. Hardly had the plan of conquest been outlined than it was observed that the country was rich in precious metals, contained an abundance of furs, and had the advantage of trade with China. It was decided to work the mines, and to do this meant feeding the miners. The Government sent across the Urals a force of Cossacks, whose individuals were both peasants and soldiers grouped in *voiska*; serfs whom their lords, when authorised after 1760 to send them to Siberia, chose from among the least profitable, so as to get rid of them; free peasants of the best type, who, together with some clandestine settlers (deserting conscripts and runaway serfs) formed a number of villages between 1838 and 1856, when the variety of the country's resources was more clearly seen and its wealth in gold confirmed; finally, deportees, some sentenced in the criminal courts and others for political reasons. The last, who became more and more numerous in the nineteenth century, consisted of Poles, Decembrists,[1] and nihilists, and were usually men of ability, who, not content with appreciably improving their own economic conditions, rendered great service to science. In spite of the great distances and difficulty of travel, the European population, which had been estimated at 229,000 in 1709, rose to 1,540,000 in 1816, and nearly 3,000,000 about 1860. But the political exiles represented only 3 or 4 per cent. of the deportees, who numbered 680,000 from 1825 to 1881. Siberia was in fact becoming a dump on to which was thrown the scum of Russia.

The abolition of serfdom changed the nature of the problem.

[1] Persons convicted of participation in the revolt of December 1825 at St. Petersburg.

Driven from home by the irritating *mir* system, hosts of half-starved *moujiks* (110,000 between 1860 and 1880; 440,000 between 1880 and 1892) set out to try their luck in Siberia. For want of guidance, this first mass emigration was fated to suffer cruel setbacks. Sickness and death played terrible havoc in the ranks of the intending settlers, and very often the survivors found the space already occupied along the usual lines of approach and wandered about miserably. In spite of this, the exodus assumed such proportions that Government circles feared that Russia might become short of labour, and measures of control and protection were imposed.

Only those who had obtained official permission were allowed to move. The State itself undertook at heavy cost to organise the colonisation. An inventory of available land was drawn up, lots marked out, railway tickets granted at reduced prices to the emigrants and their *khodoki*[1] and emigration officers were appointed to look after the crowds, officers who were for the most part as intelligent as they were human and even quite self-sacrificing. Finally, emigration centres were established, at which the prospective settlers were assembled, sorted, and distributed. As at this time that wonderful instrument of colonisation, the Trans-Siberian Railway, was under construction, 932,000 settlers arrived between 1896 and 1900; but owing to the Russo-Japanese War, only 436,000 arrived between 1900 and 1905.

At the end of this war the extreme severity of the agrarian crisis in Russia made a still more vigorous effort necessary. All the machinery of emigration was grouped under a single office which had an annual budget of £40,000,000. For colonisation by peasants the Tsar presented his immense property in the Altai region, which was nearly as large as Spain and offered wood, water, and black earth, as well as a position near the railway. Parts of the Crown Lands were parcelled out, fitted up, and distributed free of charge by the Tsar, who also had all the arable land bought, especially in the forest belt, and had lots prepared to be sold in return for annual payments. In certain cases the houses were built in advance and subsidies of various kinds allowed. Thus, it was possible to grant to every male emigrant, whatever his age, a *dolya* (= lot) of 37 acres on the average. Sometimes the grant was larger, if only part of the land was arable; at other times it was smaller; for instance, in very favourable districts like the Altai region the lots measured 27 and in some cases only 19 acres.

The results were wonderful. In 1906 arrivals totalled 217,000; in 1907 this rose to 589,000; in 1908 to 753,000; and in 1909 to 675,000. In the years following, since the pressure of population had slackened in Russia, new settlers averaged only somewhat more than 200,000.

[1] Delegates sent by bodies of intending emigrants to investigate the possibilities of settlement and to choose land in advance of the main parties.

In 1914 Siberia contained some 9,500,000 Russians, nearly half of whom were women, which was very encouraging for the future. Moreover, the *Zemstva* assisted those who wished to settle in Siberia, and the overall percentage of those who returned was no more than 3 or 4. The figure was higher in the Far East, where, owing to the climate, Russians suffered grievous disappointments and developed an incurable yearning to return home.

After the war and revolution the Soviets resumed the task which had been interrupted. They forbade free emigration as a rule and

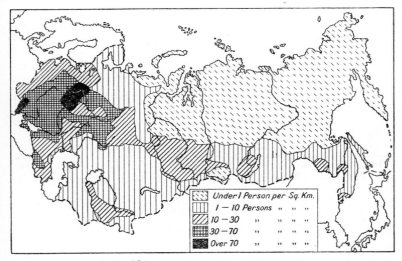

FIG. 10. DISTRIBUTION OF POPULATION.

forced all the republics to furnish statements of their available land. In spite of insufficient supplies of money, which reduced the clearing of the land, and in spite of the growing distance of the settlements from the railway, hundreds of thousands of lots were distributed. In 1926 Siberia had a population of 12,500,000, of which at least 11,000,000 were Russians.

Thus, the number of Russians steadily increased in all the outer possessions. They were, indeed, in the majority in Siberia alone. But everywhere, in the *Okrainy* as in Russia, the Government applied itself to 'russifying' the *inorodtsy*.[1] It sought to impose on them the Orthodox religion, Russian customs and the Russian language. The

[1] The term *inorodtsy*—literally, those of foreign race—originally denoted the tribes in Siberia, but has gradually been extended to mean all those of non-Russian extraction.

policy of assimilation, which often translated itself into very unpleasant persecution (in Europe more than in Asia, it is true), tended to reinforce the spread of the dominant nation.

Now, in spite of the complete change in the ideology of the Government, Russian expansion, far from slowing down, is speeding up nowadays. Nor could it be otherwise. One fact certainly dominates the current domestic history of the Soviet Union, namely, its constant increase in population. Doubtless, the hecatombs of the first world war, the civil war, and the revolution, famine, epidemics, and the

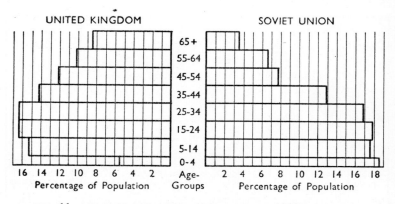

FIG. 11. AGE DISTRIBUTION OF POPULATION IN 1939 IN THE U.K. AND U.S.S.R. COMPARED.

Percentages of Population in various Age-groups based on the *Statistical Year Book of the League of Nations.*

emigration of 'White' Russians—not forgetting the loss of vast provinces—had cruelly reduced the population. Reckoned in 1914 at 140 million in the territories occupied by the Union in 1939, it is said to have fallen to 132 million in 1922. But by 1926 it had increased again to 147 million; in 1931 to 161 million; and in 1939 to 170,464,000. This increase of 23½ million people in twelve years represents a gain of about 2 million a year, or nearly 5500 a day. It looks as if during the years immediately preceding the second world war this annual increase rose to 2½ and perhaps 3 million, or a daily increase of between 7000 and 8000 persons! From 1900 to 1930 the population of the United States grew at a mean rate of 1½ million persons a year; but this was mainly the work of enormous immigration. In Russia there is practically no immigration, and the rising figures are due to a natural increase which moved at a dizzy rate. There is nothing abnormal in this, for emigration to foreign countries has completely ceased and the death rate has been enormously reduced. In

1913 intestinal typhus had more than 26 victims a year in every thousand of the population. By 1926 the figure had fallen to 8·8. In 1925 there were 22·2 deaths for every thousand persons in European Russia; but in 1928 it was 17·9, and it is claimed that the present rate is 7·2 per mil., the lowest in the world. Though during the first years of Bolshevism abortion was practised legally, the birth-rate is now very high. The mean rate in Russia varied from 43·2 to 40·5 per mil. during the period 1925–8, since when accurate statistics have only recently been published. Some say that the rate is no higher than 25 or 30 per mil.; others that it has kept up to 40 or 45 per mil. Even on the less-favourable hypothesis the annual increase is 11 per mil. compared with 5·8 in the United States; and it is destined to accelerate not only because the Government encourages this fecundity, but also because the average age of the population is very young. In 1939 those under the age of 7 formed 18·6 per cent. of the total; those under 20, according to some accounts, and those under 30, according to others, represented 45·1 per cent. In spite of a great decrease in the birth-rate during the war years, the rate of increase since 1939 has been so enormous that in 1959 the population amounted to 208,826,000; that is, to slightly more than 23 persons to the square mile of the country as a whole, and 350 persons to the square mile of land at present cultivated.

To sum up, in the years since 1939, the population of the Soviet Union has increased by an amount more than twice that of Great Britain and Ireland. This extraordinary growth has set the rulers problems of extreme gravity. It has obliged them to people and occupy the whole of the vast national territory; it has made the drive to the east, especially in Siberia, more intense than ever; and more generally, it has forced the Soviets to a systematic exploitation of all the resources of the country. Thus, it appears to be the mainspring of the immense effort which began in 1928 and which, to judge from results already achieved, seems destined to alter the face of the Soviet lands. We have now to consider the stage reached in the colonisation of the different parts of the Union on the eve of this colossal undertaking.

CHAPTER 8

POPULATION AND SETTLEMENT IN RUSSIA

1. VARIEGATED CHARACTER OF THE ETHNOGRAPHICAL MAP

The population of Russia is essentially Slav and mainly Russian. Yet the ethnographical map is pretty well variegated. The fact is that when all is said and done the formation of the Russian state is quite recent. Many parts of the country submitted to the Tsar only one or two hundred years ago, and consequently a number of minorities had not yet been completely assimilated when the old régime fell. In fact, the Soviet Union contains more than a hundred nationalities and peoples. Apart from the Slav group, these may be classed as conquered nations and immigrant or partially absorbed peoples.

(a) *The Conquered Peoples.* This group comprised Finns and Tatars. The former were the remnant of an ethnic group which had formerly been compact and had occupied the whole of northern Russia, but are very scattered today. They include first of all the Lapps of the Kolski peninsula, about 2000 in all. They are small, yellow-skinned, dark-haired, and very distinctly Mongolian in type. The same type occurs also in the 20,000 Samoyedes, or Nentse, who dwell on the Arctic coasts and who, like the Lapps, are tundra-nomads. Then come the pastoral peoples, fishermen, and woodcutters; 140,000 Zyrians in the Pechora district, 190,000 Ostiaks and 70,000 Voguls in the Ural region, both of whom are related to the Magyars of Hungary; then 605,000 Udmurts, or Votiaks, who are cultivators in the Perm district; and, lastly, the Finns, who are also cultivators and comprise the Mari, or Charemises, of the Kazan district (400,000 in 1926, 480,000 in 1939), the Mordves (more than a million in 1926; 1,450,000 in 1939), and the Chuvashes (815,000 in 1926; 1,367,000 in 1939) around Ufa and Kuybyshev. In all, 2,500,000 out of the 3,280,000 Finno-Ugrians counted in the Soviet Union in 1926. Since 1945 this Finnish group has been increased by more than a million Ests who live in the Baltic republic of Estonia. The Letts of Latvia and the Lithuanians of Lithuania, each about 2 million in number and, like the Ests, joined to the Soviet Union since 1940, are neither Finns nor genuine Slavs. They speak Indo-European languages, and that is about all one can say. The Karelians, numbering about half a million, have been added to the Union since the conquest of their country from Finland.

The Tatar group, often called Tartars in the West owing to a freak of Classical reminiscence, represents the remnants of the old Golden Horde. It is even more scattered than the Finnish and comprises the nomadic Kirghizes and Kalmucks (about 884,000) who occupy the lower valley of the Ural River and the mouths of the Volga; the 842,900 Bashkirs of the southern Urals, formerly nomadic horsemen who have become cultivators and, like the two previously mentioned tribes, have kept their Turki language and their Turko-Mongoloid appearance. Lastly, but most numerous, there are the 2,300,000 Tatars proper, who live in the regions about Kazan, Ulyanovsk, Ufa, and Kuybyshev, as well as in the Crimea. Before the revolution they were farmers, porters, waiters, and in some cases well-to-do merchants, and the Mongolian appearance had nearly gone. Their group comprises in all 4,300,000 out of the 17,000,000 Turki in the Soviet Union.

(b) *The People who have Immigrated or been Absorbed.* In 1949, as a result of the war, Bessarabia returned to Russia and with part of Moldavia, which was annexed, became the Moldavian SS. Republic. This added people of Romanian origin. There are also 190,000 Greeks in the Black Sea districts, especially around Kherson and Dnepropetrovsk (286,000 in 1939); and 1,200,000 Germans (1,423,000 in 1939), a good number of whom lived scattered in the towns as artisans, foremen, engineers, manufacturers, or merchants. Other Germans formed 'islands' in Volhynia, Podolia, and the lower Dnepr, but their most compact group consisted of the agricultural settlements on the middle Volga in the districts of Saratov and Kuybyshev, where they numbered 230,000. Though they were good Russian citizens, they had, however, not lost all recollection of their German descent, and as a precaution they were transferred to Siberia during Hitler's invasion in 1941.

But the most important element in this second category consisted of Jews, who numbered only 1,842,000 in 1920, but 3,020,000 in 1939. There was a time when their numbers, then far greater, were regarded as forming two-thirds of the world's Jewish population. Driven out of Germany by persecution in the Middle Ages, they received little better welcome from the Tsar, whose police had a fondness for a system of pogroms, and the Jews nearly always had to live in wretched ghettoes, in which they timidly isolated themselves, surrounded by the prescriptions of the Talmud. Some rose to very high places in commerce and finance. The majority of them lived in the west and south-west, whither imperial policy drove them, and particularly in Russian Poland. When the last named was lost, the percentage of Jews in the population of Russia greatly decreased. Yet in 1920 there still were 7500 in the Crimea, 573,000 in Russia proper, and 1,189,000 in the Ukraine. They were set free by the revolution and continued to carry on business and live in scattered urban colonies. They now number about 3,000,000.

(c) *The Slav Group.* The Slav group keeps an overwhelming superiority in the population as a whole. It might be termed the Russian group, for non-Russians are very few in number and consist of little 'islands' of Poles scattered in the western districts (Zhitomir, Kiev) which up to 1772 formed part of Greater Poland. In 1939 they were no longer important (627,000 persons) compared with the multitude of Russians, who formed 77 per cent. of the Soviet population. But this multitude is not strictly homogeneous, since it comprises three elements.

First, there are the WHITE, or BELO, RUSSIANS, who inhabit the region of the upper Dvina, upper Nemen, and upper Dnepr. Their language is directly descended from that of the ancient Kriviches, and, consequently, they are regarded as racially the purest of all the Russian Slavs. Perhaps they are. Anyhow, owing to geographical and historical disadvantages, they form the poorest and most backward section of the Russian group. Furthermore, they are relatively few in number. Since the annexation of eastern Poland they number more than 10,000,000 and form 5·2 per cent. of the Russian population of the Soviet Union, but cannot have a great say in the destinies of the country.

Far more interesting is the LITTLE RUSSIAN or UKRAINIAN element which includes more than 40 million persons and forms some 20 per cent. of the Russian population of the Soviet Union. Tall, in spite of their name, with brown and even black hair, quick, and active, the Little Russians add to their artistic talents in music as well as in the plastic arts a far more open and acute mind, a swifter comprehension, and a more cheerful disposition than the other Russians. They are sometimes regarded as having a relation to their fellow-Russians similar to that existing between the people of the Midi and other Frenchmen. Their original home is the Black Earth steppe, where their chief towns are Kiev, Poltava, and Kharkov.

Finally, the GREAT RUSSIANS (110,000,000 in 1956) who people the rest of Russia formed 67 per cent. of the total Russian population in 1931 and more than 58 per cent. of the population of the Soviet

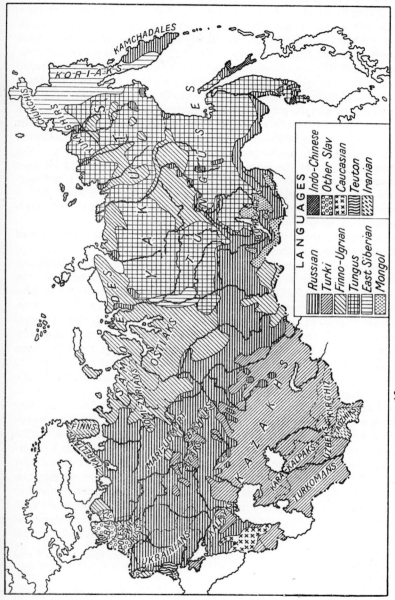

FIG. 12. DISTRIBUTION OF LANGUAGES AND RACES.

LANGUAGES

Russian
Turki
Finno-Ugrian
Tungus
East Siberian
Mongol
Indo-Chinese
Other Slav
Caucasian
Teuton
Iranian

Union in 1939. Their stature, which is often shorter than that of the Ukrainians, is not always very tall, but for the most part they have a superb muscular development and an impressive breadth of shoulder.[1] Their faces, which are frequently broad, their tendency to have snub-noses, and their slightly yellow complexions betray their infusion of Mongolian blood, in spite of their fair hair and light-coloured eyes. More serious than the Little Russians, they are also more tenacious, and their homeland, which originally coincided with the woodland steppe and the mixed forest, has spread all over the forest as well as the steppes on the east and south-east. They have become the dominant people in Russia, and their dialect, which is very different from Ukrainian, has become both the standard language and the official tongue of the empire. It is excessively complicated because it crystallised too soon, before proper development, but it is wonderfully rich and supple, wonderfully concise, perfectly flexible, and—paradoxically enough—'as musical as the languages of the Mediterranean coasts of Europe'.[2]

There are, then, shades of distinction between the three types of Russians. And yet these three types have influenced one another, and there have been intermarriages and endosmosis. No clear linguistic frontiers exist between them. Not only are there villages where the dialects are mixed, but it is even possible to find White Russians who speak their own tongue with a Great Russian accent, and *vice versa*. Stranger still, in the same family the father's language is not necessarily that of the mother and children. Owing to the action of historical factors and of economic and cultural changes, there has been formed in Russia a people whose psychology is extraordinarily attractive and at the same time deceptive, full of contrasts and even of contradictions.

The Russian combines an undercurrent of thoughtful melancholy with a gay temperament; great kindness, infinite sympathy towards pain and sin with amazing possibilities of cruelty; an almost guileless honesty with a very clear propensity to lying; a touching generosity with a fierce egotism; a humility which sometimes goes so far as to feel the need for self-condemnation[3] with an overweening disdain for others; a rare capacity for work with a discouraging apathy; so at least he appeared until recently to those best acquainted with him, though these admit that they are not sure they have understood him perfectly. These characteristics are certainly due to historical

[1] In 1916–17 the Great Russians who came to fight on the Western Front could not be equipped with French packs, which were too narrow for their shoulders and bruised their shoulder-blades.

[2] These apt phrases are quoted from the late J. Legras.

[3] This need, the famous *samooblichenye*, is, it will be remembered, one of Dostoyevski's favourite themes.

causes, which up to our own times have perhaps warped the nature of this richly endowed nation by forcing it to live in servitude. To confine ourselves to the psychological features which bear most directly on economic life and thus are most interesting to the geographer, the Russians have been accused, not without reason, of being casual and careless. The word *nichevo* (= 'it does not matter, don't worry') was so popular just before 1917 that the upper classes avoided its use, and the expression *na avos* (= 'hit or miss, have a shot') was no less common. Unconcern and even idleness, or at any rate an inability for continued effort, were regarded as their besetting sins, and these faults have undoubtedly slowed down Russian progress seriously. But what a deal of intelligence, courage, and vitality there is in the nation!

2. UNEQUAL DISTRIBUTION OF POPULATION

The exploitation of large areas has unfortunately been hindered by underpopulation. Though there are, as we have seen, densely peopled districts in the Ukraine and Muscovy, yet in 1926 the Bashkir Republic had only 6 persons to the square mile, the Kalmuck territory 2, and the Zyrian territory 0·2. These differences may be explained by geographical and historical factors.

(*a*) *Geographical Factors.* The first is obviously the climate. The centre and south-west, which are favourable to human occupation in spite of the meteorological drawbacks from which they suffer, are quite different from the north, which is too cold and afflicted with interminable winters; and from the south, which is too dry. Similarly, certain soils, like black earth and even the grey soils, give a good return to man's labour, whilst the tundra, hard-pan podzols, chestnut-coloured soils, and saline areas and desert sands give a poor return or none at all. Vegetation plays an important part too: whilst the steppe proper, the grassy areas of the woodland steppe, and the forest clearings are fairly easily tilled, the forest, though it served as a refuge at the time of the invasions, imposes on the settler the difficult preliminary task of clearing the ground.

Furthermore, relief has a finger in the pie. The ideal of the Russian farmer, according to Semionov-Tian-Shanski, is a plain as flat as a pancake, and all inequalities of relief are the work of Satan, who will have to 'answer for them to God'. Yet, except in the dry south where the damp *bliuda* attracted man, rising ground pleased him rather than the hollows and valley-bottoms, which were often marshy. Besides, it offered facilities for defence, and for hundreds of years a number of hill-tops were occupied by fortified towns. In the circumstances the seriousness of the problem of water-supply is easily understood. Whilst in the centre of the country the high ground is moderately damp, in the north it is flat and often has marshes and peat bogs, and in the south it is excessively poor in water. In both the latter cases man was induced to stay near the streams. Thus, the water-supply problem was associated with the system of communications.

It was said above that the rivers were for long the best routes, so there is nothing astonishing in the growth on their banks of many trading towns, not a few of which took the names of their rivers. Such is the case with Moscow, Vyatka (now Kirov), Vologda, Kostroma, Voronezh, Samara (now Kuybyshev), Syzran, Ufa, Mezen, and very many others. Settlement in the spaces between the valleys, says Camena d'Almeida, went on but slowly and did not begin until after the construction of overland roads in the fifteenth century.

(b) *Historical Factors.* Sparsely inhabited by poor and ignorant tribes, the north offered little resistance to the advance of the Russians from Novgorod. However, it was not Russian originally and must be regarded as an area of settlement. On the other hand, the south, which was long ravaged or at any rate threatened by the nomads, was only subdued with difficulty by the Tsar at no distant date. When this had been done, the steppe had to be re-peopled, for the conquered tribes had been expelled or massacred and had almost disappeared. Such an achievement could only be accomplished in relatively modern times. Owing to this late start in civilisation, the north and south alike can, of course, show no great density of population. In contrast with these there is a region to which from early times geographical and historical factors have combined to give a numerous population, viz. the north-west of the fertile Black Earth country, which was early freed from the nomads, and especially central Russia with its broken relief, its woodland steppes, its easily cultivable clearings, its many streams, and forests teeming with game and affording plenty of wood for building or fuel.

The old historic towns of Russia grew up in these *polye*, where resistance to the enemy from the south and the counter-offensive in the fourteenth century were organised. This middle zone, which is intensely cultivated, strongly industrialised, and humming with trade, still includes the areas with the greatest density of population and the largest number of towns, if not all the towns with the largest population.

3. CONDITIONS OF RURAL LIFE

In such a vast country as Russia, frozen in the extreme north, but semi-desert in the extreme south, the whole population is not seden-

A Ukrainian Khata

...using (new style) on
a Sovkoz

The main street in Khabarovsk, showing new and old styles of architecture

tary, and nomadism is regularly practised. The Lapps, Samoyedes, and Ostiaks of the tundra live in conical tents made of canvas or skins with a hole at the top to let out the smoke. The height of these movable dwellings varies a great deal, since it depends on the length of the poles which support them. If the marshy forest is not too stunted, the tent gains by it; but the trees may be dwarfs; and in the coastal region wood is so rare that the driftwood cast up by the waves is carefully collected. The Kirghiz and Kalmucks of the Caspian steppes live in *kibitka*, a kind of tent consisting of a trellis-like framework of wood with a covering of felt. The cohesion of the building is ensured by a series of ropes. There is an opening at the top for the smoke to escape and another, which may be hidden by a thick cloth, for ventilation. When the grass round the spot they occupy becomes temporarily exhausted, the nomads of north and south alike pack up their baggage, strike their tents, and move off elsewhere, the Ostiaks and Lapps on foot or in sledges, the Kirghiz and Kalmucks in carts drawn by horses.

But these nomads form only a minority. The great mass of the Russian people live sedentary lives, some in the towns and others in the country.

Until recently, by far the majority dwelt in the country. Estimated in 1920 at 84·3 per cent. of the population of the Soviet Union, in 1926 at 82·1 per cent., in 1930 at 81·3 per cent., and in 1959 at 52·2 per cent., the proportion of rural population was slightly less in Russia proper. It would be interesting to know the details of the mode of grouping; unfortunately, our knowledge of the subject suffers from the inaccuracy of Russian statistical terminology and from the fact that the majority of Soviet geographers prefer the sphere of physical geography to studies of this kind. It seems, however, that, to judge from the researches of Woeikof, concentration is far from being as marked in the north and centre as in the south.

But certain factors have acted uniformly throughout the country. Thus, large estates gave rise to big villages, at first because the great nobles were absentee proprietors and their stewards found large settlements easier to supervise; later, because many of the nobles built factories on their estates; for instance the foundries on the Ural, the glass-works in the Vladimir and Kaluga districts, and the numerous textile mills in the 'governments' of Ulyanovsk, Penza, and Tambov.

On the other hand, the purchase of land by the peasants encouraged scattered dwellings. The settlements in the districts of Archangel, Perm, Olonets, Vitebsk, Pskov, Minsk, and even the northern parts of those of Mogilev, Smolensk, Kalinin, Vologda, Kostroma, and Kirov are generally hamlets with not more than from fifty to a hundred and twenty persons in each 'inhabited place'. But this was perhaps because water is found nearly everywhere, though more probably because large villages could not conceivably exist in districts where agriculture was practised in clearings made by burning the forest and the land abandoned after three or four harvests. Isolated homesteads or small groupings were more suited to such an agrarian system. It should be noticed, however, that maps of this vast region of hamlets did show spots of dense concentration, with between 121 and 200 persons in them. First, there was the Novgorod district where rural settlement became concentrated in the sixteenth century owing to political troubles; then a belt of country along the Leningrad-Moscow route, where the rise of commerce and industry, favoured by the construction of canals and the canalisation of rivers, led the people to flock together; lastly, the Moscow region, where the growth of industry some time ago had the same effects.

Farther south the degree of concentration increases for reasons which vary greatly from place to place. It may be due, firstly, to an excess of water. In the Pripet Marshes really dry areas are so rare that they are sometimes occupied by large villages, and the same is true in the south of the 'governments' of Minsk, Mogilev, and Smolensk. In the Black Earth country, on the other hand, where the number of persons in each village varies between 200 and 700, lack of water, and especially of clean water, has produced the same results. Another frequent factor has been a long tradition of insecurity. This has operated, for instance, in the districts to the south of the Oka, which were settled rather late. The need to defend themselves against raiders from the steppe had forced the fathers to cluster together, and the sons kept up the custom. However, as security became assured, the tendency to concentration weakened, and the progress of agriculture encouraged big villages to send out offshoots and landowners to build new farms. In other places the sale of a portion of some estate led the purchaser to build. So true is this that the Black Earth country, being early settled (the districts of Tula and Orel, for instance), shows a greater splintering of holdings than do the more recently settled districts of Kuybyshev, Ufa, and Chkalov.

On the other hand, large villages have been fostered by intensive cultivation, notably that of sugarbeet, on the large farms which formerly belonged to rich *pomieshchiki* in Podolia and around Kiev. Many are also found in New Russia and on the Black Sea coast, where they sometimes contain more than 700 persons. Want of security has played no part here, and the effective causes have been scarcity of water, the importance of trade in many of the big villages, and the coastal fishing industry. Yet the average number of persons per village decreased by one-half between 1880 and 1910 in the

Kherson district, where the disadvantages of large villages had been conveyed by the *Zemstvas* to the people within their jurisdiction and by intelligent farmers to their neighbours.

But Russian villages not only vary in the extent to which they concentrate the population, for there is a very noticeable difference in their form and appearance in Great and Little Russia. The perfectly straight Great Russian village might be said to be concentrated or, more exactly, stretched out, for it has only one very wide, filthy street lined with a double row of detached hovels from ten to a hundred in number. Conspicuous among them formerly were the huts of the *staroste* and the tavern-keeper. The houses do not touch each other, but are separated by muddy spaces frequented by dogs and pigs. In the yard behind the house is a kitchen-garden and an enclosure in which the corn or rye mill is erected in summer. On one side is a wooden, white-painted chapel with a green roof. Usually there are no trees.

The Little Russian villages are quite different, although some exceptional ones may be seen in the Black Earth country with a single line of houses stretching for 7 miles or more. Generally, they are very large, as big as towns in some cases, and all provided with a church painted in bright colours. They are girt with a hedge of reeds or thorn bushes, and their houses are arranged not in bare, monotonous lines, but in groups shaded by trees. There are no streets. Each householder builds where he pleases, and in certain districts, especially in Podolia, the enclosure round each house covers a considerable area. Surrounded by little gardens, vegetable plots, and big orchards, the houses look almost like isolated farms amidst their dwarf willows and sunflowers 'raising their great heads full of seeds which the peasants consider a delicacy' (Baron de Baye). In fine, unlike the cheerless appearance of the Great Russian village, the aspect of the Little Russian counterpart is cool and picturesque owing partly to the trees, but also to the dazzling whiteness of the walls.

The appearance of the houses differs still more than the form of the village. Those in the forest belt are quite distinct from those on the steppe. The former type is the classic *izba* of Great Russia. Naturally, it is of wood. The wooden house is so well adapted to the climate that it has been for ages the object of a special trade, and long before the era of modern transport Russia was familiar with portable wooden houses. 'In Moscow', says the *Almanac de Gotha* for 1823, 'the peasants buy ready-made wooden houses which can be set up or taken down at will.' As a rule, however, the *moujik* builds his own house. Square, with each side measuring 13 to 16 ft., it is nearly always low and, seen from afar, appears squashed down to the ground. It has no foundation, but merely a base of stone. On this are erected the walls, made of tree-trunks, usually of pine logs, trimmed and barked, sometimes rough and at others sufficiently squared to be called balks, tied together and carefully fitted at the four corners. As a rule, the spaces are filled and the beams caulked with oakum and mud, after which a mixture of mud, straw, and reeds is spread over the walls. The roof, topped by a flanged chimney, has a low pitch, but overhangs a good deal. It is sometimes thatched, but is more frequently made of wood.

The most peculiar feature of the *izba* is the oven or stove which is sheltered in a more or less decorated inglenook and is made of several thicknesses of brick. It is used as much for heating as for cooking and even serves as a bed. Sometimes when the family is small, all its members sleep on the stove. Anyhow, old or sick people and young children normally sleep on it, so as to take advantage of its warmth. Thus, it acts as a piece of furniture.

In the *tayga* the *izba* is of the simplest type. It has a cowshed built against it and contains little more than a room or two, not counting the corridor and the storeroom which often serve as bedrooms for the children. In central Russia it is larger and, besides the barn and the loft, comprises several rooms, one of which is an unheated compartment used as an entrance and another as an attic lumber-room. Contrary to general custom, an *izba* belonging to peasants in comfortable circumstances may have an upper floor and even a sort of balcony. But as a rule, in spite of its picturesqueness, it leaves on the traveller an impression of squalid, filthy poverty. Except in well-to-do families, the scanty furniture consists merely of a double bed, a table, narrow benches fixed to the wall, and a few chests. Light and air are scantily admitted. Though in some *izby* there is a window in every wall, a number of houses have only one or two little hooded windows, narrow and low. To prevent draughts from entering in winter, they are plastered with resin and sometimes covered over with straw. If they were opened, the first odour that would greet one would be the smell of the pile of dung which is placed round the *izba* to keep it warm. In fact, fresh air is not admitted, except when the door is opened to allow one of the family to go about his business or return indoors. For weeks and months the air remains the same, close and tainted with the breath, perspiration, and exhalations of the whole family, who scarcely stir and often scorn to go out, even for what would seem to us a case of extreme urgency. The strong stench of the *izba*, in which are mingled stale odours and the smell of dust, smoke, breath, filth, dried sweat, urine, and excreta is something to write home about! The time comes when the air simply cannot be breathed, and black beetles, cockroaches, and other bugs swarm in the woodwork. In this way life may become impossible. The only remedy is to leave the house for a few days in the depth of winter with the doors and windows open. If there are no friends with whom to seek hospitality, the *moujik* and his family will wander about in the woods until the ice-cold air has done its work. Fortunately, the village is burnt down every seven years on the average, and indeed every four years in central Russia. Fire, it has been said, is the natural end of the *izba*.

River transport has enabled the *izba* to be introduced into the districts of the middle and lower Volga in spite of the extreme lack of trees there. But as a rule this type of hut is found neither in the

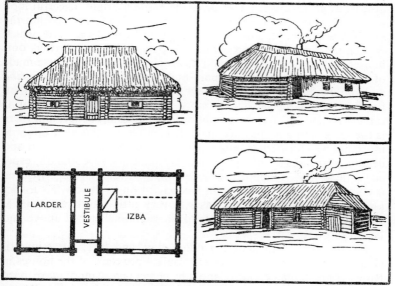

FIG. 13. LEFT: AN *izba* IN THE FOREST BELT; RIGHT: TYPES OF UKRAINIAN *khaty*.

west, nor in the Ukraine, nor in the south. These regions are the domain of the *khata* or *manzanka*, as it is sometimes called. In some cases it is made of daub, in others of turf. After the skeleton of the house, or rather the frame of the walls, has been built with skilfully plaited branches, it is sometimes plastered inside and out with a thick coat of mud. At other times, writes J. Legras, the builders 'cut parallel lines in the turf that covers the steppe. Then these strips are cut with a spade to form square slabs about 12 or 15 inches to the side and 2½ to 3 inches thick. First, they are dried, then they are placed together, with the grassy surface downwards, to form walls about 28 inches thick and 8 feet high. On the walls thus built thin beams are fastened to act as rafters running perpendicular to the direction of the street. On these rafters are stretched branches, and on the branches a double layer of turf. When this is all quite dry, the wall is plastered with clay inside and out.' The appearance of the house may vary slightly with the quantity of wood used in its construction. But whether it is of daub or of turf, the *khata* has the same external appearance. In each case its roof is thatched.[1] The eaves project a long way and on one side, supported by wooden posts, form a kind of veranda 'under the shelter of which is a ledge on the wall used as a bench' (de Baye). The clay plaster on 'the walls, external as well as internal, is carefully whitewashed every week, or at least every fortnight'. This gives the *khata* a bright, cheerful look which is lacking in the *izba*. Another point of difference is that the *khata* is not a simple house. At intervals all round the yard, which is enclosed by a fence and contains a pole-well, stand various outhouses, including a cowshed and a cart-shelter, both of course made of the same materials as the main building. Unfortunately, the *izba* and *khata* are alike in that the latter has scarcely more windows than the former and hence hardly more air and light. The interior is rather less squalid, but the conditions of life are no better, and there is the same filth and insanitariness. It is not surprising that infantile mortality was formerly so high in Russia, epidemics so frequent and deadly, and diseases of the respiratory passages so common, especially in winter. It cannot be denied that, so far as village hygiene is concerned, the Tsarist system has passed on to the Soviets a very poor state of things, which was still very little improved in 1928, although some of the dark spots of the picture sketched above had begun to disappear.

Wood, dried earth, daub, puddled clay, and turf! After investigation in 1900 it was estimated that only 4 per cent. of the houses in Russia were built of stone, and the percentage cannot have been increased between 1900 and 1917. Possibly, this almost total absence of stone may have had, as Soloviev definitely considered, a serious influence on the psychology of the *moujik* by depriving him of the sense of continuity and effort. 'There were no permanent homes which it was sad to leave, but only thatched cottages which were continually being destroyed by fire' (Massis). The relative indifference of the Russian peasant to individual property has certainly not been due to this single cause, and the ease with which he uproots himself springs from many other sources. But this extreme dearth of stone, of that material which makes our houses substantial and has given precision to the internal relations of our states, cannot have

---

[1] Hence, 69·5 per cent. of the rural houses throughout Russia were thatched in 1905, and 30 per cent. roofed with wood.

failed to induce in him that instability, that *boisak* spirit, which has for long been regarded as the most striking feature of Russian character.

4. TOWN LIFE

What has been said above concerning the peasant might certainly be repeated in a less degree about the town-dweller. It goes without saying that in the past the town house was, at least in well-to-do families, very like those in central and western Europe in its arrangement, in the number and lay-out of its rooms, in its furniture and decoration. The struggle against cold was the cause of its most peculiar features, viz. its enormous stove whose great heating power enabled the women to be dressed in light blouses in the height of winter, and its double windows which were closed in Moscow by the end of October and 'had their joints sealed with wax, only one little pane at the top remaining free to open' (Allix). But the town used the same building materials as the village. Except in the Crimea and the country round Lake Onega, which are rich in granite, diabase, quartzite, and sandstone, the use of stone is, in spite of the improvement in quarrying, a luxury restricted to great buildings, palaces, churches, and convents. Odessa has a fairly large number of houses built of marble, because many ships from Greece and Italy used marble as ballast on their outward voyage and left it behind when they sailed home laden with wheat. In the southern provinces brick has been popular for many decades, and in the twentieth century concrete has had remarkable success, for since the revolution it has been increasingly popular for new buildings. But in quite half of Russia and even in definitely southern towns like Kuybyshev and Saratov, Stalingrad and Astrakhan, most of the houses were made of wood, and the risk of fire was no less than in the countryside right up to the time when the struggle against the scourge secured the use of modern means of combating it. We know that several times 'a kopek-worth of candle has sufficed to burn Moscow' and that in the sixteenth century the lighting of fires indoors was forbidden from May to September, even for cooking, which had to be done in the open air. As far as the materials used are concerned, the only thing to be mentioned is a particularly urban feature which has often been noticed by travellers, namely, the great number of painted metal roofs, amounting to 0·5 per cent. of roofs in Russia, which is partly explained by the abundance of iron in the country.

Until recently the towns paid no more attention to town-planning than did the villages. Ideas of town-planning scarcely appeared before the end of the last century and then so slightly that the Tsarist age left almost everything to be done by its successor. In 1912, says Camena d'Almeida, no more than seventeen towns had a system of sewers and tramways; not one had an underground railway; nearly all still lit their streets with paraffin lamps; and St. Petersburg (Leningrad) had no other drinking water than that of the Neva. Numbers of them had neither pavements nor roadway; dust and mud were dreadful nuisances, especially in the south; and nearly everywhere complaints were made of the filth, absence of hygiene, and the lamentable inadequacy of the rubbish dumps.

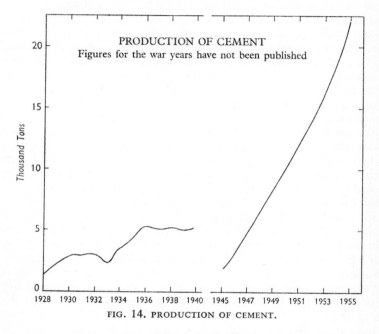

FIG. 14. PRODUCTION OF CEMENT.

Certain writers have claimed that the real distinction between the towns and villages lay in the fact that the number of persons dwelling under the same roof was greater in the former than the latter. But the truth of this is doubtful. Apart from the 'barracks' in the working-class quarters which have sprung up in the twentieth century and have multiplied since the revolution, a large number of town houses had no more, or even fewer, occupants than some country dwellings.

The occupations of the inhabitants constituted no real distinctive criterion, and the number of non-agricultural workers, the industrial activity, and the amount of business done are interesting but unreliable as tests. Many 'villages' had a large artisan population, at least seasonally, and there were some whose fairs represented a great deal of trade, just as there were 'towns' whose suburbs, and sometimes even the centres, sheltered hosts of gardeners and cultivators. In fine, the population figures are certainly the decisive factor. All the same, it must be noticed that in the eyes of official statisticians, whose records go back to Nicholas I, some agglomerations of 10,000 or 20,000 souls were still 'villages' in 1914, whilst in 1897 Kola with its 615 inhabitants was dignified with the title of 'town'.

Be that as it may, Russian towns can be placed in several categories according to their origin, it being understood that in a given town several origins may have been at work and different quarters may be recognised as belonging to different categories.

First, there are places like Kalinin, Ryazan, Vladimir, Tula, Novgorod, Gorky, Kazan, and Moscow, which are derived from former *gorodishcha* (= *oppida*) or fortified towns, snuggling under the protection of a *kreml'*, which is both a citadel, an arsenal, and a sanctuary; or under shelter of a fortified convent, such as the Ipatiev house at Kostroma, where the imperial fortunes of the Romanovs began. By a striking coincidence it was in the Ipatiev house at Sverdlovsk that the massacre took place which was fated to extinguish these fortunes for ever. The woodland steppe and the true steppe saw the foundation of a good number of such towns, most of which have decayed as security increased. Unlike those in the centre, which are so rich in churches and convents that 'the devil would not dare to enter them', these have few large buildings, but the street-names in their *slobody* (suburbs) recall their warlike past. Both types are recognised by their regular plans and concentric boulevards which, in Moscow for instance, as in Paris, have replaced the successive rings of fortifications and mark the stages of growth.

On the other hand, no military apprehension has presided over the planning of the towns in the south, which are just administrative centres. Some of those on the coast are descended from Greek or Genoese cities. The inland towns are adorned with gardens and parks of real beauty and have two features which strike visitors. First, the tiring sameness of their lay-outs. Constructed in a single mould according to a single and unchangeable idea, they have all a huge central square, with the cathedral in it, and streets whose names are as unoriginal as the lay-outs and which cut each other at right-angles. Secondly, even towns of moderate size have streets and squares of a surprising width, equal to those seen in the great European capitals. Any town of 500,000 inhabitants in western Europe or America would be comfortably placed on the area occupied by any Ukrainian city with a population of 70,000.

Towns of commercial origin are also numerous. Centres of inland water transport, large seaports dealing with exports or imports, like Archangel or Odessa, and sites of particularly prosperous fairs, like Gorky (formerly Nizhne Novgorod). As they occur everywhere and are of very different ages, their appearance is very variable, as is also their æsthetic appeal.

Finally, there grew up in the nineteenth century industrial towns which are no less commonplace than the administrative centres and are even uglier, with their factories, chimneys, and general blackness. They are to be seen chiefly in the mining district in the Urals, in the coal and iron region in the Donets, and in the Moscow basin, where textiles and metal and leather goods are manufactured. For several decades their number and importance has been steadily on the increase, and in many places vast working-class quarters with housing for multitudes and with semi-skyscrapers are curiously situated close by older buildings. In Stalingrad, for instance, there is a block of workers' flats owned by the tractor works and used to house the workers employed in the factory. The block looks shoddy by Western standards and is rather crowded inside. The standard is one family to one room. But everybody seems clean and comfortable.[1]

In Soviet times, and especially after 1945, town-planning has become stereotyped. Wealthier people have prefabricated concrete houses which are often shared with other families. These places are no better than tenement houses; but the tenants usually have a *dacha*, or wooden villa, in the country to which they resort when work allows. Urban factory and office workers are housed near their work in enormous rectangular concrete blocks of flats 'built according to socialist realism' with small windows, no balconies, and no attempt at appeal to the æsthetic sense. Nor is material comfort attained. The standard flat has only two small rooms, a tiny kitchen, and an even smaller bathroom; but, in fact, the not unusual accommodation consists of a single room for a family of four. Public buildings, on the other hand, are massive stone structures in classic style and are spacious and lavishly constructed. The Russians are proud of these marks of their achievement and especially of the Moscow underground railway with its marble-walled stations.

The urban population of Russia is rapidly growing relatively as well as absolutely. The tendency showed itself as early as the beginning of the nineteenth century. In 1926 the rate of increase was 18·4 per cent. (17 per cent. in White Russia, 18·5 in the Ukraine, and 46·3 in the Crimea) and the growth of towns exceeded all expectation. In the Soviet Union as a whole the increase was 4·5 per cent. per

[1] F. J. Erroll, M.P., in the *Royal Central Asian Journal*, vol. 42, Jan. 1955, p. 52.

annum between 1923 and 1926, but the figure was certainly even greater in Russia. From 1926 to 1939 the rate of increase in all Russian territory was 113 per cent. By 1959 the urban population was 47·8 per cent. of the total for the whole Union. This increase began by making up for the effects of a very marked falling off. From 1917 to 1920 the stoppage of industry and commerce and the acute crisis in the food supply had sent many townsfolk streaming back to the countryside. The population of Leningrad

FIG. 15. MOST IMPORTANT NEW TOWNS IN THE SOVIET UNION
(*after* Mikhailov).

fell from 2,000,000 to 706,000, that of Moscow from 1,500,000 to 1,000,000; Kiev lost 80,000 inhabitants. Odessa 63,000, Gorky 30,000, Orel 26,000, Kazan 10,000, and so on; and the urban population decreased by 1·2 per cent. But after 1920 economic recovery drew another stream into the towns. Between 1923 and 1926 Leningrad increased its population by 51 per cent., Dnepropetrovsk by 48 per cent., Ivanovo by 55 per cent., Kharkov by 33 per cent., Moscow by 31 per cent., and in 1926 twenty-four towns[1] more or less exceeded a population of 100,000. By 1955 their number had grown to 83. Indeed, since the last detailed census in 1897 certain towns have

[1] Moscow, Leningrad, Kiev, Odessa, Kharkov, Rostov-on-Don, Saratov Dnepropetrovsk, Gorky, Kazan, Kuybyshev, Krasnodar, Astrakhan, Tula, Stalingrad, Sverdlovsk, Minsk, Chkalov, Voronezh, Yaroslavl, Ivanovo, Kalinin, Stalino, and Nikolayevski.

undergone surprising growth. Thus, Gorky has advanced from a population of 95,124 to one of 876,000; Ivanovo from 54,000 to 319,000; Yaroslavl from 70,610 to 374,000; Kalinin from 53,447 to 240,000; Stalino from 32,000 to 625,000; Stalingrad from 55,967 to 525,000; Kiev from 247,000 to 991,000; Kharkov from 174,000 to 877,000; and Rostov-on-Don from 119,889 to 552,000. The terrible demographic crisis which the revolution had provoked, and which might have been regarded as irremediable when abortion was legalised and bid fair to become a custom, was overcome and the Russian population curve began to resume its triumphant upward movement. The same was true of the *Okrainy*, but in these the settlement and growth of population did not have the same characteristics.

CHAPTER 9

POPULATION AND SETTLEMENT IN SOVIET ASIA

1. SIBERIA

Of all the Russian 'possessions' Siberia differs least from Russia from the ethnographical and human as well as the physical point of view. Though on an ethnographical map vast areas are shown as non-Russian, these are without exception nearly empty. The natives are few and, since until our own times they were regarded as conquered peoples little worthy of consideration and were ruthlessly exploited, they found themselves at a low ebb after the revolution, being nearly all on the decline and usually living by hunting and fishing, with a little stock-rearing and here and there some agriculture. However, they were not all so badly off, and each of the principal peoples must be described separately. A division into Uralo-Altaic and Palæo-Asiatic groups has no real interest except for the ethnographer, and it is better to follow Camena d'Almeida and use the geographical environments and modes of life as the basis for classification and in this way to divide the peoples into tundra, forest, and steppe groups.

The tundra is inhabited almost entirely by the survivors of peoples who have been driven by invaders from better lands. The 3000 Ostiaks, or Khante, on the Yenisey, 1300 Yukaghirs on the lower Yana and Indigirka, 1200 Eskimos on Bering Strait, and even the 5000 timid, melancholy Samoyedes on the Taymyr peninsula and the lower Khatanga need only be mentioned. More interesting are the 17,000 pure-bred Ostiaks, who centre round Salekhard, but are also found under the name of Voguls in the vicinity of the Ural River and have kept their own language and customs; and, lastly, the 13,000 Chukchees, who are very Mongolian in type and visibly related to the Eskimos, and are regarded as strong, industrious, and enterprising, though very gentle in manner.

These peoples live mostly in tents, but at times in huts, lead a wretched nomadic existence, wandering up hill and down dale from the tundra to the *tayga*, fishing off the coast and in the rivers, hunting the bear, wolf, glutton, sable, goose, swan, and wild duck, and breeding reindeer and dogs. With the possible exception of the Chukchees, they are all declining in numbers. Despite their toughness, quick eye, and extraordinarily good sense of direction, most of them frequently suffer from hunger, owing to the poverty of the country, and they have had to invent 'a thousand and one ways of starving to death', eating the bast or bark of trees, searching for the hoards of field-rats, and sometimes extracting undigested green food from the intestines of reindeer in order to eat it. Moreover, the terrible climate deals hardly with them, causing frightfully high infant mortality; and they have not been helped by contact with whites, since these are mostly traders who cheat them with the most cynical greed. About 1926 it was estimated that only fusion with the Russians could save them from extinction.

In the Siberian forests also the natives often lead a miserable life. Suffering from the increasing scarcity of game and ruined by the fur traders, the Ostiaks have nearly all died of hunger, typhus, or the effects of their great consolation, drink. Less wretched are the 4000 Ghiliaks in Sakhalin and on the lower Amur, who are related to the Ainus of Hokkaido; the 5700 Kamchadals, who have nearly all forgotten their mother tongue and their religion and have adopted the Russian language and customs and been converted to Christianity; the 7200 Koriaks, who live on the coast of the Sea of Okhotsk and are very independent in character, but hospitable and obliging. Some Vogul Finns survive in the glades farther south, but they are hoe cultivators, live in *izby*, return themselves as Russians, and are counted as such in censuses. In fact, only two groups of natives still count.

The first of these, the Tunguses, who swarm on the tundra and steppe, are unanimously described as intelligent, brave, proud, resourceful and cheerful, loyal and hospitable. They are closely related racially to the Manchus and have played an interesting part as intermediaries between China and Siberia. Unfortunately, the tribes in the Amur region—the Daures, Goldes, and Oroches—fell into the hands of Chinese immigrants and were ruined by them. There are scarcely more than 14,000 of them left. The true Tunguses of the forest, who are remarkably skilful at fishing and hunting, range between the Yenisey and the Sea of Okhotsk. They have inferior rifles, but are expert in the art of setting traps and have a deep knowledge of the ways of game. Many do not have even tents, and, though they beget many children, the mortality among these is frightful, being often due to hunger rather than disease. Hence, they number scarcely 53,000 against 75,000 in 1897.

Much more important and vigorous is the Yakut group. They occupy an area of more than 1½ million square miles, or nearly one-fifth of the Soviet Union, but number only 225,000. Originally dwelling on the shores of Lake Baykal and driven thence by their enemies, the Buryats, into the basin of the Lena, this nation of herdsmen and horsemen adapted itself with remarkable flexibility to its new conditions of life. Partly giving up horse-breeding, they devoted themselves with complete success to cattle-rearing, even beyond the Arctic Circle, and to reindeer-breeding. But these wonderful stockmen are also hunters, river fishermen, boatmen, craftsmen (carpenters, joiners, basket-makers, gunsmiths, jewellers, miners), and, above all, traders. They have been jocularly called 'the Jews of Siberia'. Far from decreasing, their numbers are increasing. As the Yakuts are capable of strenuous work whenever the need arises for this, it is not surprising that they are by a long way the foremost people among the natives of Siberia.

There are, indeed, other people who live comfortably on the steppe. The chief of them are the Buryats, Mongols by race, who live mainly in the neighbourhood of Lake Baykal and in Transbaykalia. The usual account of their morals is unflattering, but at any rate they are certainly very skilful stockmen, rearing cattle, sheep, and, above all, horses. Under Russian influence they have taken to agriculture with complete success, making hay, growing cereals, manuring, and watering their pastures, and irrigating the Salenga steppe. The families which have adopted a sedentary life have given up the tent for the *izba*. Moreover, many Buryats have adopted Russian ways, which explains why the official numbers of this people have fallen from 220,000 in 1897 to 200,000 in 1926 and to 77,000 in 1939.

Their neighbours, the Tatars, are nearly as numerous and include, besides the Tatars so called, the Oirots of the Altai and the Kirghiz of the south-west. Nomadism still has many supporters among them, especially in the south-west, where there are herds of horses and camels and flocks of sheep and goats, and in the Abakan steppe from which there is a drift to the Altai in the summer for the hill pastures. But many have taken to farming or trading and, though they are Mohammedans, the very people whom the story of Michael Strogoff depicted as fierce adversaries of the Russian invaders, have to a great extent adopted Russian ways with its mode of life, its costume, type of dwelling, and even the language of the conquerors.

In fine, though the steppe natives are holding their own without too much difficulty, those in the forests and tundra are, with the exception of the Yakuts, fast decreasing. 'The extensive areas which these peoples occupy on ethnographic maps should not mislead as to their numbers' (Camena d'Almeida). Certainly, in about 1925 the natives were estimated at 93 per cent. of the total population in the 'government' of Yakutsk, at 88 per cent. in that of Kamchatka, but at only 37 per cent. in Sakhalin, 32 per cent. in Transbaykalia, 27 per cent. in the Maritime Province, 22 per cent. in the 'government' of Tomsk, and their total numbers did not exceed 1 million, or one-twelfth of the population of Siberia. Even if it is true that Soviet policy has produced an increase in their numbers, the percentage could only decrease. In 1939 Siberia had a population of 30 million. Had the native element been doubled in fifteen years, it would still not form more than one-fifteenth of the total.

This reveals the importance of the position held by the ever-increasing Russians. About 1926 there were not many Great Russians among them and the majority still came from the districts of Tula, Orel, Kursk, and Tambov, which were almost outside Great Russia. By far the greater part of the settlers originated from White Russia, from the Ukraine which, though wealthy, was beginning to be over-crowded, from the arid Crimea, and from the middle Volga where the capricious climate and the absence of industry prevented high density. It should be noted that the last-named region has sent out not only Russians, but also Germans. When all the land was taken up, the German settlements sent off swarms first into the 'government' of Chkalov, where they founded twenty-four villages, then to the Chelyabinsk region, the Kulunda steppe, the neighbourhood of Omsk, the Altai, Baykalia, etc., so that in 1926 Siberia had 108,816 German-speaking inhabitants and 503 German settlements, whose appearance was normally more well-to-do than that of the Russian village. The latter was rare in Transbaykalia in the same year, very rare in Yakutia, where the number of settlers was only 129 in four-teen years, not very numerous in eastern Siberia, far less rare in central Siberia, and very numerous in western Siberia, which had received most of the immigrants from Russia. Generally speaking, these immigrants have settled in southern Siberia, where was situated the best land, which they naturally allocated to themselves. As the immigrants now form an overwhelming majority of the population of Siberia, this population may be said to be nearly all settled on a narrow fringe along the southern frontier, exactly as in Canada, 'the Siberia of the New World'.

On the whole, conditions in the belt of settlement are like those in Russia. As the physical setting was more or less the same, the settlers had no inducement to change their habits or to give up their archi-tectural traditions. Consequently, the *izba* reappears in the wooded regions and the daub house on the steppe. However, there has been, at least in the Buryat-Mongol Autonomous Republic and the neighbourhood of Irkutsk, Tulun, and Udinsk in central Siberia, a

FIG. 16. POLITICAL DIVISIONS OF RUSSIA IN EUROPE, WITH SUBDIVISIONS OF THE R.S.F.S.R.

tendency, which has increased of late, to favour stone for housebuilding. The hard sandstones of Irkutsk and the limestones and granite of the Buryat region are much used, whilst in the Angara and Baykal regions the number of tile- and brickworks is increasing.

In general, the Siberian village is less badly kept than the Russian village and is also more pleasing to the eye. 'A little collection of wooden houses with thatched roofs and ornamented windows relieved with a coat of bright red or green paint. Between two windows there are about a dozen flower pots adding more and more red in front of the embroidered curtains. . . . Each house is prolonged by its garden, which is surrounded by a fence or hedge and is a square of ground with yellow sunflower discs swaying in it. . . . The road goes down between these houses, all of which have a family likeness and are completely painted over with flowers' (P. Dominique). But here too hygiene leaves enough to be desired for fire to be regarded as the ideal means of scavenging. It operates on the average every fifteen years.

The towns are like those of southern Russia and imitate the villages in spreading over a large area. As a rule, they were originally fortified posts established on raised river-banks, often at a confluence; and the old settlement, which was once girt with wooded ramparts that exist no longer, is a central fortress with dark, narrow streets. But around this stretch geometrically planned quarters with huge squares and extraordinarily wide streets whose maintenance, owing somewhat to the difficulties of the climate, leaves much to be desired. The railway station and its quarter with the dwellings of the employees occupy a great space, and though the gaol is large, the hospitals are vast, and schools, libraries, and scientific museums are numerous. On the other hand, there are very few churches and convents, for towards the end of the Tsarist era there was infinitely less religion in Siberia than in Russia.

In fact, there were very appreciable differences between the 'Sibiriak' and the 'Russki'. The former was physically more hardened by the severer, but healthier, climate and had a flattering reputation. Stress was laid on the fact that he had never been a serf, that he was of a prouder temper, more democratic by instinct, less superstitious, had a greater love of knowledge, was more of a realist, and more enterprising and energetic than the latter. But the roughness of his lonely, difficult life had toughened his character, and contact with so many evil elements (vagabonds, rogues, thieves, and murderers) had not been without ill effect on the settlers. 'Apart from a few notable exceptions', wrote J. Legras, 'I have met scarcely anyone here who is not coarser, more brutal, more selfish, and more indifferent to morals and religion, more habituated to the physical enjoyment of alcohol and money than most Russian peasants.' In the eyes of the latter folk the 'Siberian respected nothing'. Far from having behind him the rich poetic and impassionable tradition of Russia, he seemed as vulgar as he was commonplace and as poor in heart as in imagination and artistic feeling. But perhaps that was only a passing phase such as all colonies have experienced at their beginning, and there is no reason to believe that the faults of the Siberian will not grow less as the transported criminals are eliminated and the doubtful elements disappear under the stream of immigrants.

Be this as it may, no power, except perhaps Japan in the Far East, could after all have disputed with Russia the possession of Siberia, which is a genuinely Russian country. By a piece of good luck which would be unique but for the similar case of the United States, Russia found adjacent to her territory a gigantic and almost empty space whose natives she has easily overwhelmed by her vigorous birthrate. What was a 'colony' yesterday seemed as early as 1928 to be in process of fusing completely with its metropolis.

The same could not be said of central Asia or the Caucasus.

2. CENTRAL ASIA

Either by natural desiccation or more probably owing to the effects of war and bad government, central Asia seems to have become seriously impoverished and depopulated from the Middle Ages up to the Russian conquest. This did not prevent it from having a population of something like 14 million in 1926, which on a million and a half square miles of surface gave a mean density of 9 per square mile. This was a poor figure in a sense, but was three times that of Siberia at the same period. Vast expanses of desert were almost empty, but the oases showed densities of the order of 65, 80, and 100 to the square mile. Of this population the natives formed the great majority, about 11,200,000 persons or four-fifths of the total. Some of them are Persians, like the Tadzhiks,[1] who are the sedentary representatives of the Persian nation in Turan and speak Persian. Being perhaps the descendants of the ancient people of Sogdiana and heirs of the brilliant civilisation of eastern Bukhara, they are regarded as the most intelligent race in central Asia. They prove as excellent in farming as they are skilful in craftsmanship and prudent in commerce. In many respects they have been instructors to their neighbours.

Other natives are Turko-Mongols, who generally lodge in *yurts* and lead a nomadic life. These are the Kazaks (or Kirghiz of the Great Horde), who wander about at the foot of the Alatau, and the Kara-Kirghiz (or Black Kirghiz, the only ones who call themselves Kirghiz). The latter roam over the steppes of Kazakstan and especially in Semirechye. In 1939 they numbered 3,100,000;

[1] In 1939 they numbered 1,229,000.

and they are considered reliable, hardy, brave, honest, and industrious.[1]

Turko-Mongol in race, too, are the rough but proud Turkomans of the south, who were subdued with great difficulty and who are pastoral nomads definitely given to plundering. They numbered 685,000 in 1926 and 812,000 in 1939. Also the Kara Kalpaks, who, driven off by the Turkomans, live a semi-nomadic life on the delta of the Oxus, struggling ceaselessly with the tigers and wolves that attack their flocks and with the wild boars and locusts that ravage their crops. In 1939 they numbered 186,000. Lastly, there are the hard-working Goklens and the semi-nomadic Yomuds of the lower Oxus.

Other peoples that are mixtures of Persian and Turko-Mongol dwell on the oases in the east. First, there are the Sartes, who look like Persians, but have adopted Turkish culture, some speaking *Yagatai*, a Turkish dialect, and others Persian. They are very like the Tadzhiks with their long faces, bushy beards, and deep black eyes and hair. They are said to be timid and even rather servile in character, but they are none the less active, enterprising, and very good at farming, though they prefer trading to working on the land. Then the Uzbeks, who are thought to be related to the Seljuk Turks and whose ninety-two tribes all speak the same language (*Jagatai*, or Tatar), though they are greatly mixed with Persian stock. They are industrious, and tenacious, and their numbers[2] ensure them much importance.

Something must also be said of the 228,000 Bukharan Jews, a handsome and intelligent people who, though oppressed till 1918, had been able to amass fortunes, especially in the cotton trade. More than half of them lived in Samarkand and Bukhara. Finally, there are immigrant Persians who are traders, artisans, and wage-earners, and are particularly numerous in Transcaspia.

The great majority of these natives, of course, crowded into the oases, since these districts alone seemed to have a future. Hence, Russian colonisation was obviously less effective here than in Siberia. However, the stream of immigration, far from drying up, increased after the revolution, so that in 1926 the Russians numbered about 2,800,000 persons, or one-fifth of the population. The flow continued in subsequent years and even reached mountain areas like the Dzungarian Alatau, which it was scarcely expected to touch. But its rate has greatly slackened since then. Today, only the northern areas,

---

[1] The name Kirghiz is reserved today to the inhabitants of Kirghizistan or Kirghizia (Tien Shan and Pamirs), and the country that we are accustomed to call the Kirghiz steppes is now called Kazakstan.
[2] 3,765,000 in 1926 and 4,844,000 in 1939.

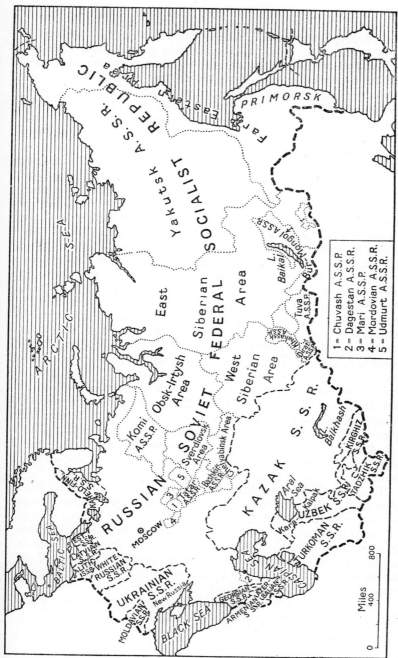

FIG. 17. POLITICAL DIVISIONS OF THE SOVIET UNION.

1 = Chuvash A.S.S.R.
2 = Dagestan A.S.S.R.
3 = Mari A.S.S.R.
4 = Mordovian A.S.S.R.
5 = Udmurt A.S.S.R.

viz. Turgay, Semipalatinsk, Akmolinsk, and above all, Semirechye from Lepsinsk to Aulya Ata, are densely peopled with Russians. Many of the villages are rather like those in nearby western Siberia, and the streets and squares of some of the towns, which are spacious, dusty, and lined with houses built of wood and brick, are curiously reminiscent of Barnaul, Ishim, or Tobolsk. In a number of other towns like Tashkent, Samarkand, Kokand, and Andizhan a vast Russian quarter has grown up next to the native town. The great width of the streets and their geometrical lay-out, the abundance of shade, the size and style of the buildings, public offices or scientific institutions, gave the quarter a very special appearance as early as 1914. But when all is said and done, the Russians were few in number. They were officials, technicians, traders, and soldiers, 60,000 of the last being sufficient in 1913 to watch over Russian Turkistan. In the villages on the oases to the east and south Russian settlers formed only a tiny minority.

Things have scarcely changed. On the whole, central Asia remains a country in which the general tone of life is still native, except in the north-east. The country does not give the impression of being Russian, as Siberia does. Furthermore, a Russian type of house is exceptional. The *yurt* of the kind seen in south-eastern Russia prevails over vast expanses of desert or steppe. It exists also in the mountains in a slightly modified form known as *kibitka*, but it is sometimes found there with huts of wood or stone which, unlike those on the plains, have something of a chimney. The house built of hardened loess prevails in the oasis belt, which is inhabited by a settled population. The higher one climbs above sea-level, the more one notices that the loess is mixed with conglomerate for building and that at the same time there is a falling off in the number of the villages and the standard of comfort. In the towns the narrow, filthy streets, the untidy arrangement of the houses, and the variegated picturesqueness of the bazaars are typically oriental.

To sum up, the population of central Asia is very different from that of Siberia and seems destined to remain so, because many natives, especially the Kirghiz and Turkomans, are turning over to a settled life. Hence, the land still available for settlement becomes less and less. Whether the country will adopt Russian culture in course of time seems doubtful therefore. In the early years of the Soviet régime there was still the appearance of a colony of exploitation rather than one of settlement.

The same remark holds good for Caucasia, where the natives had and still have a great numerical superiority.

3. CAUCASIA

The population of Caucasia is not very numerous, as may be imagined, considering the immense space occupied in the country by lofty mountains, and the aridity of many areas of moderate height, not to mention the very disturbed history of the region, its wars, massacres, deportations, and emigrations. But on the other hand, it is extremely varied.

There can be no doubt that the Caucasus was peopled from very ancient times. Remains dating from the Mousterian period have been recognised, for example at Illskaya in the Kuban province in northern Caucasia. Side by side with spontaneous settlements are often found colonies planted by governments. Among the successive empires of western Asia scarcely one failed to establish colonies near the mountain passes in order to prevent the nomads of the steppes to the north from having access to them. Thus, the Sassanides planted the Tatas in eastern Caucasia in the sixth and seventh centuries, and the Arab colonies established in Azerbaidzhan and southern Dagestan still breed camels. But a more important factor, which has been pointed out again and again, is the part played by the mountains as a refuge. The region has been troubled by a hundred invasions, and the insecurity which prevailed for long on its borders explains why so many people have sought shelter in the mountains, just as it clearly explains the character of the inhabitants.

Until recently, not only did the mountaineers always go armed with their *kinjal* (dagger) or even dressed in complete armour, as the Khevsurs used to do, but in many cases they also fortified their houses. In the lower valley of the Rion, where the houses are isolated wooden homesteads surrounded by large yards, the practice of raising the buildings on piles is no doubt intended as much for a protection from damp as against attack. But in Georgia many dwellings are placed against a natural eminence and built into the hillside, so that they have no other opening than the door. In Kakhetia, where the attacks of the Lesghians were for long a constant menace, the houses which are not more or less underground are frail and hard to defend; and so there are fortified towers in which the population could take refuge. Among the Tushes whole villages are composed of square towers built of large blocks of stone. In northern Osetia the houses are built of stone, have two or three storeys, and are surrounded by a high wall strengthened with towers. In southern Osetia the houses are of wood, but are placed several together in an enclosure defended by a strong palisade. Towers are also found among the mountain Chechens, some being used as dwellings and others purely for defence; but they are not as big as those in Svanetia, which sometimes exceed a height of 65 ft. In the lower districts inhabited by the Lesghians all the houses are surrounded by solid stone walls, and windows and doors open on to an interior courtyard. Finally, in upper Dagestan the villages, which are built of stone and snuggle against the side of the mountains on terraces cut by steep, narrow streets, are arranged so as to offer a vigorous resistance to an assailant.

The peoples who sought refuge in the Caucasus lived in fierce isolation owing to the relief of the land. As the mountain range is in an early stage of evolution, it is not easily penetrated and the valleys have poor intercommunication. Hence by reason of the difficulties of travel, the latter form little worlds of their own, in each of which the people have lived in cultural isolation and mistrustful solitude and have thus maintained their identity instead of fusing with their neighbours. The result is that the Caucasus is a museum of races, a patchwork of nationalities, a mosaic of religions, and a Tower of Babel. Scarcely any other country is more attractive to the ethnologist and the student of comparative linguistics. European, Asiatic, pagan, Jew, Christian, and Mohammedan, all mingle in this region, where even in the days of Pliny one hundred and thirty interpreters were required by the stranger who wanted to travel from one end of the country to the other. Today many a dialect is spoken by only four or five villages. In the main, apart from the question whether the 'Caucasian race' really did spring from this region, three chief groups of peoples, or rather languages, are recognisable:

(*a*) *The Khartvelian Group* inhabits the centre and west of Trans-caucasia from the Kura valley to the Black Sea. It comprises four languages: Georgian, spoken in Georgia and westwards as far as beyond Suram by a magnificent breed of Christian farmers, wine-growers, and stockmen whose civilisation dates from very early times; they numbered 985,000 persons in 1926 and 2,248,000 in 1939. Secondly, Mingrelian, spoken by 225,000 Christians in ancient Colchis, whose natural resources they turn to such poor effect that they are obliged to emigrate to Tiflis and other towns, where they live as casual labourers and porters. Thirdly, Laze, spoken by the Laze or Tsan Mohammedans between Batum and Trebizond. And fourthly, Svanet, spoken by the rough, wild mountaineers of the upper Ingun valley. In this group should also be included the Pshavs and Khevsurs to the east of the road from Tiflis to Ordzhonikidze and the Tushes on the northern slopes of the mountains.

(*b*) *The Western Caucasian Mountain Group* comprises some 60,000 Abkhases clustered around Sukhum. They are the remains of a formerly Christian people who turned Mohammedan. They have very peculiar agglutinative language, and emigrated almost all in a body in 1864. The group also includes about 200,000 Cherkhasses, whose history is much the same. Many of those who remained in Russian territory scattered to the north of the Caucasus and under the name of Kabards settled in the neighbourhood of Krasnodar. They too have a separate language.

(c) *The Eastern Caucasian Mountain Group* comprises the Chechens,[1] who occupy the northern slopes. They are Sunnite Mohammedans and were the strongest supporters of Shamil, many of them leaving the country after his final defeat. The group also includes under the name of Lesghians the 230,000 Avars, 160,000 Kurins, and 45,000 Laks who inhabit Dagestan and are terribly fanatical Mohammedans, but very industrious and most skilful in metal work, to exercise their craftsmanship in which they often migrate in winter as far as Persia.

Besides the Caucasian peoples properly so called, there are many others to be mentioned. First of all, there are the Armenians, Christians by origin and religion, who numbered quite 1,500,000 in 1926 and more than 2,000,000 in 1939. Their extraordinary commercial gifts and their influence in municipal government are well known, and a mere mention of names like those of Bagration and Loris Melikov is enough to indicate the place the Armenians were able to take in the days of the empire. Then there are Persians, including besides 50,000 scattered Persians who are especially numerous in Tiflis and Baku, the 225,000 Osetians,[2] who command the road into Georgia on both slopes of the range; the 75,000 Tats of the 'governments' of Baku, Kirovabad, and southern Dagestan; the 50,000 Talishes in the Lenkoran district; and the 55,000 Kurds of Armenia. Finally, there are some 2,000,000 Tatars, who are either farmers in the Kuban valley and the neighbourhood of the Caspian or else nomads dwelling in felt tents on the Kura and Terek steppes. To these must also be added some 100,000 Turks and 120,000 Caucasian Jews so as more or less to complete the catalogue of indigenous peoples.

As we have seen, the number of Europeans is not very great and could hardly be large. True settlers are rare in Transcaucasia. Until very recently the Russians were represented mainly by officials, soldiers, traders, and technicians. In fact, the only part they have occupied in any strength is western Caucasia. The climate of the Kuban steppes as well as the fertile soil, which is rather like Black Earth, reminds them of south Russia, and today this area forms a 'russified' district. Here the daub hut prevails, with here and there a brick house, and these are replaced in the mountains and foothills either by wooden *izby* or stone houses. But on this north slope settlement does not climb above a height of 2300 ft. The greater part of

[1] They numbered 305,000 in 1926 and 407,000 in 1939.   [2] 355,000 in 1939.

the mountain range has not adopted Russian ways, any more than have Transcaucasia and Armenia, in spite of the marks of Russian influence on certain quarters of Tiflis and Baku. In 1926 the low percentage of Russians in the total population of Caucasia could not fail to give the country a colonial character.

4. RECENT INCORPORATION IN THE FRAMEWORK OF THE SOVIET UNION

The harsh policy of assimilation practised by the Tsar's Government throughout Asiatic Russia was expected eventually to turn the other races into Russians, for this aim had already been achieved with a

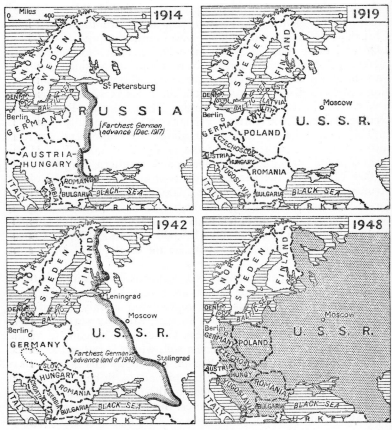

FIG. 18. FRONTIERS OF RUSSIA, 1914–48.

number of Tatars, Buryats, and Yakuts, and it was considered that the civilisation of the eastern peoples was too far inferior to that of Russia to fail to succumb to it in the end, and so the old administrative divisions of Russia, Siberia, central Asia, and Caucasia seemed logically doomed to disappear sooner or later. We have seen that physical geography in no way justified them. From the human point of view, they had some value in Caucasia and Turkistan, but no longer retained any in Siberia.

Thus, physically and ethnographically speaking, these divisions might have appeared out-of-date, or very nearly so, as early as the first year of the present régime. In 1928, they no longer had any pretext for existence, since the latest justification of them, their administrative and political uses, had disappeared. In fact, the Soviet Government has quite a different solution from that of the Tsars for the problem of racial, religious, and linguistic diversity and for that of the political inequality of the peoples. They have renounced the indivisibility of the empire together with the protection of the conquered races and foreign minorities by the Russians in order to encourage the reawakening, or even the awakening, of even the slightest degree of racial individuality. Not content with reviving the Ukrainian and White Russian languages and with fostering the use of German by the settlers on the Volga, they have—by giving them official equality with Russian—raised to the dignity of national languages tongues which until then were spoken, but never written. Soviet officials have been obliged to learn the language of the country in which they performed their duties, and the works of Gorky, for example, have been translated into Chuvash and those of Shakespeare and Maupassant into Kazak. The Russian names of towns have been abolished and replaced by old native names,[1] and local customs have been restored to honour. One district became Chuvash, another Zyrian, a third Karelian, a fourth Kalmuk. This does not mean that separatist movements are being initiated: the Kremlin will not have that at any price. The Georgian revolt was drowned in blood in 1924, and Ukrainian separatism was closely watched. But the Kremlin has regarded the cultivation of local patriotism not only as an act of justice, but also as a wise step, since it considered that to show itself in a good light to the natives was the best means of facilitating the spread of Communist doctrine among

[1] Besides this, names which suggested the Tsarist régime have given place to others which recall the past or present glories of Communism. It has sometimes happened that the new godfather of a town has fallen into disgrace (as Trotsky did), and this has sometimes led to changing the names of certain places two or three times. So far as we know, at least 115 Soviet towns have changed their names since 1917, which does not facilitate the study of the geography of the union. So far as possible, the latest names have been used in this translation.

them, and that was all that mattered. Besides, it will be seen that the Kremlin has striven to base political autonomy on a certain degree of economic self-support.

Since 1923 the former Russian empire has become a federal state: the Union of Soviet Socialist Republics. The absence of any geographical name indicates that the Union is open to any state which will accept its political and social creed. The largest of its elements, called the Russian Socialist Federal Soviet Republic, contains 92·7 per cent. of the area of the Union and covers territory including Russia and Siberia, running from the Arctic to the Black Sea and from the Gulf of Finland to the Pacific. The membership of the Union is as follows:

Socialist Soviet Republics in the Union on September 1, 1939:

Republic.	Capital.	Area in Square Miles.	Estimated Population in 1956.
Russia	Moscow	6,569,000	112,680,000
Ukraine	Kiev	231,000	40,600,000
Byelo-Russia (White Russia)	Minsk	80,000	8,000,000
Georgia	Tiflis	27,000	4,000,000
Armenia	Erivan	11,540	1,600,000
Azerbaidzhan	Baku	33,200	3,400,000
Kazakstan	Alma Ata	1,002,000	8,500,000
Kirghizstan	Frunze	76,000	1,900,000
Turkmenistan	Ashkhabad	187,000	1,400,000
Uzbekistan	Tashkent	153,000	7,300,000
Tadzhikstan	Stalinabad	55,000	1,800,000

To these have been added by annexation since September 1, 1939:

Republic.	Capital.	Area in Square Miles.	Estimated Population in 1940.
Moldavia	Kishinev	13,000	2,700,000
Lithuania	Vilna	25,000	2,700,000
Latvia	Riga	25,000	2,000,000
Estonia	Tallin	17,000	1,100,000

In 1956 Karelo-Finland, which had been made a constituent Republic of the Soviet Union in 1940, was reduced to the status of an Autonomous Republic within the Russian Republic.

But there are many subdivisions into autonomous republics, autonomous provinces, autonomous districts, autonomous territories,

FIG. 19. RUSSIAN GAINS IN THE WEST IN 1939–45.

105

etc. The republics of Abkhazia and Adzharistan, for instance, form part of Georgia, and the republic of Nakhichevan and the mountain district of Karabagh are attached to Azerbaidzhan. The federal republic of Russia is a world in itself and contains fourteen autonomous republics: Bashkiria, Buryat-Mongolia, Dagestan, Kabardino-Balkar, Karelia, Komi, Mari, Mordovia, North Osetia, Tatar, Udmurt, Chechen-Ingush, Chuvash, and Yakutia; seven autonomous regions: Adygei, Gorno-Altai, Tuva, Jewish, Kalmuck, Karachai-Cherkess, and Khakass; and ten national areas like Taymyr and Chukotka. On a different classification Russia properly so-called is divided into territories, including 'The North', 'Western Siberia', Krasnoyarsk, 'Eastern Siberia', 'The Far East', etc. It covers an area of 6,617,830 square miles and in 1956 had a population of 112,600,000. Since 1945 the Soviet Union has acquired the whole of Sakhalin, and its boundaries with Germany, Poland, Czecho-Slovakia, and Romania in the west and with China and Korea on the east have been left undefined.

Hence, on the map subdivision seems to be extreme. But it is not dangerous. Moral unity is achieved through love of the Communist doctrines—the only ones taught—and of 'the common fatherland of the proletariat'. Material unity is assured by the well-known iron grasp of Communist party dictatorship; and this unity seems assured, although the constitution formally recognises the right of any state to leave the Union. None of the members thinks of doing so; even if one wished to leave, it would not run the risk. However this may be, the Union has a very authoritarian and centralised Government. It is none of our business to describe its mechanism. Suffice it to remember that Moscow controls all its essential services. Moreover, no non-Russian state would be in a position to refuse obedience. What weight would the weak numbers of Caucasia, Turkistan, or even the 40 million Ukrainians carry against the 112 million Russians? It matters little that there are schools in which the teaching is in Yakut, that there are newspapers printed in Chuvash, and theatres acting plays in Georgian, and that a number of natives are local government officials. The Russians cannot help taking the lead owing to their enormous numbers and the superiority of their civilisation.

Nevertheless, two main principles have been laid down: the *inorodtsy* of former days have the right to retain their identity, and, furthermore, there are no longer Russians, Ukrainians, Tatars, Mingrelians, or Jews, but only Soviet citizens with equal rights and alike qualified for every office, even the highest,[1] and all due to benefit from the same care on the part of the Government. This policy has in practice proved very cunning. By removing the mistrust of the

[1] Stalin was a Georgian.

subject races it has without any doubt at all won most valuable assistance in the immense effort undertaken since 1928 to modernise the Russian world in true fashion.

The government of the Soviet Union is effected on a dual system, one section of which is political whilst the other is the Communist Party. The political section consists of the Soviet of the Union, which is formed by 708 deputies, one for every 300,000 persons, and the Soviet of Nationalities, which is a kind of senate and consists of 639 deputies, 25 from each Union Republic, 11 from each Autonomous Republic, 5 from each Autonomous Region, and 1 from each National Area. Elections take place every four years, only one candidate being allowed to stand for each constituency. Anyone over the age of 23 is eligible for election, but in practice all candidates are selected by the Communist Party. The political Soviets, which form the Supreme Soviet, meet twice a year, each session lasting about a week. To act for the Supreme Soviet between meetings there is a Presidium of thirty-three members, including the President of each Union Republic, which is always in session. Its chairman is the Head of State. Ordinary day to day business is carried on by the All-Union Council of Ministers, which is appointed by the Presidium and consists of twenty-four members. The chairman is the Prime Minister.

The Communist Party section consists of the All-Union Party Congress, which has 1355 delegates, one for each 5000 Party members, and meets from time to time. Between meetings its power is delegated to the Central Committee of the Party, which appoints the Presidium (Politburo) and Secretariat. The First Secretary is the most important person in the Soviet Union. Both Stalin and Krushchëv have held this post. The Central Committee consists of 133 full members and 122 'alternates', meets in secret, and is the true ruling body of the Soviet Union.

Part III

THE ECONOMIC SYSTEM

CHAPTER 10

THE ECONOMIC SYSTEM

A Russian scarcely ever speaks of his country without boasting with
visible pride of its ample dimensions and resources. Yet the Soviet
state used to consider itself backward economically, and the Russian
empire was terribly behind the times.

There were physical reasons for this backwardness: the severity of
the climate, the lengthy duration of the necessarily almost inactive
winter period, the aridity of vast areas, the difficulties of transport
over abominable roads in an enormous country, and the poverty
of much of the soil on the tundra, the podzol region, or the saline
steppes. Psychological reasons existed too: the people had little
attachment to the soil and readily moved from one place to another,
nomadism being for many of them a thing of the not very far past.
They therefore often showed apathy and want of foresight. In many
regions they were extremely ignorant. Lastly, the most serious
reasons of all were certain social ones: serfdom had ended in 1861,
but its abolition had left the *moujik* in great poverty. The *mir* system
was unfavourable to the modernisation of agriculture, nor had the
peasant the means to attempt improvement. Since the large estate
continued to be common, it was the duty of the 'better people' who
owned them to act as guides and instructors; but with a few brilliant
exceptions they played their parts badly. The immense potentialities
of the empire remained to a great extent unexploited. The general
poverty made it impossible for industry to find a market and so
develop seriously and make profits; and for large enterprises technicians and capital had to be sought abroad.

This does not mean that Tsarist Russia was in a state of economic
stagnation or that its production was at a low ebb. Such an assump-
tion would be flagrantly unjust. In world statistics Russian agriculture took a high place. The empire of the Tsars achieved an enormous
production of timber and furs. It owned much livestock, was the

110

leading exporter of wheat, flax, and hemp; and it sold great quantities of potatoes and beet-sugar. From the end of the nineteenth century especially, very remarkable progress was witnessed owing to the action of a real statesman, Count Witte. The textile industries in Muscovy and Russian Poland developed perceptibly; and coal was exploited with great success in the Donets basin, iron at Krivoyrog, and crude oil at Baku. At the same time some imposing railway construction was undertaken and carried out: the Trans-Siberian, Trans-Caucasian, Trans-Caspian, Trans-Aralian, and the Petrograd–Murmansk, not to mention the construction of the Nicholas II Canal in Siberia. A great stream of Russian emigration peopled Siberia and the north-east of central Asia. Foreign commerce was mainly favourable, and, thanks to the tenacity of the *zemstvas*, education made great strides, especially in the Ukraine, where 90 per cent. of the urban population and 73 per cent. of the rural population of school age regularly attended an elementary school in 1914.[1] In fact, all achievement has not been due to the Soviets, and many Russians were able to say: 'True, the foreigner goes faster than we, but that does not prevent us from making a great deal of progress.'

But besides some bright spots the picture showed many dark patches. The methods of farming were still primitive. The south-west (the districts of Kiev, Volhynia, and Podolia) was beginning to be acquainted with the scientific rotation of crops, and there potatoes, sugar-beet, and fodder crops were associated with cereals and improved by periodical manuring. But the greater part of the Black Earth country clung to the old triennial rotation consisting of winter wheat, spring wheat, and fallow. In other places prevailed the system of fallow of five, ten, or sometimes twenty years following two, four, or six years of cultivation; and in central and eastern Siberia and south-eastern Russia there was the most primitive semi-nomadic extensive cultivation. Manure was scarce, fodder-crops were lamentably inadequate, and two out of every three ploughs are said to have been *sokhy*, or poor swing-ploughs with wooden shares. The wheat crop, apparently so fine, was scarcely more than twice that of France, though the population was three times as great. Wheat exports were large only because the poverty of the peasants drove them to live mainly on rye. Similarly, the great quantity of the exports of sugar, potatoes, and Siberian butter was due to the small domestic consumption, that is, to the low standard of living, which reflected a backward social condition. The cotton crop, which was 4 per cent. of world-production, did not meet half the domestic requirements. Transport was inadequate. A country thirty-eight times as big as France had hardly twice the length of railways. Above

[1] In the rest of Russia the percentages were 82 and 57.

all, industrial production remained small. Russia had never been known to have such a great relative advance as in the time of Witte, it is true; but in 1913 the empire was producing only 29 million tons of coal a year (or 2·4 per cent. of world production), five times less electric power than Germany, and seventeen times less than the United States. It produced only 4½ million tons of pig iron a year and the same quantity of steel (5 per cent. of world production). Considering the greater progress of rivals, even of France, which was merely an average industrial power, Russian inferiority continued to increase in nearly every branch. 'We are falling behind more and more,' wrote Lenin.

There were worse things. Since the industry had been created by foreign capital,[1] and was protected by tariffs, it was usually badly managed and equipped and produced only inferior goods. Though the workmen were paid very small wages, production costs were very high, and therefore the goods could find no market abroad. The only buyer was the State, which was both producer and consumer. Hence, industry was in a condition of latent crisis and was continually threatened with bankruptcy.

Even those who did not know of this danger felt strongly that she should have done infinitely better in all the fields of economics. Lenin might be suspected of partisan feeling when he wrote in 1913: 'Russia remains a wretched half-savage country'; but many Russians of the middle classes noted with sorrow that poverty was rife among the people and that the country was losing precious human capital owing to an emigration which could quite well be avoided. They were indignant at the stupid selfishness of the governing classes and at the administrative waste, negligence, and inertia; and the catch-phrase: 'There must be a change,' was pretty generally echoed.

Then came the war and the revolution, the downfall of Russia, the redistribution of land (which brought great disillusionment to the peasants),[2] and 'war communism'[3] which had to face civil war and a nameless anarchy. The result was complete economic disorganisation, the almost complete stoppage of the transport system, the closing of a large number of mines, paralysis of industrial production, the break-down of agriculture, and a general dearth which in the districts of the lower Volga turned into a terrible famine owing to an exceptional drought. Russia seemed ruined. Even the Ukraine was heartrendingly impoverished in spite of its natural wealth. Its cereal

---

[1] The ascendancy of foreign capital was great. In 1914 only 53 per cent. of the investments in industry were Russian.

[2] Many got only an acre and a quarter.

[3] This is the name given to the years 1917–20, when the Soviet Government was simultaneously engaged in wars with the 'White Army' and foreign intervention, whilst attempting to establish Socialism within the country.

crop had dropped by two-fifths. 'There is almost a return to natural economy, each family of peasants producing just its own needs' (Grenard).

Realising the danger, Lenin backpedalled and like a good opportunist permitted at least a partial return to a free system of agriculture and domestic trade. The NEP[1] permitted the economic restoration of Russia. But at the same time the capitalist reappeared. A class of rich peasants, known as *kulaks* (= monopolists), cropped up in rural districts. Though they constituted hardly one-fifth of the peasantry, they officially owned half the land and one-third of the livestock, whilst millions of petty farmers were dispossessed, ruined, and turned into wage-earners. In the towns a new category of private capitalist, called *nepmen*, arose out of trade and the exploitation of the home-worker. These were men without culture or scruple, hard and bold. Two such classes might one day endanger the Soviet system, which had intended, in conformity with socialistic principles, to make 'the material conditions of production the collective property of the workers themselves' and in that way to use the whole working population for tasks productive for the community and not for a special few. *Kulaks* and *nepmen* seemed as if they would prevent this. In face of this danger and in spite of the opposition of Trotsky, who aimed mainly at international revolution, Stalin resolved to build up socialism in a single country. But for that he had to draw up the most precise of programmes for the organisation and renovation of the Union. He had to plan production, and he did.

[1] *Novaya Ekonomicheskaya Politika* = New Economic Policy.

CHAPTER 11

THE FIVE-YEAR PLAN SYSTEM

The year 1928 marks the important date when the Soviet Union embarked on the new scheme of five-year plans which were destined to transform the whole aspect of the country. Strong reasons had decided the rulers to take this step. The first, and not the least, was the steady, very rapid increase of the population, which made the creation of new resources essential. But it was also necessary to correct the unequal distribution of existing resources, which had led to the opposition of town and country, the inferior status of the *Okrainy* and even of the outer regions of Russia relatively to the centre, and to absurd competition between productive areas. Baku, for instance, had practised dumping against the crude oil from Emba. Finally, industry had to be protected from an attack by foreign capital. More generally, it was necessary to develop production to its utmost, passing, as Stalin said, 'from a technique which was obsolete and at times medieval to one which was modern' by creating a strong agricultural system and at the same time a foundation of industry capable of re-equipping and re-organising agriculture, transport, and industry itself.

The second reason was the need to protect and strengthen communism against its enemies at home, or, to put it another way, 'to eliminate capitalist elements and abolish class distinction in order to . . . build up a socialist society'. The interests of the new rulers required them to depend on a very large class of factory workers (and in fact they favoured factory hands for a long time at the expense of the peasants). This in turn called for a great industrialisation of the country. The Government also aimed at getting rid of the infinite number of private enterprises then existing in the Union, some industrial, but most of them agricultural. Since the revolution the peasants had been sending to market far less grain than before. This was because the Soviet Government would not at this time give the producers the equivalent in consumption goods of the grain exacted by the State. This exaction indeed constituted a very heavy tax, and the *moujiks* evaded it as best they could. The re-provisioning of the ever-growing towns thus became a difficult problem. If, however, the 25 million privately owned farms could be combined into 240,000 collective enterprises, it would become an easy matter to exact the required amount of corn from the peasants and to make them produce not merely to meet the needs of their own families, but also to supply the flax, hemp, cotton, and vegetable oils that industry required. It would, too, become particularly easy to modernise agricultural methods, increase yields, and make agriculture advance at the same pace as industry. Lastly, a scheme of collective farming was also necessary in order to eliminate the *kulaks* and easily control the peasants by organising them.

A third reason, and a very important one—whatever certain people may think—was the need to confront foreign nations with a strong Union. It was to be economically strong because, to be completely independent of world capital, of whose unyielding hostility it was aware, it had to make itself into a powerful industrial country, capable of being self-sufficient in manufactured goods and in agricultural produce not only in time of peace, but also in time of war. As the country is almost devoid of coastline, it is too exposed to complete maritime blockade not to feel an imperative need to obtain all necessary commodities on its own soil in case of armed conflict.

It was to be militarily strong too. Some people have thought that the Soviet Union dreamed of subjecting Europe by force of arms to its hegemony and doctrines. Certainly, the Union remembered the dangers to which the new system had been exposed in 1919–20 owing to the support given to the Whites by foreign nations; and it knew of Japan's eye on the far east of Siberia and of that of Germany on the Ukraine and the Caucasus. These were amply sufficient reasons, as was proved by the events of June 22, 1941, to justify a colossal effort to produce military equipment and arms, which demanded a gigantic preliminary industrial effort. 'We are encircled by a whole series of capitalist countries whose technical development is greater than ours,' Stalin would say; 'Russia's independence cannot be defended without a solid foundation of industry.'

This third reason, even more than the first two, called for very prompt action. The economy of the Union had to be transformed in an extremely short period of time. This was not the first occasion on which such a problem had confronted Russia. 'When Peter the Great, having to deal with countries more developed than his own, feverishly built factories to equip his army,' says Stalin again, 'this was his way of trying to break the fetters of a backward country.'

The dictator of the Kremlin was, we know, not afraid one day to call this Tsar his model; and indeed Peter was his forerunner in the worship of Western technique, in his confidence in the wealth and potentialities of his empire, and in his attempt to make the country into 'a vast, laborious workshop' (Massis). Resorting, as Stalin has done, to the employment of foreign engineers, Peter built in record time 233 factories and workshops, formed the metallurgical centres at St. Petersburg, on the Ural, and at Olonets (where the first mushroom town was destined to be built at Petrozavodsk), and greatly increased that at Tula, founded cloth and canvas factories capable of turning out goods for export, built arsenals, constructed roads, ports, and canals, opened mines, created a great town in a desert, and, in short, astonished foreign visitors by the magnitude of the economic changes achieved in Russia. In truth, Peter's reign was a kind of foretaste of the era of five-year plans.

Such an era had been foreshadowed and suggested by Lenin, who had wished to see the Union 'make sure of the possession of all essential raw materials, transform the geography of the country both by the construction of lines of communication and by the transfer of population, . . . and industrialise the countryside as well as the towns'. As early as 1920 he had a ten-year electrification plan drawn up; in 1923 he inspired a five-year plan for reconstructing the metallurgical industry. After his death the Government used a system of 'Control Figures' of production, which in fact strove to look ahead. But Stalin wanted more, as he considered that time was pressing.

After long consultation and innumerable reports by statisticians and technicians he made the *Gosplan* (State Planning Board) department draw up a five-year plan which was adopted by the Conference of the Communist party at the end of 1927. The document, which reflects a vast totalitarian conception extending to every aspect of life in the Soviet Union and intended to regulate everything, was less rigid than it has often been said to be. It decided in advance the whole economic programme of the Union for a period of five years. But far from being settled once and for all, it prearranged maximal and minimal variations so as to cope with uncertainties of weather, changes in technique, increase in population, and, like a delicate machine whose wheels are interdependent, it had to undergo many revisions in the course of its execution.

In principle, it was to equip the Union with a mighty heavy industry pending the time when subsequent plans would give it a light industry worthy of the country. Thus, the annual production of coal was to rise from 35,000,000 to 150,000,000 tons; that of mineral oil from 11,700,000 to 40,000,000; that of pig iron from 3,300,000 to 10,000,000; that of steel from 4,200,000 to 10,000,000; that of electrical power from 5,000,000 kilowatt-hours to 22,000,000. To feed the enormous industrial population the area of land under cultivation was to be increased from 291,000,000 to 358,000,000 acres. The yield would be increased, and fisheries would be developed. Besides, the cultivation of industrial crops would be stimulated, new railways and roads constructed, and navigation improved. Progress along these lines would permit of advance in other directions, which would be increasingly marked and rapid during the subsequent five-year periods. Soon the Soviet Union would 'overtake and pass the capitalist countries', including the United States, whose economic power obsessed the minds of the Russians. Then its military power would be such that it would no longer have anything to fear from any state or coalition. The considerable rise in the standard of living would indissolubly attach the masses to the Soviet system, and as the Union would become a 'social paradise' in the eyes of all the workers on the globe, its example would be the most effective propaganda to bring about the downfall of capitalism in the rest of the world. Was this gigantic programme realisable?

Yes: firstly, because of the Union's prodigious natural wealth. This had been known to be immense, but the reawakening of scientific research in the Union showed them to be even greater than had been thought. The numerous exploring expeditions financed by a Government which knew how to sow in order to reap were not content with making rapid progress in the knowledge of the geology and geography of the country by exploring the Arctic, the Far North of Siberia, the polar Urals, the Tien Shan, the Pamir, and the Aralo-Caspian deserts: they located previously unknown vegetable wealth, discovered many new coal- and oil-fields and deposits of iron, manganese, copper, zinc, lead, phosphates, and potash, and thus added to the purely scientific outcome of their work other practical results of the greatest importance. On the other hand, the reserve of man-power was incomparably great and was steadily increasing. The Russian's characteristic of being able to uproot easily without losing his natural fecundity was of the utmost value in the circumstances. In other countries it would have been difficult, if not impossible, to transplant to order millions of human beings thousands of miles from their homes. Here the deed was quite easily done.

Secondly, there were psychological reasons. Russian pride felt spurred on when a persistent propaganda had made it realise the seriousness of the country's backwardness relatively to capitalist states and the contrast between the tremendous potential of the Union and its meagre realisation. On the other hand, the passive docility natural to the people made submission to the Draconian privations which its rulers imposed on them less trying than would have been the case with most other nations. The slight value attached to human life by the rulers facilitated the achievement of enterprises which were grandiose but costly in life, as similar views had facilitated the construction of the palace of Versailles by Louis XIV and St. Petersburg by Peter the Great.

Lastly, there were politico-social reasons. The Soviet State owns all the country's natural resources. It directs all financial institutions, all transport, all industry; it controls foreign commerce and nearly all the internal trade. The various branches of industry, or 'trusts',[1] are under the authority of People's Commissars. That is to say, that, economically speaking, the Soviet Union may be regarded as a single colossal business and that there more than in any other country the will of the Government makes itself felt in material things. Besides, the plan has the force of law: every citizen or group of citizens who tried to avoid carrying out orders received in connexion with it would be guilty of high treason towards the new socialist system and punished accordingly. This organisation of the economic life greatly facilitates the achievement of the Kremlin's designs.

All these advantages were needed to overcome the terrible obstacles that lay ahead. Lack of time was not the least of these, for the aim was to change the appearance and character of Russia in the space of five years. The general poverty of the masses augured consumers with very slight purchasing power, and there were no luxury trades, since these had been killed by the abolition of the moneyed classes.

The country had always been very short of capital, but the supply was less than ever after the war and the revolution. As the debts of the Tsarist Government had been repudiated, there was no further hope of borrowing money abroad, especially as after 1930 the other countries found themselves hard hit by the world depression. But the estimated expenditure was gigantic: 80 billion roubles for the first plan, and 7·5 billion for State industry alone in 1931, or nearly double the real value of American investments. Actual expenditure was all the heavier because there was frightful waste. Since the State Bank automatically met all requests, at least in the first years, the managers of businesses scarcely troubled to think of prime costs. Furthermore, a lamentable inadequacy was to become apparent in transport. Goods arrived after incredibly long delays, were sent to wrong destinations, were entirely lacking in one place, whilst they piled up and rotted in another. The press did not cease from fulminating against this paralysing disorder.

The staffs, decimated by the exodus of numbers of engineers,

---

[1] These have nothing in common with American trusts, but are merely organised professions and large industrial groups; e.g. the oil trust, gold trust, copper trust, etc.

whether foreign or Russian, and by the execution or imprisonment of many Russians, could only be painfully reconstituted. Many managers and technicians showed their ill will by slowing down or stopping production so as to wreck the socialist experiment. Lastly, great difficulties were to be anticipated from the mass of the people. Industrial labour was but slightly organised, if at all. Certainly, there existed in addition to the factory workers village craftsmen who were often skilful in making household requisites, but these *kustar* (= bush) operations, though very interesting and at times endued with artistic qualities, bore no likeness to the manufacturing industries; and as for the innumerable *moujiks* who were suddenly promoted to be factory hands, the axe was the only tool with whose use they were familiar. Besides being ignorant, this labour was undisciplined, careless, and lacking in enthusiasm for the work. Above all, it was afflicted with congenital instability and readily quitted one factory to go to another or to return to the village. Lastly, the docility of the masses was not without limit and was besides offset by an apathy representing a force of inertia which was extraordinarily difficult to overcome. All those who could not bear the iron discipline or were embittered by the hardships caused by it struggled openly or secretly against the plan.

But though wreckers were not rare in the factories, the peasants were far more vigorous in their resistance to collectivisation. Lenin had strongly advised on his deathbed against applying the system to rural districts.

The process of collectivisation, which was at first fairly slow and discreet, quickened its pace and became harsh and overbearing, for, far exceeding the prescriptions of the plan which envisaged 14 million 'socialised' peasants as against 121 million who were engaged in private enterprise, it claimed 'the socialisation of the whole body of private farmers'. This roused against it not only the *kulaks*, but also the *seredniaks*, or 'average' peasants, who, not content with destroying the cattle and reserves of produce before submitting to 'collectivisation' and with wrecking their work, actually revolted in many districts. In the spring of 1930 the Ukraine, lower Volga, and more particularly the Kuban, witnessed serious disturbances, so that the Government had to give way and proclaim that admission to collective enterprises was voluntary. Nine million resignations followed this, and it was believed that only the *biedniaks* (= poor peasants) would support the new system.

Colossal difficulties call for heroic remedies. To overcome the resistance of the peasants, not only were the *moujiks* tempted by the restriction of all the advantages and facilities of work to members of collective enterprises, but the big stick was also used. Except where the recalcitrants were left without means of subsistence they were either shot or deported with their families to the icy wastes of the forest and tundra, where, as they were put to the hardest of work, they died by hundreds of thousands, if not millions. Rebels and wreckers in the factories were broken in a similar way. But, something more than executions was needed to build a new world, and the Government, knowing this, used every means in its power.

Science was harnessed to the plan, and enormous sums were allocated to the Academy of Sciences, which lost its independence and became henceforth the servant of the State. The effort was particularly intense in the field of geology. The Soviet Union has more than 6000 geologists, France only about 60. In 1933 the main department of hydrology and geology employed more than 8000 technicians and about 100,000 workmen, not counting the thousands of engineers and tens of thousands of workers in the State departments of the oil, coal, and other industries. Many zoological and botanical expeditions and innumerable agricultural surveys and laboratory experiments in physics, chemistry, and biology were undertaken.

The same anxiety to be up-to-date and operate scientifically is reflected in 'the geographical redistribution of the centres of technical and industrial training in regions suitable because of their natural facilities and the opportunities afforded for utilisation' (George). Thus came into being the system of *kombinats*, or groups of factories, which, by employing both horizontal and vertical integration, co-operate in the use of raw material, carrying the treatment of the raw material as far as possible, whilst utilising their by-products to the full. In all this an anxiety is evinced not only to secure a high yield and great efficiency, but also to attain to an ultra-modern technique equal to and surpassing that of the United States.

Nevertheless, although the Soviet Union, in common with the United States, has a taste for the colossal, there is no question of its aping the latter. 'The very essence of Bolshevism is the alliance of Russian revolutionary enthusiasm with American practical spirit', and the guiding principle in this has been 'the establishment of socialism'. Consequently, recourse has been had to the socialisation of the means of production. Not that collectivisation is complete, for in 1955 just over a hundred individually owned farms existed in the Soviet Union; nor does the State directly control all the Union's resources. The national republics and the towns have the management of industry and transport of local or regional interest, the collectivised village controls its land, and craftsmen have survived in so far as they have not harmed collective interests. But the State none the less owns all mining rights and the general establishments of transport and industry and is the proprietor of the land which is today divided between the state farms and the collective village enterprises.

The ownership of this vast wealth, actual or virtual, did not prevent the State from being faced with an extraordinarily difficult financial problem. This it could not solve by foreign loans, for with difficulty it secured only a few loans in Germany and the United States. However, foreigners granted what came to nearly the same thing, namely, big long-term credits, and the Soviet people on their side subscribed to an internal loan of some 10 thousand million roubles during the first *piatiletka*. The Soviet State also had recourse to the export of precious metals, especially gold, the production of which was increasing; but it sent abroad even more wheat, timber, and flax at such low prices that in 1930 the world cried out against Soviet dumping. In spite of the enormous universal fall in wholesale prices due to the world depression, the drive to export as much as possible continued for several years. This course was possible only by forcing enormous sacrifices on the people. As ordinary taxes brought in too little, enormous levies of agricultural produce were exacted in return for extremely small payments. Only 30 or 40 per cent. of the production of wheat, vegetables, milk, meat, beet-root, and sunflower seeds was redistributed among the peasants. Hence, when bad years occurred, there were severe dearths and in 1933–4 a famine which caused many deaths in the Kuban and western Siberia. In general, the exigencies of the plan required a levy of 40 per cent. of the national income, which involved a terrible lowering of the standard of living. Russia was said to be rationed like a country at war.

To make the people put up with this effort and suffering, the whole population had to be placed in a strait-jacket.

Twelve hundred thousand technicians were needed. All the engineers who had remained in the Soviet Union were requisitioned and sent willy-nilly wherever the State thought fit. As they were too few to cope with the immense task, multitudes more were trained by establishing technical high schools, polytechnics, and institutes of all kinds. The training was hasty and often improvised. Fortunately for some tens of thousands training was prolonged by a period in the United States. In 1939 the total numbers of the economic services were reckoned at 12 million persons. It is unnecessary to say how precious during the war this reserve of men accustomed to leadership was for the recruitment of reserve officers. In 1955 there were 584,900 engineers who had had higher education and 804,900 technicians with a secondary specialised training. On the other hand, large numbers of foreign engineers were attracted to the Soviet Union by paving their way with gold. There were few Englishmen, even fewer Frenchmen, but some 10,000 Germans, and above all there were

Americans. Dneprostroy was the work of Hugh H. Cooper, Magnitostroy that of Arthur McGee & Co. of Ohio and New York, the great tractor works at Stalingrad of John Calder of Detroit, etc.

There was no risk of failure in the labour supply, especially as there was no hesitation in the use of a large number of women in industry, both in metallurgy and mining, and even in work at the bases during the war. So the reserves of peasants were drawn on; and crowds of workmen were requisitioned for real forced labour, as in the time of Peter the Great, and their numbers were swelled by political prisoners and *kulaks*. Millions of forced workers were collected in camps and were employed in the forests and sawmills in northern Russia and Siberia and in the construction of canals and other works. The White Sea–Volga and the Moscow–Volga Canals were among those built by such labour. Gradually, as Soviet industry became able to provide sufficient machinery to render the employment of forced labour uneconomic, the use of people convicted on trumped-up charges and mass deportation decreased, though the practice of forced or directed labour has by no means ended as yet.

The worker has no right to refuse prescribed changes of work or abode. But at the same time an effort has been made to remedy the defects of the Russian workman. The restless, unstable character of the *letunes*, or flitters, was opposed by Draconian measures, such as the withdrawal of the food ration card for an inexcusable day's absence or, more recently, by fines. The Soviet worker, 'bound to his factory as is the agricultural labourer to his *kolkhoz* . . . and, like Ixion on his wheel, is free neither to go nor to stay where he pleases' (A. Gide). He has not the right to strike. Soviet trade unions exist to stimulate production by means of 'Socialist emulation' and 'stakhanovism'. They are part of the State organisation, their functions being to take part in fixing wages, in the rationalisation of labour, and in the maintenance of factory discipline. They are also concerned with the provision of social services and amenities for the workers and the improvement of their conditions of work and life. The truly dictatorial powers of factory managers and the reduction of the rights of workmen's syndicates to insignificance have once again taught him the need for discipline and obedience. By 1933 the former control of the workers had been left far behind.

To make the worker careful and industrious, as well as to remedy the lack of skilled workmen, the development of professional instruction was encouraged by opening technical courses in manufacture. And more generally, the education of the people not only in Russia, but also in Asia among tribes whose languages were reduced to writing for the first time. In many places 'centres for the liquidation of illiteracy' were formed; in very remote regions anyone who could read was obliged to teach ten other persons to do so. 'Shock parties' and teams of 'social tractors' were formed to act as advisers and trainers of the ignorant and mediocre. The best workmen were covered with praise and given higher wages and various material advantages, especially in the form of larger food rations. Another distortion of principle was the re-establishment of night-, piece-, and chain-work. But more was required; so when a miner of the Donets, Alexei Stakhanov, invented a form of division of labour in the mine which resulted in producing fourteen times as much coal as by individual working, 'stakhanovism' came into fashion in all branches of industry and even in agriculture. The indefatigable repetition of the slogan 'Socialist emulation' caused endless competitions between factories and *kolkhozy*, as much through the motive of beating 'records' and sporting honorific distinctions as to hasten the execution of the plan.[1] An indefatigable and skilful propaganda in favour of it had created a real 'war spirit', with all that is implied by the expression not only of tendentious statements, but also of enthusiasm and devotion, especially among the young elements in the population, who are more permeable to this influence than their elders. 'Young communists' from all parts of the Union themselves built 'their own town' in the Far East, the town of Komsomolsk, which in 1956 had a population of more than 169,000 persons. At the same time a veritable cult sprang up, the cult of machinery and 'record' figures. Young people, children and many grown-ups, thought of nothing but blast-furnaces, motors, turbines, tractors, production diagrams, and triumphal graphs. 'Statistics took the place of ikons,' says de Monzie. It was this enthusiasm and abundance of hope, as much as or more than constraint, that gave the Russian people the strength to hold out and struggle on in spite of hard sufferings. 'The present generation', they said, 'is being sacrificed for those to come'; and it is largely to these sufferings that are due the splendid results obtained.

The results were splendid, in spite of undeniable partial failure. Certainly, the collectivisation of the rural districts has had its disadvantages. The number of farm stock decreased by half and, in spite of the introduction of the motor engine, the quality of agricultural performance left much to be desired. Many peasants worked unwillingly or half-heartedly or even brought ill-will to their task.

[1] Since 1929 the Soviet year has been divided into twelve months of thirty days each, not counting five feast days, each month comprising five *shestidnievki*, i.e. periods of six days. Five are working days, and the sixth a rest day. The 6th, 12th, 18th, 24th, and 30th are 'days of outing'. The word 'Sunday' is dead, as are 'Saturday' and 'week'. The application of this reform was suspended at the beginning of the German invasion, for the safety of the nation was more important than social improvements.

The result, as Stalin admitted, was that neither the collective village enterprises nor the State farms were paying concerns. Russia entered a permanent system of undernourishment, and industrialisation could not be made to advance at the rate intended. Industrialisation suffered from other weaknesses. In spite of repeated efforts, prices remained high; the production of manufactured goods increased much more slowly than that of raw materials, and consumption increased little or even diminished owing to the lowering of the standard of living. Lastly, the poor quality of nearly all these articles did little to tempt foreign purchasers. Besides, foreign trade had fallen off by a half since 1913, and its state was disquieting. No more foreign credits were obtained, except on short terms and very unfavourable conditions. The financial situation was becoming frankly painful.

But on the other hand, there were many positive results, socially and economically. By 1938 the *kulak* class had been 'liquidated'; private property almost abolished, nearly all the peasants had entered the *kolkhozy*, and, thanks to the enormous increase in the number of workers, the broad political base desired by Stalin had been created. Industrial production had more than doubled, that of the means of production (coal, oil, electricity, pig iron, steel, and cotton) increasing more rapidly than that of consumption goods. Apart from many other secondary achievements, a certain number of really imposing works had been successfully carried out: Dneprostroy, Magnitostroy, the equipment of the Kuznetsk and Karaganda coal-fields and of the oil-field at Emba, the Baltic–White Sea Canal, the Turksib Railway, and the Magnitostroy–Kuznetsk Railway. Illiteracy had greatly diminished. In 1913 30 per cent. of the subjects of the Russian state could read; in 1932 the percentage of literate Soviet citizens was 90. Fine social buildings (hospitals, clinics, and sports grounds) had been constructed in many places. Lastly, the military power of the Union had very appreciably strengthened, especially in aviation. Only ignorance or falsehood could assert that the five-year plan had failed. It had been realised up to 94 per cent., and that in four years only. And the capitalist press which in 1928 sneered: 'Fantasy! Utopia! Delirium! Gigantic eccentricity! Sure to be a resounding failure!' was beginning to show a certain acid and angry uneasiness.

The work was, however, far from complete, especially in matters agricultural, and a second five-year plan came into force at the beginning of 1934. It envisaged many industrial constructions and a massive increase in industrial production. The targets were 152 million tons of coal, 47 million tons of crude oil, 38 million kilowatt-hours, 18 million tons of pig iron, 19 million tons of steel, 14 million tons of rolled iron, and 155,000 tons of copper. It also aimed at a considerable effort to improve transport, including the construction of 4500 miles of railway, some new canals, and 20,500 miles of important new air-lines, not counting secondary routes. Above all, It aimed at bringing industry closer to its raw material, at improving the standard of living by a fourfold production of consumption goods which had previously been neglected, by building a large number of houses, by extending still more the area under cultivation, by increasing agricultural yields through the completion of collectivisation, greater use of farm machinery, and the general use of manure, and by reconstituting the necessary amount of live-stock. It was estimated that these measures would bring about a rise in real wages of the order of at least 100 per cent.

In fact, the accession to power of Hitler and the growing risk of war obliged the Government to foster heavy industry still more, as it would be most necessary should conflict arise. The military preparation, pursued, as we know, with care, had to be paid for by prolonging the people's harsh privations. Nevertheless, this second plan attained very substantial, though unequal, results. Socially speaking, its success was complete. The last 'capitalist elements' had disappeared, the 'individual' peasants and the unassociated craftsmen formed only 6 per cent. of the population, whilst the workers and employees constituted 35 per cent. and the peasants in the *kolkhozy* 55 per cent. Students, the army, and pensioners made up the last 4 per cent. In industry, where production was more than doubled, the programme was almost completed in pig iron, coal, mineral oil, electricity, and, more generally, the creation of the means of production. The number of machine tools was doubled, and metallurgical and mechanical production increased threefold. But there was also an advance in light industries, and the production of consumer goods rose by a hundred per cent.

Similarly, in spite of many failures, agricultural output rose by 54 per cent. The returns of the *kolkhozy* were three times as great. The stock was reconstituted, which permitted the food industry to increase its activity by 113 per cent. and trade to regain a little of its freedom. In 1938–9 for the first time since 1917 the people satisfied their hunger. Although the standard of living of the workers was very low, it was gradually rising, as was proved by a fourfold increase in savings bank deposits, and a slight improvement in the working of transport gave hope of further progress in the near future.

In 1938 the Soviet Union had become one of the world's greatest economic powers. But it was not satisfied with overtaking the capitalist powers; it wanted to surpass them. In this way only would consumption per head in the Union succeed in equalling consumption in France, Germany, and Great Britain, if not the United States. So a third five-year plan was introduced. It aimed at almost doubling the national output and at increasing the volume of industrial production by 88 per cent. In view of the more and more pressing risk of war, the problem of increasing the means of production necessarily continued to be of the greatest importance, and heavy industry kept first place in the thoughts of the Government.

Increased production of fuel and power seemed essential. 'The third five-year plan laid the chief stress on progress in chemistry,' but the production of the chief consumer goods (cotton and woollen goods, boots and shoes, paper, sugar, and preserved foods) was to rise by 50 or 100 per cent.; and care was to be taken to distribute geographically the new enterprises so as to avoid the 'gigantomania' of the preceding period. Two or three works of normal size are constructed more quickly than a 'monster', cost less, and are more easily managed. In agriculture the value of the total production was to rise by 50 per cent. Encouragement was to be given particularly to the cultivation of fodder crops and so to stock-breeding, as well as to industrial crops, vegetables, and fruit. Mechanisation was to be carried even further, and a national system of rotation and improvement was to be successfully introduced. The functioning of the transport system was to be greatly improved. Retail trade was to be made more active; a large number of houses were to be built; and education was to be developed. In short, the work of transformation which had been begun in 1928 was to be almost complete in 1942, and the Soviet Union was to be on a level economically with the greatest nations. The Government was to be free to make a generous distribution of consumers' goods, since production would have reached the desired volume, and the Union was to pass from a Socialist to a real Communist economic system.

The third five-year plan was thus to make a decisive turning-point in the Soviet system. But before it was achieved, the German invasion took place, and a period of devastation, ruin, and indescribable suffering began in the Union. Yet the war years were not without advance. It is true that production was slowed down owing to the withdrawal of millions of men from industry. The greatest reduction was naturally in consumer goods, and the people had to undergo a further period of hardship. In 1937 the production of consumer goods had increased more than six times over the 1913 figures. The goods included clocks and watches, bicycles, sewing machines, cameras, gramophones, wireless and television sets, refrigerators, washing machines, and other articles. In 1945 production fell to half the 1913 figure. Even tractor production, of which Soviet economy set such store, fell from 48,100 in 1939 to 31,600 in 1940 and 7,700 in 1945. The same fate befell timber production, which decreased from 126·1 million cubic metres in 1939 to 117·9 million cubic metres in 1940 and to 61·6 million cubic metres in 1945. No records have been published for some industries during the war years, but the figures given show a serious falling off. Thus, the production of crude oil fell from 30·3 million tons in 1939 to 19·4 million tons in 1945. There was a slight rise in the generation of electrical power from 39·4 milliard kWh. in 1938 to 43·3 milliard kWh. in 1945; and in the seven years during which the third plan lasted 23·5 million tons of pig iron came from the furnaces. In the three years 1939, 1940, and 1945 there were raised 461·4 million tons of coal. In spite of the many setbacks, however, industrial production rose by 195 per cent. The deliberate or unavoidable destruction of buildings during the war called for much repair and reconstruction, and between 1939 and 1945 the floor space of dwellings and other houses built or reconstructed after damage amounted to 91·8 million square metres. Altogether, capital investment in building, installation, and collective farms totalled 273·5 thousand million roubles; i.e. £6,837,500,000 in exchange value on July 1, 1955.

After the war, though the Soviet Union had lost vast numbers of men, the prestige of the Red Army, its demonstration of power, and the increased confidence victory gave to the Communist leaders inspired renewed effort. This was greatly assisted by the 'cold war', which enabled the leaders to whip up enthusiasm by an appeal to patriotism. Consequently, the fourth five-year plan, which ran from 1946 to 1950, was carried out with all the vigour of a great nation fired with enthusiasm. Among the Germans captured during the war were a number of scientists and technicians, and these the Soviet authorities set to work to eke out the numbers of their own people or to make up their deficiencies. With their help industry as a whole, and in particular the chemical industries, made great strides forward. The target for output per man-year was placed at 137, that of 1940 being the basic 100. The production of pig iron was 19·2 million tons, as compared with 14·9 million in 1940 and 14·5 million in 1937. Coal showed an even greater increase, 261·1 million tons being raised, as compared with 164·1 million in 1945 and 128 million in 1937; and crude oil showed a production of 39·9 million tons against the 21·7 million tons produced in 1945 and 28·5 million tons in 1937.

Agriculture also made great progress. New State farms were made, and many of the older ones were subdivided, so that by 1950 the number of such farms, including both *sovkhozy* and *kolkhozy*, had increased to 4988 and covered nearly a tenth of the available area. Of this 95 million acres were under wheat and 12 million acres under maize. There were 58 million head of cattle, nearly half of which were cows; 22 million pigs; and 93 million sheep and goats. The number of M.T.S. (Machine and Tractor Stations) had risen to 8414. The factories had produced 108,800 tractors, as against 51,000 in 1937. From the great forests of northern Russia and central Siberia 161 million cubic metres of timber were obtained, as against 114 in 1937.

A great deal was done to improve communications. There were 72,595 miles of railway line in service, and over these were carried 834,300,000 tons of freight. A great effort was made to improve the navigable waterways, and the period of the plan ended with 80,000 miles, as against 45,000 in 1928. The vast distances from one part of the Union to another rendered the aircraft peculiarly useful for freight as well as passenger transport, regular services being instituted between the main towns, and planes being used for supplying outlying stations in the Far North.

With all this material progress culture was not forgotten. The Bolshoy Theatre was revived, many technical and other colleges established, and 4345 new schools opened.

The fifth five-year plan, running from 1951 to 1955, achieved even greater results. Output per man-year rose by 44 per cent. on the previous period. Industrial production rose enormously, 68 per cent. of this being due to the rise in the productivity of labour. The main achievements in the last year of the period were 33·3 million tons of pig iron; 391 million tons of coal (bituminous coal 276·1 and lignite 114·9 million tons); crude oil 70·8 million tons; and 163,400 tractors. With all this output of productive material the consumer was given 35 times as much of the articles mentioned above as he had had in 1913, and retail prices were reduced by 26 per cent.

In agriculture during the fifth five-year period 656 new State farms were established and 246 others formed by dividing existing ones, thus bringing their total to 5134. The area under cultivation rose to 460 million acres. Of this 315 million acres were under grain and 30 million acres under industrial crops in the last year of the period. The farms had 1,429,000 tractors, 338,000 combined harvesters, and 544,000 lorries, and the number of M.T.S. had risen to 9009. The 85,700 collective farms (agricultural 'artels') were worked by 19,700,000 peasant households. The figures for live-stock were: cattle 67,100,000; pigs 52 million; sheep and goats 143 million. Timber production rose to 214 million cubic metres.

In communications, neither the railways, with 75 thousand miles of line in service, nor the navigable waterways, with a length of 83 thousand miles, had increased strikingly; but a new feature was the great increase in motor roads. At the end of the Tsarist régime there were only 15,000 miles of hard-surface roads suitable for motor traffic. Most of the roads in the Soviet Union before 1940 had been earth tracks which in spring dissolved into mud traps. The war emphasised the need for better roads, and these began to be built before hostilities ended. By the conclusion of the fourth plan there were 110 thousand miles of motor roads and in 1955 there were 128 thousand miles. Air travel had increased out of all knowledge. Soviet aircraft construction had advanced so much that the authorities were allowing them to be shown beyond the Iron Curtain, where they were admitted to be equal to those produced in Britain and the United States.

To achieve even greater progress, more than fifty new establishments for higher education were opened, and the number of pupils who completed courses in higher education was 1,121,000. Little is known of the standard reached by these courses, however. Research workers totalled 223,900, of whom 87,500 had attained to the degree of D.Sc. or Candidate of Science (equivalent to the second degree of British universities). Besides this, the number of libraries of all kinds had been increased from 351,000 in 1950 to 392,000 in 1955.

Altogether, then, the advance made by the Soviet Union up to the end of the fifth plan was immense. Between 1929 and 1955 the capital invested amounted to 1556 thousand million roubles, 865 thousand million in industry and 128 thousand million in collective farms. The national income had increased twelve-fold per head of the population between 1913 and 1955, and the total industrial production was nineteen times greater. Producer goods had increased forty-three-fold, and consumer goods nearly eight-fold. Much of this increase in productivity was due to the fact that the output per man-year of manual workers in industry was eight times as great in 1955 as in 1913, though the working day was shorter.

In the sixth five-year plan, which was meant to cover the years 1956 to 1960, the directives of the 20th Congress of the Communist Party of the Soviet Union aimed at surpassing the material production of the Western countries. In 1960 industrial production was to be forty times as great as in 1913. The output per man-year throughout the five years was planned to be 50 per cent. above that of 1955, for more than four-fifths of the total increase in industrial production was to be achieved by the greater productivity of labour. Production targets included: pig iron 53 million tons a year, coal 593 million tons, crude oil 135 million tons, electrical power 820 kWh., tractors 322,000, combines 140,000, diesel locomotives 1630; cotton fabrics 7953 million yards, and silk fabrics 1175 million yards.

In agriculture the plan envisaged an increase in productivity in State farms of 70 per cent. and one of 100 per cent. in collective farms. The target for the grain crop was 180 million tons. This vast scale of production should make the national income 24 times as large in 1960 as in 1913. Consumer goods were to have become on the average between $1\frac{1}{2}$ and $2\frac{1}{2}$ times as plentiful as in the previous five-year period, whilst certain new articles were to be in relatively greater supply. Thus, the supply of vacuum cleaners was to be four times as great as previously, that of refrigerators nearly five times, that of television sets five times, and that of washing machines six times. The targets in transport reflect the belief that the aims of industrial production would be achieved. Taking 1955 as base, the figures of planned increase are: freights on railways 142 per cent. and on inland waterways 180 per cent. On maritime routes the cargoes were to be more than doubled, road vehicle and air transport freight were also to be doubled, and six times as much oil was to be passed through the pipe-lines.

Great though these targets may be, they are not as spectacular as the progress made in physics, which enabled an earth-satellite to be launched on October 1, 1957, and to be followed by others. This achievement together with success in rocketry has placed the Soviet Union on an equal footing with Britain and the United States in matters scientific, though the period of hardship and austerity has not yet come to an end for the ordinary citizen. It should be remembered that much of the material progress has been due to far-sighted insistence on the part of the authorities on technical and scientific education, and the sixth plan aimed at a 50 per cent. increase in the number of science specialists in secondary or higher education

In September 1957 the Supreme Soviet decided to replace the sixth plan by a seven-year plan lasting from 1959 to 1965. This step was taken partly because the various industrial targets seemed due to be reached by the end of 1958 and partly because the agricultural system was to be revised. The most important feature of this revision was the transfer of all agricultural machinery from the M.T.S. to the collective farms. This will free the management of the farm from the handicap of having two heads, the chairman of the farm and the chairman of the M.T.S. The latter has hitherto ensured that the kind of crops planted and the quantities of grain and meat delivered would be controlled by the State. This control will now be achieved by raising the prices paid to farms for produce and by reducing the quantity of produce required to be handed over to the State.

CHAPTER 12

AGRICULTURE

Agriculture remains the chief occupation of the people. Yet, whilst forests cover 3½ million square miles, only 590,000 square miles are cultivated. There is still much land which has never been touched or only slightly used, especially on the edge of the Siberian *tayga*, where the area is probably twelve times as large as France. But though there is very fertile land (alluvial soils in the Transcaucasian valleys, loess in the oases, and, above all, black earth of which it is proverbially said: 'Sow sand instead of grain: if God blesses you, you shall have bread at the end of the year'); though there is land of moderate quality which could easily be improved (soils of the woodland steppe), there are also very poor soils which take a great deal of manure (the podzols), and indeed utterly barren soils, like the acid, marshy tundra lands, the saline steppes of the Caspian, and the sandy or clayey saline soils of the Aralo-Caspian depression. Nearly half the territory of the Union consists of deserts, arid steppes which would be ruinous to irrigate (1,158,330 square miles), tundras (2,700,000 square miles), or high mountains. On the whole, the proportion of arable land is relatively small, though absolutely speaking, their area is immense.

Worse still, the length and severity of the winters preclude the cultivation of delicate plants in a very large part of the country, and the snow-cover is generally too thin to protect young cereals. Water is often not to be had or is badly distributed. There are terrible droughts which affect *chernoziom* more than any other kind of soil. Hardly 5 per cent. of the territory is sure of a good crop. The chief feature of the climate is its uncertainty from day to day; and that is serious in a country in which the long period of winter inactivity forces one to earn one's living for the whole year during the short summer. Nowhere else do climatic conditions weigh so heavily on agriculture. In so capricious a climate the sacrifices demanded by intensive cultivation cannot be risked.

131

These natural conditions were not very susceptible of improvement, but the same was not true of human conditions. Forty years ago Russian agriculture suffered from a bad system of tenure. Only 2 per cent. of the State lands were cultivated and communal property was worked so unwillingly that its yield was falling off. Only private property cultivated by farmers or free peasants could show passable returns. Although agriculture on the great estates in the Ukraine had reached a fairly high technical level, elsewhere the *moujik* did not have the means to bring his methods up-to-date, and a kind of anarchy too often characterised production. In one place there prevailed a rotational system in no way suited to the kind of soil; in another there was a one-crop rotationless system (cotton, flax, etc.) which exhausted the soil, whilst 'the competition of cheap wheat from land settled free of charge in the south-east accelerated the decline of the production of grain in the centre' (Mikhailov). In short, agriculture was backward nearly everywhere and gave a poor yield. Now, these human conditions have been properly modified, and their old characteristics transformed.

1. NEW PREVAILING TENDENCIES

The first and most striking change has been collectivisation, which is practically complete today. Nearly all the cultivated land in the Union is occupied by *sovkhozy* or by *kolkhozy*. In 1955 only 100,000 'individual peasants' remained. *Sovkhozy* and *kolkhozy* occupied 396 million acres in 1955.

Sovkhozy, of which there were 6000 in 1958, were originally immense State farms, most of which had between 75,000 and 150,000 acres, though some had more than 250,000, and the 'Giant' had 500,000. On establishing them, the Government gave them unlimited funds and ordered them to specialise in some branch of agriculture or stock-rearing and to furnish enormous quantities of wheat, beetroot, flax, vegetables, milk, or meat. In the centre there were the administrative offices, refectories, dormitories, kitchens, often an assembly room, a reading-room, a library, a theatre or cinema, repair shops, hangars, stables, and the agricultural school with hundreds of students and scores of teachers; then vast fields and, on the outskirts, a rather military-looking camp. In fact, the employees, who are workmen with a fixed wage, were and are organised in 'brigades' and treated like soldiers. These *sovkhozy* covered a total of 297 million acres in 1954 and cost the Treasury huge sums. In 1939 Mr. Molotov stated euphemistically that their returns left much to be desired. But they serve as models, spread abroad modern methods, lend their equipment to the neighbouring farms, and in their courses train specialised agricultural labourers, tractor drivers, and mechanics. The day that the country around them is won over to modern technique, the *sovkhozy* will have done their work and will be able to disappear. Its land will then be divided among the neighbouring *kolkhozy*.

Kolkhozy, or collective farms, numbered 87,500 in 1955 and covered 191·8 million acres. In some forest regions where the parcels of land are scattered among the clearings, the use of heavy machinery worked by gangs of peasants would achieve nothing. So the system of *tsoz* is applied, leaving much to individual initiative and restricting itself to collectivising the machinery, repair shops, and storehouses. But wherever there are great expanses cultivated in a single block, the old system of *artel*, or association of workers with a common stock, which was so dear to Russia in former days, resumes its place. The *moujiks* pool their lands, their seed reserves, cattle, and equipment, and thus make a collective farm. The *kolkhoznik* keeps as his private property his cottage and the garden of six or seven acres attached to it, together with a paddock for his stock, which as a rule consists of a cow, two calves, heifers or bullocks, one or two sows, ten ewes or she-goats, twenty bee-hives, and as much poultry as he pleases. This little property, confirmed as his by the statute of 1937, is naturally his main interest. He has often succeeded in adding to it illegally, and, by devoting to it the best part of his efforts, he sometimes gets 40 per cent. of his annual income from it. But in the eyes of the out-and-out Communists this is a dangerous abuse, since *kolkhozniks* ought above all to work for the group as a whole. Told off into gangs which share out the various tasks between themselves and distribute earnings according to the work, they are workers in co-operative farms rather than wage-earners or civil servants, as they have been called. Each of them owes the *kolkhoz* a certain number of days' work, or *trudodny*. After deducting the State levy and what is to be consumed locally, the agricultural produce is sold to State organisations. The price serves to pay the *kolkhoznik* according to the number of *trudodny* done, to improve the implements, expand the livestock, and endow the village with a creche, a hospital, its club, and its library, which will transform it 'according to Socialist ideas'.

The system is not without its difficulties. During the early years a large number of peasants, furious because their land and cattle had been taken from them 'for the workers' and having little liking for the kind of military control imposed on them, were careful to work as little as possible and not to do a stroke more than anyone else. As their personal interests were no longer involved, they attended the requisite time, but did little useful work. Others thoughtlessly and carelessly left someone else to do the work. But gradually the creaking of the machine grew less, and the number of opponents has greatly lessened: a generation imbued with communist ideas has grown up to manhood, whilst the hostile older men have disappeared. Middle-aged men allowed themselves to be won over more and more by the advantages of the system. The social advantages, the disappearance of class distinctions based on property, were apparent to the poor peasants only, but they all recognised the technical advantages and particularly the introduction of the motor vehicle.

The policy of introducing the tractor for farming was accord-ing to the wishes of Lenin, who, realising the need to win over the peasant by demonstrating to him the superiority of collective over individual cultivation, used to say: 'He won't be on our side until we improve his economic conditions of life. If tomorrow we could give him 100,000 first-class tractors, supply them with petrol, and equip them with mechanics, he would then say: "I am for the com-mune—that is, for communism." ' The policy accorded with geo-graphical conditions. In these endless plains the tractor found space to deploy its energy; it alone, and not the *moujik's* weak horse, had strength enough to construct a network of drains in marshy districts by drawing an excavator and to preserve for agriculture forest glades which had been laboriously cleared; it alone could break up the chest-nut soils of the south and south-east, hardened as they were by an arid climate; it alone could ensure the completion of agricultural work in the very short time which the exiguity of the vegetative period demands in this climate, either in spring between the *rasputitsy* and the great heat which threatens to burn up the crop, or at the end of summer when the harvest is scarcely over and the autumn ploughing and sowing must be completed urgently, so that the shoots of winter wheat may be able to resist early frosts; it alone could perform the deep autumn ploughing which enables the soil to store up rain-water before winter comes; and, lastly, the practice of harrowing in spring to accumulate the melt-water and the ploughing of the fallow land in summer and autumn ended in imposing too exhausting a toil on the animals, and machines alone could accomplish so much work in so short a time. Hence, steady efforts have been made to mechanise Russian agriculture. At first, the machines were mostly of foreign origin, but since 1932 they have all been manufactured in the Soviet Union. In the beginning the machinery was entrusted to either the *sovkhozy* or the *kolkhozy*, but experience led to the conclusion that it was better to restrict the latter to horse-drawn machines and to the mechanical tractors which they used constantly.

Today most of the farm machinery is divided between the *sovkhozy* and the M.T.S. (Machine and Tractor Stations). These M.T.S., which until 1958 were 'a fundamental element in rural organisation'

(Péchoux), were financed and controlled by the State, which, as the owner of the machinery, hired it out temporarily to the *kolkhozy* in return for a payment in kind and in cash according to contract. In 1913 the number of tractors in the Russian Empire amounted to a few score, and only a few *pomieshchiky* had these machines. By 1928 the Soviet Union had 24,500 of them, by the end of 1938 it had 450,000. In 1955 it had 338,000 combined harvesters (more than all other countries together) and 162,000 complex threshing machines (twice as many as the U.S.A.). Machinery performed 93·8 per cent. of the agricultural work. More than a million and a half agricultural labourers were employed in the driving and maintenance of the machinery; and milking of cows by electricity, which till recently had been a monopoly of a few countries, like Great Britain and Wisconsin, with very up-to-date agricultural methods, has for some time been in practice in many of the dairying *sovkhozy*. There is no doubt that so far as mechanisation is concerned, Soviet agriculture is today quite equal of that of the United States, if indeed it does not surpass it.

In 1954 the Soviet Government modified its agricultural system. Chief among the changes was the decision to sell to the collective farms the machinery which had been previously held by the M.T.S. and to turn the M.T.S. into R.T.S. (Repair Technical Stations). About 35 per cent. of the farms were too poor to buy the machines, so some of the M.T.S. retain their old functions. In all, out of a total of 681,000 tractors and 264,000 combined harvesters in the M.T.S. 482,000 tractors and 215 combined harvesters were sold by 1958.

In any case, the results of this mechanisation are now immense. If collectivisation helped to foster it, mechanisation has in return furthered collectivisation by lightening the toil of the peasant and by making him a skilled worker. It has increased the area of land under the plough and the production of wheat, though in certain districts wheat-growing has given way to the cultivation of oleaginous seeds, cotton, rice, or citrous fruits, which also benefited from the mechanisation. It has moved the cultivation of grain crops towards the south and east, thereby permitting the sparsely peopled regions to be put to their proper use. Finally, whilst using a minimum of labour, it has permitted a great improvement in the work of maintenance and at the same time raised the technical standard of the agricultural population, making it more permeable to new ideas in scientific farming.

In fact, another prevailing tendency is a constant effort towards an increasingly rational and scientific agricultural system. It has been decided to give every region 'an alimentary basis'. Hence, it is rare for one crop to be exclusively grown, and an attempt is being made to associate several in well-arranged rotation; for example, wheat, oleaginous seeds, and fodder crops in the lower Volga region; wheat, cereals, sugar-beet, and hemp in the Ukraine; and flax, cereals, fodder, and wheat in western and central Russia. Of course, there has been a selective choice of seed, the formation of dung-heaps has been increased by developing stock-rearing, and the most appropriate fertilisers have been sought out. An area of 10,600,000 acres of marsh has been drained in Colchis, the Kuban valley, western Siberia, the Moscow and Leningrad areas, and especially in White Russia. A system of irrigation has been introduced to deal with drought, that age-old scourge of the Russian empire. By means of this system, $16\frac{1}{4}$ million acres have been brought into use in central Asia and Transcaucasia, and vast areas in the Transvolga steppes were added in the course of the third five-year plan. It was hoped in this way not only to irrigate the fields, but also to increase the rainfall. In large areas of the lower Volga, Ciscaucasia, and Kazakstan thick hedges of trees have been planted along the sides of the fields to protect the crops from the dry and scorching breath of the *sukhovei*. Drought-resisting crops like sorghum, millet, maize, lentils, sweet clover, and sunflowers have been increased, and the varieties of wheat which are least troubled by want of moisture have been sought out. The melting of the snow has been delayed over millions of acres by means of screens and baskets; the processes of dry farming have been adapted to the arid areas; and early sowing in mud has been achieved by means of aircraft. Great efforts have been made to modify the poor soils not only with manure, but also by other improvements, such as the plastering of saline steppes, and the addition of lime to 12 million acres in the central and northern regions. Over an area of $1\frac{1}{4}$ million acres in south Russia a great effort has been made by means of plantations of little coppices to check the spread of the *ovraghi*, and hitherto shifting sand has been fixed in southern Russia and central Siberia by sowing grass and planting shrubs. 'We are remaking the soil', say the scientific agriculturalists of the Union, who are also striving to renew the flora and have acclimatised new varieties of wheat, sorghum, soya, Byzantine oats, textiles like the grasscloth plant, *kendir*, *kena*, and *kanatnik* (kinds of jute), the Algerian cork-oak, and the Chinese lacquer-tree, and have domesticated various rubber-yielding lianas.

They have tried to do more and have claimed that they have created a new scientific agricultural technique, of whose real success they are proud and which is adorned already by names like those of Vavilov, Michurin, and Lissenko. 'Dry market gardening' is a doubtful matter. Certainly, Jevinski the railwayman at Chelkar near the Aral Sea and his colleagues at the station at Repetek in the Kara Kum have demonstrated the possibility of horticulture right out in the desert, but their carrots, cabbages, potatoes, radishes, onions, cucumbers, water melons, ordinary melons, and strawberries have been obtained by irrigating the gardens with water raised from under the dunes. If we are not mistaken, it seems to us that the process was not unknown and that it has been practised on the oases for thousands of years.

Far more interesting is 'jarovisation' or 'vernalisation'. By a suitable treatment of the seeds, the growing period of cultivated plants is remarkably shortened and the bearing of fruit is brought on earlier. The discovery is of the greatest importance in the north, since it allows many cereals to ear and ripen there, though formerly they could not be cultivated at all, and since it 'increases yields through the use of varieties which could not be grown previously' (Musset). Very promising too seems the creation of an Arctic agriculture, especially in the Kolski peninsula, where, when cleared of stones, drained, neutralised, and manured, the soil has been sown with seed from northern lands like Alaska, and fodder crops, vegetables, barley, and oats are produced at enormous cost of labour and expense. At Igarka in Siberia it is reckoned that to succeed cultivation needs 100 tons of manure to $2\frac{1}{2}$ acres. Thus, nature seems to be challenged, and scientific agriculture in the Union can boast that it has got the better of her. Anyhow, the struggle seems to be turning to man's advantage.

But in thus flouting natural conditions the Soviet Government is by no means just giving way to costly whims and to the pleasure of displaying its newly acquired strength. The creation of new industrial regions demands the formation of corresponding new agricultural areas, for otherwise the costs of transport would make the price of food too high in districts like the Arctic, central Siberia, the Far East, and Kazakstan. That is why it has been necessary to perfect the methods of scientific agriculture adapted to local conditions, to transport millions of Russian peasants into those districts and to cause large numbers of nomads to adopt sedentary lives.

The effort was to lead to a steady extension of the area of cultivated land. This was in fact one of the most striking features of Soviet agricultural policy. The increase, which has been from 292 million acres in 1913 to 459 million in 1955 and to 482 million in 1958, has been possible because collective farming permitted the concentration of effort under one directing hand. It is particularly striking in central and western Siberia, Kazakstan, and the eastern portion of the district of the middle Volga, where the forest was losing ground, whilst wheat and industrial crops were advancing towards the north and east.

Lastly, it should be noticed that, though the soil is certainly better used than formerly, far greater progress in this direction is being considered. About 1920 Jakovlev, the Commissar for agriculture,

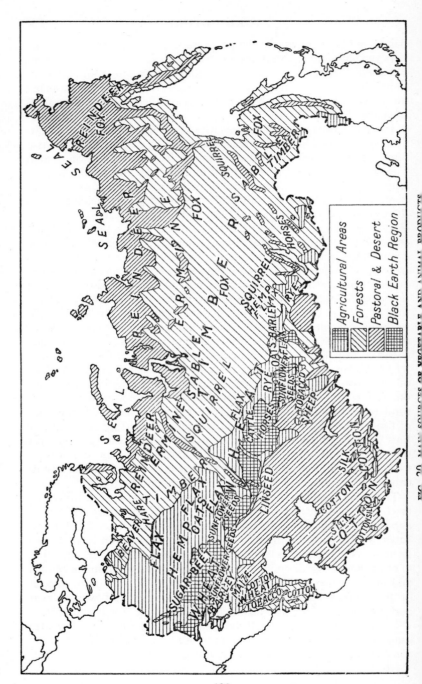

FIG. 20. MAIN SOURCES OF VEGETABLE AND ANIMAL PRODUCTS

estimated that in the regions which are to be opened up one man would have to be enough for about 500 acres and that this would be achieved by creating vast *sovkhozy* (State farms) some hundreds of thousands of acres in extent, in which the work would be completely mechanised. The idea has not been followed up. But the aim is to redistribute agriculture in a certain number of rationally delimited zones. The first region, the *tayga*, is at present little more than a reserve of arable land. The second comprises the mountainous regions of central Asia and the south-eastern Transvolga steppes and is used for extensive stock-rearing. The third runs from the southern Crimea through Caucasia towards central Asia and is the zone of sub-tropical crops, viz. cotton, tea, the vine, early vegetables, and citrus fruits. The fourth, which stretches from the Baltic through Muscovy to the Urals, is the zone for flax, milk, and vegetables. Lastly, the south-west of the Ukraine, the central region of the *chernoziom*, the north of the Kuban valley, and a portion of the eastern steppes constitute the zone of intensive stock-rearing and of industrial crops, including maize, soya, beet, hemp, tobacco, cotton, sunflower, and *kenaf*. This leaves us wondering in which zone wheat is to be cultivated on a large scale in future.

Thus, a huge effort has been successfully made to give an industrial character to agriculture and to intensify agricultural production. Certain it is that on the whole there has been an increase in the latter. Yet it does not follow that all is going well. In fact, agriculture is always more or less threatened by the very capricious climate; the lack of fodder crops, though less than formerly, is still serious; and yields, which remain generally insufficient, are increasing slowly and slightly. There is even little assurance, too, that the general increase in agricultural production has been as rapid as that of the population. However this may be, a very noticeable movement of population from the country to the towns has been recorded since 1928, though agriculture remains the principal occupation in the Soviet Union, and the rural population, with its 82 million persons, still constitutes 41·7 per cent. of the total. True it is that the value of the agricultural produce represents hardly more than 25 per cent. of the total production; but the value is calculated in roubles, and it would take a very clever man to find out the exact international value of this very independent currency. 'At the beginning of 1956 the number of manual and office workers, with their families, amounted to about 117 million persons, the number of collective farmers and co-operative craftsmen, with their families, to about 82 million, and the number of individual peasants and craftsmen not in co-operatives, with their families, to about one million persons.'[1] Yet it should be noted that,

[1] *The U.S.S.R. Economy*, English edition.

according to some authorities, the percentage of men really employed in agriculture would in 1939 have been only 46. On this reckoning 21·4 per cent. of the population lived in the country without working on the land. The figure seems enormous. Perhaps the first figures include both men and women, the second the masculine element only. The explanation is hardly satisfactory. Besides, a consideration of the variety and volume of the produce gives a rather flattering idea of Soviet agriculture.

2. CROPS

Progress has been most marked in the cultivation of cereals. The Soviet Union, which had caused the 96 million acres of virgin land ploughed since 1954 to be sown mainly with grain, devotes to them more than 212 million acres and, reckoning wheat, rye, oats, and barley together, produces an average of 4 million bushels, or more than one-third of the total world production. But these crops are of very unequal importance in the different regions.

Wheat leads today with over 45 million tons, or 48 per cent. of the total cereal crop. Its most favourable region is the Black Earth country, owing to the good quality of the soil, in spite of the severity of the winters and the serious risk of drought. All over the Ukraine, on the middle Volga, and in western Siberia it is the chief cereal by far and is increasingly so. But it is also found on the podzols of the forest clearings, where it is making appreciable headway, thanks to jarovisation and the selection of varieties which resist the cold well; in the southern part of the pre-Uralian region, where the quality of the soil is sometimes good; on the fertile lands of the lower Volga and Kuban valleys, in spite of the aridity of the climate; in northern Kazakstan, where it is clearly flourishing despite the dryness of the district; and in the Amur region, where, however, the excessively moist summers scarcely suit it. Owing to the thin snow cover and the severity of the cold, spring wheat is planted. Certain districts, however, such as the central Black Earth region, can grow winter wheat, and, paradoxical though it may seem at first sight, spring wheat predominates on the steppes in the south and east, whilst winter wheat is found farther north—which clearly illustrates the importance of the depth of the snow cover in the matter.

In an area so vast the physical and human conditions of production are necessarily far from uniform, and the same is true of the yields. In the fertile Ukraine, which is densely peopled and has an advanced technique, collectives and State farms fairly normally reap 30 bushels to the acre, and certain specially favoured districts, like Kiev, Vinnitsa, Kherson, Odessa, and the Kuban have been able in the

An Oirot cowboy with his charges on the mountain pastures of the Altai

A wheatfield on the "Communism" Collective Farm in the Vekil-Bazarsk District, Turkmenistan

Tadzhikistan.
A flock of sheep on
a mountain pasture

Tea gardens and a tea
factory near Batum

best years to reach 45, 60, and even 67 bushels to the acre. But outside the Black Earth country on the wretched podzols and in the districts short of labour the yield is often less than 12 bushels to the acre. In the Soviet Union as a whole it had not yet reached 15 bushels to the acre at the end of the second five-year plan. True, the years 1938-9-40 witnessed a successful effort which brought production to nearly 18 bushels to the acre. The degree of progress may be realised by recalling that about 1932 the yield was only between 8 and 10 bushels. But 18 bushels to the acre is still very small for a country in which bread remains the traditional prime necessity in food, though it is no longer a charm or a remedy.[1] The statement that the Russian has become an 'eater of white bread' may be treated with reserve in view of the increase in population.

In any case, the Russian did not eat white bread up to recent times, for, though the lands of the nobility produced wheat, those of the peasants for the most part produced rye. Only slightly cultivated in Siberia and still less in Turkistan, rye in 1928 reached a clear first place in cereal production in Russia. In 1955, however, it had dropped to second place. Its northern limit runs through Novgorod, Vologda, and Kirov; its southern limit through Chernigov, Tambov, or Ufa. In the governments of Vladimir, Kazan, and Ulyanovsk it covers half the area under cereals and throughout the central region the size of its harvest is the great criterion distinguishing good years from bad. The Russian harvest forms nearly half the world-production. It is, however, consumed in the country, for black bread is the chief food of the *moujik* and, besides, *vodka* is made from rye. To-day the grain is appreciably losing ground and represents no more than 13 per cent. of the cereal crop, the area under the crop being 47 million acres. But its hardiness will certainly always keep it an honourable place. Besides, it is actually gaining ground in the Far North.

The same is true of oats, the area under the crop amounting to 36 million acres, or 12 per cent. of the cereal crop. Very rare in the Black Earth country, it holds an important place to the north of a line through Ufa, Ulyanovsk, and Voronezh, especially in the districts of Tula, Ryazan, and Moscow. It is gaining ground in the northern districts, including the Kolski peninsula. Before 1914 it was an export crop and was little used as cattle-food. Today it is no longer sent abroad and, in spite of the uncertainty of its yield, it is much used for feeding man and beast, though its production has fallen off. In this land of horses its cultivation is a necessity.

Like oats, barley is essentially a northern plant and is the only

[1] The allusion is to a remark in a Russian geographical journal a few years ago.

cereal which flourishes in the Far North. In the Archangel district it formerly occupied 55 per cent. of the area under cereals. It is now gaining ground in the Kolski peninsula and also in Siberia. But it is also grown in the Crimea near Nikolay, and in Turkistan, and in small amounts elsewhere. Its main area is in the Black Earth country round Kiev, where it is found with hops. Its production not only aims at feeding man and beast, but is also of great industrial import-ance in this nation of beer drinkers. It occupied 22·6 million acres in 1955.

There is no need to stress the buckwheat grown in central Russia and in process of losing ground on the northern Black Earth country; or the millet which, on the contrary, is making headway in the Black Earth country and in Kazakstan. It plays a part of some importance in the Russian diet in the form of *kasha*, a dish of millet boiled with butter and milk. Maize has been making headway, especially in the south, where a large acreage is devoted to the crop in the Ukraine and in parts of Russia proper. It has become popular in Kazakstan, Belorussia, and the Baltic Republics, but is losing ground in Georgia and Moldavia. In 1955 the area under the crop was 22·5 million acres and in 1958 it rose to 47 million acres.

Rice, which has long been cultivated in the Ussuri district and Georgia, has greatly attracted the attention of the Soviet Government by reason of its unique food value, and its cultivation by means of irrigation has been begun not only in Tadzhikistan, Turkmenistan, and Kazakstan, but also in the Ukraine near Dneproges and Kharkov, on the shores of the Black Sea and Sea of Azov. It is stated that it would ripen very well in the Moscow district. Sowing is done by aircraft, harvesting by combined machine. Production (313,000 tons) is still very modest, however.

To sum up, the production of cereals in the Soviet Union is, except for the last named, enormous and takes first place in the world. Though the quantity exported is less than in 1914, the formation of large reserves has been possible for some years. Nevertheless, the relative position of cereals in Russian agriculture has diminished. Their predominance is weakening before the advance of fodder, root, and particularly of industrial crops.

For reasons which were mainly psychological the potato was intro-duced into Russia with some difficulty, and in the reign of Peter the Great 'the devil's apple' caused riots. Since then it has had its revenge. As early as 1913 the amount produced (34,447,000 tons) was inferior only to the quantity produced in Germany. Further progress carried it by 1939 to 64,593,000 tons, or one-fourth of world production, which far surpassed German production. Today it is grown every-where, from the polar regions to the oases of central Asia, but especially on the fringes of the great forest belt from White Russia to Siberia, and more particularly in the clearings of the centre and north-west, where it is grown on the podzols next to rye and flax. In 1957 the area devoted to the crop was 22·5 million acres, and the crop amounted to 87 million tons. In the Leningrad area it is now gaining special importance. Unfortunately, the yield is poor. Round Moscow and Smolensk this may exceptionally reach 220 bushels to the acre, but the average does not exceed 150.

Industrial crops have greatly increased. Certain textile raw materials take a prominent place. In 1913 hemp was an important crop in the Black Earth country, flourishing especially in the governments of Orel, Kursk, Penza, Poltava, Voronezh, Tambov, and Kaluga, and in White Russia. It yielded an enormous quantity of fibre and seed, not counting the oil-cake made from waste. Its production was nearly ruined by the revolution, but has revived. From 1925 to 1929 it was of the order of 300,000 tons a year and represented four-fifths of world-production. This was a marked falling-off; and the area of cultivation has shifted, mostly to western Siberia, the middle Volga (Kuybyshev), the Crimea, and Kirghizia, which are the hemp-producing regions today.

Russian flax is, of course, known the world over. Before 1914 it came from either the centre (Yaroslavl, Ivanovo, and Moscow) and north-west (Pskov, Kalinin, Smolensk, and Leningrad) or the governments of the Baltic States and Poland. The empire produced four-fifths of the world's supply of the fibre, in spite of backward methods of cultivation. In certain districts flax occupied three-quarters of the area sown in spring. Production ceased with the war and revolution. Since then, in spite of the loss of the Baltic provinces from 1919 to 1939, it rose to its old level and even beyond, owing to the use of a better rotation of crops. Instead of being planted every year in the same soil, flax now alternates with rye, potatoes, and especially with clover in the north-west. The improvement is also due to the very great mechanisation of cultivation (grubbers, beaters, specialised M.T.S.), which by economising in labour has permitted the eastward extension of the areas devoted to flax in regions that are seemingly too sparsely peopled for the crop. The total yield of 623,000 tons in 1939 represented 80 per cent. of world-production and thus made the crop almost a monopoly of the Union. The third five-year plan aimed at an advance of 49 per cent. on the figures for 1937 (i.e. 520,000 tons). The area under the crop in 1955 was 3·7 million acres. Besides, the production of flax seed is considerable in western Ukraine, around Kuybyshev, and in the north-west.

Hence, flax is of great importance not only as a textile fibre, but also as a vegetable oil. The Soviet Union is not well supplied with the latter type of crop. In addition to flax, there is sunflower, which covers large areas in the Ukraine, Moldavia, the Crimea, on the middle Volga (Kuybyshev and Solodniki), Ciscaucasia, and Kirghizia and which yields more than a million tons. Besides supplying oil that is otherwise unobtainable, it is for the *moujik* what chewing-gum is to the American. Since 1913 the area devoted to the crop has increased more than fourfold and in 1955 amounted to 10·4 million acres. There is also the mustard produced at Solodniki (Sarepta) and soya which as early as 1934 occupied about 250,000 acres in the Ukraine and Ciscaucasia, but, in spite of innumerable good qualities, is making little headway, since the methods of cultivation have not yet been perfected for want of sufficient adaptation to local conditions. It is, however, a popular crop in the Soviet Far East.

The tobacco grown in the Ukraine, the Crimea, Kirghizia, and the Caucasus is of little importance. More interesting are the latex plants. The Soviet Union contains no region in which the *hevea* will flourish; consequently, experiments have been made with latex-yielding plants akin to our dandelion, viz. the *sagiz* of the Crimea and central Asia and the *kok-sagiz* (*Scorzonera*) of the Caucasus, which seem able to yield between 8 and 24 cwt. per acre of industrially useful latex. Mikhailov claims that it is 'superior to that of the tropics'. The *kolkhozy* have therefore been made to cultivate it as well as the Mexican gladiolus. In 1940 the area devoted to it was 62,000 acres, and it was hoped to get something approaching 50,000 tons of caoutchouc on the average, whatever the weather. Certain pessimists, however, think the climate too dry for any real hope of success, and their forecast seems justified, for the latest Soviet statistics make no reference to the crop.

The two greatest industrial crops are sugar-beet and cotton. The cultivation of beet began at the end of the eighteenth century mainly on the large estates and, because of this, suffered particularly at the revolution. Its production, which had sufficed to meet the needs of the nation since 1880, fell away by nine-tenths. Since then it has recovered marvellously. As early as 1928 the area under the crop exceeded that in 1913. Five years later the 1928 area had doubled; and in 1939 the Soviet Union produced 2,362,000 tons of sugar, or one-quarter of world production. Associated with wheat in the Black Earth country, beet is there and everywhere a factor in careful, scientific cultivation. Hence, the soils of Kiev, Poltava, Chernigov, Kharkov, Nikolay, Kursk, Orel, Voronezh, Tambov, Tula, and Kuybyshev remain its best area, giving the greatest yields: 900 to 1200 bushels to the acre in the Kursk district and the Ukraine and sometimes 1500 in the Kharkov district. But since 1928 it has gained ground elsewere. Though the possibility of cultivating it in the northern districts has scarcely gone beyond the limits of theory, it covers vast fields on the *chernoziom* of western Siberia, in Uzbekistan, Kirghizia, and south-eastern Kazakstan, where the yield is between 670 and 745 bushels to the acre. Lastly, it is cultivated with complete success in Georgia and the Far East in irrigated fields. In 1955 the area devoted to the crop was 4·4 million acres, which is nearly three times the area covered in 1913. In 1957 the total production amounted to 54 million tons.

Usually, however, more attention is given to the progress of cotton. Although Tsar Alexis Mikhailovitch did not succeed in growing it to the north of the Caspian three hundred years ago, the last years of the empire of the Tsars established it in eastern Transcaucasia and especially on the oases of Turkistan after 1880, notably around the headwaters of the Syr Darya. In 1913 about 200 million acres were devoted to the crop; and the average yield of approximately 200,000 tons supplied half the demand for cotton. On the fall of the Tsars the Soviet resumed the many former plans and added others of their own. 'Water for the cotton' was the slogan, and huge dams and irrigation systems were multiplied in central Asia and Transcaucasia. These oases in Armenia, Azerbaidzhan, Turkistan, Tadzhikistan, Kirghizia, Karakalpakia, and above all in the district of Fergana in Uzbekistan are and certainly will remain the citadels of cotton in the Soviet Union, especially as the construction of the Turksib Railway has permitted central Asia to specialise in the crop by eating Siberian wheat. But other regions have taken to cotton-growing without irrigation, and this has interested the Government, since the cost price is much less. These regions are Dagestan, Nakhishevan with its hot summers, and indeed now Ciscaucasia, the lower Volga, the Crimea, the shores of the Sea of Azov and Black Sea, and even the Ukraine, where it encroaches on the wheat lands and where its cultivation is associated near Kharkov with that of rice. It there occupies more than a million acres. The yield here is naturally far less than it is in the irrigated belt; consequently, some people have called these regions a failure, whilst others think a success has been won by at last carrying the limit of cotton cultivation in the Union from lat. 43° N. to lat. 47° N. Anyhow, whilst in 1928 the Union devoted 2,400,000 acres to cotton, in 1938 it was cultivating nearly 5,000,000 acres; and production rose from 196,000 tons in 1928 to more than 800,000 tons in 1937. In 1955 the area under the crop was 5·4 million acres, and there is little doubt that the Soviet Union supplies more than a quarter of world-production. Production reached 4·4 million tons in 1957. On the figures for 1938 the United States and India were the only countries which produced more than the Union, whose needs are met by its own production. And it should be noticed that, though the bulk of the crop consists of ordinary upland varieties, fine Egyptian cotton tends to occupy more and more space in central Asia and Transcaucasia.

The situation is much less bright as regards the cultivation of shrubs, fruit, and market vegetables. The vine is not quite at home in so severe a climate; and yet grapes are produced. They ripen in a few favoured districts, viz. the Sea of Azov–Black Sea area, notably the *liman* of the Dnestr, the south coast of the Crimea, the sands of the southern Dnepr, and some of the hills of Moldavia and the southern Ukraine; some of the slopes in Ciscaucasia; the hills of Dagestan; certain valleys in Georgia, Kakhetia, and Armenia; finally, the glary, scorching oases of Tadzhikistan and Uzbekistan. Besides fresh grapes, which alone interest Muslims, these vineyards used to yield about 110 million gallons of wine. Some kinds may be mentioned, namely, *kizliar* (Caucasus), which is somewhat like claret; Kakhetian wines, which are more like Burgundy; Chabat, Alupta, and the wines from the old estates in the Crimea, and sparkling wine from the Don valley. But on the whole, though they are rich and full-bodied like Greek or Spanish wines, they are not especially good and before 1917 found little favour among well-to-do consumers. Since the disappearance of this class, the vine seems to have less future than ever in the Soviet Union, even though the standard of life improves appreciably. The masses have not acquired the habit of drinking wine and do not like it.[1]

With tea the matter is quite different. This beverage is as much or even more the national drink than beer is. For a long time it was brought by caravans from China; then at the beginning of the present century the Tsar's Government had plantations made in Colchis. In 1905 it covered 1600 acres and produced 350 cwt.; in 1913 the acreage rose to 2500 and in 1925 to nearly 12,000,000, of which more than 9,000,000 are around Batum and in Georgia, the remainder being in Addzharistan and southern Turkistan. Its production rose to 23,000 tons in 1940. Varieties from Assam and Ceylon have been acclimatised, and, though the average yield is still no more than 8 cwt. to the acre, certain specialised *sovkhozy* and *kolkhozy* have raised it to five or six times that amount. The third five-year plan aimed at considerable advance, and the extreme youth of many of the plantations suggests that the aim will be reached.

It is hoped that the same will be true of fruit. On the whole, the continental climate is rather unfavourable to it. However, apart from

---

[1] Besides, *vino* means 'wine' only in dictionaries. In current speech the word means 'brandy'. The foreigner who wishes to drink wine should ask for *vinogradnoye vino* = 'grape wine'.

small fruit like cranberries which yield an abundant crop, a fairly large amount of fruit is produced in the orchards which surround the peasants' houses, at least in White Russia, where abound the pear and, more especially, the national fruit, the apple, and in the south-west, where the apricot and plum have the advantage of warm, dry summers. But fruit plantations like those in the gullies of the Kharkov district are exceptional. To find real fruit-growing regions one must go to the lower valley of the Volga, which as early as the reign of the Tsarina Elisabeth sent its produce to Moscow and St. Petersburg by special services of fast *telegas*, the Sea of Azov–Black Sea area, and especially the Crimea—or better still, outside Russia proper on the southern slopes of the Caucasus, Addzharistan, Armenia, the oases of central Asia, and the district of Alma Ata. It is in these regions out-side Russia that it is hoped to develop fruit production, especially of citrous fruits, which in 1937 occupied 1,600,000 acres, mostly in Georgia. The slogan is that Transcaucasia is to become 'another Florida' or, according to others, 'the California of the Soviet Union'.

Vegetables are the object of a similar effort, and this is very neces-sary, for Russia has scarcely any vegetables. Tolstoy's vegetarian diet was in the eyes of his fellow-countrymen not merely the least of the old eccentric's strange whims. As a rule, production can only be reckoned on from little plots adjoining the *izby* and *khaty*, where are grown sugar melons, water melons, pumpkins, cabbages, turnips, horse-radishes, and, above all, cucumbers which flourish from the Far North to the extreme south. What Russian rustic tale whose scene is laid in rural districts does not mention cucumbers? Here and there are a few better endowed regions where the cultivation of vegetables assumes a real importance, viz. some districts in the Ukraine, the Moscow basin, the Volga country, the Sea of Azov–Black Sea area, and, better still, the oases of Turkistan, where water is plentiful. But it is also carried on in Dagestan, Yakutia, and now it is being tentatively established in the Far North. Hitherto the total progress of production has been appreciable, and the area given for the purpose has risen to 3·7 million acres. Vegetables are now much grown around the big towns.

Thus, the Soviet Union, which has a great variety of natural resources, manifests the keenest desire to be self-sufficient in agri-cultural produce and notably in the essential commodities of wheat, sugar-beet, and cotton, the production of which is encouraged as vigorously as possible. But the authorities recognise that the results remain inadequate, and a new agricultural system is now being introduced.

3. STOCK-REARING

Although the progress of agriculture has often been declared to be too slow, the complaint could even more justly be made against stock-rearing. This weakness is due to two main causes. There is, first of all, the sorry heritage of the past. Interest in stock-rearing was always secondary in old Russia owing to unfavourable natural and human conditions. Since artificial pastures and fodder crops occupied only 2 per cent. of the area cultivated in 1913 and as many of the natural pastures were of mediocre quality owing to drought or the poverty of the soil, the animals were generally underfed. At the end of the long winter they were pitiably thin. On the other hand, except on the estates of a few wealthy persons, they were often of poor breed badly selected, and inadequately tended. Their stables were ill kept, and epizootic diseases were frequent. Horses alone appeared in any considerable number.

Secondly, there was the catastrophe caused by the introduction of collectivisation. In their rage at seeing themselves plundered, the *kulaks* indulged in veritable hecatombs of animals; and the total amount of live-stock was halved. Besides, if the ill will of opponents and the negligence of the lazy damaged agriculture, these causes had a far worse effect on stock-rearing. A badly cultivated field merely gives a poor yield; but an animal, when badly tended, wastes away and dies. The damage caused by the new system was considerable, and many old *moujiks* repeated the saying: 'A child with seven nurses goes blind.' (In England we say: 'Too many cooks spoil the broth.') For years this caused extreme dearth of meat, milk, butter, and cheese, a fact which told heavily on the provisioning of the towns. A vigorous effort saved the situation. Thanks mainly to the irrigation of arid land in the south-east, the area devoted to fodder succeeded in rising from 7 per cent. in 1934 to 14 per cent. in 1938. By 1955 the area had again doubled, the total acreage amounting to 88 million. To restock the country with animals *sovkhozy* were set up to supply well-bred beasts to the pastoral *kolkhozy*. Specialised forms of stock-rearing came into use, particularly in the north, where agriculture is difficult, and on the steppes of Asia and south Russia, whose dryness is favourable to sheep-farming. But even more effective than these measures was the permission given to the *kolkhozniky* to have beasts of their own on their little plots of land; and when the reform act of 1937 allowed those in agricultural districts where stock-rearing was well developed to keep two or three cows, two or three sows with their piglets, twenty to twenty-five ewes, and any amount of poultry, rabbits, and bees; or in stock-rearing districts (Armenia, Georgia, Tadzhikistan, and Kirghizia) as many as four or five cows, two or three sows, thirty to forty ewes, a horse or two donkeys or two mules or two camels as well as poultry and bees, the growth of this private stock, which is prosperous in the Black Earth country and the clearings in the mixed forest, went on with a rush and is a most flourishing form of stock-rearing. In 1955 it included 34·4 per cent. of the horned cattle, 18·6 per cent. of the sheep, 28·8 per cent. of the pigs, 54·7 per cent. of the goats, but only 10 per cent. of the horses. These improvements have resulted in the meat available for consumption increasing from 5·8 million tons in 1953 to 8 million tons in 1958, and milk from 3·6 to 5·7 million tons. These percentages are lower than those in 1940, and the future of stock reared by the *kolkhozniky* is uncertain.

Horse-breeding is often considered to be the most important occupation. Actually, Russia formerly possessed half the horses in the world and, though the number fell from 30 to 15 million, rising again to 17½ million in 1938, this figure is still larger than that of any other country. There are some interesting breeds: the Kalmuk horse, which makes a good charger; the Anglo-Arab of the Don valley; the Orlov trotter; and the Orlov Rostopshin Anglo-Arab saddle horse. But on the whole the horse population consists of rather poor beasts of little value, small and short in the north, in eastern Russia, and Podolia, but taller and more robust in the centre; they are all, however, cheaply maintained and are willing workers. Before the advent of the machine, they played a leading part in agriculture as in transport. The *moujik* and his horse were inseparable. In the eyes of this nation, which is so ready to excuse wrong-doing, stealing a peasant's horse was the only unpardonable crime, and the offender was not seldom lynched for it.[1] Today the number of horses is increasing very slightly, and tractor policy has in no way dealt a mortal wound to horse-breeding, which remains prosperous in Bashkiria, where there is a stud-farm at Chkalov, and in the Ukraine, the Sea of Azov–Black Sea area, Dagestan, Karabagh, as well as in Turkmenistan and Kirghizia. However, though the horse carries the day on the Russian steppes, it has to compete with the camel, the breeding of which is encouraged in central Asia, with the mule in the mountainous parts of this region, and with the yak in the Pamirs.

In the Far North reindeer breeding is of great importance. For the hyperborean peoples it is the universal provider, on which their life depends. Until only recently, anyone who did not own one was a beggar, a 'fisherman'. Certainly, reindeer breeding has a long way to go, but the example of Canada and Alaska show what enormous supplies of meat scientific breeding of the animal can procure. And

[1] 'One fault is no fault; two faults make half a fault; three faults make a fault,' says a Russian proverb.

the competition of the sledge dog does not appear serious except in a few regions of broken topography, for the reindeer will always have the advantage of not eating fish, which is the only, or almost the only, food which the country affords to man.

A substantial recovery has been made in cattle-breeding, in spite

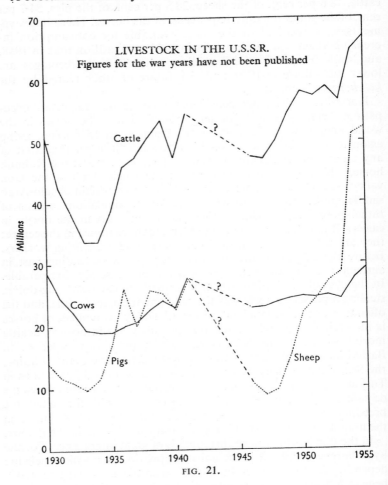

LIVESTOCK IN THE U.S.S.R.
Figures for the war years have not been published

FIG. 21.

of the scarcity of good pasture. In 1913 the Russian empire was the second country in the world in the number of horned cattle, but after the war and revolution the crisis of 1928–32 caused the number of head to fall from 70 million to 29 million. The chief cattle regions today are northern Kazakstan and south-eastern Russia, where extensive nomadic stock-rearing procures for slaughter beasts weighing between 900 and 1100 lbs.; the mountains of Georgia and Osetia, which produce meat as well as cheese and butter; the Ukraine, whose robust grey-coated animals perform miracles of ploughing and of carting sugar-beet, but fatten easily on beet pulp; and, lastly, the north-west, centre, and north of Russia, as well as western Siberia and, only recently, the Far East, which is interested especially in dairy produce. The Kholmogory breed in the Archangel district gives an average of 660 gallons a year, and the Yaroslavl breed yields nearly as much. In 1938 the Soviet Union counted 63,200,000 head of cattle. But in 1928 it had 70,000,000, and, though the number had then increased by 54 per cent. since 1924, this was not an advance, for 1955 these were no more than 67 million.

Sheep-rearing is better endowed by nature, since there are immense sheep-walks on the steppes of the Black Sea, Caspian, central Asia, and south-western Siberia. But between 1928 and 1932 the number of sheep fell from 133 to 47 million, and formerly only a few specialised regions had large numbers of the animals, viz. the dry steppes of the Black Sea and Ciscaucasia and those to the east of the lower Volga, where the Astrakhan district was very important for the supply of meat, wool, and skins. Today this area has been extended to include Dagestan, Turkmenistan, and Kazakstan, where sheep always formed the principal animals of the nomads; and it is imagined that central Asia is being made into 'another Australia'. The breeds are often poor. Though the cross-bred with its fine wool is found in southern Russia and among the Russian colonies on the Kirghiz steppes, the sheep with coarse wool still prevails in Russia and the hardy Kirghiz fat-tailed sheep in Siberia and Turkistan. A serious effort is being made to apply selective breeding to the animals and to feed them better by keeping them in one place on prepared pastures. Apart from this, the number of sheep rose in 1938 to 103 million head, though this figure includes goats. This was a great recovery compared with 1932 and an enormous increase as compared with 1913 and its 45 million head, especially as this included the figures for the then Russian Poland. Now the numbers have nearly returned to those of 1928, with 124,982,000. This includes sheep alone. Goats number 17,654,000. In 1957 the wool clip amounted to 490,000 tons.

In pig breeding the advance has been undeniable. Excluded *a priori* from the Muslim countries of the Union, pigs had formerly a certain importance in White Russia, that land of oak forests, in the Ukraine, New Russia, and the governments of Kaluga and Kirov; and even then the methods were extensive. On the other hand, they assumed an intensive character and gave a far greater return in the governments of Moscow, the north, and western Siberia; that is to say, in places where dairy produce was important and where, according to the celebrated formula, the pig tended to become 'a by-product of the cow'. Here, too, the decrease was great between 1928 and 1932, when numbers fell from 26 million to 10 million head. But fascinated by the example of the United States, the Soviets persisted in improving the situation by encouraging pig breeding to some extent everywhere, and especially around the great urban areas. Even the Jews of Birobidzhan have taken to it. In 1938 the number of pigs in the Union amounted to 30,600,000, and this had risen to 52,155,000 in 1955.

Something must be said about poultry farming, which, though of recent growth, since it was really started only between 1880 and 1890, has developed to considerable proportions in the districts of Voronezh, Kharkov, and Tambov, in the Tatar republic of the middle Volga, in the Urals, and western Siberia, giving to the empire millions, if not tens of millions, of hens, geese, ducks, and turkeys. Since the crisis caused by the revolution the poultry yards have been restocked, and progress has been all the more since concessions were made to the *kolkhozniky*.

Bee-keeping is very important. The occupation was held in honour from very early times, as is proved by the presence of a hive in the arms of Tambov, and it has spread to some extent everywhere, especially in western Siberia, where Barnaul is 'the city of honey'; in eastern Siberia, Nakhishevan, the Caucasus, the districts of Ufa, Kazan, and Voronezh, and even more in the Ukraine, where the bee is troglodyte, and in the former governments of Poltava and Dnepropetrovsk. In 1913 there were 7,000,000 hives, and the harvest was valued at 20,000,000 roubles. Today, more than 1,550,000 families keep bees, and an Institute of Apiculture has been founded near Tula.

Finally, the existence must be recorded of a very active silk-worm cultivation in Transcaucasia and Fergana. It is very promising, but hitherto little effort has been made to exploit it fully.

On the whole, in stock-rearing as in agriculture the resources are large and various. The Soviet Union has as many horned cattle as Germany, France, the Netherlands, Belgium, Great Britain, Denmark, and Poland together (1 animal for every 3 persons); a total number of sheep that rivals that of Australia (more than 1 animal for every 2 persons); a pig for every four head of the population; and it can slaughter 32 million cattle, 64 million sheep, and 21 million pigs. The corresponding figures in the United States are 24, 21, and 52 million respectively. It is estimated that stock-rearing has ceased to be the weak point of the agriculture economy. This opinion is rather optimistic, and the Soviets recognise that progress is slow and that much remains to be done, especially in improving the quality rather than increasing the quantity. The animals are generally poor specimens and their yield of meat only moderate. It is certain that the technique of stock-rearing ought to be greatly improved and fodder crops extended. The fifth five-year plan increased the area under the crops to 88 million acres, and caused the pastures in the Caucasus and mountains of central Asia to be far more extensively used. The Government is greatly interested in reindeer and has raised the number of cattle to 67,000, of pigs to 52,000, and of sheep to 125,000. Its anxiety is particularly over the pig and the cow, for the pig is a 'meat factory' and the cow 'a milk factory'. The use of such expressions—they even speak of the manufacture of wheat—emphasises quite distinctly the well-known fact that 'industrialisation is the mania of the Soviet régime'.

CHAPTER 13

INDUSTRY

The Soviet Government's mania for industrialisation certainly does not mean that a great effort has not been made to improve agriculture. But in this department success has not been striking everywhere, and industry has undoubtedly advanced at a more rapid pace: a fact which is due not only to a fierce determination to succeed, but also to some extremely remarkable natural resources.

1. SOURCES OF POWER

Magnificent coal-fields, which are continuations of those in Europe, exist on the borders of Primary strata in the Soviet Union. The Donets district, nowadays known as 'Donbass', has been worked for long years, but whilst it yielded only 22,790,000 tons of coal in 1913, its production today is 125,900,000 tons. It is still the mainstay of coal production in the Soviet Union. However, its reserves (amounting to 80,000 million tons), enormous though they may seem to us, are a trifle compared with those of the 'Kuzbass', or Kuznetsk coal-field in Siberia. The latter, which in 1955 yielded only 28 million tons, has a reserve of 450,000 million tons. The Karaganda coal-field in Kazakstan is the 'third coal base in the Union'. In 1955 it yielded only 28 million tons, but its reserves are estimated at 50,000 million tons—and even at 60,000 million, if a few small fields in the same region are included.

There are many other coal-fields besides these. In Europe are the central, or Moscow, field, whose chief centre is Borodino and the reserves of which amount to 12 million tons; the middle Volga field, with mines at Dombarovki in the Chkalov district and a production of 9·5 million tons in 1939; the Kizel field in the central Ural region, all the fields in the Urals together having a reserve of 6500 million tons; the Pechora field, which is not well known, but stretches

definitely towards the southern Urals, and to which have been attri-
buted reserves of 34,000 million tons; and the Poltava coal-field. This
is all without taking into account the beds of lignite on the right bank
of the Dnepr, in the Ukraine, at Moscow, Murmansk, and Borovichi
near Leningrad; or the beds of peat near Moscow, Ivanovo, Leningrad, Gorky, Kirov, Sverdlovsk, and in White Russia. In Asia there
is a series of coal-fields in central Siberia, at Irkutsk, and in Transbaykalia, the coal-fields at Minusinsk and Kansk (or the Tunguska
fields, with reserves of 55,000 million tons) and that at Shulim near
Krasnoyarsk, which has a reserve of 40,000 million tons. Then in the
Far East there are coal-fields at Artem, Suchan, near Vladivostok,

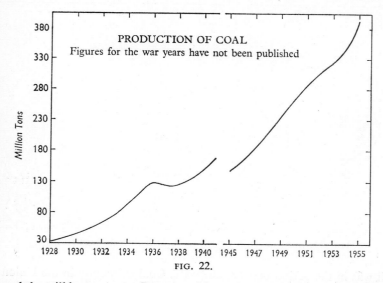

FIG. 22.

and the still larger one at Bureya, with reserves of 30,000 million tons.
In central Asia coal-fields exist at Shural in Tadzhikistan and in
Kirghizia, with reserves of nearly 4000 million tons. And, lastly, in
Caucasia there are fields at Kutaisi in Georgia and Tanabsheni in
Abkhasia, and even larger ones on the northern slopes, the region
having reserves of nearly 4000 million tons. And this list does not
include the coal-fields in Yakutia which seem to extend 250 miles
along the valley of the Lena, or those of the Ob, lower Yenisey (at
Igarka and Norilsk), Pyasina, and Anadyr valleys in the Far North
of Siberia, which, in spite of their remote position, may render great
service by providing for the refuelling of ships in the Arctic Sea.
Reserves of nearly 10,000 million tons of coal have been said to exist
in north-eastern Asia alone.

A great part of all these coal-fields remains unworked or nearly so. But it is beyond doubt that so far as coal is concerned, the Soviet Union is in a very strong position. Only the United States now, and perhaps China one day, could rival it. Russia alone could support the whole industry of the Soviet Union for 750 years at the present rate of consumption. But that part of the Union contains only 7 or 8 per cent. of the total reserves. These reserves are estimated at 1,628,238,649,810 tons, or one-fifth of the world's coal, and enough to last a thousand years and more for the needs of the whole world, assuming that the rate of consumption remained constant at what

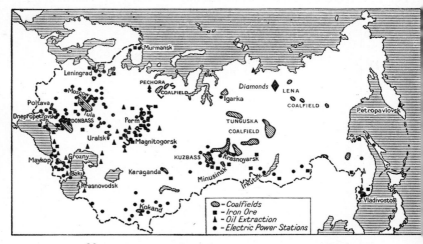

FIG. 23. DISTRIBUTION OF MINERAL AND POWER PRODUCTION

it was in the period between the wars. Coal extraction in the Union continues to increase: in 1913 the quantity raised was 29·15 million tons; in 1928 this rose to 35·5 million, in 1932 to 64·4 million, in 1937 to 12 million, in 1940 to 165·9 million, and in 1956 to 423 million.

Although the estimate of the reserves of crude oil is more difficult to arrive at and is, besides, more problematical, it remains certain that in respect of this commodity also very few countries dispose of wealth comparable with that of the Soviet Union. In 1913 Russia took second place in the world with a production of 10·3 million tons; and yet that included only the production from the Caucasus, the oil-field at Baku providing 83 per cent. of the total and those at Grozny and Maykop supplying 13 per cent. The quantity produced at Emba (to the north of the Caspian), Fergana, and Sakhalin was

insignificant. During the revolution and civil war there was a collapse
of the industry. But even before the time of the five-year plans a
great effort had been made under the direction of an engineer named
Serebrovski, 'the crude oil dictator', to rebuild and modernise the
plants and as early as 1928 the 1913 production level had been surpassed. By 1940 it had risen to 31·1 million tons. The German
invasion caused a great fall in production, and the 1940 figure was not
reached again until 1949. Since then there has been a rapid increase
in production. In 1956 this rose to 83 million tons. The Caucasus is
now the third largest oil-field, yielding 21 per cent. of Soviet production; but Emba, Ufa, and other fields in the R.S.F.S.R., which
in 1940 yielded only 10 per cent., now yield 70 per cent. In the

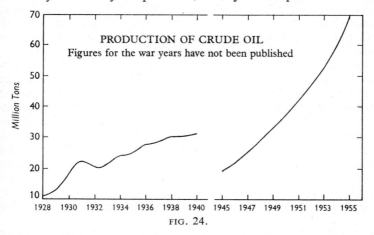

FIG. 24.

Caucasus Baku is estimated to have reserves of 1500 million tons.
The oil-field in Sakhalin yields hardly 492,000 tons and the Fergana
field slightly more than this. Since 1928 petroleum has been prospected for right into the Aralo-Caspian deserts, in the depths of the
tayga, and in the Arctic *merzlota*, and has been discovered in a host
of places: in Turkmenistan not far from Krasnovodsk, and in
Neftedagh, where the resources are said to be enormous, and there
is talk of raising 10,000 tons a day; in central Asia near Kokand; in
the north of Siberia at the upper end of the Gulf of Kronotski 190
miles north of Petropavlovsk in Kamchatka; in the lower Khatanga
valley; in the lower Lena valley; in the lower Yenisey valley; in the
lower Ob valley; in the Far North of Russia on the Murmansk coast,
where a field that has been located is perhaps connected with another
which has been reported in Karelia; not far from the middle Pechora
to the north of its tributary, the Ukhta; away in the opposite direction

on the Crimean peninsula of Kerch; and in the Ukraine at Romny near Poltava.

Most of the new fields were indeed not being worked before 1940. At Romny, for instance, the first industrial petroleum was produced in January of that year. Anyhow, it may be accepted that, when these reserves are added to those of the fields already mentioned, a total of nearly 3000 million tons is reached. But there is far more, for in eastern Russia, between the middle Volga and the Urals, an immense oil-field has been discovered extending from lat. 52° N. to lat. 60° N. It is already spoken of as a 'second Baku', and the experts attribute to it between 900 and 1100 million tons, certain enthusiasts even speaking of 2700 million tons. In 1955 this field yielded more than three times as much as the famous fields in the Caucasus. It is at present being worked mainly at Sterlitamak and Ishimbayevo between Ufa and Chkalov and at Chusovski Gorodki near Perm and Syzran near Kuybyshev.

Compared with such vast wealth the oil-field at Drohobycz-Boryslaw, which has been taken over from Poland, cuts a poor figure with its few hundred thousand tons. In all, the Soviet oil reserves probably amount to about 4000 million tons, and its current production (nearly 100 million tons in 1957) is exceeded by that of the United States alone, by which it is in fact far outdistanced. Besides, though the Government has often reproached the Neftianiks for insufficient progress in oil extraction (and this was indeed rather slow before 1941), an immense advance has been achieved in the technique of refinement, construction of pipe-line,[1] increased number of tank-waggons, and improvement of oil transport by water. Much attention has been paid to natural gas, the production of which is planned to reach 150 billion cubic metres in 1965. European Russia has fifteen fields, of which nine are associated with oil. But coal is still by far the most important fuel in the Soviet Union.

The mere possession of such a wealth of fuel would be enough to give the Union an industrial potential which would be equalled with difficulty. But in addition it is very richly endowed with electric power. Not that it is a great country for 'white coal'. Certainly, when the rivers are in low water it has hardly as much power as Belgian Congo; and just as certainly, when the streams have their average volume, it takes first place among the countries of the world, thanks to the rapids on the lower Dnepr and on the Svir-Volkhov system, to the power supplied by the Lena, Yenisey, Ob, Amur, Syr Darya,

---

[1] Their total length in 1941 was 2617 miles. The then longest—Baku–Batum—measures 1067 miles. The line from Grozny to Tuapse is 384 miles long. But the new line from Kuybyshev through Gomel into Poland and East Germany, Czechoslovakia and Hungary is nearly 2000 miles long.

and Oxus, and to the falls in central and eastern Siberia and on the feeders of the Kama. But owing to the winter freeze-up, this power is available in summer only. Besides, the distribution of these resources is very unequal. The Soviet Union is pre-eminently a country of plains and low plateaus, vast areas have only very low falls, and the real 'white coal' is too often available only at tremendous distances from the thickly populated industrial regions. Hence, hydro-electric power is only 13·5 per cent. of the total generated in

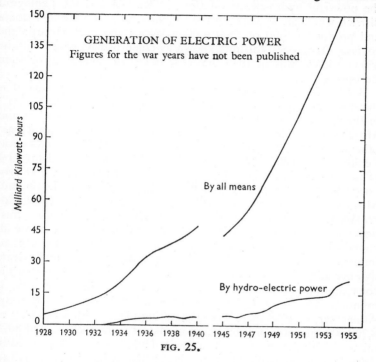

GENERATION OF ELECTRIC POWER
Figures for the war years have not been published

By all means

By hydro-electric power

FIG. 25.

the Soviet Union. But the infinitely better distribution of oil and coal resources compensates for these drawbacks, and plentiful supplies of oil fuel, lignite, coal-waste, and peat allow of an abundant production of thermo-electricity. The Soviet Union has therefore achieved an immense success in this department. Electrification was one of Lenin's fads, and the first five-year plan set itself to create in the popular masses a veritable worship of electricity. And this was necessary, too. Coal-fields like Kuzbass or Karaganda cannot find full employment on the spot for all the power produced, and they are so far from the main industrial centres that the wisest plan is to transport the power in the form of current. Consequently, innumerable generating plants have been constructed.

In 1937 the hydro-electric power stations produced in all no more than 4,200,000,000 kWh., which was only 12 per cent. of the total production. In 1940 their 5100 million kWh., 625 million of which were produced by high falls (three in Transcaucasia and two in central Asia), represented only 10 per cent. of the total. Most of the power was therefore produced by low falls of great volume, as in the powerful hydro-electric stations in Karelia and the Leningrad district, which are situated on the Volkhov, Svir, Neva, and Tuloma and produce a total of 1500 million kWh.; and even more in the colossal Dneproges, for long known as Dneprostroy, which with its 558,000 kWh. was in 1939 the most powerful generating plant in Europe and for some time was the most powerful in the world.

But by far the greatest part of the electric power produced is thermic. Some power houses, like Baku I and Baku II (270,000 kW.) in the Caucasus use petroleum; others, like those in the Ural and Moscow coal-fields, use low-grade coal; others use natural gas; others, lastly, like Gorky I (204,000 kW.) and Red October at Leningrad (710,000 kW.) use peat. In 1935 peat was used for 21·4 of the production, which is a far greater percentage than that produced by 'white coal'. The chief electrical regions are Leningrad, Moscow, the southern Ukraine, eastern Caucasus, Urals (Magnitogorsk), Kuznetsk, Tashkent-Fergana, and, lastly, Karaganda, Krasnoyarsk, and Irkutsk. Within these regions the power-houses are all connected together. Of the current generated 80 per cent. goes to industry. The rest is shared between the railways, public and private lighting in town and country, and, finally, agriculture, in which the consumption of electricity, though encouraged in every way, is infinitely less. In 1937 there were 1900 miles of electrified railway. Altogether, in 1938 there were generating plants with a capacity of 8,700,000 kilowatts, a production of 39,600 million kWh., and 8078 miles of high-tension lines. The Soviet Union has now advanced in world production from fifteenth place which it had held in 1913 to second place, and it is destined to do still better. More power-houses are being built nearly everywhere: from White Russia, where the gigantic Belges has been constructed, to Transcaucasia, eastern Siberia, Uzbekistan, and above all the Volga valley. The last district produces 23,000 million kWh., thanks particularly to the two enormous power-houses in Kuybyshev, which produce 14,000 million. Altogether a hydro-electric production of 170,000 million kWh. has now been realised, i.e. the equivalent of 120 million additional tons of coal. Hence, the Soviet Union, which is now a great producer of electricity and especially of thermo-electricity, has taken its place alongside the United States among the great producers of power from various sources. There is, however, little information of its progress in the use of atomic power for industrial purposes.

2. RAW MATERIALS

Rich as it is in motive power, the Soviet Union is not less so in raw materials. Mineral building materials are, however, not plentiful. They are found in Murmansk, Karelia, the southern Ukraine, the Crimea, on the western fringe of the middle Volga basin at Syzran, and especially in the mountain regions of the Caucasus and the ranges of central Asia and eastern Siberia, where they are being worked increasingly. Yet the Union is certainly ill provided in this respect, and hence the recent extraordinary increase in the manufacture of bricks as well as of cement and concrete.

On the other hand, the Union has at its disposal a fabulous wealth of timber—not, it is true, in the south, which except on the mountains is bare of trees and has a percentage of wooded area that varies between 0·8 and 4, but in the whole of the northern half. Apart from forests which are 'of local importance', the wooded area in the Union is estimated at 2362 million acres, which is 21·5 per cent. of the territory of the Union and one-third of the world's forests. In Russia the southern part of this forest has undergone considerable clearing. Only 13·7 per cent. of the western district is wooded still, 13 per cent. of the Moscow district, and 12·2 per cent. of the Tatar republic; but forest still covers 41·2 per cent. of the northern region: 68 per cent. of the area of the basins of the Dvina and Pechora, 70 per cent. in the Urals, 47·5 in Karelia, 22·5 in the Leningrad area, 16·8 in the districts of Gorky and Kirov; 22·6 in western Siberia; 27·9 in eastern Siberia; and 37·9 in Yakutia. In 1928 these forests yielded 71·5 million cu. yds. of timber; and in 1937 about 222 million cu. yds., of which nearly 131 million were found in Russia. The timber consisted of good oak from White Russia, walnut from the Caucasus, cedar from the Far East, but above all soft woods, among which pinewood from Olonets and firwood from Smolensk and Vologda are especially well known. This marvellous wealth is now, as formerly, used for fuel, building, the manufacture of domestic instruments, and indeed for clothing, since poverty usually forces the peasants to wear shoes of bark known as *lapty*;[1] but, as will be seen, it is also used as the basis for important industries. However, though timber is

---

[1] 'To make someone fall from boots to *lapty*' means 'to reduce him to beggary'. A *lapotnik* is a clodhopper. Notice that there is no equivalent of *sabot* in Russian, any more than in English, since the type of footwear does not exist in either country.

exploited seriously in the Far East, central, eastern, and western Siberia, and in the Karachi and Cherkesse districts of the Caucasus, the industry reaches a high degree of importance only in Russia, in the districts of Gorky, Kirov, the Bashkir and Chuvash republics, White Russia, and above all Karelia. In these areas the winter felling and the launching of log rafts on the rivers after they have thawed in spring make the forests busy and give rise to much traffic between the forests and the steppes as well as to seaports like Archangel and Leningrad from which timber is exported. This exploitation is of long standing. Up to a short time ago it was organised by associations of woodcutters. The Soviet Government has set itself to modernise and rationalise it, not only by constructing many roads through the forests and by making the motor-saw assist the hand-saw, not only by making motor tractors and lorries help the horse-carts, but also by moving the industry towards the north, north-east, and east, which have hitherto been almost untouched. Whilst production in the west has increased by only 25 per cent., in the Urals it has risen by 70 per cent. and in western Siberia by 210 per cent. Nevertheless, the Siberian *tayga* is still practically intact, and the forests of northern Russia are scarcely less so. A number of trees die of old age, and three times more wood grows than is cut; and this loss of wealth will continue so long as the roads by which the timber can be removed are not more numerous. At the same time, the Soviet Government aims at creating other timber resources, and it has made an effort to plant the Algerian cork-oak in the Transcaucasian mountains and the Crimea. The outcome of the experiment is not yet known.

The forest yields not only wood, but also furs, the pursuit of and trade in which has, we know, played a principal part in the development of the national power of Russia. Today the decrease in game is very marked in Russia, where the forests no longer harbour many valuable fur-bearing animals, except the mink and the marten. However, hunting is still fairly active there, especially in the Kirov district, in the Zyrian country, and the Urals. But the resources remain far more considerable in the Caucasus (tigers, panthers, bears, lynxes, foxes, martens, and otters), in central Asia (tigers, leopards, panthers, bears, boars, foxes, and antelopes), and even more in Siberia, where there is in the Altai, the territory of Krasnoyarsk, Yakutia, Kamchatka, the Far North, and above all in the Usuri valley a great abundance of sables, silver foxes, ermine, martens, racoons, otters, polecats, squirrels, lynxes, gluttons, bears, cheetahs, panthers, tigers, etc., which swarm there.

The abundance is great, but the supply is not inexhaustible. The Tsarist Government feared that the mad waste, which grew worse after the perfection of firearms and the multiplication of traps, might end by reducing the Siberian forest to the same state of impoverishment as the Russian. The Soviet Government has tried to avert this danger by severely regulating and collectivising hunting, which has henceforth been entrusted to associations of trappers; and it has endeavoured to struggle against the improvident greed of the individual. In particular, it has established a good many reserves, covering more than 24·5 million acres and ranging from the Caucasus to Kamchatka, from the Crimea to the Altai, and from the Urals to the Sikhota Alin. Not content with preserving in them the various indigenous species, it acclimatises foreign ones, like the musk rat, skunk, otter, and silver fox from North America and the nutria from the Argentine, and encourages their multiplication in *sovkhozy*.

Perhaps this is the place to stress the great wealth of the fisheries in the Soviet Union. The rivers of Russia are full of fish. Salmon and white fish swarm in the rivers and lakes of the north and north-west, and sturgeon, carp, barbel, etc., in streams flowing into the Black Sea and Caspian. Similarly, the Siberian rivers and Lake Baykal are wonderfully stocked, and in spring it is possible to have there, as on the Volga, a miraculous draught of fishes. The wealth has been exploited for long years, but between 1860 and 1900 the exploitation, which was organised in the capitalist manner, made great progress and moved towards the river mouths. An effort was made to establish preserving and a paying system of marketing. In addition to the foregoing the Murman coast and the coast of the Far East, where warm and cold waters meet, also abound in fish. Sea fisheries were early established in them but the White Sea fisheries have been even more prosperous. Today great success in organising and rationalising the fishing, maritime as well as fluvial, has been achieved and in 1939 the Union reckoned 142,000 fishermen. There were 810 fluvial and lacustrine fishing *kolkhozy*, distributed through the south-east (lower Volga and Astrakhan region), the north-east and south-west of Russia, the Ob, Lake Baykal, and the rivers of Yakutia, and, lastly, the Amur and Ussuri. The Yenisey and many lakes remain almost unexploited for want of local means of preserving and rapid transport of the fish. The *kolkhozy* dealing with sea fishing numbered 830 and worked mainly on the Murman coast, the White Sea, the Sea of Azov, the Caspian, and the Far East, where Nikolayevsk and Sakhalin are two large fishing centres. The former has on the average a catch of between 600,000 and 700,000 cwt., the latter between 2,000,000 and 2,500,000 cwt., and an increase on these figures is expected. By now fish holds a considerable place in the Russian diet, especially in the north, where many communities have little else to eat.[1] Furthermore,

---

[1] While travelling from Povenets to Archangel, J. Legras was surfeited with 'this exclusive ichthyophagy'.

fish forms the raw material of an increasingly busy industry of canned food.

The same may be said of a number of agricultural products whose abundance and variety have led to a great expansion of the food industry. The abundance of wheat and barley conduces to the development of flour-milling and brewing; large stocks of sugar-beet to that of sugar-making and refining; the progress in oil-seed production to that of oil-making; potato cultivation leads to distillery and starch-making; and pastoral products give rise to the making of butter, cheese, pork-butchery, and canned meat. By its variety and quantity agricultural production also provides plenty of raw material for textile industries. True, this is hardly the case with wool, of which the Soviet Union produces some 20,000 tons a year, or with leather, which in spite of very real progress is still clearly in short supply. But in flax and hemp the Union has an overwhelming superiority over other states; its production of cotton is one of the largest in the world; and it has a great and increasing abundance of raw silk, not to mention many latex-yielding plants which are capable of supplying a rubber industry.

That is, however, not the essential gauge of the prosperity of Soviet industry. Such a yardstick indeed resides in the fact that, even apart from coal and petroleum, the underlying rocks are of surprising wealth. Precious metals, rare metals, and useful ores are all found there, usually in great quantity.

Among the precious metals hidden in the rock-core of the ancient hill-masses first place must be given to gold. Its production, which was rather supine in the days of the Tsars, amounting to less than 60 tons a year, has made an extraordinary spurt recently. In 1952 the total production amounted to 670,000 lb., and many gold-mining areas have been added to the old auriferous regions in the Urals and Altai, to the lodes on the Lena and on the Vitim and Olekma plateaus in eastern Siberia, and to those in the Bureya and Amur valleys in the Far East. Mushketov described twenty-three of them in 1929. Since then more have been discovered in Yakutia, Baykalia, the Maritime Province, Kazakstan (360 veins), Svanetia, and even in the districts of Murmansk and Moscow and in the Ukraine. The lodes which have been exploited in the Kolyma valley since 1933 are the richest in the Soviet Union. The Government seems to have made the almost vertical rise in gold production one of its chief aims since 1928. 'It has invested colossal sums and made gigantic efforts in this industry' (Littlepage), which Serebrovski, formerly the oil controller and chief *glavzoloto*, has effectively striven to modernise and develop, even at the cost of doctrinal contradictions such as the payment by piece-work and the extensive employment of 'individual' gold-washers—no fewer than 100,000—who provide nearly one-third of the production. The authorities still complain that mechanisation is not carried far enough, that certain installations are defective, and that the technical employees of Soviet origin are too few. The fact remains that probably nearly 250 tons of gold were extracted in 1938, perhaps close on 300 tons in 1939, and that, according to such a well-informed person as Littlepage, it is possible to increase the quantity extracted 'very substantially'. This activity in districts which a short while ago were still uninhabited should open them, as Stalin

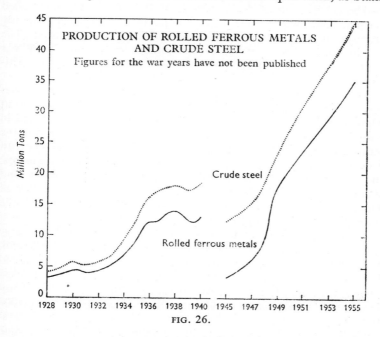

PRODUCTION OF ROLLED FERROUS METALS
AND CRUDE STEEL
Figures for the war years have not been published

Crude steel

Rolled ferrous metals

Million Tons

FIG. 26.

has said, to agriculture and industry, just as has happened in California. Besides, the importance which the possession of a vast stock of gold—certainly one of the largest in the world—has for the steadiness of national economy in times of peace and even more in time of war need not be emphasised.

The quantity of silver mined is far smaller. The metal is, however, found in the Caucasus in the silver-lead mines at Alagir, in the Urals, at Nerchinsk in eastern Siberia, and above all in the Altai region and on the Kirghiz steppes. It is thought that in 1938 the quantity mined was about 214 tons.

Another precious metal is platinum, nine-tenths (5300 tons) of the world-production of which comes from the Soviet Union. It is mined chiefly in the Urals in the valleys of the Tura, Lial, Isa, and Lozva, where it is found in a pure form in placers or else mixed with gold and other rare metals, from which it is separated by smelting and refinement carried out mainly near the mines at Mias.

Iridium, osmium, palladium, rhodium, vanadium, titanium, molybdenum, zirconium, tungsten, chromium, etc., are rare metals which are much sought after today for the preparation of special kinds of steel and are found not only in the Urals, but also in the Far East, Karelia, and especially in the Kolski peninsula. With these must be mentioned the manganese which comes from Nikopol in the Ukraine, but mainly from the unrivalled mines at Kutaisi and Chiatura in Georgia. The production in the Soviet Union (2·76 million tons) represents 40 per cent. of the world's output and has little fear of any serious competition except from India.

The Urals (especially the Mias district) are rich in precious stones also. Diamonds, which are found in several places in Russia (e.g. at Dmitrievski in the Bashkir republic), have lately been discovered in valuable industrial quantities in the Siberian plateau, especially in the valleys of the Vilnuy and its tributaries, and the stones, together with jade, malachite, jasper, opals, topazes, amethysts, emeralds, sapphires, and rubies, form 'a wonderful jewel-case unique in quality and quantity' (de Korff). Rubies are also found in the lofty valley of Gount in the Pamirs. In addition to these precious stones there is the glass produced in the old imperial works at Sverdlovsk.

Nearly every kind of useful ore is found. Lead exists in large quantities in the Urals, Ciscaucasia, Transcaucasia, Tadzhikistan, Uzbekistan, Kazakstan, and the Altai region, the output of the metal being a little more than 67,000 tons in 1938. Zinc occurs in the Donets region, the Altai, Urals, and Ardon valley to the west of Ordzhonikidze in the Caucasus, the total output in 1938 being close on 69,000 tons. Tin, which was already being extracted in Kazakstan and Transbaykalia, has lately been found in the valley of the upper Kolyma, in the north of the Chukotski peninsula, and especially in the Urals, where forty-four lodes have been discovered over an area of 4600 and 5800 square miles. Nickel occurs in the central and southern Urals and in the Kolski peninsula, the output being 2460 tons in 1938; mercury near Dnepropetrovsk and in Yakutia (264 tons in 1934); asbestos in the Urals; bauxite in the Ukraine, in the Bashkir Urals, near Ryazan, and especially at Tikhvin not far from Leningrad. Its reserves should be close on 18 million tons. Nearly 250,000 tons were extracted in 1938. Graphite is mined in the Urals and in the Tunguska valley in central Siberia. Potassium and soda form enormous beds in the Ust Urt and above all at Berezniki and Solikamsk in the northern

Urals, where it is said that there are some 16,000 million tons.[1] Phosphates are also found in prodigious quantities in the form of apatite in the Kolski peninsula (about 3·7 million tons in 1935). Mirabillite (Glauber salts) is only the principal salt extracted in the Gulf of Karabogaz in the Caspian. Not far from that place Cheleken Island and the neighbouring coast yield ozokerite, a fossil mineral wax which is also found in Fergana, in the former Khanate of Khiva, and on the shores of Lake Baykal; whilst Semiz Bugu has great reserves of corundum. But all this wealth is small compared with the Soviet Union's resources in copper and iron.

From time immemorial Transcaucasia has been famous for its copper mines, especially those at Kirovabad, the excellent ore of which contained 10, 12, and sometimes 25 per cent. of metal. Today the mines at Alaverdy, Ordubad, and Devdoraki are the most important. As early as the seventeenth century other deposits were discovered in the Urals at Turminsk, Gumishevski, and Mednorudiansk, and in our own times a whole series of lodes have been located in the middle and southern parts of the range, viz. in the Bogomolovski mines and in the deposits at Dagtiarinski in the district of Soimonovskaya, at San Donato, and Sverdlovsk. In all, the Ural region has reserves amounting to 1·5 million tons. Equally important are the deposits at Almalik near Tashkent; but far less so are those in the Manghishiak peninsula, whose cupriferous sandstones have been worked since ancient times, those on the plateau of Vitim and at Norilsk in the lower Yenisey valley (cupro-nickel), and in the Far East. But most important is the discovery of superb resources in Kazakstan in the form of rich polymetallic deposits at Predgornoye in the southern Altai, a deposit of 2 million tons at Kounradski on the shores of Lake Balkhash, and another of 5·5 million at Dzhezkazgan on the Hungersteppe. At present, extraction amounts to 1·3 million tons of pyrites, giving 106,000 tons of metal; and it is believed that the reserves would supply the needs of the whole world for ten years. But they are certainly very much less than those in America.

In iron, however, the superiority of the Soviet Union is overwhelming. The Krivoyrog deposits between the Bug and the Dnestr have been worked for a long time. Do they extend, as is suspected, as far as the Donbass? Anyhow, the reserves seem to amount to some 20,000 million tons of ore, which represent 1000 million tons of metal, the content of these ferruginous quartzites being 35 per cent. The Kerch deposits have also been worked for a long time, but are of small importance, for, even when the reserves of the Moscow and Tula districts and of the Kolski peninsula are added, they apparently only slightly exceed 1000 million tons. As for the mines at Khopiorsk

[1] Other writers say 2000 million tons of pure potassium.

to the east of the middle Don, they contain only a few hundred million tons of phosphoric ore.

Far greater are the resources of the Urals, where magnetite, with a metal content of between 40 and 70 per cent., has long been exploited in open-cast workings near Magnitogorsk. Since the revolution fabulous wealth has been discovered in this region. The Magnitnaya Gora is a veritable mountain of ore containing at least 300 million tons. Farther south the beds at Khalilovo near Orsk contain 400 million. In all, the brown and red hæmatites of the Urals would represent reserves of 1325 million tons according to some and 2500 million tons according to others.

Iron is found in many other districts in Asiatic Russia. The deposits in Kazakstan and the mountain district of Shorie in the south of the Kuzbass and those in the districts of Telbes, Temir Tau, and Tashim (200 to 250 million tons) are relatively modest. Far greater are the deposits in the Angara valley, where ore with a metal content varying between 40 and 63 per cent. is found, both to the south of the Irkutsk coal-field and a few hundred miles to the north of it (at least 500 million tons). Very important too are the iron deposits in the Far East and particularly those in the Little Khingan (reserves 600 million tons; metal content 62 per cent.), not to mention various little deposits in the north of Siberia, of which one adjoining the Sea of Laptev is very promising.

If this ended the catalogue, the Soviet Union would none the less exceed all other countries in supplies of iron. The reserves in Lorraine are estimated at 5000 million tons, those in the Lake Superior district at 1500 million. Now, the famous magnetic anomaly at Kursk, first noticed in the time of the Tsars, has given promise of a magnificent deposit of iron. True, there is no exact agreement about it: some hold that it contains reserves of at most 2000 million tons; others that it is a matter of some 200,000 million tons of ferruginous quartzite, i.e. between 80 and 100,000 million tons of metal—which would supply the world for hundreds of years at the present rate of consumption. These figures give food for thought. Even on the first hypothesis the supply is enormous. Though the ores contain a great many silicious elements, their average metal content (30 to 40 per cent.) is equal to that of the minette of Lorraine, and near Kursk they are only 500 ft. below the surface, so that when the time comes to exploit them, extraction will be easy. In short, it may be that present methods of exploiting ore leave much to be desired and cause serious waste, but yet production has made extraordinary progress in the Soviet Union; e.g. 27 million tons in 1936 against 6 million in 1928. This was surpassed only by the United States and France. In 1955 production rose to 72 million tons. Altogether, the Soviet Union has prodigious possibilities, and the dispersion of its reserves over the four quarters of its vast territory is economically very advantageous.

What a foundation is laid by the presence of all these minerals for an ambitious metal industry and a would-be vigorous chemical industry! Indeed, the gods have been generous here. True the human conditions were, at the beginning at any rate, far from equal to the natural conditions. It has been seen above what obstacles were struck, especially in industry, by the five-year plans and what measures were adopted to overcome them. There is no doubt that in spite of partial checks the Soviet system has achieved astonishing

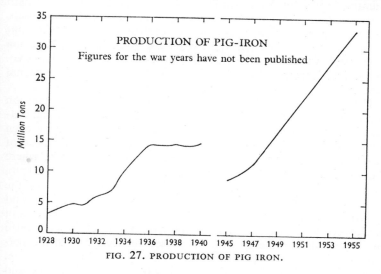

FIG. 27. PRODUCTION OF PIG IRON.

progress in this field. The figures of production do not, it is true, always appear to conform with the estimates of reserves, but besides the fact that to harmonise them would sometimes require long delay, such harmony is not always necessary or desirable in connexion with mining.

3. PROGRESS OF MISCELLANEOUS INDUSTRIES

It is a remarkable fact that progress has been least marked in the textile industry. In the days of the Tsars it was the most prosperous of Russian industries. Its organisers had secured excellent results, which were very evident in Moscow, especially in the cotton industry. But from the Communist point of view its distribution was bad, since it sacrificed the interests of the regions producing raw materials to those of the manufacturing centre. Hence, in this as in other branches, a great effort at dispersion has been witnessed. Certainly, by virtue of its former primacy the centre largely keeps its lead with its 170 mills, its 3 million spindles, and its hundreds of thousands of workmen; but spinning and weaving have sprung up in the producing areas, some of which (Transcaucasia, Armenia, Turkistan, and Siberia) are in very remote regions.

The cotton industry keeps an indisputable preponderance. Of long standing in the Moscow area, the modernised textile industry enthusiastically took to cotton, which gradually invaded the whole country, especially the east and north. Kalinin is one of the main centres. Others are Yaroslavl, which weaves various kinds of cloth, and Kostroma, which contains a large number of spinning mills. But the industry flourishes mainly between the Volga and the Klyazma at Shuya, Serpukhovo, Orekhovo-Zuyevo, and above all at Ivanovo. In all, the Moscow area yields more than 75 per cent. of the national production.

The Leningrad area was established well before the Revolution and is much smaller, furnishing only 6 per cent. of the national output. But today many other centres have appeared and have even surpassed the original cotton towns. Tashkent is now at the head of production, but there are others in the Ukraine; in Siberia, where Barnaul is supplied by the Turksib Railway with raw cotton from Turkistan; in central Asia, where besides Tashkent there are the cotton towns of Ashkabad, Fergana, Stalinabad, Leninabad, and Chardzhou; in Transcaucasia at Kirovabad and Leninakan; and in Georgia, Ciscaucasia, etc. Though the output of the former centre has increased absolutely, it has decreased relatively, since the percentage of the other regions has constantly increased at its expense. The number of spindles and looms produced in 1928 was 66 and 3700 respectively. By 1955 production had risen to 1990 spindles and 16,000 looms. The 1913 output was overtaken by 1931, but progress has been slow and irregular. There were setbacks from 1932 to 1935 and again, owing to the war, from 1941 to 1948. Since then the rate of progress has improved, and in 1955 the output of cotton fabrics amounted to 5904 million metres.

The woollen industry is in an even worse condition. It was never very strong in Russia. In 1937 it produced only 118 million yards of cloth, which was hardly more than in 1928 and was far short of the target of 240 million yards. The quantities of wool and cotton judged necessary in 1932 were not produced, whilst the population increased continually. Since the end of the war, however, production has doubled, and in 1955 had risen to 275 million yards of woollen fabrics.

The silk industry is still undeveloped. However, throwing and weaving mills have been added in central Asia and Transcaucasia to the old manufactures of the centre in Moscow and Vladimir. In 1939 about 77 million yards of material were produced, but this was increased by 1955 to 575 million yards.

Lastly, linen manufacture, which formerly flourished at Kostroma, Kazan, Ivanovo, and Moscow, and was later ruined by the revolution, has revived at Ivanovo and even more in the west in White Russia. In 1939 it produced about 860 million yards of cloth, and its future seems assured, though since that date no further figures have been given.

Nevertheless, the prosperity of the textile industries has been

FIG. 28. DISTRIBUTION OF INDUSTRY.

rather deceptive on the whole. They have made some progress in the *Okrainy*, where raw materials are produced, but are far from meeting the normal requirements of the country. Severe privation has been the consequence of this. The same is true of the manufacture of ready-made clothing, linen underwear, and knitted goods, which are still in very short supply. It would, therefore, be unfair not to take note of progress in these industries. Between 1928 and 1937 the output of clothes increased sixfold and knitted goods eightfold. The manufacture of fashionable clothes began again in 1935, and, though the factories are particularly numerous and busy in the Moscow and Leningrad areas, they occur in large numbers in distant places, notably in Tiflis and throughout Transcaucasia. These are large-scale undertakings with great numbers of workers and by no means little artisans' workshops.

The leather and fur industries may be classed with the textiles. The former, which has also seen the multiplication and spread of large enterprises, flourishes especially in the Ukraine, its ancient home, but nowadays also in the Kirov district, the Kalmuk republic, and the south-east (Azerbaidzhan), where skins are to be had. The output of shoes amounted to 38 million pairs in 1928 and was nearly 200 million pairs in 1939. This was a great increase, but quite inadequate, and the output was increased to 274 million pairs by 1955. As for the fur trade, which is carried on mainly in the Kazan and Kirov districts, it is clearly prosperous. Formerly, many Russian furs were exported raw and returned from abroad made up. Today, the Soviet Union more and more works up its own furs and even imports hides from Australia for tanning.

The food industry has clearly made more progress than the textile. As its raw materials are plentiful, it is expanding a little everywhere, specialising according to the agricultural produce of the various regions. Thus, flour-milling is prosperous in the Ukraine, the Crimea, the middle Volga, the Kursk district, and now also in the Moscow area. Bashkiria, western Siberia, Kazakstan, Transcaucasia, and the Far East, with 198 mills in all; and oil works flourish in the Ukraine, the district of Voronezh, Ciscaucasia, Kazakstan, and western Siberia. Butter (200,000 tons) and cheese (35,000 tons) are made in south-western Siberia and in the dairying district of north Russia (Vologda and Kineshma). Distillery and starch-making are carried on in the great potato-producing regions, and pork butchery of the American type in the west, where pigs are abundant. Lastly, the canning industry has expanded enormously. In 1937 the output consisted of 873 million cans, and a target of 2000 million was aimed at in 1942. Canned meat is produced in Kazakstan (Semipalatinsk), Orsk, Burmongolia (Ulan Ude); canned vegetables in Dagestan; and finally and above all, canned fish. There are as many factories as there are fishing *kolkhozy*, and their chief centres are Sakhalin (which itself has twenty-three factories), Vladivostok, Nikolayevsk, Okhotsk, Archangel, Murmansk, Zhdanov, Taganrog, Rostov, Astrakhan, and Chapayev. But others are continually coming into being even on the Anadyr, and the third five-year plan, which aimed at a substantial increase in the food industries, attached special importance to canned fish. This concerns not only man, but also the Arctic dogs, which are recommended to be fed as much as possible on biscuits made of fish waste. The industrial preparation of these began in 1934.

Appreciable progress has also been made in the timber industry. In modern times it produces not only furniture but also plywood, cellulose, artificial silk, and paper. Its traditional home is in the forest lands of the north and north-west of Russia, that is, the Archangel

The little port of Petropavlovsk in Kamchatka

Yalta and the Crimean coastline

Moscow. The River Moskva, with a modern block of flats on the right and the Kre in the background

The River Neva and the Port of Leningrad

district, Karelia (where is situated the Kondopoy cellulose-paper *kombinat*), and the districts of Olonets and Chudskoye; but it is also very prosperous in the Urals (where the Kostroma *kombinat* is situated) and in the pre-Uralian district (where Kirov has the largest European factory of school furniture). And now it is finding a footing in the *Okrainy*, where it at once assumes the most modern form; for instance, the timber-cellulose-paper *kombinats* at Bzyb in Abkhasia (Caucasus), at Krasnoyarsk in central Siberia, and at Igarka in Arctic Siberia, not to mention the great sawmills at Stalinabad in Tadzhikistan. The paper industry deserves special mention. It was formerly established in the north-west, because it imported its raw material from Germany and Finland; but now it flourishes mainly in North Russia, the Urals, and Siberia. But the output is still small: 830,000 tons in 1937. It was to have exceeded 1,200,000 tons in 1942.

The chemical industry brings us to the great success of the Soviet Government. Under the Tsars this industry existed at the ports only, where it used foreign raw materials; and, besides, it was so insignificant that it can be said to have been entirely the creation of the Soviets. Here, too, recourse has been had to the system of *kombinats* not only in the Moscow area, where the Stalinogorsk works produce synthetic ammonia and nitric acid and the Voskresensk works superphosphates, but also in the Urals, where the Berezniki *kombinat* produces synthetic ammonia, soda, and various acids, in Kazakstan, where the Aktyubinsk *kombinat* treats phosphorites. Concentration has been avoided, as usual, and the chemical industry is carried on at Kirovsk right away on the Kolski peninsula just as it is on the shores of the Gulf of Karabogaz on the Caspian. But obviously the industry has, nevertheless, preferred to be near coal, as in the Ukraine and the Kuzbass, at other times near copper, as in the Urals, or apatite, as in the Kolski peninsula, or sulphur (Turkmenistan) or phosphorus (Moscow area) or potassium (Solikamsk) or, lastly, vegetable raw materials, as in the chemical wood *kombinats* in the north. Aniline dyes and pharmaceutical products are prepared, but the three main specialities are the manufacture of artificial manure, of which Kirovsk and the Chvichikstroy factory in central Asia are the chief centres; the manufacture of rayon and *fibro*; and, lastly, synthetic rubber, or *sovpren*, which is made at Yaroslavl, Voronezh, and Dzhefremov, 52,000 tons having been the output for 1938. The Soviet Union uses twice as much of the last material as of natural rubber. The raw materials, which are chiefly alcohol derived from potatoes or cereals, are plentiful. As a whole, progress is good, and everything pointed to an acceleration during the third five-year plan; but the advance has been slight compared with the progress in metallurgy.

In heavy metallurgy hundreds of new enterprises have been formed, and the output of pig iron and steel has increased astonishingly. Since 1931 the Soviet Union has been making more pig iron than Great Britain; in 1935, with its 12 million tons of pig iron and its 12·5 million tons of steel, it ranked next after the United States and Germany. In 1936 its output of pig iron and steel rose to 14 and 16 million tons respectively, which was higher than the German output; in 1940 it rose again to 14·479 and 18·4 million tons respectively; and in 1941 to 18 and 22 million tons, and in 1955 to 33 and 45 million tons respectively. The process used is the Siemans-Martin open-hearth process, 369 Martin furnaces producing 85 per cent. of the total output. Bessemer steel represents only 10 per cent., and steel made by the Gilchrist-Thomas ('basic Bessemer') process is almost negligible. Equipment has been augmented from 69 blast furnaces in 1928 to 120 in 1938, 28 of them exceeding a volume of 1046 cu. yds. and 3 attaining to 1700 cu. yds. The average daily output of pig iron was 540 tons from the blast furnaces against 364 in Germany and 560 in the United States. Generally speaking, the Soviet iron industry is characterised by the remoteness of the blast furnaces from the coal-fields, which is clearly a disadvantage. However, this remoteness is not so great as to make the burden of cost price unbearable. There are today three great centres of production of pig iron and steel:

(1) The Ukraine, which includes the Donbass and the iron of Krivoyrog. The quasi-monopoly it once had no longer exists, but it still holds nearly half the blast furnaces and produces close on 49 per cent. of the pig iron and 36 per cent. of the steel. A good number of long-established factories are situated on the coal-field more than 300 miles from the ore. However, there is an enormous plant in Krivoyrog itself. The famous Dzherdzhinski works is on the Dnepr at Zaparozhstal, and on the shores of the Sea of Azov there are two large-scale plants, one at Kerch and the other at Zhdanov.

(2) The Urals, an old metallurgical region, still exhibit certain obsolete characteristics. They contained most of the 36 little charcoal-burning blast furnaces in use in 1937. But a great effort at modernisation has been made, and numerous factories have been built or completely renovated at Zlatoust, Verkhne Isetsk, Nadedzhinskoye, Chusovoy, and, above all, at Nizhni Tagil. The most spectacular creation, however, is that of Magnitogorsk, which has 4 gigantic blast furnaces and is regarded as the world's second iron-producing district. In all, the Urals provide 20 per cent. of the Russian output of pig iron, 8 per cent. coming from the Sverdlovsk district and 12 from Chelyabinsk. Like the Ukraine, it has a good many steel-works and rolling mills in addition to its blast furnaces. Its share of the output of steel is about the same as that of its output of pig iron and seems, moreover, destined to expand.

(3) The Altai has a large output, based on the rich Kuzbass coal-field and on the railway communication with Magnitogorsk, pending the time when the iron deposits of the Altai are worked. Here stands the famous Ural-Kuznetsk *kombinat*. Iron from the Urals is transported 1200 miles from the place where it is raised, a fact that does not lessen its cost of production. Yet the Kuznetsk district, like that of Magnitogorsk, is one of the great objects of Soviet pride. It is covered with iron-works, of which the one in Kuznetsk itself is the largest, and it produces at least 8 per cent. of the national output of pig iron and steel.

But the activity in these three main areas does not represent all the iron metallurgy in the Soviet Union. A centre has come into being in the Leningrad area, and now the Moscow area has one with thirteen blast furnaces, large workshops in Moscow, Voronezh, Tambov, and Tula, steel-works many of which are independent, and an output of pig iron and steel representing 4·6 and 13·9 per cent. respectively of the total from the Soviet Union. Transcaucasia in its turn is entering the industry with the great works at Dashkesan, and the Bureya district in eastern Siberia is preparing to follow with an output of pig iron which should amount to about 600,000 tons per annum.

On the whole, it may well be that the heavy metallurgical industry has some defects, viz. slowness in constructing new material, and lack of skill in the workers, who cause frequent breakdowns, damage, and loss. The output appears very moderate, and M. Pardé notes that in 1936 the Soviet Union 'produced with 285,000 workers (24,000 of whom were at Magnitogorsk) just under one-third of the pig iron and steel produced in the United States by 420,000 workers'. The Union has nevertheless gained second place in world output, and proof that the industry satisfies the national needs is given by the fact that the five-year plans have authorised a great slowing-down of its expansion.

Manufactures using iron and steel have of course greatly benefited by the development of the heavy metallurgical industry. Under the Tsars it was very backward; to such a degree, in fact, that most machine tools had to come from abroad; and it was restricted to the Leningrad and Moscow areas and a part of the Ukraine. The first five-year plan, which aimed especially at increasing the means of production, paid particular attention to the manufacture of machinery, owing to the growing threat of war. The second plan continued in this path more perhaps than might have been desired. Nevertheless, other branches of this industry also expanded.

The districts in which iron and steel manufactures are produced are far more numerous and more evenly distributed than formerly. They are often located near blast furnaces and steel-works, but even more so near big towns, where there are reserves of labour and many consumers. The chief centre is still in the Moscow area, with Moscow, Kalinin, Bryansk, Gorky, and Tula; but the Ukraine, with Kharkov, Kiev, Voroshilovgrad, Kramatorsk, and Dnepropetrovsk, is scarcely less active. Between them they make more than 50 per cent. of the output. But now there are many other centres, viz. the Urals, with Chelyabinsk (where there is a large tractor factory) and Nizhni Tagil; the middle Volga, with Kuybyshev, Saratov, and Stalingrad; Transcaucasia; and the south-west of Siberia.

The manufacture of machinery destined for the heavy industry maintains a fair output. It is located around Moscow and Leningrad; at Kiev, Sumy, Kramatorsk, and Gorlovka in the Ukraine; at Grozny, Tiflis, and Baku in Caucasia; at Ufa, Chelyabinsk, and Sverdlovsk in the Urals; at Kuybyshev on the Volga; and at Omsk, Novosibirsk, and Irkutsk in Siberia. In 1956 there were 1,760,000 metal-cutting machine tools and 365,000 units of forging and pressing equipment.

Another main branch of the industry was the manufacture of building materials and railway equipment, including framing, metal bridges, sluice valves, girders, turntables, rails, trucks, and locomotives. The production of railway material has its chief seat in the Moscow area and is also carried on near the iron mines in Russia.

The output of locomotives rose from 654 in 1913 to 1700 in 1938. No information has been given of more recent production. Production is firmly established in Moscow, Bryansk, Gorky, Sormovo, Kharkov, Novocherkask, Orsk, and Kolomna, which specialises in petrol-burning locomotives for waterless regions; at Koshira, which like Kolomna and the 'Dynamo' shops in Moscow, construct electrical locomotives; at Rostov-on-Don, Kuznetsk, and, above all, at Voroshilovgrad, whose annual output of 1080 units nearly equals that of the Baldwin Company of Philadelphia. No other country manufactures as much, and the needs of the nation would be completely met but for the rapid deterioration of the goods. The same is more or less true of the waggons built, as locomotives are, at Bryansk, Sormovo, and Novocherkask, but also at Bezhitsa, Dneprodzerzhinsk, Kalinin, Zhdanov, Poltava, Tiza, Voronezh, Leningrad, Sverdlovsk, Nizhni Tagil, Irkutsk, and Udinsk. Production has risen to 76,000 a year.

The manufacture of farm machinery has been an equally striking success. It is carried on mainly in the Black Sea belt and the steppes, with the Leningrad and Moscow areas playing only a secondary part. Strangely enough, the Red Pontilov factory at Leningrad gave Russia the first tractors in Soviet times, but as a whole the factories in the centre and west situated at Liubertsi near Moscow, at Tula, Orel,

Voronezh, and Gomel, have obsolete works which were marked down for modernisation before the war, but were destroyed in the fighting and have since been rebuilt. On the other hand, the south and east of the Russian Black Earth country is covered with new factories at Kharkov (heavy caterpillar tractors), Kiev, Odessa, Kherson, Krivoyrog, Dnepropetrovsk (farm machinery), Zaporozhye, Rostov-on-Don (where the enormous Roselmash proudly stands), Stalingrad (formerly called Tsaritsyn—heavy tractors and machinery), and Saratov (combined harvesters). Chelyabinsk at the gateway into Siberia supplies tractors and machinery to western Siberia, Kazakstan, and the Far East. In Turkistan there is the Tashselmash factory at Tashkent; hence the region manufactures its own cotton-ginning machinery. Already the output is enormous and in 1956 consisted of

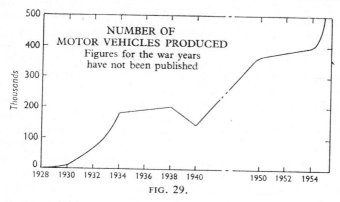

NUMBER OF
MOTOR VEHICLES PRODUCED
Figures for the war years
have not been published

FIG. 29.

163,000 tractors, 282,000 harvesters, large ploughs, grubbers, cotton gins, and innumerable little machines. The Union does not seem to boast when it claims to have equalled the United States in this industry.

A very great, but hitherto less successful, effort has been made in the motor industry. The condition of the roads and the absence of individual wealth are unfavourable to the manufacture of private cars. All the same, there has been great development. In 1929, when manufacture began, the output was 2000 vehicles; in 1932 it had risen to 26,800, and in 1937 to about 200,000, of which 188,000 were lorries. In 1942 it was planned to turn out 300,000 lorries and 110,000 cars a year, but in actual fact in 1937 there were only 449,000 lorries and 65,000 cars on the road, which were very small numbers. This limited stock wore out quickly and was repaired with difficulty. Anyhow, the manufacture of motor-car parts has been undertaken on a large scale at Kuznetsk, Kuybyshev, Ufa; and coach-building at

Stalingrad and especially at Gorky, Yaroslavl, Kalinin, and Moscow. The Molotov factory at Gorky is reputed to be the most extensive in Europe and the third five-year plan envisaged further developments in it and its satellites at Sormovo and Moron Pavlovo. In 1937 the Stalin factory in Moscow had 65,000 workers. It produced 55,000 lorries and 4000 cars and was to have had satellites attached to it. The factory at Yaroslavl was of similar size. Since the end of the war there has been great expansion in production, and in 1955 the number of lorries produced amounted to 329,000.

With the manufacture of motor vehicles may be associated that of aircraft, which is said to occupy more than a hundred factories. Production figures are not available, but it seems established at least that Soviet commercial aviation is as good as any in the world.

The extraordinary development of electric power demanded a corresponding expansion in the manufacture of electrical goods, and this has not failed to come about. At Leningrad, Bryansk, Ufa, Sverdlovsk, Tokmak near the Black Sea, and especially at Moscow the manufacture of motors, turbines, and electrical apparatus has experienced a remarkable development. In 1955 the generation of electric power totalled 23,000 million kWh.

Finally, shipbuilding has awakened after a long sleep. Perm, Rybinsk, Gorky, and various little Tatar towns build river boats, whilst the shipyards at Leningrad, Nikolayev, Sebastopol, Astrakhan, Vladivostok, and Komsomolsk construct seagoing vessels. The tonnage launched in 1937 amounted to 1,281,000. But since the end of the war in 1945 the shipbuilding industry has been greatly expanded, and Russia's naval and merchant marines have been vastly enlarged. It is said that a submarine warship is being built which will be driven by atomic power.

In short, the effort expended for the benefit of the metallurgical industry in its various forms has had impressive results. The quantity of products may certainly leave much to be desired in many cases, and costs may be extravagant; but these are faults which better organisation may hope to lessen gradually.[1] The fact remains that the metallurgical industry of the Soviet Union, which a short while ago was very backward, is now almost unrivalled. For accuracy's sake mention should be made of the aluminium industry which has just sprung up in the Kolski peninsula and which is rapidly developing at Zaporozhye in a *kombinat* modelled on the Dneproges; of the manufacture of tin goods, which is carried on mainly in Burmongolia,

---

[1] According to M. Lecerf, an eye-witness, 'nowhere else have the worship of incompetence and the dislike of responsibility been carried so far as in Russia. In the mines, for instance, any number of engineers can be found for surface and office work, but scarcely any for work below ground.'

where the Sherlovo Gorsky *kombinat* handles 45 per cent. of the tin in the Soviet Union; of the copper industry, which is organised at Kounradski and in the Kalkashstroy in Kazakstan and which will be greatly furthered by the proximity of the Karaganda coal-field.

It is scarcely necessary to stress the fact that the general rise of industrialisation and urbanisation has caused an extraordinary expansion of the building trades. The output of cement has risen from 2 million tons in 1928 to 22 million tons in 1955, and in the same year the various industries connected with building used more than 6 per cent. of the output.

Nothing has been said of the many industries which make accessories, like clocks and watches, scientific apparatus, cameras and photographic materials, gramophones, musical instruments, and wireless equipment. These industries were for the most part due to the second five-year plan and were located preferably in the Leningrad and Moscow areas, where more than anywhere else skilled labour was to be had. The output is inadequate, but is gradually improving in quantity and quality. The list of main consumer goods to be available by 1960 includes washing machines, vacuum cleaners, refrigerators, television sets, and bicycles.

Thus, a real industrial revolution is in full swing. In the Union industry has increased both on the surface and below. The number of workers in industry alone represents 8·5 per cent. of the population, and 31 per cent. of the total labour force of the Soviet Union. Though in the past Soviet statistics have been accused of exaggeration, Russia's known achievements lead one to believe that they are fairly accurate.

Certainly, many little businesses exist; that is, businesses in which not more than thirty persons and no machinery are employed. But since 1938 *kustar* industry has disappeared, and all industry is carried on either by the State or co-operatives. At least during the first two five-year plans the tendency was towards the ultra-modern and gigantic, like the factories at Kramatorsk and Voroshilovgrad.

But besides this, great changes have come about in the distribution of industries. Formerly, they were confined almost entirely to the centre and the Ukraine in Russia, and the 'possessions' served as sources of raw materials and as outlets. The Communist Government has aimed at a more reasonable distribution together with the disappearance of the inferiority of the *Okrainy*. By a 'phenomenal expansion' (Allix), due to geography as much as or more than to politics or strategy, industry has constantly spread towards the south and east, has flooded Asia far and wide, and has imposed itself on peoples who but yesterday were still nomadic and almost in a state of barbarism. Furthermore, instead of restricting itself to the towns, as it did formerly, manufacturing industry readily establishes itself in country districts, and many factories have been so placed. Notwithstanding Marxian doctrine, an effort has been made to avoid congestion in the larger towns. To distribute production better and to give the non-Russian peoples an economic foundation for their political independence, the factories have been carefully scattered, many being located outside the main centres and indeed outside the great traditional regions of industry. Certainly, there are still some great industrial regions—and very big ones too—such as the Moscow and Leningrad areas, south-eastern Ukraine, and the central and southern Urals, to which may be added the much more recent northern fringe of the Altai. But in the intervals between them large industrial centres have grown up at places like Stalingrad, Saratov, and Kuybyshev. In this way production is diffused throughout the territory and has increased relatively faster in the *Okrainy* than in the metropolitan districts. Industry holds an increasingly important place in the countryside and is found on the fringes of the burning desert as well as in the Arctic wastes, at Balkhashstroy as at Kirovsk.

It should not be concluded from this development that all is going very well. The commodities produced are often poor in quality and in addition are very dear. Hence, they are unlikely to tempt the foreign buyer. But this the masters of the Soviet Union have hitherto declared to be of small importance, since they have been interested solely in the home market. On the other hand, consumer goods have not succeeded in increasing at the same rate as the means of production, and light industries are far from having expanded as much as heavy industry. Commodities in everyday use, which were formerly supplied mainly by *kustar* industry, are in shorter supply than anything else. Hence, in spite of recent improvement, the people lack many things which are regarded as necessities in the West. According to Mr. Molotov, just before the war everyone could have 17·5 yds. of cotton cloth, 6·5 ft. of woollen cloth, a pair of shoes, 11 lbs. of paper, 6·5 lbs. of soap, 31 lbs. of sugar, 8 lbs. of preserves, and five tins of canned food a year. This was no longer the severe restriction of the first five-year plan, which resembled war-time rationing; but was still an extremely modest standard of living. No similar figures of rationing have been published recently, but the *U.S.S.R. Economy* states that 'by 1954, State retail prices had been reduced to a level 2·3 times below that of 1947; foods were 2·6 times below that level and manufactured goods 1·9 times'. The price of clothing fell only 15 points between 1947 and 1954, but clearly the people were much better off than they had been.

The harmonious development of industry demands good communications. It is not enough for the Soviet Union to have varied and abundant wealth. It must also be possible for places in situations remote from the exploitation of that wealth and from the working up of the raw materials to profit by their existence. This is a difficult problem, since the country is so vast. A consideration of the geography of the Union always comes back to the central idea of the enormous distances involved, and the incompletely mastered vastness of the country is just what too often hinders the efforts at economic restoration. Want of space forbids a description of the postal system. Before 1917 the Empire had scarcely 12,000 post offices, most of which were situated in towns, and only 3 per cent. of the population had their letters delivered at their homes. After 1932 the percentage rose to 90. Similarly, the problem of communications has taken a long stride forward since the invention of wireless. Sending and relay stations are counted by tens, receiving stations by hundreds; and, in spite of the general poverty, there were more than 2 million wireless sets in 1939, and the Union had 67 broadcasting and 6860 relay stations. Broadcasts are made in about sixty languages. Wireless communication certainly has a particularly brilliant future in this country owing to its immense area and the dispersion of its inhabitants. Even now a training in the use of wireless telegraphy is held in great respect. Besides, there exist 335,000 miles of telegraph and telephone lines. The most serious defects are to be found in the transport system.

CHAPTER 14

TRANSPORT AND COMMERCE

1. PRESENT INADEQUACY OF TRANSPORT

The problem of transport is all the more important because in Siberia and Turkistan, and indeed in Russia, there are between the favoured regions in which wealth and power are concentrated very large belts of uncultivated land almost devoid of population. The existence of these empty belts makes communication difficult and increases the expense of building and exploiting the main lines. The same difficulty is encountered in the desert crossings in the west of the United States. Furthermore, the establishment of communications is often rendered difficult by the climate, soil, vegetation, and at times even by the relief. Apart from the lofty ranges of the periphery, central and eastern Siberia have, owing to the rejuvenation of the relief, steep gradients, deep valleys, and narrow gorges, which require a number of bridges and tunnels and compel much grade-making. It is noticeable as a rule that, though Siberia has big rivers flowing from south to north, there is no natural route connecting the west with the east and that once the Yenisey is reached, travel becomes very difficult across the wooded heights. This fact has greatly lowered the value of the central and Far Eastern regions.

Transport, which is a serious matter at all times, has become more important than ever since the great task of 'socialist reconstruction' was undertaken. Formerly, whilst foreign relations had endowed the west with a fairly close-meshed transport system, the economic opposition between the metropolis and the *Okrainy* had given rise to a centralised network of communications which mainly consisted of routes connecting the former to the latter; e.g. the Trans-Siberian and Trans-Aralian railways. Later, during the first five-year plan the various regions began to be specialised economically. Thenceforth they were obliged to be able to exchange their products directly, and hence the construction of arteries like the 'Turksib' railway. The recent industrialisation of the remoter regions has given them fresh needs which have called for the construction of a system of local routes. Hence, the railway joining the iron-mines in the Urals to the coal-field in the Altai, or the copper-mines near Lake Balkhash to the coal-field at Karaganda. These local systems are one day to be 'connected to the centre by main federal routes'. When the dispersal of industry is sufficiently advanced, the carriage of heavy goods to great distances will be less necessary than today. The Government has long been aware of the extreme gravity of the transport problem. Hence the many efforts to solve it. But the task, which is of overwhelming dimensions, is sometimes very difficult, at least as regards the roads.

(a) *The Road System.* Indeed it is very difficult to maintain good roads. The extremely violent rainstorms and especially the two *rasputitsy* and the severity of the frost in winter damage them terribly. Besides, as there is little road-metal in most parts of the plains, the construction of a proper carriage-way demands the transport of enormous quantities of material over long distances and involves an exorbitant cost. The expense is all the harder to bear because, owing to the low density of population, the villages are often far apart. It is natural that there should be some hesitation to construct, and then to maintain at high cost, immensely long roads on which the traffic will necessarily be small. Geology, climate, and the distribution of population combine to impose on the Union a road system which is as inadequate as dilapidated. In 1914 the roads were a disgrace to the empire. With few exceptions, the highways were broken by potholes which were filled with water or mud and jolted

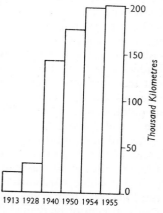

LENGTH OF
HARD-SURFACE MOTOR ROADS
FIG. 30.

the carriages so much that after a journey of several hours the first thing offered to the exhausted and battered traveller was a bed. A landowner who lived three or four miles from a *chossé* was considered fortunate. Local roads in the country districts were merely tracks in which vehicles sank to the axles during a thaw. Overland transport was busy only in winter when the trodden snow formed a hard surface. In autumn and even more in spring a journey by *tarantass* involved real danger. Furthermore, the road system in the time of the Tsars had a mileage of barely 18,000. This means that the road mileage was, relatively to area and population, one-hundredth that of western Europe. The carriage roads, which were the only ones at all comfortable, still had a mileage of less than 7000, and the 'government' of Moscow, which was the most amply provided, had only some $4\frac{1}{2}$ miles in 40 square miles. In those days there were only about 10,000 motor-cars in Russia.

Of course, the situation merely grew worse during the revolution. In the time of the New Economic Policy it became rather better. In 1928 the Union had 20,000 miles of metalled or cobbled highways and 5600 miles of 'improved' roads. But the real effort began with the first five-year plan. Between 1928 and 1932 nearly 60,000 miles of new roads were constructed, more than 7000 miles being metalled. Whilst in 1929 only 2500 miles were made, the figure rose to 20,000 in 1933. At the end of this year there were 117,000 cars in the Union.

Local roads built at the expense of various federal republics and by the labour of peasants[1] gave satisfaction as a rule, especially in Chuvashia, a country which, though formerly almost inaccessible, had some 500 miles of carriage road in 1933. The trunk roads, on the other hand, which were paid for by the Union, gave rise to much criticism on the score that their 'gradients were badly planned, the bridges unsound, the construction defective, and the work carried out too hurriedly'. Yet the plan was far from being completed. Besides, as the maintenance service was miserably equipped, it wholly abandoned some 25,000 miles of road and did next to nothing for the rest of the system.

Accordingly, the second five-year plan had to follow up the work energetically. On the eve of the German War of 1939 there were 150,000 miles of all-season motor roads,[2] but only 40,000 miles were provided with a hard surface. Progress was still inadequate, and the third five-year plan envisaged the construction of a great many more roads. It cannot be denied that a creditable piece of work has been accomplished not only in Russia, where, for instance, arterial roads have been constructed between Moscow and Minsk and Moscow and Kiev, but also in Siberia, where similar roads have been made from Yakutsk through Aldan to Irkutsk and from the same centre to the ports of Ayan and Magadan on the Sea of Okhotsk. Caucasia, where the road from Dagestan to Georgia 'passes through a district of broken relief in which the dialects of the mountain folk do not even contain a word denoting a carriage road' (A. Pierre); and

[1] In 1934, for example, 'the average task of each rural area was fixed at 600 metres (656 yds.) of road construction and 4 kilometres ($2\frac{1}{2}$ miles) of maintenance, the individual labour representing only six days a year' (A. Pierre).

[2] Theoretically, the system had 850,000 miles of road; but 700,000 miles of these 'roads' consisted of little more than tracks metalled here and there.

central Asia, where, for instance, roads have been constructed from Osh through Pishpek to Tashkent, from Stalinabad through Ura to Tiubé, from Krasnovodsk in Turkmenistan to Kunye-Urgench, and above all the road from Osh to Khorog, 435 miles long, which climbs the Pamirs and rises to a height of 15,000 ft. above sea level. But the present road system, quite incomplete and badly maintained as it is, remains lamentably inferior to requirements, which have greatly increased since 1928. Hence, except on a very few trunk roads, highways played only the modest part of feeders to the railway, and the 700,000 cars and lorries which passed over them were not able to carry more than 2 per cent. of the goods to be transported.

The third five-year plan flattered itself that it could triple the number of motor vehicles and train 2 million drivers, a programme which logically implied the construction of many new roads and the energetic improvement of the existing system. But the work was interrupted by the German invasion. The war, however, had demonstrated the need for good roads, and strenuous efforts were made to search for road metal among the Quaternary rocks (alluvium, moraines, scree) and to construct all-weather motor roads joining the main towns. By 1958 the length of such roads was 210,000 miles, and the quantity of goods carried by lorry amounted to 3730 million tons. This was 12·3 per cent. of the goods carried by all forms of transport.

(b) *Waterways.* These are clearly better than the roads. Some rivers, like the Dnepr, can be pointed at as having rapids and all may be decried for being frozen over for five months, for having enormous floods in spring and low water in summer, for being full of dangerous pieces of drifting ice at the beginning of spring and autumn, and, in short, for being navigable on only 150 to 200 days in the year. But, as has been seen above, they have some excellent qualities: adequate depth, a usually fortunate course, and in particular an extremely gentle gradient. The services rendered by them in the past are well known. Today, in spite of the evolution of technique, they are still able to play an important part, and it is quite easily possible to travel by water from Astrakhan to Leningrad and Archangel.

The Volga is the lynch pin of this magnificent system of natural waterways which has a length of nearly 70,000 miles and is even longer, if canals are included in the reckoning. From this river branch out the various parts of the system connecting the Caspian linking of the river basins. Further connexion was necessary if the full value of the system was to be realised. Under the Tsars the Government understood this and bent itself to the task. Though it could not construct the Volga–Don Canal, it completed the Nicholas II

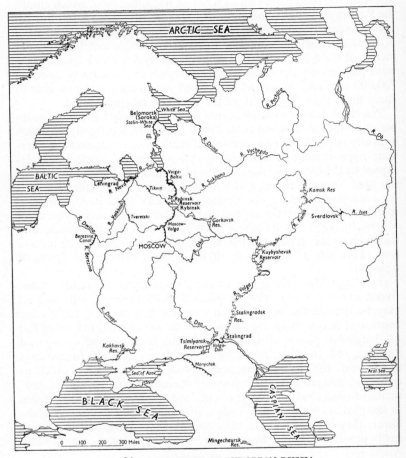

FIG. 31. WATERWAYS OF EUROPEAN RUSSIA.

Canal between the Ob and Yenisey and above all it created the Marinskaya system, now known as the Volga–Baltic Canal, in order to join the Volga to the Baltic. The system, from Leningrad to Rybinsk, measures 695 miles, of which 389 are in open rivers, 113 in canalised rivers, and 193 in canals. Its summit level is 400 ft. above the sea; it boasts 38 locks capable of admitting barges of 800 tons capacity, a length of 338 ft. and a draught of 6 ft. One after the other it uses the Neva, Lake Ladoga, the Svir, Lake Onega, the Marinskaya Canal proper, Lake Beloye, the Duke of Wurtemburg's Canal, and the Shexna, and thus connects Leningrad with Rybinsk on the Volga. Lastly, the Tikvin, which connects the Tikvinka, a feeder of the Sias, with a sub-tributary of the Volga, linked this great river with Lake Ladoga.

In spite of defects in the moorings and locks, the system as a whole does yeoman service. Vyshni Volochek, at the beginning of the Tveretski Canal, was one of the busiest river ports in the days of the Tsars. However, it was overtaken by Rybinsk, which in 1911 was the busiest of all, with an annual traffic of 1,800,000 tons weight. Similarly, Cherepovets on the Suda was a typical winter haven in which boats found shelter and defence from the break-up of the ice.

But from Siberia to the Ukraine many other rivers carried a great deal of traffic. Chief among them was the Volga–Kama. As early as 1820 a steamboat service ran between Astrakhan and Nizhni Novgorod (Gorky), and in 1914 fast, well-appointed passenger boats plied along it. But above all, the river carried upstream many lighters, boats, and barges laden with salt, wheat, fish, fruit, and petroleum. Downstream went timber rafts 1700 ft. long and 330 ft. wide, formed of *bieliany*,[1] large river-boats nearly 350 ft. long, close on 70 ft. wide, drawing 14 ft., and capable of carrying nearly 7000 tons of wood, as well as between one and four *izby* intended for sale on arrival as dwelling-houses.

The revolution and the civil war completely disorganised river traffic. Hence, the days of the five-year plans witnessed a serious attempt to restore this activity too. Efforts were directed at repairing the boats, at the improvement of the chief river ports of Gorky, Rybinsk, Kuybyshev, Saratov, Astrakhan, Rostov, Kherson, Kiev, Leningrad, and Yaroslavl; and especially at the construction of new waterways, with the result that in 1955 the total mileage of the system was well over 70,000. This increase was due to the canalisation of many rivers, but also to the construction of several canals.

---

[1] As these are neither painted nor tarred, they are of a whitish colour, which explains the name. When their wood cargo is discharged, they are broken up and sold. Sometimes their materials are used for building boats for use on the Sea of Azov.

The Stalin, the Volga–Don, and the Volga–Moskva Canals deserve special mention.

The first, constructed in the record time of eighteen months by an army of political prisoners and convicts, has connected Leningrad with Soroka since 1933, linking the Baltic with the White Sea by way of the Neva, Lake Ladoga, the Svir, and Lake Onega. It is 140 miles long and has 18 locks, of which the one at Povienets allows boats to be raised 250 ft. Although its importance seems to be strategic rather than commercial, since 1933 it has transported 886,000 tons of cargo and 12,000 passengers.

The enthusiasm which this success caused accelerated the construction of the Volga–Moskva Canal, which was opened in July 1937. With a length of 79 miles, a breadth of 177 ft., a depth of 18 ft., and capable of taking vessels of 10,000 tons displacement and a draught of 15 ft., it starts from Ivankovo, enters the gigantic reservoir at Ucha, approaches Moscow from the east, and feeds its conduits with one branch, whilst the other passes through a five-stage lock and reaches the Moskva in the region of the Sukina marshes above the town. In another direction the removal of the rapids of the Dnepr by means of the famous dam has opened the lower course of the river to regular navigation. The Marinskaya system and the old Berezina Canal have both been renovated, thus improving the links between the Volga and Baltic and the Dvina and Dnepr. These works are the beginning of an immense enterprise, viz. the 'Five Sea Ship Canal System', linking up the five Russian seas: the Arctic, White, Baltic, Black, and Caspian. The project involves in particular the construction of a Volga–Don canal. The second five-year plan hoped to carry out this work, but the desire to associate its execution with the general treatment of the great river and with the irrigation of the Volga steppes prolonged the preliminary studies by several years. Eventually the canal was opened in 1936. Water has been supplied by damming the Don at Kalach and is renewed by four reservoirs along the course of the canal.

On the whole, there has certainly been an improvement. Besides a large passenger traffic of more than 80 million travellers, especially on the Volga, Kama, and the Siberian rivers, nearly 140 million tons of freight, two-thirds of it wood, was shipped in 1955; and the traffic on the inland waterways amounted to 67 billion ton-miles as compared with 29 million in 1913. But these impressive figures represented only 3 per cent. of the total traffic and the Government wants it to be far greater. There are complaints of the inadequacy of the equipment, which is often old and worn out; of the labour, which, according to Mr. Molotov, wasted half its working hours between 1937 and 1938; and of poor co-operation between the railways and the waterways. Hence, it may be gathered that the organisation of the inland navigation system is bad and falls far short of what it might be. This conclusion may well be accepted without erring too greatly on the side of optimism. Consequently, much remains to be done, and far more in Siberia than in Russia. It is true that in the former country the uselessness of the rivers in winter is seriously prolonged by boundless floods. Besides, these rivers flow into the Arctic Sea. Hence, though they are of great use locally, they will not have any important general value unless navigation in that area is organised in a really practical manner. In central Asia the part played by waterways is necessarily small; but, curiously enough, the oasis of Khorezn in Uzbekistan was reached only by way of the Oxus as late as 1934.[1]

(c) *Railways.* Owing to the cruel inadequacy of the waterways and roads, the railways play a leading part in transport. Of course, the length and severity of the winters, the relatively heavy snowfall, and the frozen ground impose some tricky problems on the engineers; so do the high temperatures in Turkistan, the crossing of more or less shifting sands or vast swamps, and also the obstacle presented by immense forests. The extreme scarcity of road metal, which makes the use of ballast difficult, was an added handicap. On the other hand, the almost general flatness of the relief is a major advantage, as few constructive works are needed and building costs are very light. Although the first Russian railway, constructed in 1833 in the Demidov workshops at Nizhni Tagil in the Urals, was intended for the transport of ore, the system as a whole is known to have been based mainly on political and military considerations. Hence, the replacement of the normal 4 ft. 8½ ins., gauge by the unusual 5 ft. gauge, whose adoption aimed at isolating conservative Russia from progressive Europe as well as at hindering possible invasions. Hence too, the centralised character of the system, whose focus, owing to geographical conditions, was, however, not Leningrad, but Moscow. In 1914 the mileage was 41,600. This was much less than the mileage of British railways, though the area of the Soviet Union is more than seventy times that of our islands. Most of the lines were of course in Russia. A series of them radiated from the natural capital, thirteen of them connecting with foreign railway systems, and others running towards the north and south coasts or to the Asiatic possessions.[1] But there were also some important cross-country lines; e.g. Leningrad – Vologda – Kirov – Perm – Sverdlovsk, Smolensk – Tula – Penza–Kuybyshev–Ufa–Chelyabinsk, Kiev–Kharkov–Penza, Leningrad–

[1] The following may be mentioned as examples: Moscow–Leningrad, Moscow–Riga, Moscow–Kovno (–Konigsberg), Moscow–Minsk (–Warsaw–Berlin), Moscow–Kiev (–Lvov), Moscow–Odessa, Moscow–Orel–Kursk–Kharkov–Sebastopol, Moscow–Voronezh–Rostov-on-Don, Moscow–Astrakhan, Moscow–Ryazan–Kuybyshev–Chkalov, Moscow–Gorky-Archangel.

Vilna–Warsaw. The last dying effort of the Tsarist Government was
to build the Leningrad–Murmansk line during the 1914 war, in spite
of terrible difficulties, of which the severity of the climate was the
least. In certain sections it was necessary to sink 15 cub. yds. of
gravel in each yard of line in order to consolidate the surface.

The rest of the system in the time of the Tsars comprised four main
lines. In spite of its name, the Trans-Caucasian did not cross the range,
but ran from Baku to Batum through Tiflis. In central Asia Annenkov
housed 1500 soldiers in an immense train and used them to build
the Trans-Caspian Railway in order to overcome distance and sub-
due the Turkomans. This line, which was started as early as 1880 from
Krasnovodsk on the Caspian, crossed the barren, shifting sands of
the Kara Kum by mighty efforts, leaped over the Oxus, and reached
Andidzhan in 1882. In 1898 and 1916 the anxiety of the Russians
over Afghanistan and India led them to build branch lines from
Merv to Kushka and from Burkhara to Termez. A little later the
Chkalov–Tashkent line, which was completed in 1905, became 'the
cotton railway'. These railways in Turkistan have called for some
fine constructive work. The bridge over the Ilek on the Chkalov–
Tashkent line, for instance, is more than 650 yds. long.

Above all, there was in Siberia the Trans-Siberian, whose construction was being urged by Muraviov as early as 1857 and was
begun in 1891. In spite of great difficulties, including the breadth
of the rivers in the west, the absence of coal for the engines, and the
need to bore wells, sometimes through the *merzlota*, in order to get
water, it advanced at an average speed of 370 miles a year, and, by
the end of 1904 the main line ran from Chelyabinsk to Vladivostok,
a distance of 4268 miles. It was an imposing work, though it had only
a single track and, as it was too hastily built, it permitted a speed
of only 18 miles an hour. Thus, trains took ten days to complete the
journey from terminus to terminus. But the line had had imposing
results. These were, of course, not seen in its competition with the
Suez Canal, whose takings it affected in a very slight degree; or in
military matters either, for it could not prevent the catastrophe of
1905. Yet it has played a very important part in forwarding colonisation and exploitation. So well did the Tsar's Government understand the function of the railway in the opening up of Siberia that,
after the mutilation caused by defeat at the hands of Japan, they
hastened to construct a new line in Russian territory and did not
cease from their endeavours to complete it until they had constructed,
first, the Trans-Baykalian line, and then the Chinese Eastern Railway
and the Amur Railway.

But on the whole this system was far from meeting needs. Its
general plan, according to the revolutionaries, reflected only too

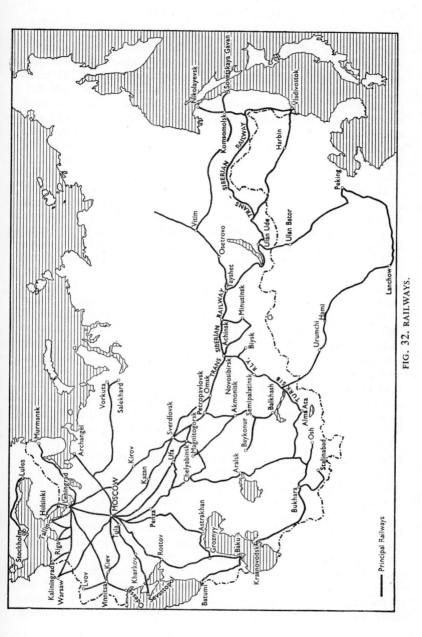

FIG. 32. RAILWAYS.

Principal Railways

191

clearly the colonial nature of the *Okrainy* and the parasitic part played, in their opinion, by the metropolis. The strain of the German War of 1914 followed by the destruction and disorders of the civil war caused frightful damage. More than a quarter of the 35,000 miles to which the railway system was reduced by defeat had been destroyed; more than 12,000 miles of rails, 7500 bridges, and hundreds of stations had to be remade; and 62 per cent. of the engines and one-third of the carriages and trucks were unserviceable. Hence, the volume of goods carried fell in 1921 to one-quarter of what it had been in 1913 and the number of passengers was little more than one-third.

The period of the 'New Economic Policy' witnessed an undeniable recovery. Not only were the ruins rebuilt, but a number of new little lines were also constructed, and by October 1928 the mileage rose to 47,000 without attracting public attention, however, by any great spectacular achievement. The first five-year plan could not set out a vast programme of industrialisation without trying at the same time to face requirements by an immense effort at railway construction. It envisaged increasing the mileage of the system to nearly 58,000; but in fact, by 1938 it had not raised it above 51,000. Russia benefited by some new lines, viz. the Kazan–Sverdlovsk, Saratov–Millerovo, and Donbass–Krivoyrog; but the greatest efforts had been devoted to the backward eastern republics and led to the construction of the lines from Troitsk to Orsk and from Akmolinsk to Karaganda and, above all, the famous Turksib (Turkistan–Siberia) Railway. The plan of this last had been studied in detail in the time of the Tsars, construction was begun even before 1928 and finished in 1930 with rather too much haste, and speeds suffer accordingly. It is 900 miles long and carries fruit, vegetables, wine, and cotton from Turkistan to Siberia by way of Semiriechye and Semipalatinsk, and cereals, hay, timber, hides, and metals from Siberia to Turkistan. In addition to this progress, the number of locomotives rose from 16,500 to 19,500 and that of carriages and trucks from 450,000 to 550,000.

Still, these figures were very small. The rolling stock had to be greatly overworked for the number of passengers to exceed 967 million in 1932,[1] and the goods traffic to rise to 104,000 million ton-miles.[2] All the same the railways remained unable to fulfil their tasks. The ballast was mostly sand, the sleepers often rotten, the rails too light or very worn, the locomotive generally weak because it had been badly serviced, the carriages and trucks were small and old-fashioned, very few modern switch-points existed, very few trains were fitted with automatic brakes and couplings, the signal system

[1] There were 248 million in 1913 and 291 million in 1928.
[2] In 1928 there were 52 million ton-miles.

was primitive and rudimentary, and the employees were too few and untrained as well as lacking in professional pride. This was the explanation of the slowness of the trains given by Commissar Andreyev. The average speed per hour of a goods train was less than 9 miles, and, when the endless halts of the trains are reckoned, the goods carried moved at about the rate of a pedestrian. But in spite of this slowness, there were frequent derailments and collisions, uncertainty on the time-tables, congestion, accumulation, and loss at depots of goods not sent on because of a shortage of trucks. In 1933 only 52,000 a day were loaded, though to fulfil the plan between 60,000 and 62,000 should have been freighted. Harsh penalties, which went as far as capital punishment, were meted out in vain to those responsible. The inadequacy of the railways handicapped the whole economic system.

Consequently, the second five-year plan aimed at another vigorous effort and decided to make an almost threefold increase in railway transport. First and foremost, traffic conditions were improved by adding to or renovating the rolling-stock and permanent way and by the introduction among the employees of the *Stakhanovist* spirit, in this case called *Krivonossist*. Progress was very slow, and the working did not clearly become better until 1937 onwards. Then nearly 7000 miles of new lines had been constructed, of which the most important was the one from Moscow through Valuyki to Donbass (742 miles), double tracked and capable of taking thirty trains a day each way; one from Magnitogorsk to Stalinsk; one from Karaganda to Lake Balkhash; and one from Lake Baykal to the Amur. But many others might be mentioned.[1] Lastly, a number of single-track railways have been double-tracked; e.g. Penza–Syzran, Syzran–Ruzayevka, Ufa–Kizel, and especially the Trans-Siberian, which it is hoped will one day have four tracks. Besides, many lines have been electrified; notably those connecting the Donbass with Krivoyrog, Stalingrad, Rostov, and Kharkov.

The results of the second five-year plan were therefore appreciable, but better was wanted. Consequently, the third five-year plan decided to build 12,000 new passenger coaches, 178,000 new trucks, and 7370 new locomotives; to electrify close on 1200 miles more; to double 5000 miles of track; and, finally, to construct a further 7000 miles of line.

In Russia a railway was built from Kotlas to the Vorkuta coalfield in one direction and to Leningrad in the other. Another line from Soroka runs to Plesets so as to join the line from Kirovsk to

[1] Novosibirsk–Kolchughvro, serving the Kuzbass; in the Urals region Kirov–Perm–Sverdlovsk; Sverdlovsk–Kurgan, Sverdlovsk–Sarapol, Sverdlovsk–Bogdanovichi, etc.

that to the Far North, whilst a third now goes from Ufa to Kazan to connect the southern Urals with the centre of Russia. In the Caucasus and Caspian regions railways now almost encircle the Caspian Sea. One line passes along the Caucasian shores of the Black Sea, a branch serving the Araks valley and joining the Trans-Caucasian to reach Baku. It was planned to extend this line to meet the Trans-Iranian Railway, but political circumstances have so far prevented the extension. Chelyabinsk is now connected with the Emba coal-field by a line which passes through Orsk and joins the Chkalov–Tashkent Railway at Kandagach. In Siberia the B.A.M. (or Baykal–Amur) branches off the Trans-Siberian at Tayshet a few miles east of Krasnoyarsk and, after serving the Bureya valley, reaches Komsomolsk, whence it continues to Sovietskaya Gavan on the coast of the Gulf of Tartary. To ease the much congested Trans-Siberian the B.A.M. is to be projected westwards from Ust-Kut through Boguchany and Abalakovo to north Russia, where it is to connect with Moscow and Archangel. This will give the great industrial development around Bratsk a separate connexion with Moscow on the one hand and the Pacific ports on the other. The new line will join the Trans-Siberian by means of a branch from Abalakovo to Achinsk, which is to continue through Minussinsk and run parallel to the Mongolian frontier to Slyudyanka on Lake Baykal, where coal and iron have been found. From Ulan Ude on the east side of Lake Baykal a line has been built through Kyakta, Ulan Bator, and Kalgan to Peking, where it joins the Chinese system and gives the Soviet Union an open-water port at Tientsin. A further junction with the Chinese system has been achieved by a line from Sergiopol through Urumchi and Hami to Lanchow.

Thus, real progress has been made. In 1955 the system had 74,998 miles of line, of which more than 1200 were electrified, a third of the lines were double tracked, and 10 per cent. equipped with automatic signalling. It could now carry 90 per cent. of the goods. In 1955 it carried 560 million tons of goods and 1,641,400,000 passengers. Although the traffic towards the metropolis is increasing still, the improvement in the railway system is appreciable in the *Okrainy*, where old and new modes of transport sometimes exist side by side in a very curious way. In Kazakstan, for instance, the train and the aircraft are found with the camel caravan. But the railway system is still far from complete, since it has 7 miles of line to every 1000 square miles of surface or eleven times less than in the United States. Its ill-assorted equipment is in general very worn, for only a small percentage of the equipment in use, can be renovated in any year. So the equipment is frightfully overworked. Every mile of line must carry nearly 5 million ton-miles, or nearly three times more than in the United States, four times more than in Germany, and ten times

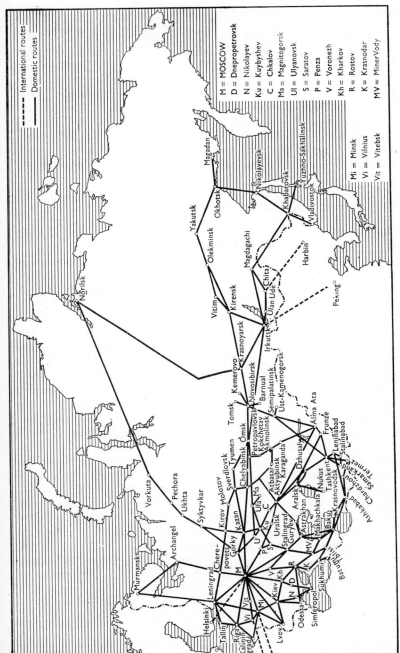

FIG. 33. AIRWAYS.

International routes
Domestic routes

M = MOSCOW
D = Dnepropetrovsk
N = Nikolayev
Ku = Kuybyshev
C = Chkalov
Ma = Magnitogorsk
Ul = Ulyanovsk
S = Saratov
P = Penza
V = Voronezh
Kh = Kharkov
R = Rostov
K = Krasnodar
MV = MinerVody

Mi = Minsk
Vi = Vilnius
Vit = Vitebsk

more than in France; and 8 million passengers, as compared with 1 million in Germany and 140,000 in the United States. It is therefore inevitable that the trains should be slow, efficiency at a general low level, and complaints ceaseless. Certainly, great efforts will be needed for some time yet, since new centres of population are being formed in many regions. The railways cannot indeed reach perfection until the distribution of population has been stabilised. Furthermore, they are now faced with serious competition from the roads. Whereas in 1928 they carried 91·1 per cent. of the total traffic and the roads carried none, in 1955 their share had fallen to 83·1, whilst that of the roads had risen to 13·3 per cent.

(d) *Airways.* Though the efforts of the Soviet Government have been especially directed to the railways, the development of civil aviation at the same time was a necessity in this gigantic country. Here, as in the vast solitudes of America and Africa, the aircraft has often preceded the train and even the motor vehicle, notably in the Far North of Siberia and the deserts of Turkistan. Alone, or almost so, with the help of wireless, it enabled the central government to keep permanent control of certain remote territories.

The Tsarist Government had, of course, no time to organise the system. But as early as 1922 three organisations were formed, two of which aimed at establishing regular air lines without the assistance of the Deruluft and the German Lufthansa, which had previously been indispensable. The third, the Osoaviakhim, which soon had several million members, aimed at encouraging the chemical industry and the construction of aircraft. Soon the new mode of locomotion aroused a passionate enthusiasm in young people and attracted many of them into aviation. In 1929 the various Soviet commercial air lines were amalgamated into a single corporation, the Dobroflot, which became the Aeroflot in 1932. Progress was very rapid. In 1937 more than 200,000 workmen were occupied in seventy-two aircraft factories, and some 1000 aircraft were in service on civil routes. The system, which was the longest in the world, had a mileage of 65,000. Russia had some of the main routes; e.g. Moscow–Leningrad, Moscow–Minsk, Archangel–Syktyvkar, Moscow–Kaunas–Berlin, Moscow–Kiev–Prague, Moscow–Stalingrad–Astrakhan. But the most important linked Moscow with Caucasia via Kharkov, Rostov, Baku, and Tiflis (1879 miles), with a branch to Kiev, Odessa, Zhdanov, Krasnovodsk; and with central Asia via Sverdlovsk, Petropavlovsk, Karaganda, and Alma Ata (2298 miles) and via Kuybyshev, Chkalov, and Tashkent (1894 miles), with branches to Kabul and Urumchi; and, lastly, with Siberia via Sverdlovsk, Novosibirsk, Irkutsk, Khabarovsk, and Vladivostok (5092 miles), with branches to Salekhard, Yakutsk, Bodaybo, Ulan Bator, Komsomolsk, and Petropavlovsk.

In 1939 more than 49,000 tons of freight, mainly postal, and 200,000 passengers travelled on the system. By 1955 the freight carried had increased more than ten times and the number of passengers had risen more than seven times.

Of course, in the past equipment and organisation left much to be desired: the airports were generally poor, the ground-lighting and night-lighting were inadequate, the repair shops badly equipped, the time-tables largely disregarded, and speeds slow. This state of things still exists away from the chief airports, which are well equipped and as good as those in the West.

In few countries is aviation as important as in the Soviet Union owing to the vast distances to be covered and the serious natural obstacles to surface transport. The maintenance of weather stations on the islands and north coast as well as other posts in the vast empty spaces of Siberia is made possible by the use of aircraft. But the aircraft is not restricted to maintaining communications. By sprinkling and powdering it combats parasites, malaria, and wood-destroying insects; it reports forest fires; in an hour it sows 50 to 75 acres with seed; and, lastly and most important, it has achieved magnificent work of geographical exploration in the Far North and in the northeast or Siberia.

(e) *Ocean Navigation.* Natural conditions are indeed unfavourable to maritime activity. As we have seen, the coasts are undeveloped and generally poor or even bad, and they are washed by seas which are landlocked or frozen for much of the year. The Soviet Union is pre-eminently a continental country and has little seafaring instinct. Even though the Russians have played a very honourable part in exploring the oceans and in particular the Arctic waters, it must be admitted that really seafaring communities are rare in the country. Only those dwelling on the shores of the White Sea deserve the epithet. Hence, it may well be imagined that Russian ocean navigation was very modest in 1913, in spite of the efforts of the Tsar to create and develop Murmansk, the sea-walls of which were begun in February 1915, and the foundation of the town was settled in October 1916. Owing to the civil war and the blockade, maritime activity fell away to nothing after the first German War in 1914–17.

In spite of the harm due to the loss of the Baltic ports, and especially Riga, seafaring recovered by degrees. All the shipping companies, except the Dobroflot, were amalgamated in a single *Sovtorgflot* with its headquarters in Moscow. This controlled the shipping lines in the Black Sea and those running from Leningrad to Hamburg, Stettin, Bremen, and Le Havre, and from Novorossisk to Odessa, Genoa, and Marseille. Of course, coastal traffic was reserved to the Soviet flag, and the central freight council had the monopoly of chartering foreign vessels. By 1940 the total amount of Soviet freight carried by sea (31·2 million tons) was rather more than double the 1913 figures (15·1 million tons). At the end of the fifth five-year plan it had risen to 53·7 million tons. According to Lloyd's Register of Shipping Soviet ocean-going tonnage in 1956 consisted of 3668 ships (1931 steamers and 1737 motor vessels) of a total gross tonnage of 2·64 million tons. This took eleventh place in the list of the world's shipping. Since then the tonnage has risen by $2\frac{3}{4}$ million tons, and the sixth five-year plan aims at adding to the Soviet merchant fleet more than $1\frac{1}{2}$ million tons of new vessels, including dry-cargo ships, tankers, and liners. How far Russian shipyards are capable of producing these new additions is not known. So far a good many of the new ships have been built abroad, mainly in Poland and East Germany, but also in Britain, France, Belgium, and Western Germany and have been intended mainly for domestic purposes: ice-breakers, trawlers, and fish-factory vessels. However, the launching of a nuclear-powered ship, the ice-breaker *Lenin*, is evidence of a high degree of shipbuilding knowledge and skill.

In spite of the unfavourable character of the coastline, there are a good number of very busy ports which have recently benefited by large additions and modernisation. First come the timber ports: Leningrad, with six miles of wharves, more than sixty landing stages, very modern equipment, a ship canal which takes ocean-going vessels right into the port, a whole system of railways, immense oil tanks and a pumping station, and numerous cold-storage establishments; Riga, which was a very busy port in 1939, in spite of being separated by a frontier from Soviet territory, and which is rising from its ruins and resuming its connexion with its backland in order to become once more the main outlet for the whole of western Russia, as it was before 1914; Archangel, at the mouth of the Dvina on a relatively busy sea; and, lastly, Murmansk, situated on ice-free water, an essential strategic port, but also a regional commercial outlet, a large exporter of timber and phosphates as well as a port-of-call on the north-eastern route. Mention should be made of Soroka, the little port at the White Sea end of the Stalin Canal, which may one day become a serious rival of Archangel. Then come the Black Sea ports, through which are exported wheat, petroleum, and half-finished or manufactured goods; Odessa, a deep-water port, which is nearly alway ice-free, well sheltered and well equipped with elevators, cold storage, warehouses, and transporter-bridges; Kherson, on a lagoon near the Dnepr; Sevastopol in the Crimea, a superb naval and commercial port with deep-water docks; Tuapse and Batum, two petroleum ports with very modern equipment; Novorossisk at the outlet of the Caucasian wheat lands; Rostov-on-Don, a river port accessible to large cargo boats and seemingly with good prospects for the future; and Zhdanov, which exports coal from the Donets. On the Caspian stands the very large petroleum port of Baku. Lastly, on the Pacific, Vladivostok, the terminus of the Trans-Siberian Railway, is ice-free on an average for 110 days in the year, but is kept open continuously by ice-breakers. Nikolayevsk and Komsomolsk on the Amur are handicapped by the bar at the mouth of the river. Close relations with China have given the Soviet Union free use of its former port of Dalny at the terminus of the Chinese Eastern Railway, and the line from Ulan Ude to Peking gives a second warm-water port at Tientsin, whilst that from Sergiopol to Lanchow opens the possibility of shipments through Shanghai and Canton.

On the whole, therefore, there has been in this department a considerable recovery. This appears very clearly in the Suez Canal traffic, where the share of the Soviet flag is increasing. It rose from 21,600 tons in 1920 to 333,000 tons in 1928, and to 1,547,000 tons in 1934. In 1938 90 per cent. of Soviet foreign trade went by sea. However, though the third five-year plan announced the creation of a fleet of ocean-going vessels, it did not give the impression that the problem of merchant shipping greatly interested those in control. Mr. Molotov scarcely mentioned it in March 1939, when outlining the main features of the plan. In fact, from the point of view of shipping, only one matter seems really to stir them, viz. the Arctic route.

Towards the end of the rule of the Tsars the Government had thought of attacking the problem, as they were invited to do by the lessons of the Russo-Japanese War. Their attempts at establishing sea communications between Russia and Siberia did not go beyond the Yenisey, but a great deal of useful information had been gathered, from which the Soviet Government afterwards profited. In 1923 it resumed the effort, which had scarcely begun, and it was partly to serve as a base for this that they equipped and developed the port of Murmansk. But the passage through the central and eastern seas of the Arctic coast, which are not warmed by the North Atlantic Drift, proved extraordinarily difficult. While the Arctic Institute in Leningrad toiled, the Siberian *Komseveroput* actively studied the possibilities of the 'Northern Sea Route'.

In 1932 the great effort began with the establishment of *Glavsevmorput*, or Chief Administration of the Northern Sea Route. A network of meteorological stations was established along the coast of the islands and mainland of the Far North. These now number one hundred, no fewer than eight being on the Chuckchee peninsula. A powerful fleet of ice-breakers was put into service, and a large number of aircraft were kept for reconnaisance flights over the Arctic

Sea. A hydrographic service was set up to chart the seas and maintain lights and buoys. These measures, which progressively grew in effectiveness, culminated in 1954, when the High Latitude Air Expedition established two drifting stations on the sea ice of the Arctic Sea and sent parties of scientists in aircraft over much of the central Arctic. The avowed object of the project was to discover the water and air circulation in order to improve ice forecasting on the Northern Sea Route. As a result of measures thus taken and of long research by the Arctic Institute the *Sibiriakov*, which left Archangel on July 28, 1932, under command of Professor Schmidt, was able to reach Bering Strait on October 1 of the same year.

Whilst the Soviet authorities no doubt have a strategical motive, they also have in view the economic development of the great northern wastes of their territory and the exploitation of the boundless forests of Siberia. So far timber, felled in these vast forests and floated down the Ob and Yenisey, has been the chief commodity carried on this route. In 1938 forty-five ships loaded cargoes of timber at Igarka on the Yenisey, a port which had grown from almost nothing in 1927 to a town of 20,000 people in 1939. Besides this traffic there was a good deal more from Salekhard on the Ob and from other little ports reached from either the Atlantic or Pacific. Most of the timber shipments were destined for the United Kingdom.

There have been set-backs, of course. In 1933 the *Chelyuskin* was crushed by ice, and in 1937 twenty-six ships were caught in the ice and held for the winter, two being lost. But success gradually came. Before 1926 the Northern Sea Route had never seen more than five ships in one season. In 1928 there were eight, and in 1930 there were fifty. In 1936 more than one hundred ships sailed on various parts of the Route. In 1937–8 three steamers from the west and two from the east did the return trip between Murmansk or Archangel and Kamchatka, and the freight, which from 1876 to 1919 had not amounted in all to 5400 tons, rose during the period 1933–8 to 1,169,000 tons. In 1939 a group of four dredgers and four tugs sailed from the Atlantic to the Pacific. They were helped at difficult places by icebreakers, but had no escort all the way. In 1940 the ice-breaker *Josif Stalin* made the first voyage from Atlantic to Pacific and back again in the same season. Now it is a mere routine matter for ships under Soviet control to go wherever they like along the whole length of the Route. This great achievement has been due to better forecasting of ice conditions and better traffic arrangements. But the success is precarious, for a very small change in climatic conditions might make the ice impassable and block the whole traffic.

The attention of the Soviet Government has hitherto been concentrated on internal affairs, and the merchant fleet and shipbuilding capacity have been largely neglected. Hence Russia, which has made herself a leader among the nations, finds herself with a small and somewhat antiquated mercantile marine. Now that she has apparently decided to undertake world-wide trade expansion, it would seem that a great increase in her maritime activities will be necessary and that for this purpose her merchant fleet should be greatly augmented.

2. FOREIGN TRADE A STATE MONOPOLY

Though most of the frontiers of the Soviet Union are land frontiers, it would be wrong to think that most of its foreign trade is overland. On the contrary, its overland traffic represents only 10 per cent. of the total. The truth is that the foreign trade in the past was small. In 1913 its value of 2899·1 million gold roubles scarcely amounted to one-fifth of that of the United Kingdom. Forced to sell a great deal to pay the interest on its heavy debts, the Russia of that time exported large quantities of wheat, flour, butter, eggs, timber, and flax (value 1520 million gold roubles); its imports consisted chiefly of cotton, wool, rubber, and machinery (value 1374 million gold roubles). That is, as a new country it sold foodstuffs and raw materials to buy mainly manufactured goods. Trade was principally with Germany, England, the Netherlands, France, and Italy. The war, the revolution, and the financial blockade, during which foreign stock exchanges refused to deal in roubles, completely destroyed this trade.

Gradually, recovery was brought about with the help of the New Economic Policy. In 1926 it had risen again to 1,288,000 gold roubles, imports greatly predominating of course. But from the very first it became a State monopoly by the decrees of 1918 and 1920. Not that the Soviets meant to live in isolation, but they soon saw the need to harmonise the volume of foreign trade with the demands of national economy, and this principle was strengthened still more when the system of five-year plans proved successful. The Government then saw itself forced to create considerable wealth in order to pay for its enormous purchases.

Two main principles guided the organisation of foreign trade, viz. to import only strictly indispensable goods and to export as much as possible so as to balance the imports. Every year a plan of sales and purchases is drawn up and is revised every three months according to the activity of foreign and domestic markets. Quotas are fixed for exports. Once the needs of the people have been calculated, surplus agricultural and industrial produce is sold, and the foreign credits thus secured are used to procure for the Union commodities unobtainable in the country. Hence, the volume of imports is determined by the funds available in foreign currencies. However, the value of imports may exceed that of the exports if an unfavourable trade balance is covered by payments. When the quota is fixed, an allocation of goods to be bought is made to the various branches of industry. The needs of current operations are satisfied first, then the equipment needed for incipient enterprises is bought, and, lastly, goods for current consumption; as a matter of principle, no luxuries.

Exports as well as imports required licences from the Board of Trade, without whose signature no foreign business can be done. Sales and purchases are arranged through the trade representatives of the Soviet Union abroad. These are established on the same footing as private companies, act as agents for the Soviet Government, and are organised into specialist departments, each of which comprises various sections for the sale or purchase of different commodities, such as wheat, flax, timber, chemical products, electrical equipment, etc. Theoretically, this trade should be unaffected by movements in the world market; but, in fact, the Union's economic independence of the 'capitalist' countries is clearly less than is often stated in Moscow. Consideration of the very marked fluctuations in this trade proves that it is influenced by economic and political factors, one or the other set predominating according to the countries and circumstances, and that external events have an evident reaction on its course. It is clear, for instance, that the Union is almost helpless in face of a fall in prices in the international market.

During the first five-year plan foreign trade greatly expanded, since the policy of industrialisation required large imports of raw materials and machinery, the latter being 89·1 per cent. of the total of 1932, and, in exchange, there were huge exports of wheat, timber petroleum, furs, and flax. In 1930 imports totalled more than' 1069 million gold roubles and exports more than 1002 million. These transactions were not always accomplished without difficulty. As the Soviet Union was often forced to accept short-term credits and high prices, it had frequent recourse to barter and to dealings which curiously resembled dumping. Between 1928 and 1932 the Union's foreign purchases exceeded a value of 1850 million roubles, which at the official rate of exchange was equivalent to £732 million. In 1956 trade with the United Kingdom amounted to a value of £81 million.

It has been rightly emphasised that during the first year of the world depression Soviet trade still increased slightly. In 1930 it had risen 16·1 per cent. over the figure for 1929, whilst world trade had fallen by 11·4 per cent. But from 1932 Soviet trade also declined, though more slowly than that in other countries. In 1933 the fall reached 53·2 per cent. compared with one of 57·4 in world trade, and exports fell to 496 million roubles, imports to 348 million. This decline was caused by the world depression, by general over-production, and the consequent fall in prices. It came on too soon to suit the Soviet Government, whose exports were extremely restricted by it. But the exports declined less than the imports, and, whilst in 1930, 1931, and 1932 the balance of trade was unfavourable to the Soviet Union, after 1933 it left a considerable margin. A huge cut in imports had been made by the Soviet Government.

This arose, firstly, from the fact that, as the Union had contracted enormous debts and, as its balance of trade was very unfavourable, amounting to 294 million roubles in 1931, everyone feared that the debt would not be paid. The Soviet Government weathered this stormy cape only by imposing Draconian restrictions on the people and by energetically increasing the quantity of gold mined. Furthermore, the success of the five-year plan permitted the suppression of a few of the imports and a reduction in the quantity of many others, at the same time as it increased certain exports. Finally, about 1935, the purchase of equipment had greatly decreased owing to the progress of industrialisation; sales tended to recover; and, as trade relations with foreign countries assumed a more normal character and was conducted with less suspicion, the Soviet Union was regularly granted credits for five years at least and at 5 per cent. at most. The balance of trade remained favourable till 1939, when imports, though much inferior in volume to exports (1·1 million tons against 8·6 million), were of greater value (1,422,000 roubles against 1,331,000). But foreign trade remained small, since most of the domestic production could henceforth be kept for home consumption.

Besides, the trade has partly changed in character. Machinery and equipment still form the bulk of the imports with 33 per cent. of the total, and delicate apparatus and surgical and optical instruments are still obtained from abroad, though the standard of Soviet technical skill has greatly improved. But there is now a greater range of goods brought into the country, including raw materials (iron and steel, non-ferrous metals, and rubber), manufactured goods (ships, paper, chemicals, and the modern textiles of rayon and nylon), and food (sugar, fish). Imports of tropical fruit, rice, tea, coffee, and cocoa have increased.

The Soviet Union is still a primary producing country, and its exports consist mainly of raw materials. But though the exports of oil and timber are considerable, industrial progress has lessened the shipments of various raw materials in favour of finished or half-finished goods, like dressed and dyed furs, linen thread and tissue, tractors and other agricultural machinery, rails, iron alloys, and electrical apparatus. In 1957 more than 75 per cent. of Soviet exports consisted of industrial materials, especially petroleum, timber, coal, and base metals. Machinery and equipment formed 32 per cent. of the exports in 1946, and metals 15 per cent. The export of grain, which had ceased in 1917, has been resumed and in 1956 formed 10 per cent. of the total. Flax, oil products, and coal have been added to the list.

The Soviet Union cannot, therefore, be said to be in economic isolation. Indeed, in 1956 the value of its foreign trade amounted to £2320 million. But the fact remains that on the whole, whilst foreign trade occupies the best part of the activities of certain nations, like the English and Dutch, it represents merely an ancillary aspect of national life in the Soviet Union. But it is increasing, and of late the increase has risen. Between 1929 and 1939 the share of the Soviet Union in world trade was between 1·39 and 2 per cent. In 1956 this share rose to 10 per cent.

The bulk of Soviet trade has been, and still is, with neighbouring countries in Asia, viz. China, Turkey, Persia, Afghanistan, and Mongolia. But efforts have been made to extend commercial relations, and trade is now carried on with European countries, where, apart from the satellite States of Poland, East Germany, Czechoslovakia, Hungary, and Romania, the chief customers are Finland, the United Kingdom, France, Western Germany, and Yugoslavia. The Soviet Union imports fish from Iceland, Norway, and Sweden and exports oil to Iceland, 30 per cent. of whose trade it monopolises. Finland receives large quantities of sugar. Trade with the United Kingdom comprises (a) exports to Russia: sugar, iron, steel, machinery, and ships; (b) imports from Russia: timber, furs, and manganese ore. Outside Europe the only considerable imports from primary producing countries are sugar from Cuba and wheat from Canada; but there have been large exports of fuel, industrial materials, and machinery, including oil, to the United States. It has been thought that recent trends in Soviet trade have had a political rather than an economic motive. To more developed countries like Denmark or the Argentine oil and other goods are offered at undercut prices, whilst to backward countries economic aid is lavishly given. Whether there is a political motive or not, it is clear that Russia means to expand her trade and to challenge the commercial supremacy of Western Europe and North America. Meanwhile, to tie her European satellites more closely to her system the Soviet Union is building a pipe-line from Kuybyshev to Gomel in Belorussia, where it will bifurcate to carry crude oil to refineries in Poland and to Schwedt in East Germany in the north and to Hungary and Czechoslovakia in the south. A branch will reach the Baltic coast.

3. A PLANNED INTERNAL TRADE

The home market is, in fact, immense and is constantly expanding since the population is visibly growing. Now, its needs are normally far from being satisfied. If it is no longer true, as Farbman wrote in 1931, that '150 million persons are, so to speak, standing in a queue to be served', the standard of living is woefully low.

Domestic trade should be very busy owing to the surprising variety of the country's resources; but the vast distances and the inadequacy of the communications weigh heavily on it. In the time of the Tsars the producer could rarely deliver the goods directly to the consumer. There was a swarm of middlemen, peddling was extremely common, and fairs were very numerous. The last included those at Kharkov and Kiev, which were 'contract fairs'; that at Baku, which was a very important factor in relations with Persia; that of Irbit in Siberia, at which furs, leather, horsehair, honey, wax, butter, hemp, and flax were sold from February 15 till March 15; and, lastly and most important, that of Nizhne Novgorod (Gorky), which, owing to the admirable position of the town, was visited by 200,000 persons between August 1 and September 15 and did business valued at close on 180 million roubles in ore from the Urals, salt from the Kama valley, furs and leather from Siberia, fish from Astrakhan, oil, wine, and fruit from the Caucasus, wheat from the Volga area, sugar and tobacco from the Ukraine, cotton from Turkistan, and timber from the Far North.

Then came the war and revolution. The decline in production, the complete disorganisation of transport services, and an unskilful attempt at nationalisation ruined internal trade. In 1921 the New Economic Policy restored trade by private firms, and these continued to exist for a time. But the Soviet Government has constantly reduced the 'private sector' of trade in favour of the 'socialised sector' by overwhelming the former with taxes and developing the co-operative movement. In 1928 private firms dealt with 23·6 per cent. of the retail trade; in 1930 the percentage had fallen to 5·6. Since then private trading has disappeared. The fairs have been suppressed, and partnerships and individual firms of merchants have shut down. Private trade as it formerly existed has been strangled between co-operative and State trading.

It might be objected that private trade is reappearing under a new form, for the *kolkhoznik* has the right to sell in the *kolkhoz* markets the produce of his garden, his byre, and his poultry-yard; and this arrangement has greatly improved the feeding of the towns. But *kolkhoz* trade does not represent more than 11 per cent. of the internal trade. As a whole, internal trade is directed and controlled by the Commissariat for Internal Trade and Food Supply, which is furnished with commodities by the supply *kombinats* and supervises their distribution among the retail centres, fixing quotas of goods according to the state of the stocks and keeping demand steady by bringing purchasing power into harmony with the expansion of the supply of commodities. And this supply is shared out between the co-operative and State trades.

The former can scarcely be said to owe its existence to industrial and financial co-operatives, but rather to the agricultural and even more of consumers' associations which existed in the time of the Tsars and have since then wonderfully expanded. Local co-operative societies and regional unions extending over a republic or even the whole Soviet Union have ended by including almost the whole adult population. Formerly, they played an essential part in supplying food to the people, in spite of their shortcomings and defects; and the system of 'endless queues in front of half-empty shops' was widespread for many years. In 1955 co-operative shops did 31 per cent. of the retail trade, which means that 69 per cent. falls to the State trader; but the share of the co-operatives is slowly growing.

State trading works in three main ways. TRUSTS are sometimes wholesale and even retail dealers, but only within the limits of their own industry; and they therefore have specialised shops. SYNDICATES can also organise the retailing of their goods. Lastly, and most important, the TORGS, which are purely trading businesses, are at times restricted to dealing in a special branch, but at other times extend their activities to the general trade of a whole region. The big department stores called *univermag* are typical of these State shops.

The system has not worked smoothly. In the course of the first five-year plan it was found to be necessary to give more food to the most 'important classes of people', viz. manual workers, engineers, and town officials; and for them were reserved ration cards which gave to them alone access to State co-operative shops, where prices were far lower than in private stores. In the same way, 'restricted retailers' or 'Closed Distributing Centres' were reserved for certain persons or classes of persons favoured on account of their special usefulness; for instance, a prominent engineer or distinguished scholar. Besides, foreign engineers obtained provisions from *Insnab*, the All-Union office for supplies to foreigners, and its branches which were fairly well stocked. Lastly, there were the *Torgsin*, in which purchases were obliged to be paid for either in foreign bills of exchange or with gold. Altogether, there were no fewer than five sets of prices, and the result of this annoying complication was necessarily speculation and a rise in the cost of living.

The second five-year plan saw a slight improvement in the situation. Gradually the 'restricted retailers', the *Insnab*, and the *Torgsin* all disappeared, which improved the value of the rouble, and by degrees ration cards were abolished for food and for a number of different kinds of manufactured goods. However, the distribution of clothing, household requisites, and various other products of industry remained subject to a quota. These measures, which did not, as had been hoped, bring down the cost of living, marked a certain improvement in the food supply and corresponded to the end of an important stage towards a return to unrestricted trade.

But 'unrestricted trade' does not mean 'trade handed back to private enterprise'. Trade is planned as much as ever, or even more so, and the third five-year plan announced the intention of the Government to extend still further the system of State and co-operative retail trade. In this system, as in everything else, the organisation is decidedly of the collectivist form of socialism. It does not escape censure, but has been charged with innumerable instances of underhand dealing and 'leakage' which it is likely to encourage. The Soviet Government has tried to find a remedy for these abuses, but they are with difficulty avoided, especially in a time of reconstruction. In any case, it is not fair to stigmatise the system as a 'riot of bureaucracy'. P. George pertinently stresses the fact that 'the trade organisation of the whole Soviet Union has 2 million employees, that is, about as many as the system of distribution by private firms in France, which has to serve one-quarter of the number of consumers'.

Certainly, in spite of the precedent of Peter the Great, such an effort at complete change has never been known to have been effected in so short a time. And it is indisputable that already very great changes have been accomplished. Some of them immediately strike the traveller who can compare the Soviet Union with Russia in former days. Where he had seen obsolete ploughs drawn by a rawboned horse or an ox of skin and bones painfully scratching the soil, tractors whirr and buzz; and nearly all the countryside is cultivated by machinery. Regions which before were almost inaccessible are connected with the rest of the country by wireless, aircraft, and the advantages of fairly regular postal services. New roads and railways have been built; the number of motor vehicles and trains running has appreciably increased; and the airways are among the busiest in the world. Industrial plants have multiplied not only in, but also outside, the towns, and their capacity often rivals that of establishments in the United States.

The appearance of the towns has been modified. Today, they generally have an immense industrial quarter; then, beyond an open, green belt of gardens, promenades, and sports grounds are blocks of tenements. Lastly, there is the official quarter. And this has all been modernised in appearance. The towns have striven to look American and sometimes succeed in doing so by equipping themselves with tall buildings of ferro-concrete whose sameness is quite trans-Atlantic. 'The advent of this new building material has given Russia what she lacked—stone' (Massis). This is particularly true of the very large towns, like Leningrad and even more so Moscow, where in 1934 there were still 31,000 wooden houses out of a total of 51,000. Today new streets, avenues, and vistas have been made; the old 'Chinese' walls of the inner cities have been demolished; a number of historic buildings have been pulled down because they blocked traffic; schools, institutes, and libraries have been built. The Moskva now flows between granite embankments; vast factories have sprung up in the suburbs and near them new quarters for the work-people; lastly, the capital has been equipped with an underground railway which is the greatest pride of its citizens.

This change in appearance of the town has, moreover, been accompanied by an astonishing expansion, and one of the things that most strike the traveller is the vast quantity of scaffolding that he sees. The population of Moscow jumped from 2,029,000 in 1916 to 4,839,000 in 1956; Leningrad increased from 1,690,000 to 3,176,000; Gorky from 181,189 to 876,000; Ivanovo from 111,114 to 319,000; Yaroslavl from 112,103 to 374,000; Kalinin from 105,710 to 240,000; Sverdlovsk from 134,355 to 707,000; Novosibirsk from 120,000 to more than 731,000; Alma Ata from 45,000 to 330,000; Voroshilovgrad from 72,000 to 257,000; Tiflis from 279,565 to 625,000; Baku from 446,832 to 901,000; Kiev from 493,000 to 991,000; Kharkov from 409,000 to 877,000; Tashkent from 320,865 to 778,000; etc.

More than this. Where there were formerly wastes have sprung up dozens of towns whose wonderful expansion recalls that of the most remarkable American mushroom growths. One may perhaps ignore the case of Stalinogorsk, which from a tiny life-centre known as Bobriki has expanded today into a town of more than 100,000 inhabitants; or of Chelyabinsk, which has developed from a little local chief town into an industrial centre with a population of 612,000. But there are also Magnitogorsk with a population of 284,000, Zaporozhye with 381,000, Karaganda with 350,000, Kounradski near Lake Balkhash with 50,000, Stalinsk, Leninsk, Prokopevsk, and Kemerovo, all in the Kuzbass and with a united total of 966,000 inhabitants, not to mention Kramatorsk in the Ukraine, Gigantia in the steppes between the Volga and the Don, and Komsomolsk on the Amur. From 1932, the date of its foundation, to 1956 the population of Komsomolsk rose from 4000 to 169,000. In the course of the war the town was one of the chief centres for the 'recovery' of armour-plate derived from captured enemy material.

But this is not all. The countryside shows a visible trend towards urbanisation. Much has been said about the efforts made by villages in the Soviet Union to reach a satisfactory standard of hygiene. It is no less interesting to notice that, except in the forest regions where evolution is slower than elsewhere, dwellings tend to collect in little townships whose appearance is rather like that of a garden city. This is due to the economic and social transformation of the countryside. Uprooted as it were from their lands, the peasants gather in the centre of the collective farm at the point where stand the silos, elevators, storehouses, manure heaps, and machine sheds, the byres for the cattle of the *kolkhoz*, the school, the community house, the cinema, crèche, dispensary, bakery, co-operative stores, etc. 'Around these are arranged the dwelling houses either without any scheme or along the roads, each provided with its paddock and garden. . . . And beyond are the vast fields which are cultivated by machinery' (George). Thus, the village is becoming modernised and, thanks to mechanisation and collectivism, it is assuming a somewhat urban appearance.

Other changes which are less immediately noticeable fairly soon attract attention. The erection of factory canteens, central kitchens, and common wash-houses simplifies the life of the work people and especially that of the women workers with children, and lessens the poverty caused by the privations inherent in the carrying out of the five-year plans. Besides, the risk of unemployment has disappeared for the Soviet worker, who benefits from a whole system of social insurance and a pension in old age. The struggle to improve public health has met with great success. Epidemics have grown rarer, infant mortality less, and the number of hospitals, dispensaries, and crèches has increased considerably, as well as that of doctors. In 1955 the birth-rate was 25·6 per mil. and the death-rate had fallen from 30·2 in 1913 to 8·4. The number of doctors and dentists had increased from 28,000 to 334,000, whilst that of hospital beds had risen to 1,290,000.

The construction of innumerable sports grounds has helped to make the people stronger and healthier. But sport is not of the amateur or professional kind enjoyed in England as a means of recreation or amusement, but is classified politically and designed to produce worthy representatives in international competitions.[1]

Finally, education has made remarkable progress. No doubt certain regions like the Ukraine were already advanced in this respect in 1914, but others were lamentably behindhand. Anxious to increase the occupational value as well as the dignity of the workers by means

[1] Thomas Preston in the *Royal Central Asian Journal*, vol. 44, April 1957.

of education, and wishing above all to solve the difficult problem of training leaders as quickly as possible and with the help of purely Soviet teachers, the Government made great efforts to improve the system of education, which was made compulsory for ten years. Children go first to primary schools, from which they pass to seven-year schools. At the latter stage the best pupils are moved to a secondary school or a secondary technical school. In 1955 there were 30 million pupils in the primary and secondary schools and nearly 2 million in the secondary technical schools. Above this there is full provision for higher education with a strong scientific bias. In 1955 the number of students who qualified for the Candidate's Degree (equivalent to the second degree of English universities) was 7607. It is unlikely that so sudden an expansion of an education system should produce a high general standard of performance, yet Russian scientists who have visited English establishments have shown an undeniable high standard of knowledge. 'Russian students have little time or inclination for social life, their spare hours being occupied by musical entertainment, visits to museums, or sport.' [1]

The Soviet Union has also striven to give a minimum of education to those whose age prevented them from benefiting by the new secondary school system. Not content with abolishing illiteracy, it has established workers' universities, the *Rabfaky* (Faculties of workers), which were continued until 1941, when the 25,000 adult students were called up for the army. Since then the *Rabfaky* have not been re-established.

The number of public libraries was increased from 25,000 in 1913 to 172,000 in 1938 and to 266,000 in 1955. These contain 892 million books, which is more than four for every member of the population, and more than eight times the figure for Germany in 1934. This seems to confirm the noteworthy fact that the Russian working man is a great reader. Altogether, provision for public education absorbs nearly one-quarter of the total expenditure of the Union in peace time, a fact of which the State may well be proud.

We shall say little of the 825 theatres or of the 59,200 cinemas, although the Soviet Government sees in the cinema one of the most powerful means of spreading culture. But it may be noted that in 1955 there appeared 54,700 books in 111 languages, 2026 journals, and 7246 newspapers in 70 different tongues.

But geography is also interested in other results which, though they do not greatly catch the eye, yet stand for great changes. One of the most significant is the undeniable beginning of a flight from the country to the towns. In 1928 rural artisans and peasants num-bered 120 million persons, of whom 11 million were independent

[1] Thomas Preston in the *Royal Central Asian Journal*, vol. 44, April 1957.

peasants, 4,406,000 *kolkhozniki*, and 5 million agricultural workers. In 1955 there were only 113 million, even though this figure included the persons employed in the Motor Tractor Stations and the *sovkhozy*. Thus, the rural population has fallen from 76 to 56·5 per cent. of the total population.

The movement from country to town is not everywhere of the same intensity. It is far less pronounced in, for example, central Asia or the northern forests than in the Ukraine or on the middle Volga; but it is everywhere noticeable, and it has resulted in an enormous increase in the urban population. During the first five-year plan the percentage of this section of the population rose from 18 to 24. Between 1932 and 1939 it went up to 33, and in the latter year the Union reckoned 55,711,000 townsfolk against 26,314,000 in 1926. In 1955 it had risen to 43·5 million. This increase is explained partly by a high birth-rate, which though falling, still reaches the high figure of 35·6 per mil. But an even greater factor is the entry into the towns of countryfolk whose large numbers are beginning to worry some observers. Not only have the ancient towns grown surprisingly, but even places that were country villages in the census of 1926 have become towns, large or small, and many new centres have arisen through the agency of a special state organisation known as *Giprogor*.

These towns are not market towns, but merely industrial centres, for market towns have ceased to exist in the Soviet Union, where the new organisation of trade makes them useless. The growth of new foci, which is to be seen especially in the region of the Urals and in central Asia, proves that the economic and industrial centre of gravity of the Union has moved from the west towards the middle area, if not towards the east. Some people have disputed the importance of this phenomenon, arguing that only the Kuzbass and Karaganda are really large new industrial centres and that the economic centre of gravity of the country remains fixed in the heart of European Russia. But the fact is that industry has largely moved eastwards and that many secondary centres, which were in an embryonic stage in 1913, have developed not only in the Ukraine, but also along the Volga, along the Trans-Siberian Railway, and in the oases of Turkistan, not to mention the Urals and even the Far East.

Undoubtedly, this industrialisation of the middle area and east has caused considerable displacements of population. The urge to colonise is today less directed to Caucasia and Turkistan; but it is stronger than ever towards Siberia. The immigrants do not head for the Kuzbass alone, but also towards Burmongolia, Trans-Baykalia, and eastern Siberia, and this is especially true in some years. Whilst the population of the Soviet Union increased by 15 per cent. in twenty years, that of the regions across the Urals more than doubled, and Asia as a whole, which benefited by a good half of the total increase, saw its numbers rise by 30 per cent. But the distribution of population is still less uniform than in 1926. People tend to concentrate in a few great foci, viz. central Russia (with about 25 million persons), the Leningrad area (6·5 million), the Ukraine (with 40 million persons, who tend more and more towards the shores of the Sea of Azov), the Donbass, and the industrial centres of the Crimea (1,127,000), the middle Volga, the central and southern Urals (10 million), the Kuzbass (6 million), and the Amur region (4 million), not forgetting the islands of population along the Trans-Siberian Railway or the industrial centre of Kazakstan. It is remarkable that, apart from Transcaucasia and central Asia where the expansion is due to natural increase and occurs in town and country alike, the recently formed industrial zones are the regions of greatest development. In them the towns have grown at the expense of the countryside, and even of very distant areas.

Thus, the gigantic mixture of peoples, which is necessary under the new economic system and which in the eyes of the Soviet Government has the advantage of completing the unification of the territory, is clearly observable. While formerly the white race lived mainly in Europe and coloured peoples in the *Okrainy* of the east and south, these races have been blended by the systematic transfer of population for forced labour as well as by colonising movements, not to mention the deportations. The Moscow–Volga Canal, for instance, was mainly constructed by Caucasians, Tatars, Yakuts, and Mongols, and in the Russian universities and institutes can be seen thousands of students from Siberia, Turkistan, Georgia, etc. Conversely, a number of Russians and Ukrainians establish themselves more or less permanently in the Asiatic republics, and shortly before the war thousands of peasants from the borders of Poland, the Baltic States, and Finland are known to have been officially transported to Siberia and Uzbekistan. Europeans in Asia, Asiatics in Europe, 'in this crucible boils a strange and wonderful mixture' (Littlepage).

Now, this commixture, which tends to fuse the various elements of the population, is accompanied more or less consciously by an increasing uniformity in the mode of life. The Soviet system, we know, aims at gradually suppressing the differences between town and country by means of the collectivisation of the land and also by the at any rate partial industrialisation of the country through the mechanisation of work. But the aim does not stop there. It intends to efface by degrees the differences between the old metropolitan country and the former colonies. The most striking result is that peoples who had been nomads since the earliest times are beginning to settle down, build houses, till the soil, and keep stock farms. Stranger still, they now dwell in towns which are fast becoming industrial. Elista in the Kalmuk country contains buildings of several storeys; Nukus in the country of the Karakalpaks has large factories; Stalinabad in Tadzhikistan has a population of 191,000; Frunze in the Kirghiz country has one of about 190,000. The fact that very diverse people are occupied with the same work in similar workshops, live in the workmen's quarters which are all alike, and, in a word, have the same mode of life, tends to abolish the original differences between them.

Still more important in this respect perhaps is the change in agriculture. It is a commonplace that the policy of the tractor has partially industrialised agriculture. But it must be emphasised that the Soviet system intends to improve the breeds of animals and species of plants, to remake the soils, and change the zonal distribution of crops if need be—reforms which will all be imposed throughout the country by the initiative of the community, that is, of a group of experts or even of a single person whose influence is sufficient to make his advice law. The practical farmer with his experience, his respect for tradition, his mistrust of novelties, his conservatism, and his personal tastes, his determination to act according to his own ideas, has scarcely any place in this system in which 'he must uniformly bow to an order from outside' (D. Faucher). This is a real revolution, a phenomenon hitherto unknown. Anyhow, nothing is better calculated to efface regional and even national differences.

The movement which tends to impose the same mode of life on all the peoples in the Union will, if it goes on long enough, constitute an irresistible factor of unification. In a number of decades which we shall not try to estimate, it will perhaps become difficult to distinguish the real Russian from the former Asiatic subjects, except by physical appearance and language. Besides, it will be noted that innumerable cross-breeds are to be expected; that, though in non-Russian areas both primary and secondary education is carried on in the local tongue, Russian is everywhere taught as a second language; lastly, that the dispersion of Russian elements over the whole territory has an assimilating effect on the natives living in contact with them, and that, on the other hand, the displaced natives working among Russians generally become 'russified' fairly easily. The old distinction between Russia and her 'possessions' is known to be very brittle physically; it is pledged to lose all its value economically; and perhaps one day it will scarcely exist from the human point of view. On that day the Soviet world would indeed be one and indivisible.

That point has not yet been reached. The work has only begun,

and the original differences between the large elements which constitute the Union are far from being abolished. Physical geography
is not the only cause of this, for the effects of history must also be
reckoned. The fact that Siberia, Caucasia, and Turkistan have for a
long time been Russian colonies cannot be undone, nor can the fact
that they still differ from Russia in many respects, especially in their
economic backwardness relatively to her. Hence, after the general
features of the Union have been distinguished, the main natural
divisions of this vast country must be considered.

Part IV

MAIN NATURAL REGIONS OF THE SOVIET UNION

CHAPTER 15

TRADITIONAL DIVISIONS AND THE NEW GEOGRAPHICAL PATTERN

It is clearly necessary to distinguish mountains from plains, tundras from forests, and cultivated steppes from the oases and the all but desert pasture lands. And there is some temptation to point out these distinctions within the framework of each of the main traditional divisions of the former Empire taken one after the other.

Russia properly so-called would come first with its tundras, its vast forests which have been to a passable extent cleared away in the west and south, its rich Black Earth country, its dry steppes in New Russia, its frontage on the Black Sea, its alleged mountain frontier in the Urals, its population of 138·5 million, which is relatively dense at least in the Moscow area and the Ukraine, its ancient Byzantine civilisation, its venerable buildings and occasional very old towns, its colonies in New Russia and in the lower and middle Volga contrasting with the provinces of Novgorod, Muscovy, and the Ukraine which were peopled of old by Russians and have an excellent agricultural tradition, and, lastly, its present-day irresistible urge towards modernisation.

Then would come Siberia, an extension of Russia, at least in its western portion, where once again are found the tundra, forest, and steppe, not to mention the mountains in the south. The west is the best part of Siberia, the one most like Europe and in which settlement has been most spontaneous. But there is a contrast between this western Siberia and a central Siberia which includes the Yakutsk Aut. S.S. Republic and the region around Lake Baykal and presents the same divisions on more broken relief, but which, in spite of its great industrial hopes, seems clearly less rich and is far less densely populated. Then there is the Soviet Far East comprising Trans-Baykalia, the Amur valley, and Pacific Siberia, a region which is cold and dry inland, damp and foggy near the coast, and wealthy in minerals, forests, and fisheries, but infertile and poor on the whole and until the last few years sparsely peopled by Russians.

This 'Canada of the Old World', where settlements have been formed for years past, but are increasing today owing to a vigorous policy of communications and development, is on the whole being rapidly peopled, its population being already 30 million, and is energetically exploiting its resources. Hunting and fishing are still very important in many districts, but timber is taking the lead more and more. Agriculture and stock-rearing have fine prospects, especially in the west. But owing to the abundance of precious metals (gold), useful ores, and fabulous stocks of coal, its oil-fields and hydro-electric power, industry seems to have a great future before it, and there is already a large production of iron. 'This great country', says Littlepage, 'is more like the Middle and North-West of the United States than any other part of the world I know. . . . If well managed, Siberia can rise superior to any other country in Europe or Asia and can rival the United States. So long as the Russians hold Siberia they need have no worries.'

Soviet central Asia is a very different country and is essentially a region of inland drainage. It is mainly desert or at best semi-desert and is composed chiefly of poor clayey steppe and sand deserts. Luckily, it has a girdle of high mountains which are a source of water and at the foot of which stretches a belt of loess dotted with oases. Five subdivisions may be distinguished. First, there are the dry pasture lands of the steppes of Kazakstan where there is great mineral wealth and at least some areas of cultivable land which have attracted a good number of Russian colonists; then the Aralo-Caspian deserts, where the vegetation is poor owing to the extreme dryness, and the population is nomadic, except in two large well-watered valleys; thirdly, the mountains of the perimeter, which are relatively well-watered and very high in places; and, fourthly, the piedmont oases of Turkmenistan, Semirechye, and especially the districts round the Syr Darya and Oxus. There, in spite of physical and human conditions very different from those in Russia and in spite of the difficulty of sending many colonists to a country which is already fairly densely peopled, important results have been obtained. First, in farming, by the development of sheep-rearing and the cultivation of cereals, fruit, and cotton; and then in industry owing to the abundance of hydro-electric power and of mineral wealth. Russian infiltration is certainly much less here than in Siberia, and it is doubtful whether this country will ever be completely russified. It is in process of being 'sovietised', however, and that satisfies the rulers of the Union, who are making great efforts to achieve it. The resources of the region are being exploited, and its future inspires confidence.

Lastly, Caucasia would close the list with its four obvious divisions, viz. Ciscaucasia, an arid land of wheat and sheep; the huge Caucasus range, abounding in forests, pastures, and oil; Transcaucasia, well-watered and warm, with a fertile soil and much mineral wealth; and finally, Soviet Armenia, a rough and rather poor land. On the whole, the region is very varied and contains resources that are unevenly distributed, but diversified. Russian colonisation has not really taken root except in the north-west. Elsewhere, especially in the mountains, the original native characteristics are very much alive. However, as it is gradually losing its colonial character, Caucasia is being progressively brought by the policy of the Kremlin into the great Soviet community.

The method of treatment outlined above would have the great advantage of showing the real form of each of the main elements which constituted the empire of the Tsars. But though Caucasia and central Asia have a very distinct character, it is difficult today to contrast Siberia and Russia. Furthermore, it would not be logical to stick to a division which was still valid in 1920 or 1930, but today is evidently obsolete and in opposition to the spirit of Soviet policy and the new geography of the country. It seems better to forget that there was formerly a Russia in Europe and a Russia in Asia and to distinguish in the Soviet territory as a whole a few main natural regions characterised at times by the relief, more often by climate and vegetation, but more and more, too, by the action of man on his environment.

Russian geographers, following L. Berg and using these principles, distinguish ten main natural regions: tundra, *tayga* (or coniferous forest belt), mixed forest, park land, steppe (or open and treeless grass plain), semi-desert, desert, sub-tropical areas, mountainous areas, and broad-leaved forest. Here it is proposed to follow these divisions with certain modifications. In the first place, the main characteristic of the park land is its black earth, and the region will accordingly be restricted to the belt in which *chernoziom* is found. Then, again, conditions in the semi-desert are merely a degenerate form of those existing in the steppes, so these two regions will be treated together. Finally, as the sub-tropical area is too small for separate treatment here, it will be included in the description of the Caucasus, of which it is indeed a part.

CHAPTER 16

THE TUNDRAS

The tundra belt is rightly thought of as flat on the whole, but it is not featureless, however. The Murmansk peninsula with its pre-Cambrian rocks is a very ancient region of Fennoscandian folds, which has been peneplaned, then uplifted and subjected to vigorous glaciation whose mark is seen in *roches moutonnées*, navel-shaped hollows, moraines, dammed lakes, etc. Here the Umptek or Khibiny Hills rise to a height of 4000 ft. above sea level.

Farther east the extreme north of the great Russo-Siberian plain is not strictly flat. Kildin Island is a plateau 900 ft. high; the heights of the Kanin peninsula rise to between 500 and 650 ft.; and the Timanski Hills, 560 miles long by 50 miles wide, to 900 ft. On the other hand, the *Bolshezemelskaya* (= Big Land) and *Malozemelskaya* (= Little Land) tundras are very low-lying, though covered with morainic deposits. The altitude increases to 328 ft. in Vaygach Island and to even more than 3000 ft. in Novaya Zemlya, then falls again almost to sea level in the north of the great plain of western Siberia which was invaded by the sea in the Quaternary period.

Furthermore, all these regions exhibit moderately characteristic glacial surface features, and for this reason even the plains often have a sufficiently broken surface to make travel difficult. The dunes found on the tundra near the Pechora and the lava flows of the Anadyr plateau are far rarer phenomena. On the other hand, the existence of the *merzlota* and the efforts of spring water to reach the surface cause *bulgunniakhi*, which are circular or elliptical swellings that are very common throughout Siberia and sometimes rise to a height of 260 ft.[1] Here and there at the mouths of the rivers are *laydy*, or little peaty and very flat plains.

The tundra round the lower course of the Pechora and the vast

[1] Known in the Canadian Arctic as 'pingos'.

flat stretches of recently submerged plain in western Siberia are very marshy, but even there the ground rises here and there to 500 or even 1000 ft. above the sea. Across the middle and lower course of the Khatanga lies a wide plain which is shut in on the south by the central Siberian plateau and on the north by the waters of Leptev Sea and the Barranga Mountains. In the last feature the ground culminates in heights of more than 3000 ft. above the sea. The western portion of the plain has a rolling, morainic surface dotted with many lakes, whilst the area east of the Khatanga is fluted with ridges, some of which exceed a height of 2000 ft. A good deal of salt and some oil have been found among the Secondary formations.

The characteristics of the climate of these regions are well known, viz. the very low altitude of the midday sun, the extremely short summer with endlessly long days, the length and severity of the dark winters, and the scanty precipitation. The mean temperature in the warmest month does not exceed 50° F. anywhere, and in winter the thermometer may fall to −40° F. There is little snow, and precipitation, which seldom exceeds 6 or 7 ins. a year, occurs mainly in summer in the form of drizzle. The expedition which studied the coast between the Lena and Kolyma rivers in 1909 suffered terribly from thirst, especially in the tundra which covers the Merkushin peninsula, 'a country whence there is no return', as the natives say. Gales often occur in winter sweeping large areas bare and piling the snow in drifts.

The soil is astonishingly poor. Its acid, peaty infertility and its frequently marshy nature allow merely of a sparse vegetation consisting mainly of sphagnum moss and lichens with tufts of grass, saxifrage, and Arctic poppy in the extreme north, but farther south low shrubs (dwarf birch and willow) are to be found and even gnarled trees (birch and spruce) exist along the river-banks. The Arctic fox, lemming, wolf, and reindeer together with a multitude of birds represent the animal life.

These difficult natural conditions have allowed the regions only a very feeble development. The extraordinarily small, scattered population is composed of Lapps, Samoyedes, and Zyrians in Russia, and of Ghiliaks, Ostiaks, Koriaks, Yakuts, Lamuts, and Chukchees in Siberia. Some, like the Samoyedes, are well on the down-grade, bullied and robbed by everyone; others, like the Chukchees, hold out in some way or other. But they all lead a precarious life of hardship. Hunting, fishing, and reindeer breeding are their chief means of support. They move about in pursuit of game and fish or to change the pastures of their animals. The latter are very poor specimens and cannot be given heavy loads, especially as they are very slow in recuperating; and some tundras are clothed with a reddish grass which reindeer obstinately refuse. Travelling, moreover, is very difficult, in winter because of the cold, in summer because the reindeer, which is changing its antlers and coat and is tormented by mosquitoes, has no strength to speak of, and because much of the ground is flooded or turned to deep mud. Needless to add, 'towns' like Verkhoyansk, Sredne Kolymsk, or Nizhne Kolymsk are insignificant.

Such were the conditions of life on the tundra, at least until recently. Perhaps it is changing, not only because the Soviet Government means to protect these peoples who were formerly exploited by the Russians, but also because the economic system of the region seems to be in process of considerable modification.

Until recently the Murmansk coast with its fjords and its warm current which keeps it ice-free was the only place of any value. The port of Murmansk has lately developed to an extraordinary extent. Conveniently linked with the interior by canal and rail, it has seen a surprising increase in its traffic. Hence, the town, whose population in 1924 lived in hutments and numbered only 4500, but increased by 1956 to 168,000, is the world's largest polar city. Formerly composed of wooden houses, it is now built of stone and has a theatre, cinemas, museums, a library, and dispensaries. Its growth is explained by its activity as a port and also by the prosperity of its timber trade, its shipyards, fisheries, and fishing industry. The population of the Kolski peninsula has increased nearly tenfold since 1926.

Owing to the opening of the Northern Sea Route the awakening of the Murmansk coast may soon be extended to the whole Siberian coast. As we have seen, ports have sprung up all along this coast, and many airfields have been constructed. To provide fuel and cargo for the ships, a successful search has been made for mineral wealth. In the Khibiny Hills on the Kolski peninsula there are enormous deposits of apatite and also some nephelite, certain rare metals (titanium, vanadium, zirconium, and molybdenum), copper, nickel, and iron, not to mention petroleum and building materials. Elsewhere, coal has been found in the lower Ob valley, in the lower valley of the Yenisey at Norilsk, on the Pyasina, lower Khatanga, lower Lena, and in Chukotski; oil in the lower Ob and Khatanga valleys; copper in Chukotski; nickel in the upper Pyasina valley; silver-lead on the Irana; iron, tin, ochre, and various polymetallic ores in the Anadyr district; gold in Chukotski and in the Kolyma valley, which now heads production in the Soviet Union; and rock salt on the Khatanga. Coal-mining has already begun at Norilsk and supplies the depôt at Port Dickson; salt too is mined at Norilsk, but these are not to be compared with the extraction of apatite in the Khibiny Hills, which has given rise to large mining and chemical industries producing artificial manure and aluminium with the help of hydro-electric power from the Nivastroy. Being near the forest, Igarka has been equipped with extensive sawmills.

But as white workers cannot live on meat and fish alone without risk of scurvy, many attempts have been made to produce fresh vegetables and fruit. Remarkable results have been obtained in the Kolski peninsula, but the lower Yenisey valley is in no way behind. The Poliarnyi *sovkhoz* near Igarka has herds of cows and swine, raises poultry, and also cultivates oats, beans, potatoes, cucumbers, lettuce, and carrots. As early as 1934 about 220 acres were sown, not counting what was being grown in hot-houses and in forcing frames. The Arctic stations sometimes even have plants growing under the ice in underground chambers of wood sheltered from the cold and lit and warmed by electricity supplied by wind-driven motors. 'The storms of the Arctic make the vegetables grow' (Smolka).

Real towns have sprung up and are expanding on these Arctic coasts; e.g. Kandalaksha in Murmanski, which manufactures aluminium; Nivastroy (pop. 13,000); Igarka (pop. 10,000, not counting the 2500 persons who live in its outport of Dudinka); and above all Kirovsk (Khibinogorsk), which was a hamlet of a few hundred inhabitants in 1930 and which by reason of its mining activities and its chemical industry has today a population of more than 40,000.

Thus, the opening of the Northern Sea Route will perhaps not be restricted to lessening the too continental character of the Soviet Union, but will possibly also bring to life the vast solitudes of the tundras. Well-informed persons like Samoilovich seem to believe firmly in their reanimation.

THE ARCTIC ISLANDS

On the continental shelf of Russia and Siberia there are a number of islands which are of no economic value, but which, owing to modern political and transport developments, have become of high strategic importance. As the crow flies, the distance from Siberia across the Pole to the nearest Canadian island is 1600 miles. Hence, the possibility of breaking the journey by air is a considerable advantage. Furthermore, the establishment of weather stations on the islands is of great assistance to ships making the passage along the Northern Sea Route.

Besides a number of small islands off the north coast of Russia and Siberia and a few others scattered in the Soviet sector of the Arctic, there are four groups: Novaya Zemlya, Franz Josef Land, Severnaya Zemlya, the New Siberian Islands; and the single Wrangel Island.

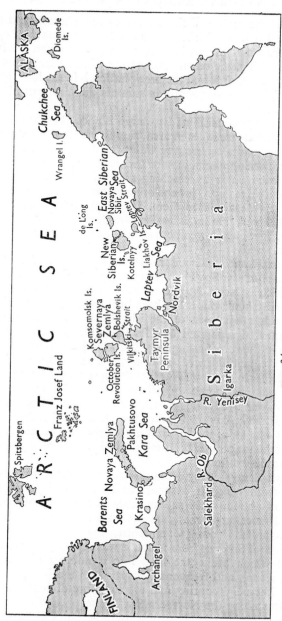

FIG. 34. THE ARCTIC ISLANDS.

Those nearest the mainland share its structure, climate, and tundra character, whilst those farther north are for the most part covered with an ice-cap and are useless for permanent human habitation. Generally speaking, the mean temperature of the warmest month is at or just above freezing, and the precipitation is in the form of snow. The fogs which occur frequently in summer are a serious hindrance to navigation.

Novaya Zemlya consists of two large islands. The South Island, which is 15,820 square miles in area, shares the tundra nature of the mainland, and has a sparse vegetation of dwarf birch and willow with some flowering plants in summer. A few Samoyedes eke out a scanty existence on it by catching seals and walrus. The largest settlement is at Krasino. Three weather stations and a wireless installation have been established there. The North Island, which has an area of 21,250 square miles, is less hospitable and mainly covered with a cap of ice. However, a weather station has been established on it at Pakhtusovo.

Franz Josef Land, which is nearer to the Pole and is the most northerly part of the Soviet territory, consists of some 800 islands, none of which is large. At one time the group evidently formed a single extensive land; but it has been broken up by a tectonic movement which has left most of the islands rising from the sea in a tabular form and separated by rifts that give greater depth in the straits than in the surrounding seas. The islands are foggy in summer, suffer from frequent blizzards in winter, and have a low precipitation, always in the form of snow. They are largely covered by ice, and their vegetation consists merely of lichens. The Soviet Union assumed sovereignty over the islands in 1926 and has established a weather station at Tikhaya Bay on Hooker Island, where the air installation is regarded as a stage in the flight across the Arctic Sea. A geophysical research station has been established at the same place by the Russian Arctic Institute.

Severnaya Zemlya (North Land) lies to the north of the Taymyr Peninsula from which it is separated by Vilkitski Strait. It has a total area of about 14,000 square miles and consists of many small islands and three large ones named October Revolution, Bolshevik, and Komsomolsk (Young Communist). In structure the group is a continuation of Siberia, from which it was separated by the tectonic movement which broke the land into a number of islands. The climate is severe, and frequent blizzards lash the islands, especially in winter. The neighbouring seas are therefore difficult for shipping which moves along the Northern Sea Route.

The New Siberian Islands are a scattered group which forms a continuation of the mainland structure. The chief islands are Kotelnyy,

Faddeevski, and Novaya Sibir. To the north-east of these is the de Long group of small islands, so named after their American discoverer. A southern group, known as the Liakhov Islands, is chiefly noted for the remains of mammoths and other prehistoric animals found on Big Liakhov, the largest.

Wrangel Island, of some 2000 square miles in extent, lies in the East Siberian Sea. It has a climate that is dry and relatively mild for its latitude, the July mean reaching 32·3° F. On it the Soviet Government has established a weather station and an air base.

CHAPTER 17

THE FOREST BELT

South of the tundras the forest covers boundless expanses between the Baltic and Pacific and between the White Sea and the Black Earth steppes. But conditions are not the same everywhere. In certain regions in the north the forest has scarcely been touched and practically reigns supreme. This is the great Russo-Siberian forest, corresponding more or less to the *tayga* belt and almost uninhabited, except in a few large clearings. On its fringes there are districts in which large areas have been cleared, and others in which the steppe is beginning to make its way into the forest. Human activity, agricultural and even industrial, has enormously increased in both. In the east they include south-eastern Siberia (i.e. the Amur valley and Transbaykalia); on the west in Russia the lake region and White Russia, with the region of Muscovy in the centre; lastly, the Urals and pre-Uralian region are to be placed by themselves, since they are rather different in their southern portions. Where the Black Earth occurs, the steppe appears, industry has taken root, and, in fact, another region begins.

A. THE GREAT RUSSO-SIBERIAN FOREST

The great Russo-Siberian forest extends over regions which vary greatly in relief. In Russia its orographic monotony is remarkable. The southern part of the Murmanski peninsula, the north of the Karelian plateau, the low Uvaly Hills, which are 600 miles long, but only 500 or 600 ft. high, and the southern end of the almost flat Timanski Heights are exceptional. Elsewhere only insignificant variations in level are noticeable. The basins of the Onega, Dvina, Mezan, and Pechora are shallow depressions imperceptibly streaked with morainic trails. Beyond the Urals much the same topography is found in the vast plain of western Siberia. Here the agents of erosion and deposition have combined to bring about an almost perfect level, and the Quaternary ice caps have left only very slight traces.

But to the east of the Yenisey appears the Siberian shield, an ancient nucleus which has resisted every fold movement since the Archæan, but after age-long denudation experienced wholesale uplift which fractured it and caused a vigorous resumption of erosion. It then underwent intense glacial action which left traces as clear as they are numerous. In the extreme south the eastern Sayan, a volcanic crystalline range which has been rejuvenated to the point of having an Alpine appearance, rises to over 11,000 ft. in Munku Sardyk. More to the north between the Yenisey and Lena is the slightly undulating Central Siberian Plateau.

Farther east is the vast upland mass of the Yakutsk Republic. Half of this spacious country of a million square miles lies within the tundra belt. Most of its development has taken place in the forest zone, where much gold is mined, some diamonds are found, and reindeer are bred. The population numbers only 480,000 and consists mainly of primitive Turkic folk.

South of a line marked by the valley of the Vilyuy, the Yakutsk basin, and the lower Aldan valley the ground rises to 8860 ft. in the Aldan plateau between the Olekma and the Aldan, to 5900 ft. in the Patom plateau between the lower Vitim and the Lena, and to as much as 9186 ft. between the Olekma and Chara. Then, forming a ridge between the Lena and Amur are the very densely packed folds of the Stanovoy Mountains (8140 ft.), which are continued in the rocky, irregular Dzhugdzhur Mountains and form a serious obstacle on the route to the Pacific. To the north-west of this line are great volcanic plateaus trenched by the gorges of the Khatanga and the feeders of the Yenisey. To the north-east lies a very broken region in which basins of subsidence alternate with folded ranges of Alpine type, like the Verkhoyanski Mountains (8500 ft.) and the Cherski range, 600 miles long, 180 miles wide, and 10,000 ft. high in Mount Chen, which was discovered by Obruchov in 1926.

Lastly, the Siberian Far East is a region of very broken relief which has been fractured, folded, and eroded, and in places shows marks of vulcanism. Beyond the Great Khingan the plateau of Zeya leads to the Bureya Mountains. This is the region of the Amur. Farther east is the island of Sakhalin, where plains and valleys lie between two ranges, the more eastern of which reaches a height of 6000 ft. There are also the hilly coasts of the Sea of Okhotsk, where the Dzhugdzhurs die away. Then the peninsula of Kamchatka, whose ancient rocks have been folded and uplifted, so that they still present a vigorous relief accentuated by a great deal of vulcanism, including 38 volcanoes, among which is Klyuchevskaya (15,700 ft.), immense fields of lava and ash, eroded cones, lava-dammed lakes, and innumerable hot springs. Lastly, there is the southern part of the Anadyr and Chukotski regions, which is little known. Here the low Kolyma plain separates the Kolyma range from the Cherski range, and the broad valley of the Anadyr lies between the Koryak and Anadyr ranges.

In this immense region which is afflicted with a dry and singularly vigorous climate, with a very mediocre and usually podzolic soil underlain by the *merzlota*, the forest reigns despotically and is interrupted only here and there by marshes, peat bogs, or bare hills called *goltsy* in Siberia. In Russia, where the forest pushes out curious tongues northwards along the valleys, it is composed mainly of spruce, pine, and fir, less often of larch and birch. Particularly dense on the upper Pechora, it is less so in the west and south, where swamps, wide river valleys, and clearings are by no means rare, but it is almost never really beautiful. It is even less so in Siberia where the larch is the prevailing species in the north, but is mixed in the south with fir, 'cedar' (*Pinus cembra*), and birch. In central Siberia this poverty in the vegetation tends to be accentuated. It is only in the Far East that, owing to the greater humidity, the forest resumes a healthy vigour. This is seen, however, not on the too windswept shores of the Sea of Okhotsk or in the south of Chukotski or the Anadyr district, but in Sakhalin, which has superb coniferous woods, and in Kamchatka, where the undergrowth is a tangled mass.

Travel is extremely difficult in these woods and is best achieved along the streams, which fortunately are assured by the low degree of evaporation of a fairly good volume in summer, in spite of the scanty precipitation. But the forest offers man an inexhaustible supply of timber, enormous quantities of game and furs, and streams full of fish. In spite of this, life is very difficult and unattractive to prospective settlers largely because of the attacks of swarms of mosquitoes, and, as we have seen, the extremely sparse population is mainly Asiatic, except in places where minerals are worked. The resources of the forest are exploited in Russia by Zyrians and in Siberia by Tunguzes and Yakuts reinforced by a small number of genuine Russians.

Hunting continues to be really important. Even in Russia it gives a good return in winter, especially in the Zyrian country. The same is true in western Siberia. However, the high-priced pelts which were formerly haggled over at the fairs at Tyumen and Irbit have become scarce in both regions and can be found in abundance only in central and eastern Siberia, although the Siberian forest seems originally to have had less game than its Russian counterpart.

The supplies provided by the rivers have been far less used up, and fishing continues to be a very important occupation in Siberia as well as in Russia, an importance which increases as one goes northwards. Raw, powdered, salted, or frozen fish is an essential food for man as well as dogs. The former keeps for himself the sterlet, perch, salmon, sturgeon, and burbot, giving to his dogs the less valuable part of the catch. River fishing brings in a big return. Some female sturgeons have been known to yield more than $17\frac{1}{2}$ lbs. of pure caviar. An important fishing industry is developing on the Pacific coast.

Then the forest itself represents great wealth. Its exploitation is far advanced in Russia, where there are many sawmills along the streams, and nearly the whole population works in these establishments as soon as work ceases in the fields with the advent of winter. Though timber is less important in Siberia, it is immensely valuable for building, heating, firing locomotives, and wood industries.

Other industries may be established some day, for the rocks are not without minerals. The Pechora region has oil and coal; Verkhoyansk district lead, zinc, and silver; the lower Tunguska valley coal, graphite, mica, magnetite, and Iceland spar; the Olekma valley Iceland spar, salt, and oil; the Olenek valley coal; the Yakutsk district coal and lignite; the Kolyma and Aldan valleys gold; Kamchatka oil; and the plateau of Zeya gold. But the importance of the deposits is as yet unknown, and hitherto the stage of hope has scarcely been passed, since realisation is infinitesimal, except for the gold-mining in the Aldan and Kolyma valleys. The latter, which began to be exploited in 1933 and is notorious for its labour camps, is the chief producer of the metal in the Soviet Union. A motor road connects it with the port of Magadan on the Sea of Okhotsk.

On the other hand, agriculture is of ancient date in the clearings and is tending to develop more and more in Siberia and Russia. Since drought is less of an enemy here than in the Black Earth country, the podzol gives yields at times greater than those of the *chernoziom*, though the technique is still based on burn-beating and fallow. There is little spring wheat and still less winter wheat; but rye, oats, barley, and, in some areas, potatoes, rice, and soya beans play an appreciable part. Flax and hemp are also cultivated, and, though with the exception of a few apple-trees, fruit trees are almost non-existent in Siberia, and except for apples and cherries rare in Russia, garden vegetables (turnips, kohl rabi, cabbages, carrots, cauliflowers, cucumbers, melons, and indeed water melons) are fairly popular.

Finally, stock-rearing is carried on in the islands of steppe which occur everywhere in the forest, especially in Russia, where the water meadows adjoining the rivers feed a large number of horned cattle.

The Vologda district is a great producer of butter and cheese. But in western and central Siberia the cow does not easily become acclimatised. In the Far East agriculture and stock-rearing suffer, even near the Amur, from the excessive humidity which is accompanied by cold; so that these districts have little prospect except in industry.

In short, the *tayga* is only moderately productive. Furthermore, it suffers from want of transport. Though the rivers, including the Lena, are very useful in summer, roads are few and the railway system poor. To cap it all, the region has scarcely any contact with the ocean, which it reaches only on the shores of the Sea of Okhotsk and the coast of Kamchatka. The former is astonishingly empty and poor, and the latter has only two little seaports, Petropavlovsk, in a busy fishing area, the catch including, besides fish, crustacea and molluscs of various kinds, and Bolsheretsk, which is the centre of fish-canning on the east coast.

More important is the White Sea coast, which is also reached by the forest. Its activities include not only fishing, lumbering, and fur trapping, but also the overseas trade which is concentrated in Archangel. This port dates from the end of the sixteenth century; but its growth made a spurt forward under Peter the Great and has been even more rapid since the construction in 1897 of the railway linking it with Moscow. It imports large quantities of fish, and tropical goods, and exports flax, hemp, timber, coal, tar, resin, fish-oil, and suet. There are extensive industries, notably shipbuilding, which has expanded at a great rate since 1928. Archangel is now much bigger and finer than formerly. Its population has risen from 70,000 in 1926 to 238,000, and its importance can but increase with the improvement in communications.

But this case is exceptional in the *tayga*. Vologda, which is a Russian railway junction and a great centre of dairying, has a population of only 127,000; yet it far surpasses all the other towns: the port of Onega (pop. 2000), Ust-Tsylma (pop. 2000), Syktyvkar (Ust Sysolsk, pop. 5000), and even Velikie Ustyug (pop. 20,000). In western Siberia the valleys of the Ob and its feeders alone have agglomerations of a few thousand souls, like Narym, Singut, Beryozov. In central Siberia Vilyuisk, Vitimsk, and Olekminsk (pop. 2500) are quite small mining centres. The only place that counts is Yakutsk with a population of 15,000, which has developed as a market and tends to grow because of the increase in mining. Lastly, in the Far East Petropavlovsk with a population of 2000 and Aleksandrovsk, the capital of Sakhalin, are tiny places. The occupation of the Kuriles and the recovery of the southern part of Sakhalin will probably lead to the growth of these towns, for oil, coal, and timber are being exploited and fish-canning factories set up. In 1946 alone, some

100,000 Soviet citizens settled in the island to take the place of the expelled Japanese.

Apart from these little townships which stand out as landmarks in the valleys, there is almost total emptiness. The vast Yakutsk Republic, with a population of 400,000, has a density of about 0·26 persons to the square mile, and Kamchatka has 130,000 persons in all. In fact, the Russo-Siberian forest is almost uninhabited.

B. THE INHABITED FOREST LANDS

But on the fringes of these vast solitudes are forest lands which have attracted settlers unevenly, but in places very greatly.

(1) *South-eastern Siberia*. This comprises roughly the Baykal region, Transbaykalia, and Primorsk (the maritime region). The first of these lies between the valley of the Yenisey and Lake Baykal. It is the southern portion of the Siberian Shield and has the appearance of a very ancient peneplain rejuvenated by recent uplifts, by numerous fractures, and by glacial erosion. Rejuvenation is most noticeable in the eastern Sayan Mountains, which form the south-western border of the 'Irkutsk amphitheatre'. Here the Tukinsk Alps and Munku Sardyk (11,600 ft.) are capped with snow and ice and have remarkably bold outlines. But farther north there is a maze of ice-eroded horsts and rift valleys like those through whose veritable gorges and famous defiles flow the Lena and Angara. The latter, which has a maximum volume of 9400 cu. yds. a second but an average of only 2100 cu. yds., is the sole outlet of Lake Baykal. A series of rift valleys is occupied by this gigantic lake, which, appreciably larger than Belgium, is 400 miles long, between 30 and 50 miles wide, and at least 2000 ft. deep throughout, often reaching a depth of 3000 ft. and indeed at one point nearly 6000 ft. The little inland sea, fed by 336 streams draining a basin 113,000 square miles in area, is visited by terrible storms. It cools the summer and lengthens the spring in its immediate neighbourhood, and it moderates the winter and prolongs the autumn.

Even in summer the surface waters away from the shores never rise above a temperature of 50° F., and from a depth of 800 ft. there is homothermia, the temperature remaining at 38° F. In winter the lake is covered for 116 days by ice three or four feet thick. The fauna, which includes a peculiar species of seal (*Phoca Siberica*) and a small viviparous spider-fish, is of great age. Economically, Baykal is important for its fishing and as a waterway.

West of the Irkutsk region and lying in the angle formed by the Western and Eastern Sayan Mountains lies the Tuva Autonomous Province which was absorbed in the Soviet Union in 1945. It occupies the area drained by the headwaters of the Yenisey and covers 69,700 square miles. Cold in winter and hot in summer, it has a plateau climate with a high diurnal range of temperature. In the north-east, where precipitation is abundant, there is forest, but elsewhere the climate is dry and grassland prevails. The country is rich in minerals, especially in gold, silver, asbestos, and copper, but so far it is almost undeveloped. It has a population of 168,000 and a capital in the little town of Kyzyl. Adjoining Tuva on the west is the Gorno-Altay Autonomous Region, peopled by Oirots and having its capital at Gorno-Altaysk. Both of these countries are intended by Moscow to be holiday resorts for the industrial towns of central Siberia.

In Transbaykalia the relief is generally fairly low because of a very long period of degradation. The Yablonovy Mountains (8240 ft.), whose worn, rounded summits are in contrast with their young valleys, separate the valley of the Selenga, which reaches Lake Baykal after crossing the Khamar-Daban Mountains (4600 ft.), from Dauria (2000 ft.), in which rise the headwaters of the Amur. The chief of these are the Argun and the Onon, which both rise in Mongolia.

Lastly, Primorsk comprises two depressions, the lower Amur valley and the valley of the Ussuri. In the former the river, swollen first by the Sungari (Sung-hua) and then by the Ussuri, spreads out widely and divides into a number of arms which flow round grassy islands before reaching the sea over a broad sand-bar. The Ussuri valley with its flat surface and fertile soil is separated from the Amur valley by a ridge lying within Manchurian territory. Primorsk also includes the Sikhota Alin (6000 ft.), the uplifted edge of a submerged horst which consists of a series of eight parallel ridges with an average height of between 2500 and 3000 ft. The ridges separate the valleys of the Ussuri and lower Amur from the sea, but are easily crossed through cluses cut by a long period of erosion. The coastline facing the Gulf of Tartary is broken and contains a number of harbours, of which Sovietskaya Gavan (Soviet Harbour) is the most important.

In south-eastern Siberia the climate is not everywhere the same. Between the Yenisey and Lake Baykal it is only moderately humid, and it is even less humid in Transbaykalia; on the other hand, in the maritime country it is very rainy and misty, but vigorous and cold throughout. The Yablonovy Mountains form a definite climatic and floral dividing line between the humid and dry regions.

This country does not belong exclusively to the forest. Certainly, forest covers vast areas in it. In Baykalia, where the woodland is interrupted by clearings, swamps, and grassy valleys, it is like the forest in the Ob valley. But it is less luxuriant and has less game, though it is just as difficult to travel through. In the well-watered

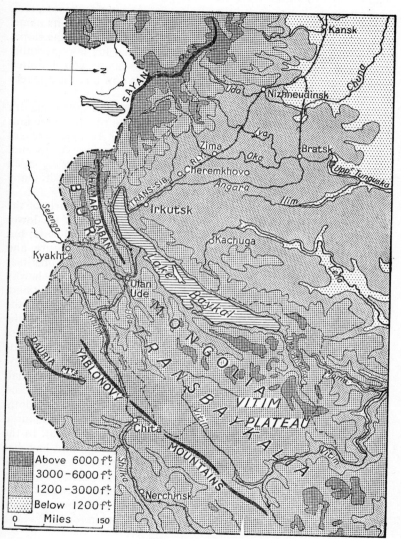

FIG. 35. CENTRAL SIBERIA.

233

Yablonovy Mountains there are dense stands of species which do not occur between this area and the Urals, viz. oaks, elms, walnuts, and, above all, the wild apple-trees which have given the range its name. Lastly, in Primorsk the forest becomes really luxuriant in the slopes of the Sikhota Alin, where vegetable and animal life is remarkably exuberant. But in places the forest gives way to steppe, which, dotted with frequent clumps of birch and pine, occurs now and then in very large expanses to the west of Lake Baykal.

In western Transbaykalia steppe reigns almost undisputed, its dry expanses contrasting with the damp meadows that run along the foot of the Yablonovy. In Dauria one can walk 9 or 10 miles without meeting a spring, and thin grass covers the occasionally salty ground. The humidity of Primorsk explains the fact that naturally open spaces are rare there; but man has cleared away the forest in many places.

Unfortunately, there is no black earth, except in the parts of the plain drained by the Zeya and Bureya. In the districts of the lower Amur and the Ussuri there are some fairly good alluvial soils; but to the west of Lake Baykal the prevailing relief is very mature, and the soil has had a long leaching, is generally sterile, and sometimes marshy. In eastern and western Transbaykalia the soil is hardly better; besides, drought very often makes irrigation a necessity and, in gardens, forces the watering not only of the earth, but also of the leaves. Two districts are exceptional: the Zeya-Bureya plain and the area south of Lake Khanka, in both of which a moderately dense rural population produces crops of wheat, maize, and soya. The former centres on Blagoveshchensk, the latter on Vladivostok.

It may well be imagined after what has been said above that, whilst agriculture in Baykalia is no great success, wheat, oats, and vegetables being produced in quantities sufficient for local consumption only, it is definitely poor in Transbaykalia, especially in Dauria, where only the north-eastern district can grow spring wheat. In the Sikhota Alin the excessive humidity, which rots grain and hay, has discouraged many men from settling there. Agriculture has had little success so far. And yet crops of buckwheat, oats, rice, soya, and fruit are grown. Luckily, stock-rearing is less handicapped, and considerable profit is made in Baykalia from cattle and horses, and in Transbaykalia from sheep, which constitute the main form of wealth among the Buryats.

In Primorsk fishing has assumed great importance, and the region has now surpassed the Caspian Sea in production. Salmon and crabs form the main catch. The Keta salmon of the Amur yields red caviar. Vladivostok is the centre of a canning industry.

In fact, in a country as remote and of such moderate fertility as

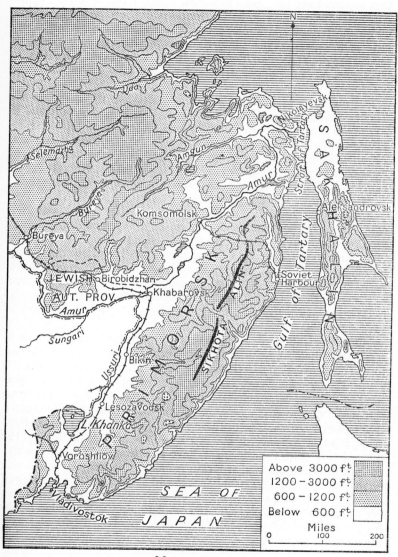

FIG. 36. EASTERN SIBERIA.

this, settlers have only been attracted by the mineral wealth, by the advantageous position for trading, and by very definite official action. Only where these conditions existed have Russian elements, which have in fact been rather slight till recently, been superimposed on the earlier population of Tunguzes, Buryats, Daurians, Goldans, or Orochans. Yet as a whole Russian settlers greatly outnumber these natives.

The region is in fact fairly rich in minerals, especially in the Eastern Sayan, where there is much gold, iron deposits estimated at 20 million tons, and some nephrite jade and mica of good quality. The graphite of the Sayan Mountains (the Alibert mine) and Turukhansk in the forest proper is no longer important.[1] But the Irkutsk district has salt and coal; Transbaykalia has salt and, in the Nerchinsk district, mercury, copper, tin, iron, zinc, precious stones, a little gold, and, above all, silver.[2]

After having given rise to the notorious convict stations at Nerchinsk (silver) and Kara (gold), this wealth attracted settlers along the Ingoda–Shilka line and the Trans-Siberian Railway. Their moderately tidy, comfortable villages are sometimes large, but the biggest centres are Kyakhta (the terminus of trade with China), Nerchinsk, and Chita, which now has a population of 162,000. These are, however, smaller than Irkutsk. Ulan Ude, whose population rose in thirteen years from 27,000 to 150,000, is a route junction in Transbaykalia.

Irkutsk is an old fortress and trading centre which, though it retains much of the character of a frontier town, has become an intellectual capital and an industrial focus. Its population of 314,000 comprises Russians and Ukrainians together with some Buryat-Mongols. Huge hydro-electric power stations will make the town the centre of one of the large industrial districts now being created in the Soviet Union. One of these stations on the Angara just above Irkutsk has a capacity of 600,000 kWh., whilst that at Bratsk 150 miles downstream is designed to have a capacity of 3,600,000 kWh. A third has been planned at Krasnoyarsk on the Yenisey, which will have a capacity of 4,000,000 kWh. It will suffer from the freezing of the river in winter, a drawback from which stations on the Angara are free. When these projects are complete, they will provide power for the new aluminium town of Shyelikov near Irkutsk, for electrifying stretches of the Trans-Siberian Railway, and for other enterprises

[1] But formerly they were of great importance. When this Irkutsk deposit was discovered, its owner made an agreement with Faber, the famous pencil manufacturers at Stein near Nürnberg, by which the graphite produced was reserved to the firm in perpetuity.

[2] Or at any rate there used to be a great deal. Today, the lode of silver appears to be nearly exhausted.

including ferrous and non-ferrous plants, a new coal-mine, a new iron-ore field at Korshanov, and an aluminium *kombinat*. There are plans for establishing an oil refinery and for bringing oil by pipe-line from Bashkiria, for getting more gold from the Lena valley and more mica from the hills by the River Mana.

Farther east, in the extreme south of the middle Amur region, Blagoveshchensk, which links Transbaykalia with Primorsk, is a supply centre for gold prospectors and a focus of trade with Manchuria. It is of very modern appearance, has a population of 58,000, and is growing rapidly. Also on the Amur, but farther downstream, is Khabarovsk at the confluence of the Ussuri with the main river. This town, whose population of 280,000 is a great mixture of Russians, Chinese, Koreans, and Japanese, is an important market for fish and furs as well as an administrative centre. The influence of Jewish agricultural settlers in Birobidzhan, where there is a population of 90,000, of whom 25,000 are Jews, may bring about great changes in the district. Changes are more certain to be made by the great metallurgical *kombinat* at Bureya, the establishment of which has been made possible by the local supplies of iron and coal.

The newly founded (1932) Komsomolsk on the lower Amur is not far from the sea. The rapid growth of its population to 169,000 clearly demonstrates the intensity of Soviet efforts to make settlements on the Pacific coast. In fact, activity in this area is continually increasing and is illustrated by the rise of Nikolayevsk at the mouth of the river and even more by that of Vladivostok. The latter port, the terminus of the Trans-Siberian Railway, is of great value, although frozen over for nearly four months, and its rapidly increasing traffic cannot but prosper if the Northern Sea Route, of which it will be the terminus, succeeds in being properly organised. Hence, the town has reached a population of 265,000 and is now the fourth largest city in Siberia. Not far away, Voroshilov (formerly Nikolsk) on the Ussuri has a population of 101,000.

Somewhat neglected for a long time, the south-east of Siberia has been the object of the Government's keen interest for several years past. Efforts are being made to introduce settlers, establish the large-scale production of potatoes and vegetables, to set up numerous industries, including coal-mining, metallurgy, mechanical engineering, wood-working, and cement-making, and to construct a railway system including the new lines from Ulan Ude to Peking, from Ust-Kut on the upper Lena to Komsomolsk, and from Sergiopol (Ayaguz) through Urumchi and Hami to join the Chinese system at Lanchow. Progress is only beginning, but even now there is justification for great hopes.

At the other end of the Soviet Union a vast area likewise escapes from the absolute grip of the forest. It comprises the Baltic Republics, White Russia, the region of the Great Lakes, the Moscow area, the Urals, and the pre-Uralian zone.

(2) *The Baltic Lands.* These evidently form part of what might be called western Russia, and there is great temptation to include them in the region of the Great Lakes. But physically and even more so humanly they have an individuality of their own.

Geologically they are mainly of Primary formations (sandstones, shales, and limestones). These outcrop very seldom, because the great Scandinavian ice-cap has left its impress everywhere by planing off the surface or laying down rock-waste. Æsars, drumlins, moraines, erratic blocks, wide fluvio-glacial valleys, and deposits like the boulder clay in England occur in profusion. Hence, the drainage is very young and inadequate, as is shown by the abundance of peatbogs, marshes, and lakes. The fact is, a whole crowd of valleys have been blocked by moraines, and the general appearance of the topography reminds one of a draught-board with some of its squares raised in relief and others hollowed out. Furthermore, the variations in the Baltic Sea since the melting of the ice-cap have clearly distinguished two parts of the coast: the north coast of Estonia is rocky and jagged, whilst the rest, whose chief feature is the large Gulf of Riga, is fringed with low, muddy beaches, brackish lagoons, or dunes.

In the interior the grain of the relief runs east-and-west in Estonia and north-and-south in Latvia and Lithuania. But the relief is everywhere marked by extreme modesty. Estonia rises to 1060 ft. in the plateau of Hanja, Latvia to 1030 ft. in the hills of eastern Vidzeme, and Lithuania to 820 ft. in the Zarasai Hills; and these are maximum heights. Quite often the altitude is less than 330 ft.; which, however, does not prevent some districts, like the Alps of Courland and the Alps of Livonia, from offering a broken and picturesque landscape. The profiles of the rivers, even those of the Nemen, its feeder the Vileya, or the western Dvina, are irregular and broken by rapids, if not by falls. This, like the defective drainage of the country, is explained by the glacial morphology.

The streams are moderately well fed. Yet the climate, with a mean annual rainfall of between 19 and 24 ins., is not very moist. The maximum occurs in summer, which proves that the transitional climate of central Europe is tending here to give way to the climate of Russia.

In fact, the winter is appreciably more severe here than in north Germany. Dvinsk (Daugavpils) has a January mean of 21° F. At Kovno (Kaunas), which has a January mean of 23° F., the Nemen is frozen over for 77 days in the year and, whilst the coast of Lithuania is as a rule ice-bound for a very short time, that of Estonia is frozen every year for between 33 and 48 days. On the other hand, summer is not very hot; for instance, the July mean at Tartu is 62° F. But as a whole, although the north is harsher than the south and the coast is moister and cooler than the interior, the climate of the Baltic Republics is still relatively temperate. Nevertheless, it is rather unpleasant owing to its late spring, the uniformly high temperature in summer, and its wet, sultry autumn. The struggle between the influence of the ocean and that of the continent is revealed in the vast area of the forests and in their composition, birches and conifers being both abundant. But in respect of its fauna, with plenty of game including wild boars, wolves, foxes, stags, and even elks, as well as regards the flora, the Baltic lands are more closely related to central than to eastern Europe.

So far as population is concerned, there has been a collision here between the Germanic, Oriental, Nordic, and, indeed, Mediterranean peoples. In the north are the Ests, who are Finnish in race and language. The Letts and Lithuanians of the centre and south speak extremely ancient Indo-European tongues. In the thirteenth century they were all very backward, the Lithuanians being especially so. But the German *Drang nach Osten* brought sailors, traders, and artisans in the wake of the Brotherhood of the Sword-Bearers and the Teutonic Knights. In 1914 immense estates were still in the possession of the Baltic barons; banking, industry, and commerce were mostly German; and the intellectual influence of the Teutons was very strong. Although this ascendancy resulted in great economic and cultural progress, the Baltic peoples on the whole bore it impatiently. But they were also threatened by Sweden, by Poland (which made Lithuania into a satellite and kept it within the Roman Catholic faith, whilst Latvia and Estonia adhered to the Protestant Church under the influence of the Swedes and Germans) and, finally, by Russia, which annexed all the Baltic States in the eighteenth century and then endeavoured to russify them. The downfall of Russia in 1917 and the defeat of Germany in 1918 gave them back their liberty, and Estonia, Latvia, and Lithuania became three independent states. Between 1919 and 1939 they made real progress, although Lithuania was handicapped by her chronic diplomatic struggle with Poland over the possession of Vilna, which they both claimed.

In 1920 and 1933 treaties with Russia confirmed the independence of the Baltic States. In spite of this, the three countries were occupied in 1940 by Soviet Forces and became parts of the Soviet Union. All commercial and industrial enterprises and the whole of the land were taken over by the Communist Government which had been set up by the Russians. At the same time the savings of the people were wiped out by the introduction of the Russian rouble at a very unfavourable rate of exchange. About 60,000 men, women, and children were deported from Estonia, 25,000 from Latvia, and 40,000 from Lithuania. In 1941 the Baltic States were invaded by the Germans and held by them until 1944. On reoccupying the States the Russians perpetrated a further mass deportation, when tens of thousands of farmers were taken to Siberia. Collectivisation has had disastrous effects on agriculture, but there has been considerable industrial expansion.

In 1946 the district of Memelland was incorporated in Lithuania, and the port of Memel renamed Klaypeda. The neighbouring district around the old town of Koenigsburg was added to the R.F.S.S.R., and the name of the town was changed to Kaliningrad (188,000) in compliment to the then President of the Soviet Union.

This chequered history explains the existence of racial minorities and the mixed character of the populations of the towns, or at any rate of most of them. About 1938 Swedes were few, but there were some 125,000 Poles, 200,000 Germans, and nearly 375,000 Russians, not to mention 275,000 Jews. The Jews were exterminated by the Germans in 1941–4, and large numbers of Poles and Baltic peoples were deported by the Russians, as said above. It may be assumed that the place of all these peoples have been taken by Russians. But both absolutely and relatively the population of the three States was, and is, small. Estonia, with nine persons to the square mile, has a total of 1,100,000; Latvia, with eleven persons to the square mile, has 2,000,000; and Lithuania, with seventeen persons to the square mile, has 2,700,000.

In the past more than two-thirds of the Baltic peoples were country-folk, which means that the countries were mainly agricultural. This is still so, although under Soviet rule industry has increased and the town population doubled. Forest covers nearly 23 per cent. of the surface, and timber is one of the chief products of the region; yet agriculture is the chief occupation. The introduction of the Soviet system has included the collectivisation of the land, virtually all the agricultural area being divided between 4100 collective farms and 297 State Farms. The area under cultivation has been increased by a good margin, but waste land, moor, and marsh still occupy too much space. In Lithuania half the land is under the plough, but in Latvia little more than a third, and in Estonia only one-fifth. Production used to be fairly varied, with rye, oats, and barley in the lead, but the chief corn crops now are wheat and maize. Artificial fodder crops, beet, and, above all, potatoes are increasing and are leading to a better use of manure. Flax, which formerly held a very important place, has lost ground. In stock-rearing before 1940 the main animal was the cow for the purpose of milk production. Since 1941, however, the number of cattle has fallen off and the number of pigs and sheep increased. Efforts have been made to increase the yield from land both by the use of farm machinery and by the employment of agronomists, live-stock specialists, veterinary surgeons, and forestry officers. In 1955 there were 311 M.T.S. and 4300 combines in use and 5300 specialists whose services were available and whose number was more than double the 2000 available in 1941. How far the yield has been increased by these measures does not appear from Soviet statistics, but that there has been some increase is shown in the modest, but appreciable improvement in housing.

As elsewhere in the Soviet system, industry has been expanded. The Baltic States are handicapped by having no coal or oil for fuel and no opportunities for producing hydro-electricity. Raw materials are not plentiful, flax and beet being the only industrial crops. But the production of cement has greatly increased, especially in Lithuania, where it rose from nil in 1913 to 204,000 tons in 1955. Refineries in Lithuania and Latvia produced 70,000 tons of sugar in the same year. Raw materials imported from other parts of the Soviet Union result in a modest production of tin-sheeting, a considerably increased output of unbleached cotton cloth and cotton fabrics, and a large quantity of mineral fertilisers. The last of these industries is new to the Baltic States.

Trade with countries outside the Soviet Union is arranged by the central authorities. In general, the aim of agriculture is to supply local needs, but timber, flax, eggs, bacon, butter, and paper are produced in excess of such need and are exchanged for coal, oil, and machinery. Inland transport is poor in Lithuania, but roads and railways have been generally improved to enable the Soviet Union to use the important ports on the Baltic. Riga in Latvia, Tallin (Reval) in Estonia, and Klaypeda (Memel) in Lithuania all have good harbours and are busy, well-furnished ports.

As may be imagined, the big towns in the Baltic States are nearly all ports. Thus, Liepaya (Libau; pop. 61,000) as well as the abovementioned Klaypeda (pop. 34,000) and Tallin (pop. 257,000), the economic as well as the political capital of Estonia. Besides being a very great focus of commerce and industry and a political and cultural centre Riga (pop. 565,000) is not only the capital of Latvia, but also the largest town in the Baltic States. Kaliningrad, whose district lies outside the Baltic States, has like Riga a long tradition of maritime trade. Like Riga, therefore, it is clearly indispensable to Russia and may be expected as a Soviet port to advance by leaps and bounds. Clearly, the possession of the Baltic States and the Kaliningrad district rounds off north-western Russia very satisfactorily and greatly strengthens the position of the Soviet Union in Europe.

The inland towns are shopping and administrative or cultural centres and are far smaller. In Lithuania, for example, may be mentioned Kaunas (Kovno; pop. 195,000), the capital of the State between the wars; and Vilnyus (Vilna; pop. 200,000) a genuinely Polish town set in a Lithuanian countryside and included in Lithuania after the Russian occupation. In Latvia Yelgava (Mitau; pop. 33,000) and Daugavpils (Dvinsk; pop. 43,000) are both declining. In Estonia the famous university town of Tartu (Dorpat) has a population of 70,000.

On the whole, though Lithuania remained poor and backward in 1939, Estonia and, even more so, Latvia were fast progressing. The re-annexation of the republics by Russia and the introduction into them of the Soviet system has considerably modified their economy. Whilst there is evidence of dissatisfaction among the people with the Communist régime, it is true that material conditions have improved. This is especially so in Lithuania, where improvement has also taken place along other lines. In this State the number of pupils in 'general' schools is three times greater than in 1914 and those in higher educational establishments nearly four times as many. Since 1914 the number of public libraries has risen from 200 to 4500.

(3) *The Region of the Great Lakes of Russia.* This corresponds more or less to the districts of Pskov, Novgorod, Leningrad, and Olonets. In the north it is formed of gneiss and granite, the beds of which are an extension into Russia of the Finnish plateau; and in the south there are less resistant clays and primitive limestones; and, at the junction of two geological regions, a peculiar feature of the relief consists of a northward facing escarpment which rises to the east of Leningrad, passes south round the town, and extends to the Estonian coast along the glint ridge. At the foot of the escarpment runs a depression dotted with lakes and forming the line of contact between an ancient rock mass and younger and less resistant beds which separates the Fennoscandian Shield from the Russian platform.[1]

Apart from the escarpment, which varies in height between 140 and 540 ft., the land forms are glacial. Traces of the ancient Caledonian and Variscan folds are negligible, as is also the evidence of faulting. The main features are moraines, æsars, and circular hollows, which are better preserved here than in any other part of Russia.

[1] North America affords an analogy in the junction of the Laurentian Shield in Canada with the younger rocks farther south. Here too there is an escarpment broken by falls (Niagara is similar, but on a larger scale, to the Narva Falls) and a peripheral depression in which there are lakes. Lake Superior and Lake Huron correspond to Ladoga and Onega, and Lakes Erie and Michigan to Ilmen and Chudskoye.

The work of the ice explains the many rapids in the streams and more especially the incomplete and defective nature of the drainage. Marshes are very numerous, and above all there is in Karelia a veritable profusion of large, deep lakes. Two of them are the biggest in Europe. Onega, 3860 square miles in area and 740 ft. deep, is joined by the Svir to Lake Ladoga, which is also fed by the overflow of the great Finnish lake Saimaa and by the Volkhov, which flows from Lake Ilmen. Lake Ladoga, which is 850 ft. deep, has an area of about 7000 square miles and is thirty-one times the size of Lake Geneva with twenty-five times its volume. Ilmen (less than 400 square miles) and Chudskoye (1400 square miles) differ in being much less deep (33 and 56 ft. respectively) and in having been formed not by ice erosion, but by morainic dams. The same is true of Lake Beloye some distance farther east.

A severe, damp, and foggy climate prevails over the whole region. The extremely unhealthy winter may bring dense fog at the same time as temperatures of 10° F. or 14° F. The forest, which was originally very extensive, is without many of the species of temperate regions, especially the poplar, elm, maple, and ash. The general infertility of the soil gives little encouragement to agriculture. But, says Camena d'Almeida, the region forms 'a junction of routes between all the Russian seas'. Such a corridor is all the more favourable to trade along it because it is the only Russian outlet to the Baltic. Finally, the growth of a capital city naturally gave rise to considerable industries, which were helped by certain mineral resources and an abundance of waterfalls.

In a detailed survey several sub-regions must be distinguished. Firstly, there is SOUTHERN KARELIA, a rough forest country in which settlers from Novgorod largely swamped the Finnish substratum. They still engage in hunting, fishing, and lumbering, but they are improving their methods of stock-rearing, modernising their modest attempts at producing oats, barley, wheat, and potatoes, and beginning to exploit the local iron, copper, vanadium, talc, marble, and coal. The presence of wood, peat, and waterfalls like that on the Svir furnishes electric power. Though Olonets (pop. 69,000) has greatly declined, Kalinink (formerly Petrozavodsk) is taking on a new lease of life and is increasing its old metallurgical industry, and Svirstroy is a new industrial centre, small, but very vigorous. New towns engaged in chemical industries are springing up along the Baltic–White Sea Canal and the Murmansk Railway. The Karelian Republic has been somewhat enlarged at the expense of Finland, the whole district between Lake Ladoga and the Gulf of Riga having been handed over to Russia, and Vyborg (Viipuri; pop. 80,000) has become a Soviet town. Similarly, in the far north Finland has ceded to the Soviet Union the port of Petsamo and the nickel-mining district around it.

THE BALTIC FRONTIER, which is also naturally poor, has had its glorious moments. In the fifteenth century Pskov was a large trading centre with a population of 80,000; Novgorod the Great especially was an enormous commercial *entrepôt* and intellectual centre with a population of perhaps 400,000, a real capital city, and the coloniser of the whole of the north of Russia as far as across the Urals. But history was cruel to them both, for the foundation of St. Petersburg dealt them a grievous blow, and today the former has a population of no more than 60,000, the latter one of 45,000. They are, however, the two chief centres in this poor country. Hunting and fishing bring in but a small yield, and wheat and flax only a modest return. Yet agriculture and the rearing of cattle and horses are making headway in the parklands; and, in fact, there is some mineral wealth: iron at Cherepovets, stone, fireclay, bituminous shale, and lignite at Borovichi, bauxite mainly at Tikvin; and the Volkhov hydro-electric power-house has given rise to the aluminium *kombinat* of Volkhovstroy.

Finally, between Karelia and the Baltic frontier lies the Leningrad area. The creation of a capital city in this land of bare conical hillocks, morainic heights,sandy plains, and marshy ground, amidst pine forests and in a harsh and unhealthy climate might have seemed to be a gamble; but the Russian state needed a capital on the Baltic, a better-placed Novgorod built quite near the sea on a navigable river and at the junction of trade routes. The first twenty years were very difficult, but by 1725 the city had a population of 75,000. Founded as a citadel in war-time under the Swedish cannon, St. Petersburg had the circular plan of a fortress, with concentric streets and avenues, like the famous Nevsky Prospekt, radiating from the centre. But at the same time the Tsars gave it fine buildings and attracted a number of immigrants not only from all parts of the Empire, but also from abroad (Germans, Englishmen, Dutchmen, French, and Jews); and they strove to improve its communications by water, road, and, later, rail and to foster various industries which received further help from the presence of transport facilities and abundant supplies of labour. So much so that in 1915 Petrograd had a population of 2,347,000. As the revolution cost it its position as capital and made it a victim of famine and massacre, its population fell to 722,000 souls.

Today, the population of Leningrad is 3,176,000. The fact is that the city is more than a mere large provincial capital, and its functions are many. Admittedly, it is still an artificial city with a rather frigid appearance and in character more European than genuinely Russian, but of real grandeur with its cathedrals of Preobrazhenski and Saint-

View over the grim interior of Kamchatka

White Russia. The River Pripet flowing through its marshes

Isaac, the Kazan Museum (until 1929 the Cathedral of Our Lady), its Winter Palace, its museum-palace of Hermitage, its splendid granite quays, its majestic bridges, and its immense avenues. Though it is somewhat lacking in charm, the same is not true of its suburbs of Leninsk (formerly Peterhof), Pushkin (formerly Tsarskoe Selo), Krasnogvardeisk (Gatchina), etc., which have inherited a number of villas and smart residences from Tsarist times. Leningrad is also a great intellectual city, with many institutes, schools, libraries, and museums. Thanks to the commercial port of Kronstadt and even more to the Neva ship canal, it is the greatest Soviet emporium on the Baltic and the Union's chief point of contact with Europe. The ship canal brings the city within sixteen miles of Kronstadt Bay and the Gulf of Finland. Leningrad is, in fact, becoming more and more of an industrial centre. Metallurgy (witness the Putilov works), textile manufacture, tanning, saw-milling, the food industry, and brick- and glass-making have long flourished there; but since 1928 there has been a striking expansion of metallurgical industries and notably of shipbuilding, and the abundance of hydro-electricity in the neighbourhood is stimulating the growth of chemical industries. The shipyards are said to be producing an atomic-powered ice-breaker and a non-magnetic survey vessel, and the factories include Electrosila (chemical equipment) and the Red Triumph Rubber Foundry, both of which are the largest of their kind in the world. On the right bank of the Neva and even more to the east and south-east of the city immense new housing estates have just been built, and the tendency does not seem to be slackening. The housing estate for Electrosila's 13,700 employees alone covers nearly two square miles. As may well be imagined, a great effort is being made for a long distance around Leningrad to develop the production of milk and meat as well as of potatoes and other vegetables and fruit, for the feeding of this enormous city imposes difficult problems.

Altogether, the sub-region is blessed with few natural advantages and is poor and on the whole sparsely peopled. But as a corridor and a lung breathing the air of Europe, it is indispensable to the Union. Russian settlement built solidly here. In 1918 the Slav world greatly contracted, and Russia lost Finland and the Baltic States; but she firmly held the region of the Great Lakes until the German War of 1939–45 enabled her to recover the Baltic States and even to advance her frontiers some way into Germany.

(4) *Western, or White (Belo), Russia.*[1] Bounded on the west by

---

[1] Officially White Russia does not include Smolensk. It is considerably smaller than the geographical region to which the name Western Russia can be applied; but it expanded in 1939 to cover vast territories which had previously formed the eastern portion of the great plain of Poland.

Poland, on the south by the Ukraine, on the east by the Muscovite industrial region, on the north by the morainic rampart of Velikie Luki, and on the north-west by Latvia, this sub-region is of varied geology, but the underlying rocks and the few tectonic features which have affected it are almost everywhere masked by a coating of glacial waste. The normal landscape shows morainic hills, vast sandy stretches, erratic blocks, lakes, and marshes. The principal feature is a huge morainic wall which runs a little to the north of Minsk and Smolensk and, resting on an offshoot of the central Russian platform, reaches a height of over 1100 ft. in Sviataya Gora at the point where it bends northwards towards the Valday plateau. Right in the south-west, too, there is an east–west terrace which was caused by an ancient dislocation. The fracture thus produced in the cretaceous upland of Volhynia separates the southern portion of that country, which is an extension of the rich soils of Podolia, from the northern portion, which is a barren plain of glacial sand and pebbles and is geographically related to Western Russia.

The climate, which is transitional between that of Poland and that of central Russia, is drier and more extreme in the east than in the west. On the whole, it is moderately damp, and the soil is often saturated with water. Owing to the very gentle gradients, streams and rivers flow sluggishly in wide meanders, and they cut through or pass round the moraines to move from one hollow to the next. The western Dvina (Duna) is an instance of this, as are also the Dnepr and its feeders: Sozh, Desna, Berezina, Pripyat (Pripet). They are unable to drain the country, which has a profusion of lakes and marshes, the best known of which are those of the Pripyat. The surface of the sub-region, which is 125 miles long from east to west and 90 miles wide, consists sometimes of spongy and more or less peaty grassland sprinkled with small clumps of trees, at other times of vast expanses of blue-green water shining among reeds and rushes, and at other times of drier areas which are often ridged by dunes. The dampness of the climate and soil explains the very wooded nature of the country. Pinewoods and mixed forests cover vast areas, especially in the basin of the Pripyat, which is known as the Polesye, or wooded land. The area of dry, cultivable soil is far less than that of the virgin forests which are often flooded and the immense swamps in which movement is only possible by boat.

In spite of its unproductive character and the difficulty of communications, this sub-region has been peopled from early times. A number of Magdalenian, Azilian, and Neolithic remains have been found in the dunes and moraines, and the sparse villages stand on these same sites today. But, being a frontier belt, it was for centuries furiously disputed between the Russians and the Poles and suffered devastation countless times. As the White Russians were cut off for a long time from the main Russian family, they developed their special characteristics more freely, but isolation accentuated the natural poverty of the country. Almost up to the present day the people—especially in the area which was Polish from 1919 to 1939— were scarcely known to the Russian officials and led a life of almost prehistoric standards. Through the efforts of General Zhilinski some three million acres of the marshes of the western part of the Polesye have been drained and made into pasture or arable, a few roads have been built, some mainly strategic railways have been constructed, and the serious endemic disease known as Polish plait (*plica polonica*) has been checked. In spite of this, the Polesye is still a wretched country, especially in the west. Except along the waterways, travel is only possible on footpaths made of faggots, logs, and duckboards leading to the fords. The villages consist of miserable log huts. The meagre crops of oats and rye feed only four to seven persons to the square mile on the borders, and the central area is almost uninhabited. The primitive character of the mode of life always astounds the Western traveller. In other parts the poverty is less, and progress not so behindhand. But owing to its geography as well as its history, the country is none the less poorly endowed and naturally unfavourable to human life.

By its very position between the Dvina and Dnepr western Russia formed a trade route along the Berezina and was a portage country. Hence the motley character of the population, which consists of 70 per cent. of White Russians with an admixture of Poles, Ukrainians, Lithuanians, and, lastly, Jews, who form 40 per cent. of the urban total. Members of the Orthodox Church rub shoulders with Roman Catholics, Lutherans, and even a few Muslims. But the country is still only moderately peopled with 100 persons to the square mile in the White Russian Republic. Between 1926 and 1929 the increase in population in White Russia was only 12 per cent., which was less than the average for the Soviet Union. Between 1940 and 1945 the total population fell from 9,200,000 to 8,000,000. Emigration seems to have been particularly active here, however, and towns of any importance are rare. In the area which was formerly Polish the only ones to be mentioned are Kovel (pop. 21,000) in northern Volhynia, Brest Litovsk (pop. 50,000) a little farther north, and then the modest little town of Pinsk (pop. 32,000) in the Polesye. To the west of the former frontier the largest are Orsha on the Dnepr, Bobruysk (pop. 84,000) on the Berezina, Polotsk (pop. 25,000) on the Sozh, Vitebsk (pop. 128,000) on the Dvina, Smolensk (pop. 131,000), which is almost Great Russian, and Minsk (pop. 412,000). They are all grown up as market towns, route and railway junctions, or stages in the river-boat traffic, but some have industries in addition. Thus, Minsk has motor-car and tractor works, flour mills, distilleries, and sawmills, and Gomel makes farm machinery. Here and there spinning and weaving are carried on. On the whole, industrial activity has greatly increased since 1944, official figures giving a rise of two and a half times. Before the German invasion there was little industry, but the Soviet Government has seen that industrial towns are most easily defended, and so Minsk and other towns have been packed with factories. The powerful hydro-electric plant called Belges was important even before 1940. Textile mills and metallurgical shops had been built around Smolensk, and the local peat resources had been used for generating electricity in several power stations. These were all destroyed in the war, but have been restored.

Before 1944 the greater part of the production was, therefore, supplied by the traditional resources. Hunting and fishing played a minor part, but agriculture (wheat, flax, and vegetables) was striving to increase its yield. Similarly, stock-rearing was making headway, and milk production had considerably increased. But local wealth in the former eastern districts of Poland as well as in White Russia proper was based essentially on timber, the exploitation and floating of which were reorganised in 1928 and occupied a large number of wood-cutters and raft-men, without counting the workers employed in the cellulose and match factories and the woodwork establishment which were combined in the Dvina trading estate. The Polish Government, conscious as it was of the danger it would run by leaving vast areas of eastern Poland with a population composed mainly of White Russians, had entered on a policy of methodical drainage, by means of which it intended to improve these districts preparatory to placing Polish settlers on them. The Soviet Government has resumed the task of drainage, which it had some time previously tried in Russia, and it is peopling the country with Soviet citizens, the few Poles having returned to their native land since the end of the war. But the task is immense and will demand long effort. It is likely that for a number of years to come western Russia will certainly remain what it is today, viz. one of the most backward parts of Soviet territory in Europe, though very great progress has been made since the end of the war. Anyhow, when the German army entered the area, it was able to confirm the statement of Hitler's propaganda which had represented the Russian nation as wretched and backward.

(5) *The Muscovite Region.* On the other hand, the Muscovite region is the real heart of Russia, not only through its geographical position, but also owing to its exceptional density of population and its commercial, industrial, and administrative activity. The 'Moscow basin', well named so since its strata are arranged in circles and

make the outline of a basin breached towards the east, usually presents the appearance of a flat and dismal plain. Moscow itself is some 380 ft. above sea level, but Ryazan is only 190. End moraines, however, crown elevations in the foundational rocks here and there and may thus rise fairly high. For instance, on the Valday Plateau, where the country is a mass of humps all strewn with moraines and dotted with lakes, Kamennik reaches a height of 1056 ft.

The importance of the region lies mainly in the fact that it is a zone of transition. Firstly, as regards the soil, in the north glacial deposits cover most of the surface, including clayey morainic drumlins and a litter of erratic blocks; whilst in the south immense stretches of sand are succeeded by loess and weathered *chernoziom*, the harbinger of Black Earth. Secondly, though the climate is severe throughout the country, the north-west has more rain than the south-east (24 ins. against 18), a shorter period of frost (4 months against 5), and less extreme annual ranges of temperature (49° F. as against 56° F.). Thirdly, the region is transitional from the hydrographic point of view. Its northern position is particularly well provided with lakes, peat bogs, and swamps both in the plains with their covering of fluvio-glacial drift and on the plateaus, which are dotted with clayey knolls and streaked with moraines. The streams have neither well-defined sources nor clear-cut banks. On the other hand, the country to the south of the Volga is better drained and drier, and its streams have real sources and well-marked right banks. And lastly, the vegetation-type is also transitional. To the north of the Volga the country is still definitely forested, with resinous species predominating. Between the Volga and Oka the conifers are greatly mixed with birch, oak, maple, and ash, and the clearings become wider and wider and are more and more easily enlarged. Farther south limes and poplars appear, and broad patches of steppe vegetation penetrate into the woods. In the end the woods are reduced to mere copses, that is, to woodland steppe which gradually turns into pure steppe.

This varied region is given a certain unity by its river system. Its axis may be regarded as marked by the valleys of the Moskva and Klyazma rather than by those of the Volga or Oka. The Volga rises in a swamp on the Valday Plateau and, though theoretically navigable from Kalinin, is in fact of little depth, and, besides being obstructed by rocks and sandbanks, suffers from a very variable volume until reinforced by the Suda and Oka. It flows near the northern limit of the Muscovite sub-region. The Oka, on the other hand, runs along the southern boundary. Rising on the central plateau in the Black Earth country at a height of 840 ft. above sea level, it is fed by swamps and big springs in the chalk. It is a fine stream with a good volume and is longer and wider than the Volga above Gorky.

Since Muscovy is a transitional belt in the middle of Russia, its population is necessarily mixed. In spite of the rather unproductive soil, it has had life-centres from early times, at least on the higher ground. The original Finnish population, the wide distribution of which is attested by the place-names,[1] and which was reinforced later by Karelians and Tatars, was submerged by Great Russians, who seem to have rapidly increased in number. The need in historical times for refuge from the Tatar and Polish invasions gave rise in the *polya* and high river banks to many towns which quickly expanded. They were market centres for the produce of hunting and fishing,[2] of field and forest, as well as for raw materials (flax and hemp) and manufactured goods. Industries sprang up in the form of the manufacture of textiles, pottery, woodwork, and ikons. The ports of the upper Volga, like Rybinsk, Kostroma, Yaroslavl (the 'Russian Nürnberg'), and above all Gorky (Nizhni Novgorod), throve on this trade. At the last named a fair, destined to be the most important in Russia, was inaugurated in 1817, but has been discontinued since the Revolution.

Spared from foreign as well as civil war from 1812 to 1941, the Moscow area developed its resources in a remarkable manner, and the return of the Government to Moscow made it once more the undisputed centre of Russian life. Today its activities are very varied. In the south especially it is still prosperous agriculturally and is trying to do even better still. Rye and oats flourish in the north, where wheat is rarely cultivated; but the latter grain is fairly abundant in the south on the approaches to the Black Earth country. Industrial crops, hemp at Vyazma and Kaluga, flax at Rzhev, Yaroslavl, Rostov, and Morom, and potatoes which are produced everywhere are of far greater importance, however; and the cultivation of market vegetables and fruit round Suzdal, Tula, Kolomna, and, above all, Rostov has expanded to an extent seldom equalled in Russia.

In spite of the changes which have come about in the organisation of the distribution of goods within the country, trade is still very important. Though Gorky no longer has its fair—which had anyhow declined since 1880—its river port is still very busy, as is also that of Rybinsk. The activities of the State shops and the co-operatives now form a greater part of the business done in important towns, notably in Moscow. And the growing transport facilities certainly imparts increasing vitality to this business.

But today the Moscow basin is pre-eminently industrial and is

---

[1] The very name *Moscow* (*Moskva*) is the Zyrian for 'water for the cows'.
[2] The name Rybinsk is derived from *ryba* = 'fish'.

the chief manufacturing centre in the Soviet Union. Raw materials, however, are not plentiful, and the rather poor coal-field at Ryazan and Tula was soon exhausted. The real causes of success have been the abundance of skilled craftsmen who had built up *kustar*[1] industry; the many railways which converged on Moscow, carrying thither trade which encouraged industry; and, lastly, the protection of the State, which since the days of Peter the Great and especially since the time of Alexander II has fostered the growth of industry in the traditional centre of Russian life. Today the discovery of new supplies of coal in the Moscow basin and the re-establishment of Moscow as the capital of the Union could not but hasten the tendency and, in spite of the loudly proclaimed intention of the Soviet Government to develop industry in the remote regions, whether Russian or not, rather than at the centre, the policy of the five-year plans has caused a fresh and vigorous expansion in the Moscow area.

But this industrial activity has not benefited all the towns. Many historic cities, like Suzdal, Vladimir (pop. 66,000), Rostov, Morom, Uglich, and Pereyaslav have utterly declined and produce little more now than market vegetables. On the other hand, some ancient towns have expanded considerably owing to the growth of industry, and many villages have become veritable towns.

The textile industry is predominant. It began with the local flax and hemp which are worked up today in Yaroslavl, Ivanovo, Rzhev, and Kostroma. Woollen manufacture also has a long, though less successful, history in Muscovy; and silk goods are made at Yaroslavl. But cotton, which has invaded the whole basin, easily takes first place. It is milled mainly at Ivanovo (Ivanovo Voznesensk) and notably in the district between the Volga and Klyazma at Shuya, Serpukhov, and the twin towns of Orekhovo and Zuyevo, but also at Yaroslavl, Kostroma, and Kalinin. Besides, Yaroslavl makes *tulups*[2] of sheepskin; Kaluga and Kimry make boots and shoes; and there is scarcely a town which does not to some extent engage in manufacture.

The metallurgical industry, which at first worked up iron ore from the marshes between Gorky and Kaluga and later ore from Krivoyrog, is also very flourishing. Bryansk on the borders of western Russia engages in mechanical engineering. Tula has large factories and makes knives and machines, not to mention samovars. Not far away, Ryazan manufactures farm machinery and Koloma railway material, tractors, and boilers. Finally, on the lower Oka the Gorky group comprises Pavlovo, which makes iron goods, cutlery, ironmongery, and surgical instruments; Sormovo, which builds steamboats, locomotive boilers, and railway carriages and Gorky, the 'Detroit of the

[1] Home industry of small craftsmen.
[2] Coats made of rough sheepskin with the wool on the inside.

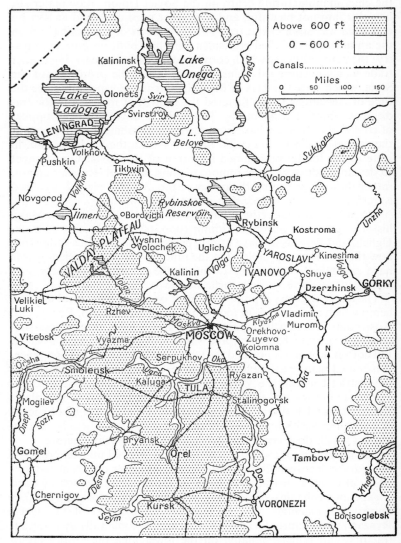

Above 600 ft.

0 – 600 ft.

Canals...........

Miles
0   50   100   150

FIG. 37. THE MOSCOW REGION.

252

Soviet Union', which specialises in the construction of motor vehicles. Finally, Yaroslavl manufactures motor engines.

Chemical industry, on its part, is fast expanding. Formerly, it flourished only at Kineshma; today it represents the greater part of the activity of Stalinogorsk (Bobriky) and is rapidly developing at Gorky, where there are in addition large oil refineries. The food and paper industries, book publication, the manufacture of musical instruments and scientific apparatus should also be mentioned, since they are growing fast.

The foregoing is a remarkably strong list of industries, and its attraction of a very large and regularly increasing working population is therefore not surprising. This part of central Russia, which contains nearly 25 million people, is now urbanised to a great degree, as the following list will show:

Rzhev	54,000	Orekhovo-Zuyevo	99,000
Vyshni Volochek	63,000	Ivanovo	319,000
Kalinin	240,000	Kolomna	75,000
Rybinsk	139,000	Stalinogorsk	109,000
Yaroslavl	374,000	Ryazan	136,000
Borisoglebsk	52,000	Bryansk	111,000
Kostroma	156,000	Kaluga	122,000
Kineshma	75,000	Tula	320,000
Shuya	58,000	Sormovo	95,000
Serpukhov	95,000	Gorky	876,000

The development of the area is summed up in that of Moscow, which is representative of it. Situated in the heart of Russia at the focus of her natural routes, the city has neither a particularly strong defensive position nor a very remarkable waterway. At first it was an asylum rather than a centre of expansion, and its existence was due to history rather than geography. Owing to the capture of Vladimir, its princes were able to assume the title of grand-dukes. The headquarters of the Russian Church were established at Moscow, and the protection of the Khans, skilfully used and then thrown off in due course, enabled the town to become the capital of the whole of Russia. Henceforth, its fortune was assured. Immigrants constantly reached it from all the Russian provinces, and its growth was almost uninterrupted, its population numbering 150,000 about 1750, 381,000 in 1861, 1,035,000 in 1897, nearly 2,000,000 in 1915, only 1,000,000 in 1920, but 2,029,000 in 1926, 2,740,000 in 1931, 4,137,000 in 1939, and, excluding the suburbs, 4,839,000 in 1955. This enormous expansion in the past, and even more in our own times, springs from several causes:

First, the political function of the city. True, it suffered eclipse for two hundred years, but the *diminutio capitis* of Moscow was so contrary to the nature of things and to historical tradition that Peter the Great himself dared not proclaim it officially, and the revolution at once gave back to the old capital its rightful leading position.

Secondly, its intellectual function. This was for a long time less than that of St. Petersburg; but in 1755 the city had its university; gradually it was endowed with many museums of art, ethnography, and science, with an observatory, with various institutes, libraries, and theatres; and this wealth of intellectual opportunity has been strengthened in recent years. A great centre of printing and of the book trade as early as the time of the Tsars, Moscow is more than ever the great spiritual focus of the Union.

Then, its commercial function. This was already well marked two hundred years ago and was very important in the last century, as is shown by Ostrovski's description of manners, the scenes of most of his plays being laid among the tradesmen of Moscow. The town was so obviously the great national market and the necessary focus of communications that the railway system was obliged to use it as its centre. Before the revolution it had many shops; it still has, and the city is the seat of a busy trade which is increased still further by the traffic on the Moskva–Volga Canal.

Finally and most especially, its industrial function. As early as 1850 it contained 650 factories and 40,000 workmen, and these figures have constantly increased. At first industry was confined to the suburbs, but later it began to invade the city itself, and the enormous increase in the population since 1929 is explained by the prodigious industrial expansion. The textile industry (cotton, wool, silk, and mixtures), dyeing, the manufacture of clothing and footwear, tanning, the metallurgical industries (railway equipment, motor vehicles, tools, ball-bearings, and precision instruments), the food industry (distillery, brewing, biscuit-making, and food canning), paper-milling, printing, and the manufacture of electrical fittings, occupy more than a million men and women.

These changes have greatly modified the appearance of Moscow. Its lay-out is like that of Paris in certain respects: there is a river, the Moskva, with islands; some hills, like the Lenin Hills and Borovitski Hill; a central kernel around which concentric circular zones separated by boulevards have grown up one after the other in the course of time. The city, however, did not begin on an island, but on the dominant north bank, where the Kremlin (or Kreml') was built, whilst a bridgehead was constructed on the south bank. Today the centre is still occupied by the Kremlin and the Kitai Gorod, the 'City of Refuge'.[1] Around them are the Bielyi Gorod (= White City), the

[1] In spite of the name, this quarter has never been connected with the Chinese. *Kitai Gorod* does not mean 'Chinese town', but 'strong town', from the Tatar word for fortress.

Zemlyanoi Gorod (City of Earth), as far as the outer boulevards (*Sadovaya* or Garden Boulevard), and, lastly, various suburbs which are extending farther and farther today with railway stations, barracks, many factories, and parks. In this very extensive city gardens, copses, and, till recently, fields and waste ground occupy a large space. The description of Moscow as a large village is unjust, however, for, though the town has been burnt down many times, it has a number of fine buildings like the Kremlin, a wonderful collection of forts, palaces, convents, and churches, the Tower of Ivan Veliki, and the splendid Cathedral of St. Basil on Red Square, where the mausoleum of Lenin now stands. It is a great city by reason of its size and the volume of its traffic, and, though it lacks the imposing appearance of Leningrad, it has a genuinely Russian hallmark which always charms foreigners. Its maze of little streets with their low houses is an attractively picturesque feature.

Since the revolution Moscow has indeed changed a great deal. Owing to the endless, frightful housing shortage, the city has continued to grow and has become one huge building-yard. But demolition is also taking place. Not satisfied with cutting many main streets through the old quarters, the authorities have pulled down a number of ancient buildings, religious or otherwise, like the monasteries of Chudov and Voznesenski, the church of 'The Saviour in the Pinewoods', the Chapel of the Virgin Iverskaya, the Church of Christ the Redeemer, the Tower of Sukharev, and many others. The appearance of the city has lost by this, and, though squalid slums are not obvious to the eye, the large workmen's quarters, skyscrapers, and administrative and commercial buildings do not go well with the swarm of palaces, towers, steeples, and the many-coloured onion domes of the churches which offer an imposing sight from the top of the Lenin Hills; and the efforts of the Soviet Government to construct a new architectural style do not seem to have had great results.

But these are growing pains, and Moscow remains nevertheless the most Russian of Russian towns and the symbol of the national past as well as the most modern city in the Union. Furthermore, it deserves its title of capital not only on account of its geographical position, the size of its population, and its economic activity, but also because it is the centre of the most complex economic region in the Soviet Union, the most European by its blending of agriculture and industry, and, lastly, because it was the cradle of the race which has conquered this gigantic empire whose language has become the medium of Russian civilisation and its vehicle of thought.[1]

[1] 'The people of Moscow like to say that good pronunciation of Russian does not go beyond the shadow cast by the steeple of Ivan Veliki!' (Tesnière).

Thus, the forest margins bordering on the steppes are clearly distinguished from the great forest proper. Within the latter there is another region on which intense human activity has conferred a rather peculiar character. This is the Ural region.

(6) *The Urals and the pre-Uralian Region.* (*a*) *The Urals.* This mountain range, more than 1500 miles long, but at most only 112 wide and 5600 ft. high, is completely isolated in the middle of the Russo-Siberian plain. It is 'the belt of the world'. Its eastern slopes, which are composed of very dislocated crystalline rocks, have no foreland. Its western face, formed of Primary beds of limestone, arkoses, conglomerates, metamorphic schists, and quartzites sometimes interlarded with granite, spreads out in a broad, undulating, and broken plateau without bold peaks or high summits. Hence, the Urals are an asymmetrical range caused by a tangential thrust from the east. As the thrust came up against the Carboniferous plateau of Ufa, the range is not straight-lined, but curves away eastwards opposite this buffer, to the north and south of which the folds clearly run in opposite directions. The folding seems to date from the end of the Primary, since when the Urals have known no further movement of the kind. The age-long erosion to which the mountains have been subjected, without other rejuvenation than a few local uplifts and the occurrence of some faults, has therefore caused extreme wear, and the range is only a broken ruin. Even if we hesitate to believe that it was formerly joined to the Tien Shan, we must admit that it was once far broader. Whether its eastern foot represents the coast of a former Tertiary sea resting on a surface which has suffered marine denudation, or whether it rises from a surface that has undergone sub-aerial erosion, the Urals are clearly only a remnant worn down by the agents of disintegration and only just escaped total destruction. Hence, the traveller from the west scarcely notices that he has entered a mountainous country, so featureless and monotonous is the relief. The disintegration by the action of frost of certain quartzite hill-tops and their transformation into jagged ridges or an expanse of boulders alone preserve a noticeable feature here and there.

Though not lofty, the Urals have a very severe climate owing to their latitude and distance from the sea. The winters are dry, but the summers definitely wet, and the clouds and rain which often envelop the mountains in the latter season explain the luxuriance of the forest. Except in the Far North,[1] the hill-tops alone are bare. Elsewhere, a sea of pines and firs, larches and birches covers nearly the whole surface.

But in such a severe climate and with such poor soil agriculture is

[1] The forest does not go beyond lat. 65° N. on the western slopes or beyond lat. 67° N. on the eastern slopes.

bound to be at a low standard, and stock-rearing is very difficult, as the damp prevents hay from drying. The great attraction for man was the presence of fur-bearing animals (bear, Arctic fox, brown bear, wolf, glutton, squirrel, and ermine) and also the abundance of timber in the district. A dense layer of Russian settlement was imposed on a primitive ethnical foundation consisting of Voguls, Ostiaks, Samoyedes, Tatars, and Bashkirs, but did not overwhelm it. The settlers were not long in noticing the mineral wealth of the range and began its exploitation in 1623. Besides, when Siberia became Russian, the Urals became a passageway leading to it, especially in the middle portion between Perm and Irbit.

The region performs this function more than ever now that Russia and Siberia are in process of fusion and trade between them is increasing. It is also becoming more and more a great mining and industrial region. But its relief is not everywhere the same, any more than the climatic conditions and vegetable and mineral wealth or the population. Several fairly clear subdivisions are to be distinguished. Little is known of the ARCTIC URALS. It is recognised, however, that, though the range is very narrow at the Arctic Circle (25 miles), it is nevertheless composed of two chains and, farther north, of three, viz. the Obdorsk Hills on the east, the Timanski Hills on the west, and in the centre the Pae Khoy, a long ridge 1850 ft. high, worn by former glaciers, and now occupied by tundra. In its marshy valleys and on its bare hills live Ostiaks and Samoyedes, who keep reindeer and hunt the lemming. The presence of rock-crystal, iron, copper chromium, and also platinum and gold has been proved.

Farther south the fir forest appears, marking the beginning of the NORTHERN URALS. These are considerably better known and are formed of a series of little ranges running parallel and sometimes temporarily interrupted, between which lie splendid valleys like those of Shchugor and Podcherem. There are no longer many glaciers, hardly a score and all tiny—*névés* rather than real glaciers—in the hill-masses of Sablia, Narodnaya, and Khaima. The biggest, Hofmann Glacier, covers nearly 91½ acres. But ice action was formerly intense, and a mantle of morainic deposits covers huge areas. The central part of the range consists of broad, flat ridges,[1] the minor features of which have been more or less carved by mechanical erosion, and often look down from their tundras on to wide U-shaped valleys. This section is called the 'Pebbly Urals'. On the flanks stretch tame, but wooded, features forming the 'Wooded Urals'. Dry in some places and swampy in others, the forest gives way here and there to little grassy or peaty glades. Its resources are almost untouched. The Northern Urals are practically uninhabited. Apart

[1] e.g. Tiolpoz Tiunder, in which Tiolpoz Iz reaches a height of 5556 ft.

from a few Russian stockmen, no one lives there except Voguls, Ostiaks, and Zyrians who wander with their reindeer from the lowland tundras to the hill-pastures or hunt the bear and squirrel. The district has deposits of bauxite, which are as yet unexploited. But the presence of coal, potassium, salt, phosphorites, and sulphur pyrites has given rise at Berezniki (pop. 63,000) to a large chemical *kombinat* which produces synthetic ammonia, soda, and acids. This industry also exists at Krasnouralsk, which has a *kombinat* for the treatment of copper.[1] But these are mere exceptions. If the whole range was like this sector, the Urals would differ little from the great Russo-Siberian forest.

It is far otherwise in the MIDDLE URALS. This sub-region seems to have undergone several successive reductions to the graded line interspersed with uplifts and renewals of erosion. Fluviatile deposits have masked the inequalities of relief in many places, and today the forms are mostly those of the peneplain. The relief is far less marked than in the Northern Urals, for, whilst Yurma rises to 3500 ft. and Kachkanar to 2820 ft., the average height is not more than 2000 ft. The far gentler relief resembles the Vosges not only in its *'ballons'*, or rounded hill-tops, but also in the large number of lakes. Its moderate altitude and lower latitude give it a climate decidedly less severe than that of the Northern Urals, and in the valleys agriculture benefits from soil of good quality which is related to loess, if not to *chernoziom*. Hard cereals and vegetables do fairly well, and stock-rearing has made some headway. On the other hand, though the forest has been violently attacked, it still represents a great source of wealth owing to its timber as much as to its furs. But the greatest form of wealth lies in the ores that early attracted many Russians.

As far back as the seventeenth century the Strogonovs began working these ores. In the eighteenth century, the Demidov brothers put new energy into the work; and since then expansion has constantly increased, especially since the beginning of the five-year plans. The vigour of the industrial activity is due to various mineral resources, viz. copper found at Mednorudyansk, manganese at Lebiaga, platinum at Nizhni Tagil, gold formerly very abundant, magnetic iron at Nizhni Tagil and the enormous mountain Blagodat.

Until recently the industry seemed to be scattered about in a host of centres, but now certain places have definitely taken the lead, and, in spite of their rejuvenation and expansion, Kabakovsk (formerly Nadedzhinsk; pop. 64,000) in the north, Lysva (pop. 30,000) on the western slopes, Chusovskoy and Isetsk are of little

---

[1] *Kombinat* has a special meaning in the Soviet Union, viz. a large unit of enterprise including a number of industrial works.

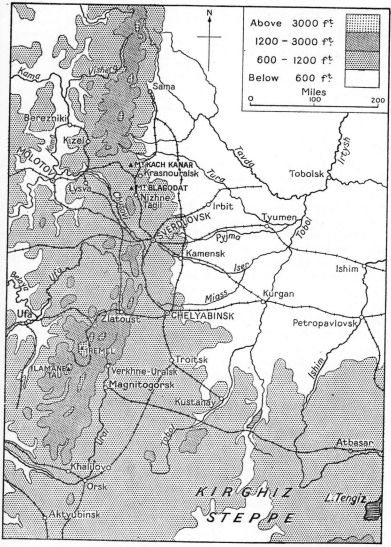

FIG. 38. THE URALS AND WESTERN SIBERIA.
Molotov has now reverted to its old name of Perm.

importance compared with Tagil (Nizhni Tagil) and Sverdlovsk (formerly Ekaterinburg).

In 1926 Tagil had a population of 39,000; today this has grown to 297,000. Its blast furnaces, great waggon works, cellulose factories, sawmills, and cement works make it one vast workshop. Sverdlovsk increased its population from 134,000 in 1926 to 707,000 in 1956. Situated at the lowest point of the Middle Urals on the ridge between the valleys of the Chusovi and Pyshma, this old imperial foundation was always a stage on the way to Siberia and in time it became the capital of the Ural Province and the starting point of the Trans-Siberian Railway. But to this function of wayside station it increasingly adds that of a great metallurgical centre. Like Tagil, Sverdlovsk has a large *kombinat* including blast furnaces and workshops for the manufacture of railway material, machine tools, and electrical apparatus. The district of which it is the centre is rich in gold, platinum, tungsten, copper, and asbestos. Its factories employ more than a million persons. The old city with its peaceful wooden houses and its industry of cutting the precious stones found locally is now an enormous town with huge buildings and extensive housing estates. It has the melancholy interest that in it the last Tsar, Nicholas II, and his family were murdered. The industrial expansion of the Middle Urals cannot but continue more rapidly since the use of the coal from Kizel which contains copper pyrites and is more abundant than was thought, but of poor quality, has been combined with that of coal from the Kuzbass.

But this activity is less than that of the SOUTHERN URALS. Here the mountains become higher again and form three branches which open fanwise towards the south. These ridges of resistant rock have a mean height of between 3200 and 3600 ft., but the most western includes some still loftier peaks, like Iremel (6245 ft.) and Yaman Tau (5600 ft.), which the action of frost continues to disintegrate and erode. The upper valleys, however, have broad, mature forms and at times marshy bottoms. The range is fairly wide here; the depth of the valleys emphasises the relief; and, though transverse valleys often connect the longitudinal ones, the Southern Urals are not easily crossed, in spite of their advanced state of denudation.[1]

At any rate, the climate is tolerable, for the sub-region borders on the woodland steppe. Although formerly ice-capped, hill-tops are now boulder-strewn or mottled tundras, and moderate elevations have only fairly open forest in which broad-leaved trees and conifers grow together. In the valleys the surface is often quite bare naturally, or at any rate the trees are easily cleared away. This has been done

[1] Only one railway crosses this part of the range, viz. the Kuybyshev–Chelyabinsk line, which climbs to a height of 1948 ft.

The heart of Moscow. The Red Square with the Vasiliev Cathedral, now a museum, in the centre of the middle ground. On the right is a corner of the Kremlin and the Mausoleum of Lenin

all the more frequently because the soil is good. In these steppe-like lowland areas *chernoziom* often appears, and, when the climate is too dry for agriculture, there are still good prospects for stock-rearing. This led to the nomadic Bashkirs being deprived of their best land, to consequent repeated revolts, and a military control almost up to our own times by the Cossacks of the Urals and Chkalov. Today, although the Russian and the natives have little liking for each other and though their villages scarcely ever have anything to do with one another, complete peace reigns in the district, and the resources of the sub-region can now be exploited.

These resources consist of the produce of the forest, agriculture, and stock-rearing. The breeding of sheep, cattle, and horses, which was more or less killed by the German War of 1914–18 and by the revolution, is beginning to recover. The growing of cereals and vegetables, which has been resumed with the aid of modern technique, is making appreciable headway. But in this sub-region, too, the resources are chiefly mineral.

At one time the only mineral worked was the iron ore on the western slopes, where the Bakal mine was situated; and there were many pig-iron foundries in the districts of Mias and Belaya. Nowadays these are no longer important, and Zlatoust is the only large centre on the western slopes. Beginning as a gold-mining town, it became a big metallurgical centre flourishing by the manufacture of arms and ironmongery, not to mention the cutting of precious stones. At the present time, heavy industry is developing fast, and the population rose from 48,000 in 1926 to 143,000 in 1956. For the sake of completeness, mention should be made of the non-ferrous metal *kombinats*: copper at Karagash, Kyshtym, and Bliav; nickel at Rezh and Ufeley.

But the principal part is now played by the eastern slopes, where the iron ores are far richer, having 65 per cent. of iron content in some places. Its prodigious abundance is illustrated by the existence of the huge mountain of iron called Magnitnaya Gora in the upper basin of the Ural River. For long years the development of metallurgy in the sub-region was prevented by the poverty of the country in mineral fuel, the competition of the Donets basin and of the oil-burning factories in the lower Volga basin, and, thirdly, the uncertainty of the labour supply. Today it is possible to use coal from the Kuzbass, not to mention lignite and peat from Chelyabinsk, oil from Ishimbayevo, or electricity from the new plants built on the Iset, Chusovaya, and Mias. Furthermore, the entry of a large number of settlers into the sub-region has supplied the labour. Hence, the district has become one of the chief industrial areas in the Union. Chelyabinsk, which but yesterday was a little sleepy provincial town, today boasts coke ovens, enormous blast furnaces, rolling-mills, the largest and most modern steel-works in the Old World, lead and zinc foundries, and plant for making farm machinery, heavy tractors, and military tanks. Its population has jumped up to 612,000. Even more striking is the case of Magnitogorsk, created *ex nihilo* at the foot of Magnitnaya Gora, but also connected with the Kuzbass. In the midst of the forests of this uninhabited district has sprung up in a few years one of the Soviet 'giants' with five huge blast furnaces, coke ovens, steel-works, rolling-mills, and an enormous electric power plant. The town has a population of 284,000 and its factories continue to increase in size. Finally, right in the south another 'giant' is in process of formation. This is the Orsk-Khalilovo group, which is supplied with oil by pipe-line from Emba and engages in chemical industries as much as in iron and nickel metallurgy.

For ages the Urals were regarded as a region of difficulty, too cold, incapable of feeding itself, having poor communications with the rest of the Empire, and a lamentably primitive standard of living. Today the northern half is almost uninhabited, except at some few points, and leads a miserable life. But the southern half, where the forest is no longer supreme, is nearly self-supporting in food, and its industrial possibilities, which for a number of years the experts thought to be mythical, are in process of becoming realities. Of course, the population is still scattered. Vast spaces are nearly empty, and the population is moving from the villages into the towns, which, owing to the enormous stream of newcomers, are visibly swelling; and their very needs will add to the value of the countryside. Already the Urals have a population of at least 10 million, and expansion certainly will not stop there. As their mineral resources are as considerable as varied and as the region lies in the heart of the Union, it may one day very possibly become the chief metallurgical region in the whole Soviet Union, as it was during the war, when the Germans occupied the Donbass and the Krivoyrog district.

(*b*) *The pre-Uralian Region.* With the Urals may be included the pre-Uralian foreland, the basin of the Kama and its feeders, the Vyatka and Belaya, and that of the upper Samara, for it shares in the same industrial region. The relief is weak, but all the same fairly broken. At one point the upper Vyatka flows between steep banks; at another, between the Vyatka and Kama, the surface is extraordinarily flat. Between the Kama and Belaya are erosional undulations, in which some hard strata project as ridges; whilst on the karstic plateau of Ufa fluted escarpments rise in contrast with gentle slopes. Elsewhere, between the Samara and the River Ural the ridge of Obshchii Syrt, which runs west-south-west of Chkalov, reaches a height of 850 ft. These small features are of less import than the local shades of climate, which towards the south-east becomes drier and drier, hotter and hotter in summer, and colder and colder in winter.

What is more important, these minor features matter less than the differences in soil and vegetation. From the Vyatka to Chkalov one passes from podzols to a poor clayey soil through a transitional belt of grey soils in the valley of the lower Kama and black earth in the valleys of the Belaya and Ufa, just as one passes from the coniferous forest to the halophilous desert vegetation through mixed forest, woodland steppe, and almost treeless steppe.

In this region the primitive basis of the population is Asiatic: in the north are pagan Finns, the Mari, Permians, and Votiaks; in the south are Muslim Tatars or Bashkirs. But Russian settlement has to a great extent overwhelmed these peoples. First, there were the Novgorodians who founded Vyatka (now Kirov) in the twelfth century and, later, the Muscovites, who came from both north and west towards the Urals. To overcome the obstinate resistance of the Bashkirs and Kirghiz, they built many forts, like Chkalov, under the protection of which Russian settlement continued, being, moreover, favoured by the policy of improved communications.

Today, except near Chkalov, the steppe is the chosen home of the Bashkirs; but, whilst a short while ago they lived by hunting, fishing, and nomadic pastoralism, many of them have now adopted a sedentary life and grow cereals, at the same time continuing to rear horses and sheep and to keep bees. Their huts, which were constructed of branches, have given place to proper *izby*, and a number of Bashkirs may be seen toiling in the Ural mines.

On the other hand, the population of the forest belt consists of Russians and almost 'russified' Asiatics: Permians, Votiaks, Mordves, Mashcheriaks, and, above all, Mari. The forest has been more or less cleared away and produces timber, cereals (rye in the north, wheat in the south), flax, hemp, and vegetables. Cattle, horses, and poultry are reared, and beehives abound. Besides, the deposits of potassium in the upper Kama valley, the wonderful reserves of which have already been mentioned, soon attracted the attention of the Russians, and today Solikamsk is a great mining town and also a main centre of the manufacture of soda and artificial manure. In the upper Vyatka valley iron was worked. Some outcrops of copper occurred near Perm. But further resources are now recognised, viz. coal at Dombarovka, which will be useful to the industries at Orsk; petroleum at Chusov and Sterlitamak-Ishimbayevo on the slope of the Urals, where it is already an advantage to factories in the region.

Of course, the towns in the pre-Uralian sub-region are growing, thanks to these resources. Chistopol (pop. 20,000) is a river port on the lower Kama and a market for cereals. Izhevsk (pop. 252,000) has arms factories; and Sarapol makes boots and shoes. Kirov, a river port and railway junction, has very varied industries (wood, leather, soap, paper, candles) and a population of 211,000. Perm (pop. 538,000), whose industries are equally varied, has, however, a predilection for metallurgy, including shipbuilding. Ufa, the Bashkir capital, is a river port, a centre for flour-milling, and a great market, and has become an important focus of the petroleum industry, which has made its population jump up to 265,000. Orsk is an industrial town with a population of 157,000. Lastly, Chkalov (formerly Orenberg; pop. 226,000) is a market town and an intellectual centre that is as much Asiatic as Russian. The rapid growth of these towns is clearly related to the industrialisation of the district under the influence of the neighbouring Ural region.

(7) *The Carpathian Ukraine and the Russian Carpathians.* After the war was won in 1945, the Soviet Union annexed the Hungarian territory of the Carpathian Ukraine which had belonged to Czechoslovakia up to 1938, and it also took a portion of the Carpathians which had previously been held by Hungary, Poland, and Romania. These districts do not belong geographically either to western Russia or to the Black Earth country, and they must be treated separately as a sort of appendage to the main body of Russia.

(a) *The Plain of the Carpathian Ukraine.* This might also be termed sub-Carpathian Russia or sub-Carpathian Ruthenia. It is part of the great plain of Pannonia, which was formed by subsidence, and its altitude normally varies between 300 and 400 ft. above sea level. Well sheltered from north winds, but not from those from the south-west, it has a continental climate, yet one that is fairly moist with a rainfall of between 30 and 33 ins. a year and relatively moderate in temperature,[1] so that work in the fields can proceed during 240 days in the year. This means that conditions are approaching those of the plain of Hungary with its vast cornfields, its vineyards on the hills, its scattered copses, and its big villages with their little, low, reed-thatched houses. Unfortunately, especially near the Tisza, the lower ground is always being threatened with floods, so shallow are the valleys; and at the melting of the snows or in time of prolonged rainfalls, the district becomes a marsh. The task of regulating the channels of the streams was begun nearly a hundred years ago, but is still far from being complete.

Whilst agriculture occupies little space in the mountains, it covers nearly the whole of the plain. The crops are very varied and include maize, oats, wheat, rye, clover, hemp, tobacco, beans, peas, and the

---

[1] At Užhorod the July and January means are 95° F. and − 7·8° F. respectively.

vine. It is a pity that methods are still primitive and the yields very small. Although a third of the surface is used for livestock (oxen, horses, pigs, sheep, and goats), the grazing is very poor and consequently the quality of the animals is low. Similarly, the exploitation of the forests is crude and thoughtless. Apart from the function of supplying timber to saw-mills and firewoods to the distilleries, the industry is negligible. The chief centres, Užhorod and Munkačevo (pop. 26,000 in each case), are scarcely more than market towns. Although the district possesses some railways, its connexions with the neighbouring states are still uncertain.

However, mountain roads are numerous and easy enough for the people of the two slopes to be of the same stock. On the eve of the war in 1939 Hungarian landowners, German settlers, and thieving gipsies were only minorities. The main body is Ukrainian and speaks Ruthenian, a Slav dialect. Very poor, yet outrageously fleeced by Jewish moneylenders and traders, extremely ignorant and quite incapable of improving their agricultural methods by their own initiative, and intellectually isolated owing to the use of a clumsy language which is understood only with difficulty by the few educated persons in the towns, these Ruthenian peasants form one of the most backward communities in Europe.

Between 1919 and 1938 Czechoslovakia had taken charge of them and was trying to develop the resources of the country, whilst faithfully guaranteeing its cultural independence. This was a singularly difficult task, since it was almost impossible to find teachers on the spot, and they had to be got from Bohemia or Moravia, which were Czech countries, not Ruthene. Reverting to Hungary in 1938, the district is Ukrainian today. In this way the Soviet Union has found a footing in the Danubian basin, and at the same time the unification of the Ukrainian peoples is completed and the community reinforced by some 725,000 persons (22 to the square mile).

(b) *The Russian Carpathians.* About 190 miles long with an average breadth of between 60 and 90 miles, the Russian Carpathians consist mainly of sandstone and schistose flysch of small resistance, but, on their western border, the subsidence of the plain of Hungary has caused a number of fissures through which laval flows have issued. The range has been thrust eastwards on to the foreland and often contains long basins which are more or less connected by the trenches cut by the streams and are very favourable to human settlement. The effects of glaciation are scarcely to be seen, at least in this part of the range, but erosion acting over a long period has worn away the summits. The outer ridge on the east is merely a hilly district. The inner ridge, along which the frontier formerly ran, contains ridges from 4000 to 4250 ft. high in the north-west, whilst in the centre the summits usually rise to 2300–2600 ft. But farther south-east on the borders of Bukovina the mountains begin to tower up. Hoverla in the Cernahora hill-mass reaches 6750 ft., and not far away Pop Ivan rises to 6642 ft. Here the traces of former glaciers are very clear. Elsewhere, heights like those of Svidovec (6176 ft.), Polonina Borsova (5231 ft.), or Arszyca (above Borislav; 5112 ft.) are exceptional; and very often these Beskids, as this part of the range is called, are no more imposing than the Vosges, sometimes even less so. The hill-tops, which of course do not reach the snowline, are rounded into *ballons*, as in the Vosges. The impression of mountain scenery is mainly due to the valleys, which are often deep, narrow, and precipitous at the sides and have been carved by a vigorous erosion stimulated by the presence nearby of two low base-levels.

A precipitation of at least 80 ins. a year, including an appreciable fraction in the form of snow, which remains for some time on the high ground, takes place especially on the western slopes which are exposed to the south-west winds; and this heavy rainfall clothes the mountains in a rich mantle of green. The flora, in which definite Balkan affinities are noticeable, is mainly of the forest-type, with pine, fir, beech, and birch. Not very extensive in the north, where it has suffered from much felling, the forest almost regains its original vigour right in the south, except on the gentle ridges in the Polonina which are covered with extensive areas of grass. So the economy in the north is not exactly the same as that in the south. In both parts the occupations are stock-rearing and the winning of forest products, but all in a more primitive way in the south than in the north, where Polish influence is stronger. In the south there are few crops (oats and potatoes, mainly), whilst in the north agriculture is more important, and the crops include potatoes, cereals, and even beet in some of the particularly favourable inner basins and lower valleys. The south has only a few little villages, whilst the valleys and basins in the north sometimes have a population density of 20, 25, or even 30 persons to the square mile.

In spite of all this, the Russian Carpathians with a population of ignorant, rough, and poor Ruthenians form on the whole one of the most remote and backward regions in central Europe, on the eastern slopes as well as in the mountainous portion of Carpathian Ukraine. It has, however, one peculiar and really important industry, viz. mineral oil. The oil-field stretches for 340 miles from the Romanian frontier of 1939 to the neighbourhood of Cracow. The local people had long noticed and used the numerous oozings of crude oil, but the first borings were not made until 1888 near Kolomyya and around Borislav. The geological conditions make the exploitation a fairly delicate matter and require the use of very resistant metals.

Few of the wells are gushers, and pumping is the usual process. Anyhow, the oil is of the most various kinds and is generally of very good quality. Its presence has given rise to a crowd of workings and a forest of derricks right in the heart of the woodland and in tiny hamlets; and it has also caused the appearance of a swarm of refineries. Unfortunately, as in the area still left to Poland, production in the Ukrainian portion has been falling off continuously for many years now, and one gets the impression that this form of wealth will sooner or later approach exhaustion. However, Drogobych and more especially Borislav (pop. 30,000), a horrible place full of hovels and wine-shops and perpetually under clouds of blackish smoke, are very busy centres of the oil industry; and thanks to this field, which perhaps has not had its last word and may have lucky surprises in store, and thanks also to reserves of hydro-electric power, the Carpathians are playing and will continue to play in the life of the Soviet Union a part which is not only industrial, but also agricultural, pastoral, and connected with the tourist business.

CHAPTER 18

THE BLACK EARTH COUNTRY

Signs of another vegetation belt, that of the steppe, were mentioned above as appearing in the pre-Uralian sub-region. Actually, this so-called 'steppe', or, rather, this grassland, is not very dry and, more-over, assumes a peculiar appearance in this northern zone on account of the presence of *chernoziom*. More or less perfect according to locality, *chernoziom* prevails over a large area of the woodland steppe and the barren steppe as far as the true steppes of New Russia. From west to east it crosses the whole of Russia diagonally, passing the Volga, bending northwards, and reaching Siberia across the Urals. But the Black Earth belt is not uniform all over. The Ukraine is not the same as the middle Volga, nor is the latter identical with south-western Siberia.

1. *The Western Region, or Ukraine.* Politically speaking, the name Ukraine denotes a greater area than that to which we apply it. Eastern Galicia and the eastern slope of the Beskids, both of which areas had been Polish until 1939, were added to the country in that year. This was followed by the addition in 1940 of northern Bukovina, which had been Romanian since 1919, and in 1945 of Ruthenia, which was ceded by Czechoslovakia. But as well as this the Ukrainian Republic includes nearly all the dry steppes of New Russia, together with the Crimea, and reaches the Black Sea and Sea of Azov. On the other hand, neither Orel nor Kursk nor Voronezh belong to it.

The relief of the Ukraine is not uniform. The extreme western portion crosses the middle section of the Carpathians, where the range is relatively low and narrow. Here are the passes which led the Asiatic hordes through the mountains in the Middle Ages: the signi-ficantly named Tatars Pass in the south and Veretski Pass farther north. The possession of this section of the mountain range is of considerable strategic value to the Soviet Union. The heights are wooded, but the lowlands of what was formerly known as Ruthenia, though now called Transcarpathian Ukraine, have been cleared for agriculture. The pre-Carpathian depression, which is clearly marked in Poland in the districts around Cracow, Tarnow, and Yaroslavl and is relatively wide between the Vistula and San, contracts from Przemysl onwards into a low, narrow belt about 1000 ft. above sea level at the foot of the Carpathians. This belt forms the upper valley of the Dnestr. But the river, which has doubtless been pushed away north-eastwards by the great quantities of silt brought down by its Carpathian feeders (the Siretul, Lomnitsa, Bitritza, and Prut), has been moved by pseudomorphism on to the ledge of the Podolian–Bessarabian platform. Hence, the upper valley of the Dnestr is paralleled by that of the Prut, which flows south-eastwards through Kolomyya, Suaty, and Chernovitsy as far as the latitude of Khotin, at which point it turns south and forms the frontier between the Soviet Union and Romania. The pre-Carpathian depression is bounded on its left by a declivity which is almost a cliff, but the right bank of the upper Dnestr, followed by that of the Prut, rises in a gentle slope to the Carpathians. The ramp which runs along the foot of the mountains has been cut up by the streams into plateaus and hills. Farther west the plateau of Volhynia is a fragment of the crystalline *massif* of the Ukraine, which has been overlaid with Secondary and Tertiary beds. Southern Volhynia is a hilly region of marly limestones with *cuestas* here and there and undulating plateaus, in whose gullies chalk appears.

More to the south, after crossing the plains of the upper Bug and Styr, with their marshy valleys separated by bare watersheds, there is a climb over the Rostocze (1350 ft.) and Gologory Hills (650 ft.) on to the northern edge of the plateau of Podolia. This plateau is formed of marls, Cretaceous limestones, and Miocene gypsums, but the ancient crystalline substratum is revealed in the deeply carved valleys. In fact, owing perhaps to recent uplift, the valleys, which farther north are relatively wide and damp, are rapidly becoming deep and narrow, and the streams flow at the bottom of veritable canyons topped by cornices of sandstone. This is true of the Strypa, Seret, and Bug (and much farther east it would be true, though less so, of the Dnepr), but the best-known example is that of the Dnestr, whose fine, deeply trenched meanders are 500 ft. deep. Between these huge cuttings the relief of the plateau of Podolia is fairly varied. In the west broad furrows cut it up into narrow strips. In the east near the Zbarazh runs a long ridge of coralline formation 1500 ft. high. In the centre are limestones in which *lapiés*, circular hollows, caves, swallow holes, Vauclusian springs, and other karstic features are numerous; and the triangular plain of the middle Dnestr has a markedly asymmetrical valley cross-section. Whilst the right bank of the river is bordered by high cliffs, the left bank is low and of alluvial origin, and liable to floods. East of the Dnestr the surface consists of high ground dissected in many places by the forces of erosion and rising towards the north, east, and, even more, the south, whilst reaching considerable altitude to the west of Starokonstantinov (980 ft.) and Vinnitsa (1225 ft.) and to the south-east of Ternopol (1400 ft.).

Farther east the ground falls away in the zone of the 'Dnepr Hills', which rarely rise above 800 ft. or fall below 650 ft. Then comes the broad valley of the Dnepr, which, like those of its feeders, is badly drained in many places, so that the districts around Kiev, Chernigov, Cherkassy, and Mirgorod abound in lakes and marshes. After that the mean altitude once more gradually exceeds 300 ft. on approaching the central Russian plateau. Here the ground, rising to 970 ft. near Tim, is dissected by the deep valleys of the Oka, Seym, Desna, Psiol, Sosva, and even more by a multitude of *ovraghi* (= gullies) cut by heavy rainstorms. Lastly, away in the east is the valley of the upper and middle Don, where a striking asymmetry is also to be seen between the high right and the very flat left bank.

Over the whole of this area there prevails a climate even more continental than that of the Muscovite region. The annual range of temperature is of the order of 75° F. to 77° F. The winters are not so long as in Moscow, but are very cold, with a January mean of −25° F. at Lvov and one of −21° F. at Ternopol. The days are fine and sunny, but the nights are freezingly cold, and snow lies on the ground for three or four months on end. The summer is very warm, practically the whole region being included between the July isotherms for 68° F. and 70° F., but it is windy and liable to thunderstorms. Spring is earlier perhaps, and autumn late and dry.

There are local shades of difference. For instance, the valley of the Dnepr has milder temperatures than the plateau of Podolia; and that of the Dnestr is rather dry and mild owing to the shelter given by the Carpathians from the rainbearing west winds and to the protection afforded by the plateau of Podolia against cold north winds. But such peculiarities are less important than pedological differences. In succession from north to south there occur, first, the dusty grey forest soil, then the grey soil of the woodland steppe, and, thirdly, near Orel the genuine *chernoziom* is foreshadowed in southern Volhynia by the appearance of loess. But the last soon assumes the dark colour characteristic of true 'black earth' and occurs everywhere except near the streams.

More importance is likewise to be attached to the changes in the appearance of the vegetation than to the differences in climate or relief. In the north beyond Kiev and Tambov there prevails the broad-leaved forest interrupted by vast open spaces. Farther southwards the copses in the woodland steppe steadily become smaller and fewer. South of the Seym in Volhynia and Podolia they have almost disappeared, and the yew and pear tree found in the Lvov district and western Podolia are replaced in eastern Podolia by the peduncular oak in the north and in the south by the pubescent oak together with the beech. In the end comes the steppe, at one time the favourite haunt of the Cossack, over which he could gallop at will.

Inhabited from early times and very rich in prehistoric relics which lie hidden under countless *tumuli*, the Ukraine has suffered many invasions, that of the Mongol Tatars in the fifteenth century being only the most famous. Across the loess plateaus of Podolia passed the *Czarny slak* (Polish = black road), which has been followed by many invaders on their way to Poland, and the inhabitants of this district have many a time had to take refuge in the local limestone caves. Consequently, the population is very mixed; but the vast majority, especially in the plain of the Dnepr and its approaches, consists of Little Russians, of whose bright, attractive qualities we have spoken above. Before 1941 there were also Poles and a large Jewish minority, but these elements are practically non-existent today, for the systematic extermination of the Jews by the Germans in 1941 reduced their numbers to a very low figure; and the Poles, on the other hand, were transferred from 1945 onwards to the western provinces of Poland, which has been taken from Germany. The western part of the Black Earth country is mainly Little Russia, a land in which the outlook on life is milder and broader than in Great Russia.

In fact, nature has richly endowed it. Admittedly, forest produce is very scarce, except at the immediate approaches to the Carpathians, and for long years wood has been sold by the pound weight. But though the soil is a little too friable and easily cut into gullies by rain, it is easy to work. It has a high content of humus, nitrogen, and phosphates, and it is wonderfully fertile. This last quality has attracted people and firmly kept them, in spite of the devastation caused by many invasions; consequently, labour is abundant and the soil cultivated by willing hands. The Ukraine has long been a land of smallholdings, and the Little Russian peasant, who is less ignorant than most of his kind, soon adopted a three-year rotation of crops and tried to modernise his methods. In fine, the produce of the intensive agriculture of the region is as plentiful as varied.

First of all, cereals. The north with its rather poor soil yields a little millet, buckwheat, barley, and rye, to which potatoes are often added on sandy soils. But in the south of the Dnestr trench on the loess in southern Volhynia and especially on the genuine *chernoziom* in Podolia, the southern part of the Dnepr plain, the central plateau, and the plain of the Don wheat is king. It covers vast expanses and is produced in ever-increasing quantities. This is one of the most productive areas of wheat in the world.

Then come industrial crops. Beginning in southern Volhynia, the cultivation of sugar-beet becomes extensive and alternates with that of wheat. The potato is a favourite crop in the Dnestr trench. Though flax is not found in the north, the districts of Orel, Kursk, Poltava, Voronezh, and Tambov have enormous hemp fields, and to the east of the Dnepr tobacco is a popular crop. A more peculiar feature is the importance of the kitchen gardens which add to the food supplies of the large population. The plots around the villages produce a large number of cucumbers, melons, onions, and pumpkins. Huge fields of sunflowers, from the seeds of which oil is extracted, are characteristic of the Ukrainian landscape. No less peculiar are the abundant fruit crops in the orchards near Kursk, in the vale of the Dnepr, and especially in the valleys of Podolia. In a few well-sheltered spots the vine is sometimes added to the apple, pear, cherry, and plum. Stock-rearing gives great returns without being as profitable as agriculture. Sheep are not numerous, but the region still contains a number of carthorses, and advantage is taken of the abundance of potatoes in the Dnestr trench to raise large numbers of pigs. Horned cattle, though bred mainly as draught animals, are of a breed that gives excellent butcher's meat. There is plenty of poultry, and bee-keeping is one of the specialities of the Black Earth country.

The great majority of the population work on the land. This is due to the fertility of the soil, but also to the absence of minerals in the underlying rocks. Of course, in recent times coal has been found at Poltava, oil at Romny, and, above all, iron at Kursk; and the prospects are good. These minerals, particularly the iron, have been intensely exploited, and another metallurgical centre has been made around Kursk. But so far, apart from lumbering on the fringes of the Beskids, the quarrying of granite in Podolia, the preparation of chalk products in the same province, and brick-making in Kiev, industry in the provinces that were Polish until recently as well as in the Ukraine as it existed in 1938 has been restricted to those based on agriculture, viz. leatherworking and, above all, the food industries of flour-milling, sugar and oil refinery, fruit canning, and jam-making. Their widespread distribution is very striking.

In spite of the inadequacy of river traffic and of the depth of the valleys in southern Podolia, which has often hindered communication and forced the several sections of the plateau to live a rather isolated life, its commerce long ago gave life and vigour to many towns. Numerous fairs, of which the one at Sorochinsk celebrated in song by Gogol and Musorgski was only the most famous, marked this activity, and the construction of railways greatly increased the briskness of the trade.

On the whole, the country is a fine one. True it is that to some extent everywhere a feeling of painful monotony is inspired by 'the overwhelming bareness of the flat horizon' (Legras) which fades into the distance in these never-ending cornfields. Even on the plinth of the Carpathians there are vast treeless spaces without running water or visible habitation, the villages clustering down in the folds of the ground where water may more easily be found. But these villages are far more prepossessing than those in Muscovy; the standard of living is higher and food more plentiful; and education was far more advanced in the time of the Tsars. In Volhynia and Podolia the Ruthenes clearly seemed less advanced in 1939 than their Ukrainian brothers in Russia. In spite of the agricultural wealth of the country, their standard of living was very modest. Their low, thatched huts often had only one room for the family and that next to the cowshed. The Poles were few, but occupied leading positions as big landowners, officials, etc., and it seems that they made little effort to raise the social condition of the Ruthene countryfolk, who heartily detested them. The great density of population is easily understood. In 1926 it normally ranged from 23 to 29 persons to the square mile, sometimes reaching or exceeding 31 or 32, in spite of much emigration to the Caucasus and even more to Siberia. Today, the Ukrainian Republic has a population of 40 million souls, but the rural density tends to decrease, since the attractions of the industrial districts, and notably of the Donbass, are gradually emptying the countryside. In the Kursk district the rural population lost 10 per cent. of its total between 1926 and 1939, and the rural areas of the Ukraine proper seem to have been even more affected. There the loss probably amounts to 26·5 per cent.

However, as the region is far less industrialised than Muscovy, it is less urbanised. All the same, it has a good number of towns which are centres of busy trade and an appreciable amount of industry. Rovno in southern Volhynia has a population of only 30,000 and Lutsk one of 20,000; but farther south is the far more important city of Lvov (Lwów in Polish, Lemberg in German), a focus of routes from Podolia, Volhynia, and the Dnestr trench. Situated at the point of contact between plateau and plain, it is a great commercial town, a by no means negligible industrial centre, and until 1939 was a centre of Polish culture, Roman Catholicism, and Western civilisation in the Eastern marches. Two-thirds of the population of 387,000 were Poles and the remainder Jews, Ruthenes, Armenians, and Russians. So it was a veritable Tower of Babel. Of the towns situated on Russian territory before the annexations of 1939, Zhito-mir (pop. 95,000; flour-milling and tanning), Berdichev (pop. 66,000), Chernigov (pop. 67,000), Vinnitsa (pop. 105,000), Poltava (pop. 129,000; woollens and blankets), Orel (pop. 128,000), and Kursk (pop. 179,000) are all important railway junctions and large trade centres standing on the plateaus.

Those in the valleys are generally more vigorous. Kolomyya (pop. 32,000), Stryy (pop. 27,000), and, above all, Stanislav (in Polish Stanislawów; pop. 32,000) are very busy market towns for agricul-tural produce in the pre-Carpathian trench. Away in the south is Chernovitsy (Cernauti in Romanian and Czernowitz in German), the capital of Bukovina. It is mainly a university town, but also has industrial and commercial activities owing to its command of an easy crossing over the Prut. Until 1941 it was far more Jewish and German than Romanian or even Russian, but its total population of 142,000 included 35 per cent. of Ruthenes. On a tributary of the Dnestr farther north is Ternopol, which has grown up as a market town and a centre of Polish culture in a Ruthenian countryside. On the eastern side of the 1939 boundary there are Michurinsk (formerly Kozlov; pop. 70,000), Tambov (pop. 150,000), Voronezh (pop. 400,000), of whom 40,000 are factory hands), which adds brick-making and the manufacture of machinery, cement, and synthetic rubber to its ancient military, religious, commercial, and intellectual activities; and, most important of all, Kiev. The admirable situation of this town has made it a great military headquarters, a wonderfully frequented pilgrimage centre, a brilliant intellectual focus, and a very busy commercial city. Furthermore, even before the revolution it had become the seat of flourishing food industries. Now it has large metallurgical workshops; its railway carriage repair shops employ more than 12,000 workers; and its chemical factories are fast devel-oping. Today this great regional capital has a population of 846,000 persons.

In short, the western portion of the Black Earth country is par-ticularly rich and precious to the Soviet Union. At one time certain parties, arguing from historical data, linguistic differences, and dis-similarities in civilisation have urged the Ukraine to secede from Russia. Had these attempts at secession been successful, the result would have been catastrophic for the Soviet State. Anyhow, it is understandable that in the course of history Poland should often have coveted these territories and that Hitler's Germany should also have wanted them. Certainly, the Ukraine is one of the most favoured countries in Europe.

2. *The Central Region: Districts of the Middle Volga.* Broadly speaking, this corresponds to the Volga plateau and the middle valley

of that river; but it is prolonged on the right bank towards the Urals, narrowing as it proceeds. *Chernoziom* appears in many of the southern sectors of the Ural foreland, where the pre-Uralian and Black Earth regions touch each other. In the strict sense of the word, the latter does not go beyond a line passing between Kazan and Ufa, and between Kuybyshev and Chkalov.

The relief of these adjacent districts is not very broken, but is moderately varied. To the west of the river the Volga plateau, dissected in different directions by the valleys, presents a few modest ridges with very gentle slopes. The highest form the Dzhyguly Hills, whose crest line rises between 100 and 1300 ft. above the valley. The latter is of recent formation. In the Quaternary the Caspian certainly reached Kazan, and the river in the basin of central Russia, that is, the upper Volga, hardly flowed beyond the present site of Gorky. As the Caspian retreated, the Volga followed it and, lowering its base level constantly to that of the sea, it cut a deep trench, made a hollow, deposited alluvium, and formed terraces which have been incised again today. As the ice-cap never occupied the area, erosion proceeded regularly, and the existing gradient is as small as the longitudinal profile is smooth. But the asymmetry of the cross-section is striking. Whilst the western slope is steepish, as the river tends to work its way westwards, the left bank, from which it is gradually moving away, is remarkably flat, pitted with mortlakes, backwaters, and swamps to the east of which it rises extremely slowly towards the Urals.

This variety scarcely appears in the climate, which is everywhere continental, severe in winter with six months of frost at, for instance, Kazan and five at Saratov; and in summer very hot with slight precipitation, of 15·75 ins. at, for instance, Kazan and Kuybyshev. But on the other hand, much variety is to be seen in the nature of the soils. Away in the north the *chernoziom* is degraded and poor and more or less podzolised. In the centre the genuine *chernoziom* reaches the river between Kazan and Khvalynsk and continues to the Ufa and Sterlitamak districts. Though thinner than in the Ukraine, it is actually more fertile. In the south there are 'grey soils' which are clayey, but rich in lime and really fertile.

Hence arises the diversity of the vegetation types. In this extreme north large remnants of forest still resist the extension of the clearings; farther south stretches the woodland steppe; and finally, there is the steppe country which today is cultivated.

The whole sub-region is one of Russian settlement. The basis of the population was formerly Asiatic; but now only one-third of the total is of that origin. A large number of Chuvashes remain in the north-west, and many Tatars in the north-east, whilst Mordves, some of whom are partly 'russified', are found to some extent everywhere.[1] But these minorities scarcely count in comparison with the Russian majority. The flood of colonisation which began as early as the sixteenth century, only reached its peak under Catherine II. Though mainly Russian, it was strongly reinforced by Swiss, Dutch, a few French, and, above all, by Germans, who were joined in the nineteenth century by Lithuanians from Prussia and Mennonites from Danzig. The policy of turning them into Russians, which was very weakly pursued in this area before 1917 and has been completely forbidden since then, left almost intact the ethnical, linguistic, and cultural peculiarities of the Volga-Germans, whose capital city was Engels (Petrovsk). In 1941 they were transferred to Siberia so as to remove the temptation to remember their affinity with Hitler's advancing troops.

The motley character of the ethnographical map does not prevent the Russian imprint from predominating incontestably, as is proved by the system employed in exploiting the gifts of nature. In the north the Volga plateau is still sufficiently forested for woodwork to continue to have real importance there; but farther south on the Black Earth there are fine crops of flax, hemp, and, above all, cereals. There are no important industries apart from flour-milling. The asphalt diggings in the Dzhyguly Hills, brick-making, and the manufacture of linen or rope cannot occupy large numbers of workmen. Hence, the plateau is not very densely populated, though the villages are big. The only notable town is Penza (pop. 231,000), a railway junction, an important market for farm produce, and a centre for textile manufactures and flour-milling.

The Trans-Volga steppes have also been corn lands for a long time, and they are so more than ever today. Furthermore, stock-rearing does not do badly, especially to the south of the latitude of Saratov, and there sheep, cattle, and, above all, horses are a real form of wealth. Between Kuybyshev and Ufa there is a hill-station at Shafranovo, 1400–2000 ft. above the sea, where patients go for a treatment of *kumiss*, a preparation made from mares' milk. Unfortunately, the risk of drought is serious, and catastrophes, like the terrible famines of 1891 and 1921, are not rare in the agricultural world here. Industrial activity is negligible and consists of a few dairies, cheese-making establishments, and meat canneries. This will continue as long as the hope of discovering rich oil-fields here is not realised. The farmers must therefore be given more security; hence the great plan

---

[1] Camena d'Almeida places the autonomous Republic of the Mari in the district of the middle Volga, a view that is supported by a good deal of evidence. However, it has seemed logical here, on account of the definitely forest character of the Republic, to include it in the pre-Uralian sub-region.

for irrigating these steppes. The construction of the huge Lenin–Volga dam on the Volga at Kuybyshev and another at Kalach on the Don and of a large number of irrigation canals should permit the cultivation of nearly 10 million acres capable of yielding close on 100 million cwt. of wheat. Whilst the villages are large, towns are few and small, the only one of any importance being Uralsk (pop. 66,000), which is a market for farm produce.

The link between these districts is the valley of the Volga, an essential feature of the sub-region. In spite of its drawbacks, the river has played a very great historical part. Its valley was an excellent route along which military and later civilian colonists could advance. Today, the flourishing state of the fishing and the great deal of traffic both on the river during the summer and at all seasons on the railway which runs along it bring much prosperity to the valley, in which, furthermore, the alluvial soil yields good harvests. Hence it may be guessed that the valley is the site of important towns. Till recently, trade was the only reason for their existence, but for a few years past industry has been established in them with complete success. Working downstream, they are: Kazan (pop. 565,000), an old intellectual town equipped now with a number of factories, mainly tanneries, distilleries, textile mills, and metallurgical workshops; Ulyanovsk (formerly Simbirsk; pop. 183,000), an historic town and an important railway junction, which has textile mills and metallurgical workshops; Kuybyshev (pop. 760,000), a former fortress, an important depôt for river traffic, and the seat of metallurgical and chemical industries; Syzran (pop. 72,000), of similar origin, which has been enriched by its trade in agricultural produce and its shale, clay, slate, and white metal quarries and by its heavy industries; finally, below the German towns of Marx (formerly Ekaterinstadt and later Baronsk) and Engels (pop. 73,000) stands Saratov (pop. 518,000), a large trade and university centre which has flour-mills, shipyards, and factories for making farm machinery.

Thus, industry is transforming the Volga valley and fast expanding its towns. Whether it will benefit from the discovery of 'the second Baku' at Emba in the pre-Uralian coal-fields is an open question. Anyhow, the dam at Kuybyshev will supply enormous hydro-electric power to it as well as to the whole district. But until things change, the middle Volga country will be merely agricultural, and the risky uncertainty of the climate, together with its industrial weakness, does not allow it to support more than 23 persons to the square mile. Consequently, this sub-region has for long sent many emigrants to Siberia. Few Russian provinces have a record of movement from the country equal to this, and between 1926 and 1939 the rural population of the Penza district fell by 18 per cent.

3. *The Eastern Region: The Siberian Black Earth Country and its Mountain Border.* Beyond the Urals stretches the plain of western Siberia. The area has undergone recent subsidence, and some parts are clearly due to erosion and others to deposition. In the south it is formed of horizontal Tertiary beds of sand and clay and in the north of Quaternary lacustrine and glacial deposits which bear witness to the occurrence of several ice ages whose effects have modified the courses of many of the rivers. But all this has had little influence on the altitude, normally between 300 and 500 ft. above the sea, or on the absolutely flat character of the topography. Hence, little lakes are as numerous on these steppes as marshes are in the forest belt. Such, for instance, are Lakes Chany, Karachi, and Ik in the Baraba steppe, or Lakes Tagarskoye and Uchum near Minusinsk. As a rule they cover only a few hundred acres and are only a few feet deep. Their bottoms are often carpeted with mud which has healing qualities for the treatment of rheumatism. Consequently, spas have grown up near them. The ground does not rise until near to the Altai Mountains, whose proximity is announced by long south-west-to-north-east undulations, or else south-westwards towards the Kirghiz Steppe. Such a relief has but the slightest influence on human life. Of a like insignificance are the local shades of difference in climate, the main feature of which is its extreme continental character.

What really matters is that south-western Siberia belongs to the belt of Black Earth. It has been seen above that *chernoziom* appears here and there in the valleys of the southern Urals, attesting in a way the connexion between the Black Earth in Russia and that farther east. In western Siberia, in fact, it forms, if not a continuous belt, at least some vast expanses. It is often degraded in the north where it is in contact with the woodland, at times it is interrupted in the south by hollows filled with saline soils, and it gradually contracts towards the east, being practically never found beyond the Yenisey; but on the *grivy* (ridges) in the south it is of a fertility unequalled anywhere else.

Originally, the northern part of this region was occupied by birch-copse dotted woodland steppe, which at times resembled the Baraba steppe in being damp and ill drained and in having a rather poor grass cover. In other parts the region was an open steppe, like that round the Ishim, with *kovyl*, sheep's-fescue, and *stipa capillata*. Less completely cultivated than corresponding areas in Russia, this steppe still exists here and there with its brilliantly coloured wild flowers in spring, its abundance of woody vegetation, its patchy grass, and its giant nettles; but it has for the most part been replaced by tilled fields.

Yet it is not altogether attractive to man. In some parts settlement is discouraged by clouds of gnats and mosquitoes bred by the marshy soil and in others by the dryness of the gypsous, clayey rock in which deep wells must be dug to reach drinking water. Nevertheless, Yermak and his Cossacks entered it in the sixteenth century; through it passed the *trakt*, the trail, with its relay posts, which crossed southern Siberia and was eventually replaced by the Trans-Siberian Railway, and to it went the stream of migrants after the abolition of serfdom and even more after the building of the Trans-Siberian Railway. The country was too much like Russia for the settlers to feel exiled, and they flourished exceedingly, thanks to the magnificent harvests yielded by the virgin soil. The colonising movement has turned almost the whole steppe into cultivated land or pasture, and it has even pushed back the forest at various points.

Wood is rather scarce in this region, and a timber industry is carried on at Krasnoyarsk only because the town is nearly beyond the eastern limits of the Black Earth and the timber comes from the forests of central Siberia. But agriculture, which had for long been primitive and practised on an extensive system, was beginning to adopt modern methods even before 1914 and yields very great returns. The production of cereals (barley in the north, oats and rye between the Tobol and Irtysh, and wheat between the Irtysh and Ob and even as far as the Yenisey) greatly exceeds local needs; and the same is true of dairy produce and potatoes. Flax production is very important.

Stock-rearing is not restricted to the nomads who keep horses and sheep in the ordinary course of their rounds, for the settled people also rear goats, sheep, countless horses (particularly in the districts of Tomsk and Tobolsk), and herds of horned cattle (especially round Kurgan, on the Tobol, and in the great wheat region). Hence, there is a great production of milk, butter, and pigs. Besides, poultry is plentiful, and the sale of eggs is one of the main sources of income in south-western Siberia. So also is that of honey.

The abundance and variety of this agricultural produce is the cause of the fairly dense population of the Black Earth belt in Siberia. Here and there large and relatively well-kept villages break the former monotony of the steppe, and several towns of real importance have sprung up. A few of the older places, like Tobolsk and Irbit, which were once flourishing, have lost their importance, since they were not touched by the railway. Tyumen (pop. 125,000), not far from Irbit, has kept a good deal of its life because it is on the Perm–Omsk railway and, thanks to this, has various industries. But others, usually those situated at points where the Trans-Siberian Railway crosses a river, have grown rapidly and since the Revolution, that is, since the beginning of the great efforts at colonisation and industrialisation, have experienced a still more remarkable expansion. Typical of these is Omsk, a former fort, administrative and intellectual centre, important railway station and junction, commercial focus, and industrial centre making farm machinery and mining equipment. It has a population of 505,000 as against 120,000 in 1926. Other instances are Tomsk (pop. 224,000), a large commercial and university town, which was connected subsequently with the Trans-Siberian Railway; Barnaul (pop. 225,000) on the Turksib Railway, a large market town with tanneries, spinning mills, and metallurgical workshops; Biysk (pop. 112,000), a commercial and industrial town; and, lastly, Krasnoyarsk (pop. 328,000) on the borders of central Siberia, a large railway station and river port, and an industrial centre with flour- and paper-mills, cement works, and factories for making vehicles and railway equipment. Novosibirsk (pop. 731,000), the capital of Siberia and the terminus of the Turksib Railway, has grown up since 1900 into the largest town in Siberia. It produces a large variety of manufactures, of which electric light bulbs is the most important, and is a metallurgical research centre.

Industry at Krasnoyarsk is based on the coal-fields of central Siberia, and also on those at Kansk and Minusinsk. The latter two belong to the mountain rim of south-western Siberia which begins in the west with the Alatau of Kuznetsk and the Salair Hills and ends in the western portion of the Sayan Mountains, a range composed of rather soft shales and characterised by moderate height and gentle outlines.

In the middle rises the lofty Altai which is ten times the area of Switzerland in its Soviet portion alone. Formed of Primary shales and limestones mixed with eruptive rocks, it was folded, worn into a peneplain in early geological times, then uplifted, dislocated, fractured, and vigorously carved by glaciation, which here even more than in the Sayan and Alatau of Kuznetsk has left countless traces of admirable freshness, such as U-shaped valleys, hanging valleys, rock dams, shoulders, corries, moraines, and ribbon lakes like Lake Telet, the source of the Ob, capable of holding Lake Geneva three times. Hence, boldly cut ridges and lofty peaks like Bielukha (15,900 ft.) are found beside old mature uplifted surfaces. The sector called the 'Alps of Katun' fully deserve the name of 'Alps', owing to its snow-clad peaks, its countless *névés*, and its 249 glaciers.

This range, with its very rich flora, grass-clad in its lower slopes, then higher up covered with mixed forest, higher still by conifers, and then alpine pasture land variegated with wild flowers, and lastly in mountain tundra, was inhabited in very early times. But today the natives form scarcely a tenth of the population. They are Tatars, peaceful Kalmuks, and Oirots who, besides engaging in some slight

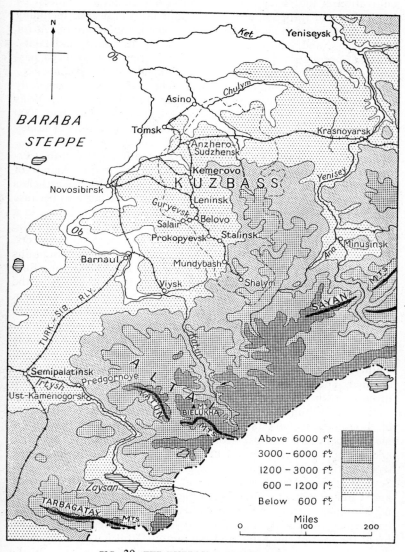

FIG. 39. THE KUZBASS AND DZUNGARIA.

The map legend reads:

Above 6000 ft.
3000 – 6000 ft.
1200 – 3000 ft.
600 – 1200 ft.
Below 600 ft.

Miles
0   100   200

cultivation in the valley bottoms, collect nuts, exploit the forest by lumbering and trapping, engage in minor local industries including the working-up of skins and leather and the manufacture of felt for yurt covers, and, above all, rear horses, cattle, sheep, and goats. This last occupation is gradually predominating, and artificial pastures are developing rapidly under the influence of the *kolkhozy*.

Russians are very numerous here. Their villages are generally well kept and fairly clean, and they engage in the same occupations as the natives, together with bee-keeping. A settler once had 2000 beehives, and a certain village collects more than 46 tons of honey a year.

The chief attraction to settlers has been the mineral wealth. Certainly, the copper, silver-lead, and gold mines in the Alatau of Kuznetsk and in the Altai have greatly declined; but nevertheless some people still firmly believe in them, and all the more so because zinc has been discovered in these parts. Coal, however, brings in a magnificent return. The coal-field at Minusinsk at the foot of the Sayan Mountains seems to be very rich and to have good prospects. The one at Kuznetsk between the Alatau and the Salair Mountains is certainly among the largest in the world. Though known for a long time, it was not exploited until the Soviet Government took the matter in hand; but the expansion has been prodigious since then. Originally, by means of the iron ore from the Urals and its own coal, this 'Kuzbass' became a gigantic metallurgical workshop. Now, however, large quantities of ore are obtained from the Kondoma district, a relatively short distance to the south, where it is raised mainly by open-cast mining. A great cheapening of the production has resulted. The largest blast furnaces stand near coke ovens, Martin furnaces with rolling-mills, chemical factories with electric power stations, and munition factories with railway workshops. Hundreds of thousands of workers are occupied, the towns of Stalinsk (formerly Kuznetsk), Leninsk (formerly Kolchughino), Prokopyevsk, and Kemerovo (formerly Shcheglovsk), which recently sprang up from nothing, alone have an aggregate population of 966,000. Several others—Mundibash, Belovo, Anzhero-Sudzhensk (116,000), and Chulym—deserve more than mere mention. They have textile mills, refineries, flour-mills, meat *kombinats*, boot and shoe factories, and cement works. An unusually large industrial region has grown up at the foot of the Altai, and the famous Ural-Kuzbass *kombinat* definitely seems to be one of the most astonishing successes of the Soviet system, though its conception was apparently so paradoxical.

In short, the Siberian Black Earth country is remarkably rich, though its value seems far from having been fully assessed. The development of its industry is destined to be colossal, and this cannot fail to spur on the exploitation of the agricultural and pastoral resources of the country, the process of which was in full swing even before the discovery of the Kuzbass. There is no doubt that southwestern Siberia is one of the main pieces of mechanism in the Soviet economic system.

CHAPTER 19

THE STEPPES

To the south of the Black Earth country the *chernoziom* thins out. This circumstance makes it less favourable for agriculture, which besides is not generously treated by the climate, because the insufficient rainfall greatly exposes the region to drought. This is particularly true of the central area: i.e. the Caspian and lower Volga districts; but it is scarcely less so of the eastern area known as the Kirghiz steppe, and it is also true to a great extent of the west in New Russia. Hence, exploitation has been slower and more difficult and has not yet advanced very far, especially in the Caspian and Asiatic portions, which were occupied by the Russians not so very long ago.

1. NEW RUSSIA

New Russia is the best part of this belt of steppes. Though clearly inferior to the Ukraine proper, it has a remarkably vigorous economic life. On the whole, the surface has been made terribly flat and treeless by the climate. On the human side it is a sort of Russian colony which was not conquered and brought within the limits of civilisation until the reign of Catherine III, who colonised it with Russians and a certain number of Swiss, Germans, and Greeks. Its towns are scarcely more than a hundred and fifty years old, and settlement is not yet complete. This explains the rather sparse population of the region, which nevertheless has great industrial wealth in addition to its agriculture.

Under an apparent uniformity New Russia presents many local variations. Its relief, which at first sight is so monotonous, is not everywhere the same. Besides real mountains like those of the Crimea in the south, there is in the north and west a series of eroded plateaus which tilt down gently towards the south-east and are deeply trenched

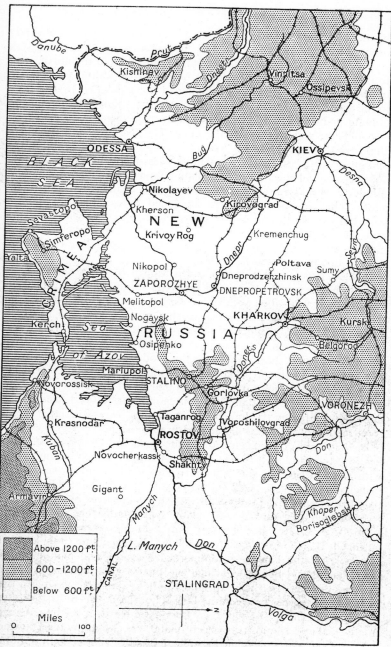

FIG. 40. SOUTHERN RUSSIA.

285

by the valleys of the Dnepr and Bug. Farther south is an area of sandy or limestone plains, very flat and easily crossed, like the Nogaysk steppe. Winter is slightly shorter in the south than in the north, with four months at Kharkov, three at Voroshilovgrad and one or two on the coast; and the rainfall is higher in the north (17–18 ins.) than in the south (15·5 ins.). The peculiarity of the almost Mediterranean climate of the Crimea has already been mentioned.

Nor is the soil everywhere the same. The *chernoziom* of the north thins out towards the south, becomes less and less fertile, and in the end gives way to ordinary, but definitely less-fertile loess. Still farther south is a belt of chestnut or chocolate-coloured earth of little fertility. Similarly, the appearance of the vegetation changes from north to south. The grassland areas are succeeded by expanses of country covered with scrub and coarse grass. Here trees exist with difficulty and are short-lived, and the low grey-walled houses seldom have gardens attached. As a result of all this, exploitation has not advanced at the same pace everywhere.

In New Russia the system of cultivation is of the extensive type, but the north is more favoured than the south. Its relatively well-watered and well-tilled valleys are better than the dry plateaus, in many parts of which only stock-rearing can flourish, and in which there still survive in places vast strips of steppe whose aridity discourages cultivation. As routes the valleys are of course better than the plateaus, and they alone have the food supplies to be had from fishing. Lastly, mineral wealth is very unevenly distributed. Hence, there are perforce great differences in density of population. High in industrial districts and moderate in good agricultural areas, it is definitely sparse on the unproductive steppes. New Russia is, therefore, made up of several distinct natural divisions.

In the north of the region the route from the Dnepr to the Don lies through the DONETS VALLEY and the plain which connects this with the Dnepr. It is an historic route of first importance and a principal region of Cossack and, later, foreign settlement. The eastern part has neither large towns nor industries, but lives by agriculture, river fishing, and stock-rearing on the grass plains. The western part is far richer and produces wheat and vegetables as well as rice and cotton. It is also more densely populated. Kremenchug (pop. 89,000) is a port on the Dnepr, a commercial *entrepôt*, and manufactures farm machinery; Belgorod, which was once a great producer of wax candles, devotes itself to soap- and candle-making; Kharkov, in the heart of the steppes between the Dnepr and Don, was at first a route junction and the site of very busy fairs. Afterwards it became a great intellectual and administrative centre and was chosen by the Ukraine as its capital. Now it is a very great industrial centre, milling flour and manufacturing textiles, felts, soap, sugar, tractors, farm machinery, motor vehicles, turbines, locomotive and electrical apparatus. Its population has jumped up from 409,000 in 1926 to 877,000 in 1956.

Farther south stretch the stumps of some ancient hills forming the plateaus of the Dnepr and Donets. It is a bare steppe, whose former population consisted for the most part of Cossacks and, later, of Serbs, Bulgars, Swedes, Greeks, Albanians, Czechs, Moldavians, Germans, and Jews; and it does not afford very good conditions for agriculture, because the *chernoziom* is too thin and droughts frequent. Yet wheat and a little maize are cultivated together with tobacco and water melons; fruit-trees and a few vines grow on slopes with a good aspect; cattle-rearing is not negligible, and there are also sheep, horses, and swarms of bees. But its wealth lies mainly in its industry.

The Dnepr plateaus have the superb deposit of iron at Krivoyrog in addition to manganese mines, and the Donets plateau contains the splendid coal-field called 'Donbass'. When the district was equipped with the means of transport and was sufficiently colonised, a great industrial region was created with the help of foreign capital and technicians. From 1880 onwards it was 'the industrial basis' of Tsarist Russia. Restored after the revolution, it has benefited by the immense efforts at improvement made since 1928, and electric power from the Dnepr has been added to the resources of iron and coal. A dam, which is almost the only one of its kind in the world, has been built at the rapids, and the hydro-electric plant, known as Dneproges, has enabled a gigantic electro-chemico-metallurgical *kombinat* to spring up nearby. It was largely destroyed by the Germans in 1942, but has been restored and expanded since the end of the war.

The whole of this natural division has become one immense workshop. The little ancient city of Kamenskoye, now Dneprodzerzhinsk, on the Dnepr has a population of 163,000; Nikopol supports 57,000 persons by mining and working manganese; Dnepropetrovsk (formerly Ekaterinoslav), an old river port, is now the site of dozens of chemical works and metallurgical workshops engaging 50,000 workers, and its population has risen from 233,000 in 1926 to 576,000. Not far from the Dnepr *kombinat* has sprung up also Zaporozhye, a symbol of triumphant venture. It has blast furnaces, aluminium and manganese workshops, and an output of 60 per cent. of the steel used by the Union. It has a population of 381,000, and is steadily growing.

West of the Dnepr the iron-mining in the KRIVOYROG DISTRICT is contantly increasing. Besides the mines it has many blast furnaces fed by the Donbass, to which it is connected by a direct railway. The town of Krivoyrog itself has a population of 322,000. By the third five-year plan several more factories were to have been built in it. Kirovo (formerly Elisavetgrad), which is some distance away, is a market town with a large population (99,000).

Away in the east of New Russia THE DONBASS is experiencing a like expansion. Besides rich deposits of peat, it has not only several hundred coal-mines with an ever-increasing output, but also many ranges of coke ovens, a number of blast furnaces, and enormous steel-works; and 'the latest prospecting has so greatly extended the mining area that the authorities no longer know where to lodge the workers in the congested towns and villages' (Slonim). Old centres, like Novocherkassk (pop. 81,000), formerly the chief town of the Don army; Slavyansk (75,000), a town of salt springs and a watering-place; or Artemovsk (formerly Bakhmut; pop. 55,000), an administrative town with large porcelain manufactures, are totally eclipsed by the new industrial cities like Konstantinovka (pop. 95,000) and Makeyevka (pop. 311,000), with their numerous metallurgical workshops; Gorlovka (pop. 240,000), a big mining town; Kramatorsk (pop. 117,000), with its gigantic rolling-stock factories; Voroshilovgrad (formerly Lugansk; pop. 251,000), which also makes thousands of railway carriages and locomotives a year, not to mention munitions of war; and Stalino (formerly Yuzovka), which was founded in 1871 by John Hughes, the son of a Welsh blacksmith and was named after him, is the heart of the Ukrainian 'Black Country' with its mine-shafts, blast furnaces, steel-works, and rolling mills. With hive-like activity the last-named town raised its population from 105,000 in 1926 to 625,000 in 1956.

On the whole the district is 'an ugly scene of rocks, bare slag, signal-boxes, tracks, pitheads, and chimneys' (Slonim). But by joining the iron from Krivoyrog to the coal of the Donbass and the hydro-electric power of the Dnepr a first-class industrial centre has been created, which grows more and more complex, since alongside the metallurgical workshops have been established chemical works, textile mills, and food factories, and since furthermore the continually increasing need for electrical power calls for more and more power plants. It may well be imagined that when in 1941 Hitler laid hands on this region, the largest metallurgical centre in the Soviet Union, he thought he had dealt the U.S.S.R. a blow from which it would not recover.

Still farther south is THE COASTAL REGION OF THE BLACK SEA AND SEA OF AZOV. In the south-west between the Dnestr and Prut stretches Bessarabia, which was formerly Romanian, then Russian from 1878 to 1918, Romanian once more from 1918 to 1940, and since the latter date attached to the autonomous Soviet republic of

Moldavia. It consists of a plateau averaging between 650 and 1000 ft. above sea level and cut up into long strips in the centre and north. The south is lower and has been gashed by a number of *ovraghi*. Its warm climate with its broiling, dusty summers is clearly steppe-like and yet moist enough for agriculture to flourish. In the north where the population is mainly Ruthene, live-stock is reared on the water-meadows in the valleys, but the chief products are barley, wheat, and maize, the last being used to feed pigs and poultry. Beltsy (or Balti; pop. 30,000) is the principal market town. Nearby, Soroki (or Soroca; pop. 15,000) and Bendery (or Bender; pop. 32,000) began as Turkish fortresses in the Dnestr valley. Tiraspol is a fairly busy town farther downstream. The central area, a district of *côtes* and bare hills, is on the contrary very Romanian. Its cornfields and the orchards in its valleys produce much wealth, and, accordingly, it contains the only large Bessarabian city. This is Kishinev (pop. 190,000), which has hitherto been an administrative and commercial centre and in no way industrial, and before 1939 it was Romanian or Jewish rather than Russian, but was very oriental in appearance. Lastly, the south, or 'Ismail region', is an undulating steppe with boundless horizons and a fertile soil. After 1815 it was settled in by Romanians, Bulgarians, Germans, Ukrainians, Armenians, and even French-speaking Swiss, and the population is very mixed, especially on the coast. Many of the individual villages have mixed populations. The coast, low and indented with lagoons, is worthless and is of no interest to the district, except for some very modest fishing. The former Venetian port of Akkerman on the *liman* of the Dnestr is its only town. But nearly all the interior is now under cultivation, and its production of wheat, barley, fruit, vegetables, and tobacco is considerable.

Though greatly neglected during the time of the Tsars, Bessarabia made real progress under Romanian administration. But the progress was inadequate, and in 1940 the country's economy was still archaic in many respects. Today it has to fall into line with the 'collectivised' economy of the Ukraine. Besides, since from 1918 to 1940 all its traffic as well as its intellectual life was oriented towards Galatz and Jassy,[1] it has since had to reverse the direction of these currents, turning its back on Romania so as to fuse into the Soviet Union.

East of the Dnestr the Odessa district is followed successively by the districts of Nikolayev, Zaporozhye (i.e. 'situated beyond

[1] Geographically speaking, this was quite logical, for Moldavia and Bessarabia form a single physical region. Humanly speaking, the mixed character of the population rendered the attachment of the country to Romania as disputable as its attachment to Russia is today.

the rapids' (of the Dnepr); *za* = beyond + *poroghi* = rapids), and Rostov. Almost perfectly horizontal, the plain often reaches the sea in cliffs between 100 and 130 ft. high, but is nearly quite flat and presents only insignificant undulations. Its surface, which is without *chernoziom*, is covered with a kind of loess and is generally very permeable, a fact which is all the more serious because the rainfall is low (12 to 15 ins.), the summers very hot, the winters very severe, and the winds extremely violent. It is even possible that the sub-region may be in process of desiccation. Anyhow, the natural vegetation is a thin, low steppe whose tufts of grass are sometimes so far apart that one is tempted to describe the country as semi-desert. Springs are rare, and settlement is with difficulty established, except near ponds and in the valleys.

Away from the lower courses of the great rivers these steppes look desolate and, settlement on them, whether by Cossacks or foreigners (Serbs, Greeks, and Germans), has been difficult. Wheat, vines, water melons, and fruit have been grown by dint of great efforts. And yet in our own times a more up-to-date technique has had satisfactory results and has even succeeded in introducing the cultivation of cotton. However, the rearing of horses and sheep on an extensive system is in its right sphere here, for it has the use of vast pastures on the almost empty expanses of Tauria to the south of the Don. Besides, the very development of the Donbass encourages agriculture and pasturage by its steadily growing demands for food. Moreover, the industry of the interior is gradually spreading like a spot of oil and is tending to unite the coastal districts.

In fact, this region is Russia's main frontage on the Mediterranean. The coast is pretty poor and is fringed with spits along the shore or running out into the sea, lagoons, delta lakes of which the largest is the Sea of Azov, crumbling cliffs, and low-lying valleys which are often flooded and are blocked by reed-brakes. Such is the ordinary landscape, and it is by no means inviting.

Consequently, the people of the region turned their backs on the coast, which was frequented only by foreign sailors: Greeks, Turks, and Italians. But southern Russia needed ports and she continued to construct them as her economic system grew. There is one on every estuary, and all the towns are ports on the sea or at least on *limans*. Some are very small, like Melitopol, Nogaysk (one of Richelieu's failures), and Azov, a decayed fortress. But Rostov-on-Don, a great intellectual as well as industrial centre and a river port, has grown extraordinarily and has a population of 552,000. Taganrog (pop. 189,000), a busy port, also has metallurgical workshops (military tanks), tanneries, and factories for making precision instruments. Zhdanov and Berdyansk have fairly good anchorages. Their trade is growing, and their whole district is fast increasing its population owing to the development of its industry. Zhdanov has gone from a population of 41,000 in 1926 to one of 273,000 in 1956. Berdyansk, which changed its name in 1940 to Osipenko, has a population of 51,000. Kherson (pop. 134,000), with its commercial annexe of Aleshki, still specialises in the export of wool and wheat. Its industrial activity is far less than that of Nikolayev (pop. 206,000), originally 'the Portsmouth of Russia', which has added to its shipyards the manufacture of farm machinery.

Lastly, Odessa, which was founded by Catherine II, but developed by Richelieu, is a great focus of overland routes as well as a very large and remarkably well-equipped port. Before 1914 it had some fine buildings and was a brilliant intellectual centre with a motley population of more than 500,000 persons. The civil war did it immense damage, and, in spite of the efforts of the Soviet Government to revive it, the town has only just recovered its former activity and its population of 607,000. It is none the less a great university town, a moderately large industrial centre with flour-milling, soap-making, brewery, and distillery. Above all, it is the principal Russian port on the Black Sea. But the fall in the export of wheat appreciably reduced its trade.

On the whole, all these ports are intensely busy, and their flow of trade, whether to the Caucasus, Europe, or Suez, is vitally important to the Soviet Union. For this reason one may rest assured that this difficult coast has a great future.

THE CRIMEA formerly played the part of a go-between with the Mediterranean world. Phoenicians, Greeks, and Romans had colonies there, and later the Genoese had trading posts in it. Geographically speaking, it has a very special appearance. It consists of three distinct parts: the northern plain occupying three-quarters of the peninsula, a southern rim of hills rising to more than 5000 ft., and the peninsula of Kerch. Joined to the mainland by the five-mile-wide isthmus of Perekop, its northern plain is an arid sparsely peopled steppe composed mainly of grassland. The only town here, Yevpatoriya, was until recently more Muslim, Armenian, and Jewish than Russian and is still a populous trading place as well as a spa with thermal mud baths. In the southern rim of hills a belt of limestone escarpments, pierced in many places by caves and cut into natural bastions, is transitional to the heights of Yaila Dagh, which are a kind of karst honeycombed with underground passages, trenched with canyons, and sloping down gently towards the north, but standing up southwards in what look like battlemented walls. Here Chatir Dagh reaches a height of 5060 ft.

This hilly area, covered with thin grass on the karstic heights and lower down with fine broad-leaved forest, has in its upland belt meadows, well-watered gardens, and fields skilfully cultivated by a well-to-do population. Bakhchi Saray, the former capital of the Tatar khans of the Crimea and dear to Pushkin, holds its place as the 'Granada' of Russia owing to the splendour of its buildings and its oriental population; but the important towns are Simferopol (pop. 158,000), once a big Tatar town and the present capital of the Autonomous Republic of the Crimea, which has a large industry of fruit canning, and Sevastopol (pop. 133,000), which adds to its business as a naval and commercial port large dockyards and engineering works, not to mention the scientific life of its institutes.

Finally, the southern face of the peninsula is marked not so much by its somewhat broken relief, the clear outline of its coast, and its semi-circular areas of subsidence as by the peculiarity of its climate and vegetation. In the time of the Tsars many towns and country houses had sprung up there amid flowers and fruit trees in gardens and orchards jealously tended by Tatar gardeners. Today, Yalta, Alucha, and Alupka are holiday resorts abounding in sanatoriums and 'preventoriums'. Besides being 'a Soviet rest-house and hospital', the coast is also a tourist centre which is being visited more and more and is therefore being more and more densely populated.

As soon as the Crimean Hills disappear, the dry and thorny steppe reappears near Feodosiya and the barren Kerch peninsula is reached. In the latter there are hot springs, quarries, and, above all, a rich deposit of iron which has given rise to metallurgical workshops at Kerch (pop. 99,000); and oil has been found there. In short, the Crimea, which is not devoid of agricultural produce and has now added a vigorous metallurgical industry to its old occupations of fruit-drying and the making of jam and wine, is fast developing and in 1939 had a population of 1,127,000 as against one of 714,000 in 1926. No further statistics have yet been published.

Though the south coast is a 'lucky accident' in the dull frontage of New Russia, it must be admitted that this country, into which people are crowding more and more, is today one of the best mining areas and one of the chief metallurgical workshops in Europe, and that its possession is of inestimable value to the Soviet Union.[1] Possibly its transport system leaves something to be desired, but at least the country looks on to the Black Sea, an advantage denied to the lower Volga district.

[1] This review of the industrial as well as the agricultural resources of the Republic of the Ukraine, together with the consideration of the number and activity of its mines and factories, should give the full measure of the colossal lie of German pre-war propaganda in trying to represent the country as a mere source of raw material.

2. THE WHITE STEPPE: THE LOWER VOLGA AND URAL RIVERS

This country is far less well endowed by nature. It corresponds to the Caspian plain, which is fairly uniform in relief in spite of the existence of a few dunes and, more especially, of the Ergeni Heights, a line of hills stretching for 220 miles from Solodniki to the Manych Depression and rising to 625 ft. at their highest point. The most marked feature in the sub-region is the lower Volga valley. Like the Ural, this river has followed the Caspian in its retreat and runs through a long course in country that is below the level of the ocean.

The soils in the sub-region are generally poor in quality. In the north fairly fertile grey earth is found, but farther south are expanses of far less productive clayey-sandy chestnut soils, followed by definitely bad sandy and, finally, saline soils. Similarly, the climate is unfavourable. Though frost lasts only three months near Manych and four at Astrakhan, temperatures of −20° F. are common and the rainfall (9 ins. at Astrakhan) is all the more inadequate because the summers are extremely hot. Hence, it is not surprising that agriculture is difficult in these semi-desert areas.

Nevertheless, there are slight local differences. The north is more or less cultivable, at least to the west of the Volga and up to within 250 miles of the Caspian. Originally, this part was covered with tall grass and in spring was speckled with wild flowers of many different colours, but was quite bare of trees, except for an occasional clump of wild pear-trees. But in 1750 the steppe began to be broken for agriculture, which is here possible without irrigation. By 1870 the original landscape no longer existed, and nowadays this is the country in which some of the biggest wheat-producing *sovkhozy* are situated; e.g. 'The Camel' (pop. 125,000) and 'The Giant', where the town of Gigantia has sprung up with its public buildings, theatres, schools, and libraries.

Farther south the barren steppes begin. Near the Ergeni Heights there is still some rain, but elsewhere water exists only in temporary pools. Black or white wormwood steppe prevails on the clayey Caspian sediments, the gypseous hillocks, and the sand which predominates near the sea and is often formed into dunes. The soil is impregnated with salt; numerous salt lakes (Baskunchak and Elton) are sprinkled about the desert, and the vegetation displays a halophilous character.

Only pastoral nomads could find a home in such a country. Hence, though Russian settlers have infiltrated into it, the mass of people is still Asiatic and yellow in race, Kirghiz in the south-east and Kalmuk elsewhere. In recent years there has been a decline in the number of

European settlers in various parts and a counter-attack by Asiatic nomadism. Apart from the exploitation of the salts of Baskunchak and Elton, the chief means of earning a living is still fishing, together with the rearing of sheep, goats, camels, and horses. Living during the winter in mud huts or holes in the ground covered over with planks and during the summer in portable *kibitki*, the nomads follow their herds and flocks, which are too often decimated by epizootic diseases and bad weather. It should be noted, however, that thousands of natives have become sedentary for a part of the year, when they till the moist soil in the bottom of such valleys as afford the most favourable conditions. The Soviet Government is encouraging this

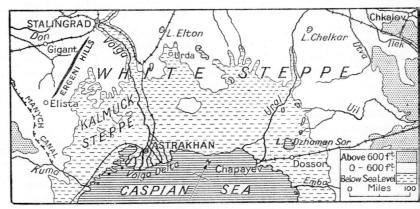

FIG. 41. THE WHITE STEPPE.

Elista has been renamed Stepnoy (see also Fig. 46).

tendency to settle, which is certain to increase now that the irrigation of the Trans-Volga steppes has been completed through the control of the Volga and that the irrigation of the Kalmuk steppe has been made possible by the construction of the Volga–Don canal. Meanwhile, a number of Asiatics are working in the Urals. The Kalmuk capital, Stepnoy, which was recently founded, has a population of only a few thousand, and Urda (Khanskaya Stavka) in the Kirghiz country has still fewer.

The Ural River, whose mean rate is 530 cu. yds. per sec. at a distance of 480 miles from its mouth (Pardé), has too small a volume to give its banks much vegetation. Chapayev at its mouth engages in fishing and oil-drilling, but has a population of less than 20,000. It is the only real town downstream from Uralsk.

In the whole sub-region, therefore, the only really productive district is the valley of the lower Volga, which is productive in spite of the very marked dryness of the climate and the broiling summer heat. The river divides at this point into several branches and wanders between eyots and sandbanks. In the end, there is more dry land than water surface, and the delta begins with its countless ramifications, its some two hundred mouths, of which about half a hundred are in regular flow, and its maze of former and newly formed islets which are all submerged during the floods. Every year the map must be redrawn, and, besides, the delta advances into the Caspian about a hundred yards every twelve months.

This lower valley was originally a Cossack military colony, but was later occupied by Russian peasants, Germans, and Moravian friars, the last of whom founded Sarepta. Today, under the name of Solodniki, it is thoroughly Russian in population and is vigorously exploiting its resources. Its garden vegetables and fruit are in a flourishing state, and its tomatoes, melons, water melons, and peaches are famous throughout Russia. Its fishery is exceptionally prosperous, especially on the delta, where it supports nearly the whole population. This is mainly river, but also sea fishing, for the fishermen on the delta constantly exploit the northern part of the Caspian. Grouped into 'fishing *kolkhozy*', they have a whole flotilla of motor-boats, and their work has assumed the character of an industry. Molluscs, shrimps, crabs, pilchard, carp, perch, catfish, sterlet, beluga, and, above all, sturgeon bring in an enormous return.

Besides this, there is the well-known busy traffic on the river along which timber, wheat, salt, fish, fruit, passengers, and nowadays oil pass incessantly. Nor is there less traffic on the railways. Consequently, it is not astonishing that a large population crowds the area and that the towns are flourishing.

Sarepta, the old austerely pious Moravian 'oasis', renamed Krasnoarmeisk Gorod, but now Solodniki, still remains fairly small. It manufactures tobacco products and mustard. But Stalingrad (formerly Tsaritsyn), a railway junction, river port, and busy market town famous for its stubborn defence in 1942, has become a very great industrial centre with sawmills, chemical factories, metallurgical workshops, and factories making farm machinery and tractors. As a result its growth has been amazing, the population rising from 150,000 in 1926 to 525,000. The discovery of deposits of iron and apatite to the west of the town cannot but encourage its future development.

Astrakhan, which is at the other end of the valley and situated amidst the vast reed-brakes on the delta, is not merely a great port on the Caspian and a big fishing centre. This old half-oriental town, which has to some extent lost its monopoly of trade with the other side of the Caspian, does a busy trade in fish, salt, fruit, and, above all, oil. Its factories in which fish is canned and caviar prepared—the most famous of Russian caviar—employ thousands of workers, and its population amounts to 276,000. The valley of the lower Volga is therefore remarkably vigorous and wealthy. The connexion of the town with the Baltic by the Volga–Don Canal has removed the drawback of the situation of the mouth of the river in an inland sea and has given a great fillip to business in Stalingrad and a large increase in population.

3. THE KIRGHIZ STEPPES

Siberia and central Asia come into contact on the Kirghiz steppes which occupy part of Kazakstan. There is too little relief for a clear distinction to be drawn between the natural divisions and between Siberia and Turkistan; nevertheless, there is some variety in the surface.

Right in the west, a little to the east of the Ural River, the very ancient crystalline range of Mugadzhar seems to prolong the Ural Mountains southwards. It is much denuded and well on the way to peneplanation, its highest point rising to about 2000 ft. Farther east is the plain of Turgay, a slight swelling in the surface scarcely rising above 500 ft., which seems on relief maps to form the boundary between central Asia and Siberia. It forms a steppe which is clayey in the north, sandy in the south, saline in the east, and from which stand out here and there little groups of hills whose denuded ridges rise to between 2000 and 2500 ft. high. In this country of ancient peneplained folds which have been more or less uplifted and fractured and whose rocks are extremely varied in age and character, erosion has uncovered the hardest beds and made them prominent.

Lastly, right in the east there reappear ancient uplands, like the Karkaralinsk Hills (4800 ft.) and especially the Tarbagatay (9400 ft.) on the upper Irtysh, which forms part of the dislocated belt showing both uplift and subsidence between the Altai and Tien Shan. This is where the great mountain ranges begin.

As a whole these barren steppes have a rather special morphology. In the south the sandy areas have features like those of the Aralian deserts. But in many parts features devoid of sand largely predominate, and in such places in addition to valleys, erosional or depositional terraces, and residual hills, which are all the work of normal erosion, there are hollows worn by corrasion, *tertkuly* or little flat-topped four-sided hills, *mielkosopochniki*, or undulating surfaces whose hills have the typical outline of a volcano, whilst between them hide little depressions which are often without an outlet for the drainage. It seems clear that these features are due to æolian erosion rather than

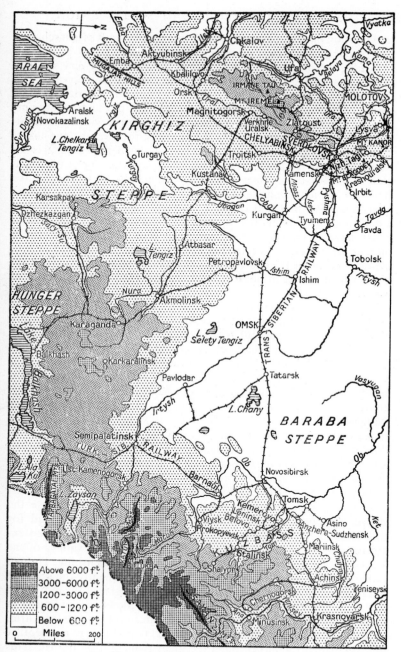

FIG. 42. THE STEPPES OF WESTERN SIBERIA.

to the action of running water, and in this connexion Russian scholars have spoken of a 'deserto-steppic cycle of erosion'.

In fact, the place of and part played by water seem very slight in these areas today. The Emba reaches the Caspian at intervals only; the upper Tobol is very small; the Ishim, which is a little bigger, is certainly in process of losing volume; and most of the other streams die away or have only a subterranean course dotted with wells. Similarly, there is an appearance of shrinkage in the swamps and lakes, the latter being extensive, but shallow. Lake Selety Tengiz is an example and so is Lake Zaysan, which is a local widening of the Irtysh with a surface three times the area of the Lake of Geneva. Lake Balkhash, which is a mere broadening of the River Ili, has a surface area thirty-six times that of the Lake of Geneva, but only two and a half times its volume. It is fringed with marshy, reed-grown shores which have no definite outlines, and it is certainly the remnant of a once larger body of water. In spite of the variations in lake and stream, the desiccation of the sub-region seems undeniable; and, apart from pools which collect in hollows, vast expanses are without a drop of water.

The fact is that the climate is dry to the point of being nearly of desert type. Semipalatinsk and Akmolinsk have an exceptionally high rainfall of 13 ins., but Irgiz gets only 6·6 ins. In the hot season evaporation is greater than precipitation, and in winter there is far less rain than in summer. But in the central and northern parts at any rate the Mugadzhar Hills have some fine stands of birch and aspen, the little heights on the steppes have fairly numerous copses, and the Tarbagatay Hills have forests and hill-pastures below their ice-fields; but as a whole the country is steppe dotted with little clumps of conifers in the neighbourhood of the Altai and with thickets of elm, lime, and oak near the Urals, and is elsewhere absolutely bare. *Kovyl* (*stipa*), fescue, and wild marjoram predominate in the west; *dyrisun*, artemisia, and various other species of wormwood in the east; and *dyrisun* and saxaul in the south.

The natural tendency in these areas, therefore, was to use the steppe for nomadic pastoralism; and in fact the people had for thousands of years restricted themselves to stock-rearing on an extensive system, as did also their brothers in the lower valleys of the Volga and Ural. Their secondary source of food was fishing. Though Lake Balkhash has few fish, Lake Zaysan is frequently the scene of miraculous draughts, as much on account of the size of the individual fish as of the number caught. This kind of life is still practised in many areas by the Kazaks and Kirghiz. But in others, the least arid, they have turned over since the end of the Tsarist rule to a sedentary life, persuaded thereto through the great reduction by the Russians of the area of their pasture lands. They have become agriculturalists as well as stockmen and have sometimes managed to earn a comfortable living.

Nevertheless, the districts which were formerly prosperous were those in which Russian settlement had taken root firmly. These were, first, the Emba valley with its cattle-rearing, millet cultivation, and fishing; then, the few well-watered valleys in the Turgay, in which were situated the little administrative centres of Irgiz and Turgay, the villages spaced out along the Trans-Aralian Railway, and the important station and market town of Aktyubinsk (pop. 40,000); then, the upper Tobol valley with its black earth and the town of Kustanay (pop. 40,000); the districts of Atbasar and the more important Akmolinsk, former Cossack garrison towns, the latter of which is an agricultural and trading centre and had become a market town with a population of 13,000. Farther east in the direction of the upper Irtysh there are the old mining centres of Karkaralinsk and Ust Kamenogorsk, and the district of Pavlodar. There, too, is the more important district of Semipalatinsk, which was a wretched village at the time when Dostoyevski lived there in exile, but today is an important route junction, a port of call for river traffic, and a very busy industrial centre with flour-mills, slaughter-houses, meat-canning factories, and a population which rose from 56,000 in 1926 to 136,000 in 1956. Lastly, there is the district round Lake Zaysan, where market gardening is carried on by irrigation, and the district round Ayaguz, Lepsinsk, and Dzharkent not far from the Chinese border. The truth is that these districts, which are generally fertile, relatively well watered, not devoid of trees, and densely peopled with Russians, are scarcely to be included in central Asia. With their rivers flowing northwards, their corn crops, and their towns of wooden houses, the valley of the upper Tobol and particularly that of the upper Irtysh are indeed almost Siberian.

Their prosperity continues to increase. But many places outside this favoured zone are awaking. It has been realised that, though *kovyl*-clad steppes are incapable of yielding more than pasture for sheep and camels, much of the land can be tilled; and in fact it is being cultivated by people who but yesterday were nomads, but today reinforced by a few Russians, have become a settled population. On the borders of Siberia many *sovkhozy* concentrate on growing corn; and on the river terraces appear rows of garden vegetables and hay-fields whose harvest enables the country's production of milk, meat, and wool to be increased.

This is not all, for northern Kazakstan is in process of becoming an industrial country. One day there will certainly be at Ust Kamenogorsk on the Irtysh a hydro-electric plant of greater power than that at Dneproges. Meanwhile, the lower Emba valley possesses, in addition to rock salt and fluorite, a superb oil-field which has long been known to exist, but whose true importance has only recently been realised. The raising of the oil is in full swing, and the town of Emba is growing. The Karaganda coal-field, which is known to have wonderfully large reserves, was found, but only slightly exploited before 1917, and its full development did not begin till 1930. It has about thirty seams, some of which are more than 26 ft. thick. Furthermore, its excellent coke is relatively near the Urals. Oil has been found in the district; hence, in 1956 Karaganda had a population of 350,000 and was the centre of a large industrial complex. Ores occur in plenty. Not far from the Altay gold and silver have given rise to many towns. Lead, zinc, and copper are mined and treated, and sulphuric acid is prepared at Zyryanovsk, Ust Kamenogorsk, Glubokoye, and, above all, Predgornoye, whilst along the Turksib Railway wolfram, vanadium, and gold are being prospected for, notably at Semipalatinsk. Nickel and phosphorites are mined at Aktyubinsk. In the Ulu-tau range there are manganese mines which began to be fully exploited during the last war to make up for the mines in areas occupied by the Germans. A magnificent deposit of copper near Lake Balkhash has given rise to large *kombinats* of copper at Kounradski-Pribalkhash, which shows promise of great things; and there are extensive copper deposits at Dzhezkazgan. In short, northern Kazakstan is clearly much better endowed by nature than used to be thought. Even now its transformation has begun not only in agriculture, but also in industry. Sugar refining, meat and fish canning, and the manufacture of chemical products are being added around the big towns to mining and metallurgical activities, and modern methods of working up wool are being organised. At the same time, new railways are being built, like the Karaganda–Kounradski line, and population is on the increase.

Thus, even in its eastern parts the belt of steppes has real value. Unfortunately, the rest of Soviet central Asia must be admitted to be far inferior in its resources to this northern strip. South of the Kirghiz steppe the desert begins.

Steppe country in a valley among the foothills of the Altai

sia's Mediterranean corner. Bakhchissarai, or the "Palace of Gardens". The Khan's
palace, built in 1503, is famous for its "Fountains of Tears" described by Pushkin

The tomb of Tamerlane in Samarkand

CHAPTER 20

THE DESERT AREAS AND THEIR MOUNTAIN FRINGE

1. THE ARALO-CASPIAN DESERTS

These cover nearly half of Soviet central Asia and form an immense plain, flat—at least to the eye—and so gentle in gradient and uniform in appearance that the wrinkles and furrows are scarcely seen from a distance. The most striking feature of this vast expanse of steppes and clayey or sandy desert is the existence of two great sheets of water which were formerly joined by a strait of moderate breadth along the present course of the Uzboy and which have deposited around themselves very extensive Quaternary marine deposits.

The smaller, the Aral Sea, has an area of 24,400 square miles, which is about four and a half times the size of Yorkshire. It has a maximum depth of 220 ft., an average depth of 50 ft., and the modest volume of 1,334,624 cu. yds. Its water-supply depends entirely on its two great feeders, the Syr Darya and Oxus. Its salinity, which is 10·3 per mil., shows a tendency to decrease. Rich in sulphates, but poor in chlorides, it quickly freezes, at any rate in its north-eastern portion. Its fairly plentiful fauna includes both fresh- and salt-water species. The few coastal dwellers, including the inhabitants of Aralsk, a town founded in 1905 at a point where the Trans-Aralian Railway touches the shore, are mainly engaged in fishing; and this will continue to be the chief occupation, unless shipping is started on this sea—which seems unlikely, unless the developments mentioned below are realised.

Though the Caspian is growing smaller, it still covers an area of 168,000 square miles and is thus the largest lake in the world. But whilst its southern part is a few hundred fathoms deep (1064 at most), the lead finds a bare 13 fathoms to the north of a line joining the mouth of the Terek to Fort Shevchenko. In the last twenty-five years, however, the level has fallen 8 ft. owing to the growing use

FIG. 43. TURKISTAN AND THE STEPPES.

of the waters of the feeder rivers for irrigation and other purposes. Except in some of the bays on the east coast, notably the Gulf of Karabogaz, its salinity is low, especially in the west and in the north around the mouth of the Volga. Its abundant fauna is rather peculiar owing to isolation from early times. The Sea is 'a real natural fishpond', said Woeikof; and the catch is often wonderfully large, especially on the submarine plateau in the north. It would be even more so if in the eastern part of the sea the fishermen did not suffer from lack of drinking water and from swarms of mosquitoes. To this ichthyological wealth its eastern shores add deposits of ozokerite, the great oil-fields at Neftedagh and Cheleken Island opposite Krasnovodsk, and the deposits of salt in the Gulf of Karabogaz, where every pint of water contains 190 per mil. of salt and at the bottom of which the layer of salt is 6 ft. thick. The population is certainly scanty. Uritski (Fort Shevchenko) is only a little settlement, and Krasnovodsk, the terminus of the Trans-Caspian Railway, is a mere port of transhipment. But the district is certainly destined soon to have a busy oil trade, and even now an industrial settlement has sprung up on the shores of the Gulf of Karabogaz to extract and refine various salts.

Outside the districts around the two seas the Aralo-Caspian subregion is marked far less by the monotony of its relief than by the dry, harshly extreme, and definitely desert character of its climate, which is healthy, but so severe that 'it takes a man of iron to stand it' (Prjevalski). Water is to be found in few places. Here and there occur *chors*, or salt marshes; *takyrs*, or clay-lined ponds, that dry up in summer; and occasional little lakes whose water remains during the hottest weather under a crust of salt covered over with sand and dust. As a result the vegetation consists mainly of bushes and thorny plants like saxaul. Even on the 'grass steppes' the tufts are widely spaced out. Hence, a nomadic life is the only one possible for man and his domestic animals.

Three divisions may be distinguished in these Aralo-Caspian deserts: the Ust Urt in the west, the Kyzyl Kum in the north-east, and the Kara Kum in the south and south-east. THE UST URT PLATEAU, which rises 650 ft. above the eastern shore of the Caspian, is a block structure bounded by lines of fracture and is reached only by climbing the peripheral escarpment. In spite of the extreme variety of its rocks, among which Cretaceous and Jurassic limestones predominate, the scenery is unusually monotonous and oppressively gloomy. Absence of running water, brackish wells, more or less sulphur-impregnated springs, vast steppes dotted with artemisia and baked by the sun—such is the eastern part. The Mangyshlak peninsula, with the peaks of Ak Tau and Kara Tau overlooking the

Caspian, is a real desert. The centre, in which 330 fresh-water wells have been located, is rather better, for here and there it has pasture on which camels and sheep browse in spring, and certain plants yield excellent dyes which are preferred to aniline dyes by some people. But on the whole the Ust Urt is a very poor country, and its population has quite clearly been sparse for hundreds of years.

The Kirghiz steppe shades off into the real Kyzyl Kum through THE HUNGERSTEPPE, or Betpak-Dala. This expanse of clay or sand and clay, 4000 square miles in area, does not deserve the forbidding label that has been attached to it, nor do the natives know it by this name. Certainly, it has no surface water, and, except for a few clumps of willows and poplars, trees are unknown in it. The heat withers everything in summer, flights of locusts are a regular plague, and the poisonous spider called the *karakul* spares neither man nor beast. But the fertility of the soil, which is related to loess, has long been acknowledged; the wells are seldom more than 10 ft. deep and are relatively numerous, and the grass is luscious enough in spring to attract a crowd of Kirghiz encampments with flocks of sheep and herds of horses and camels, which in summer return to the banks of the Syr Darya or the *piedmont* strip.

Between the arms of the Syr Darya and Oxus extends a kind of Mesopotamia which constitutes THE KYZYL KUM proper. It is formed in the north by vast alluvial plains ridged here and there with dunes; in the centre lies a thick mantle of sand which hides a fairly broken relief; and in the south rise flat-topped ridges of Primary formation reaching up to 3000 ft. The effects of wind erosion can well be studied here: grooved sand- and lime-stone, 'caldrons' and basins of corrosion, and sand deserts covered with ever-shifting barkhans. The Kyzyl Kum is nevertheless a very bad country, for water is seldom to be found and game is almost as scarce. The least-objectionable part is the south-east, where there are stretches of steppe less barren than the rest of the country and where nomadic tribes graze their sheep, goats, and camels.

THE KARA KUM, which lies to the south of the Oxus, is even worse. Formerly its northern portion was thought to be a pebbly, monotonous plateau formed of Tertiary sandstones, about 650 ft. high, and cut in the south by a fault whose escarpment rose some 200 or 250 ft. above the Kara Kum proper. In fact, the northern Kara Kum is formed of long north-to-south sand-capped ridges separated by troughs between 150 and 250 ft. lower; and its altitude is not greater than that of the southern Kara Kum. The southern portion is very broken in the south-west. The Great Balkan Hills, which seem to continue the Caucasus on the other side of the Caspian, touch the Ust Urt in the north and the Iranian mountains in the south. The greater part of the Kara Kum is formed of sand of various origin. Like the Kyzyl Kum, it is a museum of æolian morphology with its basins formed by corrasion and the scooping action of the wind, its dunes which run like wheals across it, and its barkhans standing isolated or in long groups. But certain it is that very often the topography of these 'sandy' areas is really formed, just as in the Sahara, by a rocky base which was once carved by fluvial erosion and then mantled with a covering of wind-blown sand. The hydrology, like the morphology, is typical of the desert. Here and there *takyrs* and *chors* are visible but, except perhaps in Transcaspia where the frequently brackish wells number about 10,000, the lack of water is cruel. Consequently, the vegetation is wretched and consists of bunches of thistles, low prickly plants, occasional clumps of saxaul, and a few hardy plants with immensely long roots, like *selev* or *kandym*, which sometimes manage to fix the sand.

In these conditions the Aralo-Caspian deserts have until recently been almost exclusively peopled by nomads. The Kirghiz were scattered throughout the north in *auls* of some ten families; the Turkomans drove their herds across the desert in the south; and the Karakalpaks in the centre were scorned for their far less dislike of agriculture. At the present time, nomadic life is far from having disappeared, and it is doubtful whether it will ever completely go; but efforts are being made everywhere to settle the natives either by helping them to establish farms or by inducing them to till the soil. Not only has the use of underground water enabled kitchen gardens and orchards to be planted right out in the desert, but the Hungersteppe has also been irrigated with water from the Syr Darya and has been settled by an agricultural population. Following an encouraging local experiment, a project to turn the lower Oxus through the valley of the Uzboy towards Krasnovodsk is being closely examined. It would redeem a large portion of the Kara Kum from its sterility. A little administrative town has sprung up at Nukus in Karakalpakia.

In some places the rocks have revealed considerable mineral wealth. The southern Ust Urt seems to be very rich in potassium, and the Hungersteppe has a very rich copper deposit in the district round Dzhezkazgan and Karsakpay. A railway now connects it with the Karaganda–Kounradski line. A factory for treating copper ore has been built at Karsakpay, whose neighbourhood also contains coal; and a real *kombinat* is in process of construction.

As things are, this progress has a limit. Since the Aralo-Caspian sub-region constitutes the greater part of Soviet central Asia, this country may well be said to have been shown little favour by the gods. In truth, what now gives it any value it may have is the mountain border, whose waters dispense a prosperous livelihood to the valleys at the foot.

But the Soviet Government is said to have imposing plans for improving the communications and economic conditions of the sub-region. To maintain the level of the Caspian and to provide irrigation, the diversion of the upper waters of the Onega, Dvina, and Pechora into the Volga has been suggested. A still more grandiose scheme involves the building of a dam at Belogorye near the confluence of the Ob and Irtysh, 256 ft. high and 37 miles long. The water thus trapped would form a lake 96 square miles in area and would raise the level of the Tobol and its feeder, the Ubagan, to that of the base of the watershed between Western Siberia and the Turgay district. A canal 575 miles long would be constructed across the watershed on a course shown by a line of shallow salt lakes to have been a former watercourse leading to the Aral Sea. The water thus added to the Aral would raise its surface level and revive the River Uzboy, which would flow into the Caspian Sea. Should this scheme be realised, large areas could be irrigated from the revived rivers, a great deal of hydro-electric power could be generated, a waterway 5000 miles long would connect the Caspian with Lake Baykal, and the climate of Kazakstan, Turkmenistan, and Western Siberia would be improved.

2. THE MOUNTAIN FRINGE

In the south and east a gigantic mountain barrier closes the horizons of central Asia. The Tien Shan, Alayski, and Pamir were little known until recently, but they were zealously explored in the closing years of the Tsars, and the work has been even more vigorous since the revolution. Though the mountains are far from having yielded up all their secrets, we are nevertheless beginning to have a relatively precise idea of them, at any rate as far as their physical geography is concerned.

Though generally regarded as Tertiary in origin, most of them were in fact formed by very ancient folds dating from the end of the Primary in the case of the Altai and central Tien Shan and from the beginning and middle of the Primary in the case of the northern Tien Shan. Forces acting in two directions, one north-east–south-west and the other south-east–north-west, met here, and their combined action produced mountain arcs which turned their concave sides to the north. Erosion through the ages reduced them almost to the state of peneplains, as is proved by the existence of *syrts*, or fragments of wide and almost levelled areas still found today at more or less elevated altitudes to which they have been raised by orogenic spasms in the Tertiary era. At the time of the Alpine folding these old mountains were again uplifted and rejuvenated. Some, like the Kopet Dagh, the Alayski, and the southern Tien Shan, were then folded more violently than before; the others, including the central and northern Tien Shan, seem to have been uplifted by simple vertical movement. In the Pamirs the horizontal and vertical thrusts seem to have been combined. The uplifts did not end with the Tertiary, but appear to be continuing even today. Evidence of this is given by the formidable earthquakes which destroy whole towns, as Alma Ata was in 1887 and 1911, or cause landslides capable of blocking valleys and thus forming large lakes, as happened in the Murgab valley in 1911. Fault lines are numerous in the mountains and are often marked by hot springs, but not volcanoes. The great Alayski valley, through which flow the Vakhsh, Surkhob, and Kyzyl-Su, has been formed along an immense fault.

But erosion is mainly responsible for the topography of these ranges and plateaus as they now stand. Vigorous uplift was followed by vigorous denudation, as is proved by the extraordinary depth of the detritus at the foot of the Pamirs. The destructive work of glaciers, which, to judge from the countless traces they have left, formerly covered a far greater area than they do today, has been immense, but should not make us forget the effect of normal erosion, which in many worn plateaus and ridges has dug gorges of imposing depth and steepness of sides, whilst at the same time silting up a number of lakes situated on the uplands.

So far as conclusions may be formed of a climate that is still largely unknown, what has been said above does not necessarily imply that the mountains are subject to very heavy precipitation. There is no doubt that the temperatures recorded on the lofty plateaus are severe, that there is a great diurnal range, that inversion of temperature is frequent, and that the occurrence of a foehn has very often been observed in April. Similarly, it is certain that the rainfall maximum occurs in summer, the minimum in winter; that enclosed basins are marked by drought; that precipitation is not very great on the high peaks, but chiefly favours the lower slopes. The mean rainfall is unknown, however, for only a very few recording stations are available. Some of these are well sheltered and very dry; e.g. Kheirabad with 14·37 ins., Przhevalsk with 15·90, Narynsk with 12·05, Irkeshtam with 6·50, and Pamirski Post with 2·32. Others which are more exposed to moist winds show moderate figures; e.g. Lake Iskander with 23·82 ins. and Zerafshan glacier with 27·76; or even fairly high ones, like 59·05 ins. on the southern slopes of the Hissar Hills in the western Tien Shan. Aspect is the decisive factor, and it seems certain that slopes facing west or north are far more

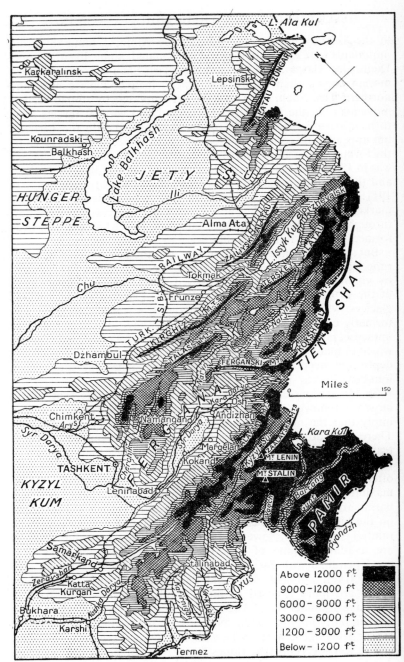

FIG. 44. SOVIET CENTRAL ASIA.

favoured than other parts, especially between elevations of 10,000 and 15,000 ft.

However, it is an exaggeration to say that the mountains as a whole are 'an island of damp in a sea of drought'. Though some real icefields, one 25 miles long by 5 to 6 miles wide, exist in the Terskey Ala-Tau, though the Fedchenko glacier in the Seldy Tau is 48 miles long, and the Inylchek glacier on Khan Tengri is 40 miles in length, glaciers rarely have a length greater than 6 miles even in the gigantic Za-alayski, and on the whole seem rather poorly fed.

This impression is strengthened by the appearance of the vegetation. North-facing slopes are often covered with luxuriant grass and splendid firwoods, but those facing south are nearly bare of trees and are invaded by Aralo-Caspian plants, unless they have vast thickets of *arsha*, a juniper peculiar to this country. 'The steppe climbs up from every direction to attack the mountain,' says Camena d'Almeida. This relative drought explains the high altitude of the snowline in summer. With the help of very surefooted horses and even more surefooted yaks man can cross these huge ranges with less difficulty than might be imagined. The military road from Fergana to the Pamirs is passable for two or three months in the year, though it rises to a height of 15,000 ft.

But these general characteristics do not appear equally throughout the region, and it should be noted that, as Camena d'Almeida has said, 'the Alayski valley' separates two different worlds. The north is better watered than the south, its mountain masses have severer outlines and larger forests, and their more luxuriant pastures feed more cattle. But at the same time dwellings and tilth definitely stop at a lower level than on the southern mountains.

(a) *The Tien Shan.* The northern ranges form the colossal group known as the Tien Shan. It begins to the north of the Ili valley with the Dzungari Ala-Tau, which rises to 15,000 ft. This old peneplain, which has been uplifted, dislocated, and fractured into asymmetrical blocks, this 'gigantic staircase on whose topmost step is spread a mantle of eternal snow' (Kalesnik), has few glaciers, but the lofty altitude of the passes make it difficult to cross.

South of the Ili stands the trans-Ilian Ala-Tau, which rises to 15,600 ft. in Kalgar. Though its glaciers are small, they seem to threaten to overwhelm the town of Alma Ata with icefalls; but none the less they are useful to the cultivation of the plain, which their melt-water irrigates.

Separated from the foregoing by a long rift valley, the Khrikunghy Ala-Tau, which rises to 17,000 ft. in Choktal, is formed of rounded ridges. Between these lie little glaciers on the far side of the dizzy gorges of Buam which have been carved by the Chu. These mountains have a western extension which goes by the name of the Kirghiz (or Alexander) Range and, like the main range, is of crystalline formation. It rises to 15,400 ft. in Mt. Semionov and is adorned with many *névés* and glaciers.

South of this long rampart stretches a valley in which sleeps Issyk-Kul, 'Warm Lake', 2250 square miles in area, 380 fathoms deep, and slightly salt. On its southern side it is dominated by the Terskey Ala-Tau, which rises to 18,000 ft. in Mt. Alexander and forms the central portion of a range 800 miles long. Westwards the Terskey Ala-Tau is continued in the Ala-Tau of Talass, whose 16,000-ft. peaks stand up above innumerable glaciers. Eastwards it is continued by a chain of shale and limestone ridges and joins the great orographic knot of Khan Tengri, the giant of the Tien Shan, which towers to 22,900 ft. at the Chinese frontier over large glaciers, among them that of Inylchek. From this same mountain knot the Kok Shaal Tau range runs out towards the south-west (19,300 ft.) and curves round to the north-west under the name of Fergana Mountains (16,200 ft.) to join the Ala-Tau of Talass.

These ranges, which are perpetually snow-capped and bedecked with glaciers, have few peaks that definitely stand out above the rest. They give the impression that they are connected with the *syrts* that are so common in the Tien Shan, and this impression is made more definite on seeing enclosed among them the plateau of Aksay and its worn surface gashed with young valleys.

Finally, to this grand Kok Shaal–Fergana arc is connected the lofty Alayski range (19,000 ft.). This great mountain wall, whose average height is 13,000 ft. and which is only slightly breached by passes more than 11,500 ft. high, is crossed only at a cost of very difficult climbing. It is continued westwards by three ranges which are roughly parallel to each other and in a fairly advanced state of denudation, but difficult to cross, viz. The Turkistan (17,000 ft.), Zeravshan (18,300 ft.), and Gissar (17,700 ft.) Mountains.

As a rule the first foothills of these mountains have an almost desert flora in which desert sedge predominates among the meadowgrass and many bulbous plants. High up the prevailing vegetation is steppe with couchgrass, barley, bulbs, and *inula*. Still higher there is steppe with fescue and feathergrass. At a height of about 5000 ft. the woodland steppe begins with phleum and hairy or plumose feathergrass, but is sometimes replaced by broad-leaved woods (walnut, apple, maple, or else mountain ash, ash, white birch, and poplar). The topmost belt is disputed by sub-alpine pasture, grasses, compositæ, and umbelliferæ on the one hand and on the other by coniferous forest in which there are no pines or larches, but large numbers of spruce and fir. In some places both of these types give place to junipers. Above the forest stretches the alpine pasture dotted with many-coloured flowers. Here the prevailing plant is the creeping juniper, after which comes the sedge *cobresia*; and as a rule the grass is not more than 4 or 5 ins. high. Near the snowline grow gentians, saxifrages, and speedwell.

The Kazaks and Kirghiz have made fairly good use of the natural resources. They get an appreciable return from hunting roebuck, maral stag, mountain sheep, lynx, ermine, panther, and bear, not to mention countless marmots and birds; and also from fishing, Lake Issyk alone giving 390 tons of fish a year. In the lower valleys where the bulk of the people live and into which most of the *auls* are crowded, there is more agriculture than one would imagine. Rye, barley, millet, pumpkins, and water melons are much cultivated, though not cotton or rice; and the Russians have introduced wheat, sunflowers, and of course cucumbers. But stock-rearing is still the chief means of livelihood.

There is little or no poultry, but there are cattle, horses, a large number of sheep, camels near the plains, and yaks at high altitudes. Wool, leather, meat, milk, and cheese supplied by these animals are of inestimable value to the mountain folk. Naturally, the climate makes the latter practise *transhumance*, which is a step forward from primitive nomadism. In summer they leave their winter quarters, or *kishlau*, and drive their beasts up to the snowfree pastures, where they install themselves in *jailau*. Here they spend 'the best days of their lives', according to Semionov, on the luscious pasture among the hundreds of thousands of oxen and sheep which they have brought up. As soon as the weather turns cold, they return to the lower valleys and to their *auls* with their little clay huts. Moreover, for some decades now there has been a noticeably distinct tendency to adopt a sedentary agricultural life. Many Kirghiz combine stock-rearing with tillage and are only half-nomadic with limited displacements. In fact, not seldom one part of the *aul* goes with the animals into the mountains, whilst the other remains behind to keep an eye on the crops that have been sown and to weed the fields. Hence, they have traditional trading places, like Karkara, a town of tents and wooden huts situated 20 miles from Przhevalsk and at a height of 6500 ft., whose summer fair, which was held until recently, used to be the scene of gathering of a crowd of Kirghiz, Russians, Sarts, and Kashgarians.

(b) *The Alayski Valley.* The Tien Shan is bounded on the south by the Alayski valley, whose trough is dominated from the north by the crystalline or volcanic formations of the Alayski Mountains, and from the south by the Cretaceous and Eocene folds of the Zaalayski range. It is a trench bounded by faults and is more than

370 miles long by 6 to 9 usually, with a maximum breadth of 13½. In it the Kyzyl-Su flows towards the west, taking the name Surkhob farther downstream in the Tadzhik country. The river rises in the Taun Murun Pass (11,000 ft.) near the Chinese frontier. Descending slowly as far as Daraut Kurgan (8300 ft.), it is almost literally strangled, but recovers a good width in the lower levels of Karategin. This district, which leads to the plains, has a sedentary population of both Tadzhiks and Kirghiz. The inhabitants, who are scattered about in hamlets and little villages, grow cereals, cultivate flax to make linseed oil, and rear animals. The district is regarded as a paradise by the people around, who often visit it for supplies. Yet its chief town, Garm, is only a country village with a population of 2000. Farther upstream the Alayski valley proper is not cultivated above Daraut-Kurgan, at which point barley and lucerne disappear; but its chestnut soil yields thick, succulent grass which, being well watered by mountain streams and warmed by moderate summer temperatures, forms green pastures. Thousands of nomads from Fergana visit it with their horses, camels, oxen, sheep, and goats, staying there from June to September and dotting the grass with countless tents.

(c) *The Za-alayski Mountains and the Pamirs.* A lofty barrier of red sandstone studded here and there with diorites and crystalline schists and known as the Za-alayski rises to the south of the valley. Though its vegetation is poor and its slopes often bare, its mean altitude, which is 5400 ft. higher than that of the Alayski, gives it a perpetual snow cover over far larger areas and glaciers that are much bigger than those in the latter range. In the east Lenin (formerly Kaufmann) Peak, which was climbed in 1934, rises to 23,400 ft., but the western part of the range which is crossed by the military road to the Pamirs through the Kyzyl Art Pass (14,600 ft.) is clearly lower.

The Za-alayski range is continued south-westwards by a set of three ranges whose forms are as varied as their geology. They are Scientific Academy range, Darvas range, and Peter the Great range, in the last of which Mt. Seviortsov reaches a height of 18,400 ft. On these mountains the snowline is never below 13,000 ft., and yet, owing to the very high mean altitude, glaciers are numerous, especially in the Seldy Tau group, which overlooks the western road into the Pamirs. A large icefield has been found there as well as many valley glaciers, one of which, Fedchenko, is among the largest in the world. Not far away, at the point where the three ranges meet, is Stalin (formerly Garmo) Peak, which was climbed in 1933 and is the highest point in the Soviet Union, since it rises to 24,580 ft.

South of the Za-alayski range stretch the Pamirs, a region of lofty tablelands (or 'pamirs') separated from each other by mountain ranges which have few passes. In spite of their relatively low altitude these mountains contain a few glaciers, though these are so narrow as only recently to have been discovered. Among them is the Fedchenko glacier, which is said to be the largest in the world outside Antarctica. In the eastern Pamirs, where most of the valleys are at least 13,000 ft. above the sea, the snowline remains at a height of 14,700 ft. The country has only recently been freed from glaciation, and glacial topography is well preserved in it. A thick carpet of drift covers the ground nearly everywhere, and topographical features are rounded and worn.

On the other hand, the western Pamirs are deeply gashed, cut with V-shaped valleys which are narrow and without alluvium and whose steep, pebbly sides rise up to narrow, jagged ridges. But this type of feature occupies little space, for 'the Pamirs remain firmly persistent in their forms and in the depressing monotony of their scenery' (Camena d'Almeida). Generally speaking, the streams erode but little, the drainage is ill defined, and the many glacial lakes in the east (Rang Kul, Kara Kul, Zor Kul, Yashil Kul, etc.) appear to be in no danger of being emptied.

The truth is that the Pamirs are a high-level desert in which erosion is weak owing to the lack of water. Except above the snowline, precipitation is slight: 2·33 ins. at Pamirski Post (0·07 in. from October 1, 1913, to September 30, 1914), and the lower valleys in the west have scarcely 8 ins. The air is rare and very dry, violent winds frequently blow, the annual and diurnal range of temperature is enormous, the sky is constantly blue, and the glare is fierce. The soils too smack of the desert and are often gypseous or salty, never loessic. Hence, the vegetation is very poor. The valleys have little water and are therefore far from verdant in spite of their lakes and marshes. Elsewhere there are no trees, but only mountain wormwood and tufts of grass struggling for life here and there among the pebbles; *tereken*, which are climbing salsolaceæ of shrub-like appearance; lichens; mosses; and sometimes alpine pasture. These afford poor food for the wild goat and the huge mountain sheep, the flocks of which are attacked by wolves. The white panther, bear, tailed marmot, red lagomys, Tibetan hare, and a number of birds of passage, like the capercailzie, mountain goose, and steppe hen, complete the fauna, which is related to that of Tibet.

Hunting is naturally an important means of livelihood. But the Kirghiz population, which is extraordinarily sparse and scattered, and numbers between 1500 and 2000 persons, is mainly engaged in stock-rearing and drives its horses, sheep, camels, and its many yaks seasonally from the plateau on to the mountains and down again. Yaks, which supply meat and milk, are essential for transport on steep gradients.

However, the Pamirs include one district that is more favoured, viz. the series of valleys which notch the western edge. These are Darvaz, Rushan, and Shugnan. They face the Pendjeh (Pyandzh), form a southward continuation of Karategin, and are drained respectively by the Vanch, Bartang, and Gunt. As they are deeply incised, communication between them is difficult. Whilst the winters are severe, the summers are very hot owing to the latitude and the lower elevation (between 5000 and 10,000 ft.). Hence, as irrigation is possible, the Tadzhik villagers engage in agriculture. Wheat, barley, millet, peas, beans, and melons are the main crops, but the vine also grows in some places and there are many gardens in which flourish the pomegranate, peach, apricot, pear, cherry, and more rarely the apple, without counting the walnut and mulberry, the fruit of which is eaten. Scattered under the shade of these trees are the villagers' mud huts coated with a kind of stucco and resembling those in the Ukraine.

(d) *The Mountains of Turkmenistan.* Finally, to the south of Turkistan runs the Iranian northern mountain border, a fringe of which belongs to the Soviet Union. The Karabil and Badkhiz ranges (4000 ft.) are denuded, stony ridges connecting the Hindu Kush with Kopet Dagh. The latter begins at Tedzhen Pass and runs northwards for 465 miles. The range is formed of big recumbent folds very recently uplifted and scored with faults, the echoes of which movements being still felt in earthquakes. Its structure is of ridges of sandstone, limestone, and marl arranged in parallel lines. Its highest peak in Soviet territory is Mt. Riza, which rises to 8200 ft. Greater height would be needed so far south and in so cloudless a climate to reach the snowline. Even the forest belt is missing; and there are only arid steppes with clumps of junipers or in the gorges hawthorn, eglantine, wild plum, and blueberry, and in some places walnut trees, willows, maples, and poplars. In short, these heights can give only poor grazing and feed for but few animals. Of far greater value is the line of alluvial fans which spread out at the foot of the range. There irrigation is possible, and carefully selected fruit-trees flourish.

On the whole, the mountains in Soviet central Asia certainly have some value, though the area of useless ground in them is extensive. The Soviet Government has tried to exploit this wealth. *Kolkhozy* have been organised; large stock-rearing *sovkhozy* have been formed, each one of which covers thousands of square miles of alpine pasture; attempts have been made to introduce agriculture into the Pamirs by establishing experimental stations to cultivate wheat and potatoes at a height of 11,800 ft. in upper Badakhshan in the western Pamirs; mineral wealth has been found in the form of precious metals and coal in Kirghizstan, iron, lead, zinc, and sulphur in the Pamirs, arsenious ores in the western Tien Shan, and phosphates in Kara Tau. Kirghizstan is rich in uranium, mercury, and tungsten. The chief uranium mines are at Maylysay and Tyuya-Muyun, where large quantities of the mineral are found. The control of waterfalls for the production of hydro-electricity has begun; and the preparation of a network of communications has been started by the improvement of the trails used by stockmen and by the construction of real roads and modern bridges. The first results of this effort seem encouraging, and it may be considered that so far in the main as pastoral matters are concerned, the mountains have a rosy future. In the meanwhile, their essential task is to supply water to the areas situated at their foot, to that favoured belt of country which was until very recently the only part of Soviet central Asia worthy of the name of cultivable land.

3. THE CULTIVABLE AREAS

It would scarcely be an exaggeration to say that the cultivable parts of central Asia are restricted on the one hand to the belt of loess which runs almost uninterruptedly along the foot of the mountains and when irrigated makes wonderful breaks in the desert, and on the other hand to the valleys of the big rivers and their flood plains—the *tugay*.

There is doubt whether the loess is of contemporary æolian origin or a geological formation derived from glacial deposits. Whatever the case, the yellowish, friable, powdery mixture of clay and limestone which smothers the details of topography under a bed 100 ft. or more thick in places, dominates the landscape with its characteristic deep fissures and steep faces. 'A sea of slippery yellow mud during the rains and the origin of clouds of impalpable dust in dry weather, it is only too familiar to the clothes, eyes, ears, and mouth of the traveller' (W. Rickmer Rickmers). But whilst its natural vegetation is grassy steppe, it has only to be irrigated to reveal its wonderful fertility. Wherever there are *aryks*, or irrigation ditches (which are seen even on slopes), the soil is covered with grass, spinneys, flourishing crops, and villages. The Sarts and Tadzhiks have clung to this favoured soil, in spite of countless devastating invasions, and 'three-fourths of the people of Turkistan live on irrigated loess land' (Camena d'Almeida).

The *tugay*, which are formed of moist alluvium, stand out in contrast with the adjoining desert by reason of their verdure. Low islands and banks which are liable to be flooded are covered with a vegetation of poplars, willows, ash, liquorice, clematis, *dyrisun*, etc., not forgetting the vast reed-brakes haunted by stags, wild boars, and even tigers. Less sought after than the loess, the *tugay* attract population through their good water supply. The soil is saturated, and lakes and pools occur in plenty. True, they are not sure to last, for a flood may destroy them or the river may sweep over them again; but the stream may also turn away and form fresh *tugay* in new areas, and, so long as the river does not dry up, the old *tugay* will be capable of bearing crops on its fertile soil. This fertility induces many of the natives to face the dangerous neighbourhood of the tiger and the risk of seeing their crops uprooted by wild boars.

The cultivable part of Soviet central Asia consists of three large divisions. First, in the north there is Dzhety-Su, or Semirechye, which borders on Siberia; next, right in the south is the series of Turkmen oases reaching to the Caspian; lastly, between the two are the lands of the Syr Darya and Oxus with the upland valleys of Fergana and Zeravshan.

(a) *Dzhety-Su, or 'The Land of the Seven Rivers'*. This lies between the Chinese frontier, Dzungari Ala-Tau, Lake Balkhash, the Kirghiz range, and the Khrikunghy Ala-Tau. Its climate is continental, fairly dry and cold in winter, dry and warm in summer. For example, Alma Ata has a mean rainfall of 22·45 ins. owing to the proximity of the mountains, but Arasan gets only 12·62 and Kopal 12·21. Arasan, which is 3100 ft. above the sea, has a mean January temperature of 13·46° F. and Kopal, whose altitude is 4570 ft., has a mean of 18·68° F. Kopal has a July temperature of 69·98° F., Alma Ata one of 73·4° F. In the mountain forests the soil is formed of black earth and on the plains of loess. The water which flows down from the mountains enables cultivation to be successful.

The district was originally inhabited by Kazaks, but, since the end of the ill-starred attempt at settling Cossacks here, the country has been patiently and methodically colonised by Russian peasants, who have increased the number of *aryks* and built villages on the plains or on the lower slopes of the mountains. They have not been successful everywhere. Much of the valley of the Ili, for instance, is marshy and saline, shifting sands hinder the irrigation of the cultivable land and the draining of the marshes, and there are swarms of mosquitoes and poisonous spiders, which are more feared by the settlers than are the tigers in the reed-brakes. But large areas especially to the south of the Ili, which were originally covered with steppe vegetation and had wonderful colours in spring, have been brought under cultivation. 'In May the steppe to the south of the Ili is perfumed with the scent of flowers. Red poppies cover miles and hide the green grass. In places belts of blue myosotis stand out against the background, making a really fantastic picture' (Sapojnikov). Hamlets and villages, nestling in the green of elms and poplars, harvest wheat, rye, flax, hemp, poppy and sunflower seeds, water melons, tomatoes, cucumbers, and enormous fruit, like the famous apples of Alma Ata,[1] the biggest in the world, though their taste is not equal to their size. Furthermore, hunting and, to a greater extent still, fishing especially in the Chu provide the means of livelihood.

Villages are especially numerous along the road to Tashkent. But there are also towns which must be mentioned: Dzhambul (formerly Aulie Ata; pop. 30,000), which grew up as a market town for agricultural produce and nearly became the capital of Russian Turkistan; Frunze (formerly Pishpek; pop. 190,000), at the foot of Kirghiz range, which grew up for the same reason, but which, as it became the capital of the Kirghiz Republic, has libraries, academic institutions, tanneries, textile mills organised in a *kombinat*, meat-canning factories, and sugar refineries; and, lastly and chiefly, Alma Ata (formerly Vyerni), the capital of Kazakstan, whose wide streets, low wooden or brick houses, and Russian shop signs remind one of Siberia, but which with its green gardens, its canals running through the yellow steppe, and its avenues lined with elms and poplars, produces the same impression of coolness as does oriental Samarkand. Hence, Sarts, Kirghiz, Kazaks, Kalmuks, and Chinese are numerous. It has always been a busy trading town; but today it is also an intellectual centre with a university and many printing presses as well as the seat of chemical and food industries. Its population has increased since 1926 from 46,000 to 330,000.

Dzhety-Su seems to be a vigorous country which has already advanced economically owing to the large Russian element in its population. Its development has accelerated since the towns have been on the Turksib Railway. Frunze is joined by a branch line to this railway, whose locomotives burn coal raised in the Ili valley.

(*b*) *The Oases of Southern Turkmenistan.* At the other end of the region there is between the mountains and the desert a narrow strip of greyish loess near to alluvial fans which by means of their wonderful fertility have attracted man since the Neolithic Age. Both agriculture and stock-raising flourish on it, and in the days of the Seleucides there was built in Morgiana[2] a town of Antioch which, with its gardens, is said to have been girt with a wall 170 miles long and which was the ancestor of the modern Merv. In the time of the Sassanides and Seljukides other towns with many aqueducts, palaces, and mosques sprang up in these parts. But the Turkmen invasion and domination ruined the country less by war and pillage than by the carelessness of the government and neglect of the irrigation system. When the Russians arrived, the situation was deplorable.

[1] The name means 'Apple Town'.
[2] i.e. the valley of the Margos, the present Murgab.

In many areas it has remained so up to the present. Near the Caspian the country round the River Atrek, which was formerly well cultivated, has largely reverted to desert, and once big villages are now but ruins. The valleys of the left-bank feeders of the Atrek are the only parts that still carry on agriculture. The northern slope of Kopet Dagh has been better treated. It is fringed with a line of oases 160 miles long and wonderfully fertile.[1] A few towns exist on it, viz. Kizyl Arvat, on the Trans-Caspian Railway, which has long traded in an old type of Turkmen carpet of extraordinary richness of design and colour; Geok-Tepe, a huge village with several thousand houses; and above all, Ashkhabad, which stands amid gardens and cotton fields.

There is the same degree of fertility in the Tedzhen delta where, long before the revolution, the rebuilding of the dykes and the repair of the canals much increased the number of farmers. Cotton has been long in taking hold, but wheat, barley, and lucerne have flourished, especially round Tedzhen.

Still farther east the Murgab district, which was the object of great care on the part of Alexander III, has to some extent repaired its ruins. In spite of many difficulties—malaria brought on by ill-regulated drainage, broken dams, and reservoirs silted up—it has again begun to cultivate rice, wheat, barley, lucerne, peas, melons, and cotton, and to make cotton-seed oil and soap. Though the new Merv lacks the glory of its predecessor, yet the fertility of the district around and the presence of a junction of the Trans-Caspian Railway with its branch into Afghanistan have made it a very busy centre. On the whole, in spite of its broiling summers and unhealthiness, the Murgab district is the best part of the strip of southern oases. As early as 1928 the irrigated area amounted to 170,000 acres.

The construction of the Trans-Caspian Railway, which was carried out some time ago, was certainly beneficial to these districts, through a good part of which it passes. Besides, the five-year plans have not neglected them. The area under cultivation rose from 785,460 acres in 1913 to 911,430 in 1955. Cotton cultivation has spread over thousands of acres hitherto untilled. In Turkmenistan there were 792,850 acres so used in 1955, most of the raw cotton produced being sent to Tashkent or along the Turksib Railway to Siberia for manufacture. Other crops (mainly wheat, millet, rice, and potatoes) occupied 118,580 acres; and orchards are extensive. On the edge of the desert a semi-nomadic population rears horses, camels, and sheep. Forage crops are grown in the Turkmen oases, and this enables stock-rearing in the country to become more and more a

[1] 'Its white soil', says Semionov, 'is in no way inferior to that of the Nile valley. An ordinary harvest gives a yield of fiftyfold, a good harvest eightyfold.'

settled occupation. Selective breeding gives wool of good quality and in greater quantity than is had in Kazakstan, where the wool is too often poor in quality and quantity. Industry has been greatly encouraged. Carpet-making has been reorganised by co-operatives and has increased its production sixfold, but, however, without recovering its old quality. Factories have been built to can fish, make soap, and manufacture textiles. A hydro-electric power plant has been built at Ashkhabad (pop. 142,000), which is now an industrial and intellectual centre as well as the capital of Turkmenistan. However, there is a vast amount of work still to be done, especially in the way of irrigation, and the value of these Turkmen oases remains even now far less than that of the country round the Syr Darya and Oxus.

(c) *The Country round the Syr Darya and Oxus. The Syr Darya and its Surroundings.* To the south of Dzhety-Su lies the region watered by the Syr Darya. Two streams, the Naryn and the Kara Darya, have joined to form this river in the basin of subsidence known as Fergana. This basin is wholly shut in by high mountains, but opens westwards in a breach through which the river escapes. Following a steep gradient, so that at Leninabad it is little more than 850 ft. above sea level, the Syr Darya is joined by the Cherchik and Arys, two right-bank feeders; and when in flood may have a volume as great as 1700 cu. yds. per second. But at the town of Turkistan it enters the desert and begins to shrink rapidly. No feeder flows in to compensate for the effects of intense evaporation, and some of its water is constantly running off into the *tugay* along its banks. In the course of geological ages and even in modern times, it has shifted its bed again and again. Today it is pressing against its right bank and wearing it away fast. At Kzyl-Orda it winds about and splits up more and more, causing huge swamps which are very hostile to man and abandoning more or less dying arms. Finally, a much-reduced stream enters a delta which is streaked with backwaters and covered with an endless and—in spite of the lack of water in the river—constantly spreading expanse of reeds.

With its surroundings the valley, 1785 miles long, is reckoned among the best districts in Turkistan. The soil, which is loess with grey earth, is excellent. The climate is warm in summer, with temperatures between 80° F. and 84° F., and cold in winter, when the thermometer registers from 29° F. to 26·5° F.; and it is relatively humid, at least in spring, when Tashkent has a mean of 13·7 ins. and Chimkent one of 19 ins. On the whole, the district is favourable to agriculture, and the proximity of relatively well-watered mountain ranges has made great irrigation systems possible.

In the valleys of the Cherchik and Arys to the south-west of

Dzhety-Su, wheat, rice, and cotton are cultivated now, sheep are reared for their wool, and cattle for their meat, milk, and butter. Chimkent (pop. 130,000), which is in the heart of a flourishing oasis, has grown up as a market for agricultural produce and has almost a monopoly of the production of santonin. Furthermore, the discovery in Kazakstan of many deposits of copper (at Almalyk), lead, zinc, and even oil has made the Soviet Government decide to establish in this town a polymetallic *kombinat* with large foundries. Hence, the population has nearly doubled in ten years.

But of far greater importance is Tashkent, the largest town in Soviet Asia and a city with a glorious historical past. Its native quarter, which is devoid of public buildings and without much interest, 'still keeps its houses which are windowless on the street side, its maze of passages and blind alleys smelling of flowers, skins, and mildew, its houses of puddled clay, its covered bazaar, its gutters murmuring with the flow of water' (Slonim). But there is also a regularly built Russian quarter with fine avenues shaded by poplars and acacias, with magnificent gardens, official buildings, and big shops. Tashkent has become a route focus and a railway junction too since the Turksib Railway has been joined to the Trans-Aralian. It is an intellectual capital provided with a university, many schools, learned societies, libraries, a museum, an astronomical observatory, and a theatre. Lastly, it is an industrial centre. To its petty native crafts have been added today flour mills, distilleries, breweries, printing-presses, and tobacco factories. To these the first two five-year plans added machine shops which turn out agricultural machinery intended for local cotton cultivation and textile machinery for both spinning and weaving. There are also railway repair shops and, above all, a flourishing textile industry. The town affords a good example of the way in which the national republics have been equipped with industry. Today a big *kombinat* works up on the spot locally grown cotton, and the third five-year plan intended to develop this activity still further. This industrial expansion explains why, unlike so many towns in Turkistan, Tashkent has copied the towns in the Urals by greatly increasing its population, which has risen from 320,000 in 1926 to 778,000 in 1956.

Tashkent is not merely an industrial town, for it has become the core of a cluster of new towns. Farkhad is a hydro-electric producer on the Syr Darya near Begovat; Chirchik also produces hydro-electric power, but is mainly important for the production of nitrogen fertilisers; Almalyk, near Angren, has copper refineries. Tashkent itself is an ancient city, but shows few signs of antiquity, and its only building of any note is the ornate opera house. It is used as a centre for showing Indians and other Asiatics the results of Communist planning, and large numbers of these visitors are taken to see the cotton mills and the irrigated fields in the neighbourhood.

The resources of the country round the Arys and Cherchik are far smaller than those of Fergana. Although the centre is a sand desert and the loess belt on the periphery is interrupted in places, the crops are very good. Within a frame of walnut forests with luxuriant undergrowth the basin has, thanks mainly to the Kara Darya and to the canals it feeds, many fields of rice, millet, wheat, barley, lucerne, as well as vineyards and orchards which supply a great deal of dried fruit for export. Stock-rearing is carried on, and the mulberry is cultivated for feeding silkworms, Fergana being the main district of sericulture in Soviet territory.

But cotton is more than ever the most important crop. Interest was taken in it during the time of the Tsars, but the Soviet Government has gone much further, and since 1930 food crops have largely retreated before the invasion of this plant which, besides the fibre that forms the basis of a great local industry, yields oil-cake for stock-feed, twigs for fuel, and seed for oil. Fergana has become the land of cotton.

In addition, it has industrial resources. For a long time the natives have been mining gold and using the sulphur springs. In recent years the coal- and oil-fields and the deposits of lead and sulphur have been attacked. Lastly, several hydro-electric power plants have been built. Consequently, besides the old native crafts of making carpets, scarfs, embroidered caps, beaten copper articles, and pottery, modern industries have sprung up, and these are mainly gins, mills for spinning and weaving cotton, electro-metallurgical and electro-chemical factories, fruit-canning factories, distilleries, and dairies.

Hence, the regular development of the towns. Except Tashkent, none of them is very big, for, as the middle of the basin is a desert, there can be no common centre. But to their historic memories and old buildings they have been able to add the wealth arising from industry and commerce, and, though Osh and Margelan scarcely count and the town of Fergana has little life, Namangan (pop. 104,000), Andizhan (pop. 115,000), Leninabad (pop. 70,000) at the entrance of the basin, and, above all, Kokand (pop. 84,000) show remarkable vitality. In short, Fergana is 'the pearl of Uzbekistan', and the energy with which the policy of irrigation and the modernisation of agricultural methods has been pursued is a guarantee of future progress.

The valley of the Syr Darya farther west is much less remarkable. It has suffered not only from the river's loss of volume and the shifting of its course, but also from countless wars. Yet, compared with the Kyzyl Kum and even the Hungersteppe it is a happy land. In the belt of meres and reed-brakes between 12 and 30 miles wide, which the river forms on its banks, the *tugay* provides man with wood, fish, game, and with forage for his beast, and these resources are greatly utilised. Unfortunately, the Syr Darya, which is shallow and impeded by banks of mud, is a very poor waterway. Though it helped the Russian conquest, its navigation is slow, uncertain, and dangerous. It is no wonder that neither Chinaz nor the town of Turkistan has really been prosperous and that Kazalinsk and Kzyl-Orda, which in any case are very small places, should have owed their growth mainly to their situation on the posting route which was replaced at the beginning of the present century by the Trans-Aralian Railway. The full use of the middle and lower course of this valley has made very slight progress.

The Oases of Zeravshan and Kashka Darya. Farther south the Zeravshan dies away in the desert before reaching the Oxus. This river, which has been likened to the upper Rhone, rises in a glacier in the Alayski Mountains and is 1025 miles long. The strip which it waters increases in breadth from a mile and a quarter at first to more than 20 miles near Samarkand. Well fed in its early course, it is much tapped after reaching the plains and in addition suffers from the dryness of the climate and the intensity of the evaporation. It reaches Bukhara with great difficulty and in a state of exhaustion and dies away about 60 miles from the Oxus. But at any rate it is inestimably valuable to the districts upstream.

From ancient times this country of Sogdiana was renowned, and its irrigation system as well as the flourishing oases created by the river were enthusiastically praised in the Middle Ages by the Arab geographers. Today the river is no less important. In 1913, 126 oases on which wheat, vines, fruit-trees, and cotton were grown, owed their existence to it. Whenever agriculture depended on the rainfall alone, it was precarious and of poor quality.

The irregularity of the régime of the river was reflected in the irrigation, which used to be as a rule rather badly regulated. Hence, there would at one time be too much water, flooding, and even swamp conditions, whilst at other times the irrigation was inadequate, the fields and animals suffered from thirst, and the oases were threatened with invasion by sand. Some of the oases were nevertheless very beautiful. The most famous, on which stands Samarkand, had until recently preserved from its very ancient past the most wonderful buildings in Russian Turkistan, but they are now in a poor state of preservation. The most famous is the tomb of Tamerlane (see photograph facing page 301). The native town has long had various industries and a flourishing commerce. Its Russian quarter, with gardens even more beautiful than those of Tashkent, has distilleries, cotton gins, large flour-mills, wine-presses, factories making packing-cases and lead-paper for packing tea, silk-weaving mills, machine shops, and a large hydro-electric power plant. The town is the capital of Uzbekistan and has a population of 170,000. In the neighbourhood there are extensive orchards and much wheat is grown.

The oases farther downstream are less remarkable. After Katta-Kurgan, which is situated in the heart of the cotton area, comes Bukhara (pop. 50,000). This old intellectual Muslim city has long been the capital of a semi-independent Khanate as well as a great commercial centre. Today, whilst the native town keeps its picturesque scene of busy trading, the Russian quarter has but few industries. Bukhara is connected by a branch line which joins the Trans-Aralian Railway at Kagan. As the district around it suffers from want of water, agriculture cannot be very good.

The story of the Kashka Darya is rather like that of the Zeravshan. Rising in the Gissar Mountains, it dies away in the sand after having watered several oases. The finest is the 22-mile-long Karshi, where wheat, rice, cotton, tobacco, and fruit are cultivated. The town is much greener and shadier than Bukhara and was formerly really important as an intellectual and commercial centre and even had industries, thanks to native metallurgical crafts. Today its star has paled somewhat.

Finally, though the strip of loess between the Kashka and Oxus is narrower, it once had a very dense population. The Mongol invasion ruined the district, which has only partly recovered since the advent of Russian-imposed peace. The irrigation system has been partially restored and fertilises a good number of oases which are remarkable above all for their fruit-growing that now competes with cotton. The most important of them is Stalinabad (pop. 192,500). The town, which now has brickfields, sawmills, machine factories, and even a *kombinat* for making underclothing, is the capital of Tadzhikistan and as such is endeavouring to become an intellectual centre and a focus of native culture.

The Oxus Valley. The Oxus flows 1560 miles from Lake Victoria in the Pamirs to the Aral Sea. It is formed by the junction of the Pamir, Pendjeh (Pyandzh), and Vakhsh. The volume of the river at Chardzhou measures 1125 cu. yds. per sec. in February and 6200 cu. yds. in July, with an annual mean of 2600 and a highest record of 12,635 cu. yds. Farther downstream its tributaries fail to reach it, since they are used up by irrigation. From the confluence with the Vakhsh, which is 1100 ft. above sea level, the gradient is gentle, and the river, whose waters are very muddy, deposits a great deal of silt. On the plain it is 760 yds. wide on the average; but in places a mile and a quarter, when it includes a number of mud banks and low islands. Its course is very variable, for the stream greatly undercuts the high right bank, threatening crops, villages, and towns; whilst the deposition of silt is intense on the flat left bank and constantly forces the *aryks* to be lengthened. Hence, it is very difficult to use the water of the river conveniently, which is all the more to be regretted, since there is plenty of water in spite of the desert climate and the absence of feeders.

Consequently, the valley under the threat of the river's shifting its course and made dangerous by quicksands is mostly an unhealthy *tugay* full of reed-brakes and swarming with wild beasts. Few people live in it, except the semi-nomadic Turkomans who take refuge there during the winter. A good number of ancient towns have disappeared in consequence of the displacements of the Oxus. The ones which survive are situated on the right bank, where the bed is fixed in hard rock. Termez, Kilif, Kerki, and Chardzhou, an important station on the Trans-Caspian Railway, are all instances of this. Then there is Turtkul (formerly Petro-Alexandrovsk), an old Cossack fortress, which is the first town on the oasis of Khiva.

The last-named town lies in by far the richest area in the valley. True, irrigation is difficult, owing to the extraordinary muddiness of the water. The canals are quickly silted up and displaced. But the soil is fertilised with a mixture of alluvium, sand, dung, and weeds and is very fertile. *Chighirs* (chain-pumps) creak everywhere, and cotton, lucerne, rice, maize, onions, melons, water melons, and other fruit give good crops. To this is added sheep-farming. Khiva (pop. 25,000) was a great slave market before the Russian conquest and up to 1918 was the capital of a Khan 'who lived in a cage which Russia had hung with velvet'. It has beautiful gardens, but no noteworthy public buildings. It is little more than a mart for the agricultural produce of the oasis and is expanding only very slightly.

Formerly the Oxus flowed towards the Caspian through the valleys of the Kunye and Uzboy. The shifting of its course destroyed Kunye Urgench, which used to be the capital of the oasis. If modern engineering restores the former course, the town may revive. Meantime, the river ends in a delta which is slowly advancing. Its northern portion is covered with reed-brakes and is inhabited only by wild boars and tigers, and its southern part is covered with ruins and has only a few decayed villages. The mouths of the Oxus are constantly shifting, navigation is very difficult on it, and the agricultural exploitation of the district as a whole is not easy.

In short, these so-called cultivable lands vary greatly in importance. Even in the best parts marsh fever and parasitic diseases like filariasis are too frequently rampant. The use of the water is often badly controlled, particularly at Khiva, though there is no country in the world in which human life depends so much on irrigation as it does in central Asia.

The Soviet Government has understood this and has made strenuous efforts to solve the problem. That is why the third five-year plan intended to complete the irrigation works in the valleys of the Vakhsh, Zeravshan, Chu, and Murgab. Furthermore, the Government is going to great expense to electrify these districts. The two hydro-electric power plants of Chirchikstroy, with a total of 400,000 kWh., will supply a number of factories, among which will be large works for making nitrate fertilisers for the cotton fields. Prospecting for mineral deposits has been assiduously carried out, and, lastly, efforts have constantly been made to improve communications, since their importance is scarcely less than that of irrigation.

Great results have been obtained in this direction, but the efforts are not being relaxed, as is proved by the recent construction of the Karaganda-Balkhash Railway, following the building of the Turksib; of the Khorezm-Chardzhou line, and of the Kunye Urgench-Krasnovodsk road, not to mention various mountain roads. It has been rightly emphasised that four great railway lines now converge on the south-eastern oases, attracting settlers and increasing the exploitation of central Asia. This demonstrates their value.

CHAPTER 21

THE CAUCASUS

In the whole of the Soviet Union there is certainly no part more distinctly marked off from the rest than the Caucasus. For this reason the great mountain range and its surroundings constitute a single region which must be studied separately. Owing to the climate and natural vegetation of the northern part, one might perhaps be tempted to tack it on to the great belt of arid steppes. But Ciscaucasia shares the features of the Caucasus as a whole in many respects, and when Russian geographers still distinguished Russia from her possessions, they used to reckon that Russia proper ended at the Manych and that beyond this river Asia began. We shall see later that this traditional division is not without some value.

'The Caucasus as a whole', we have said; but there is no question of unity here. The Caucasus is not a unit either by relief, climate, vegetation, population, or mode of life, but is universally recognised as having four divisions, viz. Ciscaucasia, the Caucasus Mountains, Transcaucasia, and Soviet Armenia.

1. CISCAUCASIA

To the south of the Kalmuk steppes runs the Manych depression, which connects the Sea of Azov with the Caspian. On the west the drainage is towards the Don, feeding the western Manych. This river issues from the long narrow sheet of Lake Manych, 62 miles by 5 or 6, and thus descends from 85 ft. above sea level to little more than 3. On the other side of this slight water-parting the eastern Manych is much smaller and is scarcely more than a string of little salt or brackish pools, the last of which is 50 miles from the Caspian.

The country through which these streams flow is dry, sandy steppe of little value, since the water of the two Manych rivers is not drinkable. Between the rivers there are recognisable signs that the eastern

Manych was once a branch of the western. These take the form of lakes and remnants of watercourses with varying amounts of water in them, all of which join up in time of flood. Hence, a project has long been cherished of reviving the connexion which existed between the rivers in the Pontian (end of the Miocene) and thus to unite the two seas by a canal along the valleys. This immense task, which will save the Caspian from its isolation, is half completed and, if the scheme for turning the headwaters of the Ob into the Aral Sea is carried out, will provide a waterway from Siberia to the Black Sea. Part of the scheme for constructing the Manychsk Canal is the leading of water from the Kuban by the Nevinnomysk Canal and the River Egorlik into the Manychsk depression. The watershed between the Caspian and Black Seas is 85 ft. above the level of the former. The total length of the Manychsk Canal will be 364 miles. The water will be used for irrigation as well as for navigation. Perhaps it may be possible to develop stock-rearing on these steppes, since in spring they contain large pools of water fed by a subterranean water-table which is swollen temporarily by the melting snow.

This depression, which was formerly occupied by the sea, marks the northern boundary of Ciscaucasia mainly by its man-repellent poverty. The basement rocks of Ciscaucasia belong to the Russian platform and have been somewhat affected by the upfolding of the Caucasus. But the surface beds are not continuations of those of the great northern plain. The Miocene clay and sand formations have for the most part been covered over by more recent deposits, alluvial and æolian, which have been brought from the great mountain range through long ages of erosion. Ciscaucasia is in short the foreland of the Caucasus and has rightly been likened to the Alpine and Pyrenean forelands. In a way it is derived from the Caucasus and forms a supplement.

Twice during the Quaternary the area was uplifted and reduced to a peneplain. A last epeirogenic movement, which is so recent as to have been witnessed by man, caused the dissection of the second peneplain, the carving of new valleys (of which that of the Kalaus is 650 ft. deep), and the formation of terraces. Yet the general appearance of the country is that of a plain gently sloping up towards the mountains. Stavropol is quite 2000 ft. high, and the right bank of the Kalaus is lined by cliffs rising to 2200 ft. But the only noteworthy features of positive relief are laccolithic hills in the neighbourhood of Pyatigorsk, among which Bash Tau is 4600 ft. above sea level. But they are of less importance than a very modest anticlinal ridge 2300 ft. high which forms a buttress to the Elbrus (Elbkis) and dies away in the plain shortly before reaching the Kalaus and Manych. This humble swelling has been enough to turn in opposite directions the streams flowing on the one hand into the Sea of Azov and on the other into the western Caspian.

(a) *Western Ciscaucasia.* This is the basin of the Kuban. This river, rising at the foot of the Elbrus and 400 miles long, is well fed by melting snow and ice as also by autumn rains and consequently has a good volume, but is muddy. It has a delta, and has now made the former island of Taman into a peninsula. For the rest, the whole coast is low, flat, and fringed with haffs and spits. It is in course of being straightened, as the haffs gradually change into lagoons and are quickly silted up.

Behind this coast stretches a plain of fertile soil, a *chernoziom* which is as much as 6 ft. thick along the Kuban. The climate, however, is relatively humid. Stavropol gets 26·31 ins. of rain a year, and precipitation is evenly distributed, with a definite summer maximum and a comfortable winter minimum. The summers are hot with a mean temperature of more than 77° F. The winters, though cold, are not excessively severe. The mean January temperature at Temryuk is 29° F., at Tamanskaya 31° F., at Krasnodar 28° F., and at Stavropol 24° F.

These conditions are similar to, but more unfavourable than, those of southern Russia, and the natural vegetation is that of the steppe, except on the hills leading to the Caucasus, where poplars, willows, beeches, and oaks make their appearance. As may well be imagined, this type of country has attracted the Russians, for it is similar to their own. After several fruitless attempts which were foiled by the Mongol invasion and the resistance of the Tatars, success rewarded the efforts of the Cossacks of the Dnepr in the time of Catherine II. Gradually they advanced to the borders of the mountains, where villages of wooden houses stretch out today along the roads. Behind them swept veritable waves of migrants. The year 1872 alone saw 54,000 Russian settlers arrive, so that the present population of the Kuban district is almost entirely Russian and is distributed in colonies large in area as in population, but fairly far apart.

The *moujiks* have found good pasture here on the marly soil and in the valley bottoms which are liable to floods; and stock-rearing has been successful. The animals are cattle of the Circassian breed, ordinary Russian or fat-tailed Kalmuk sheep, and horses of the steppe breed. Herds of 10,000 head of cattle and more are not uncommon, and stock-rearing *sovkhozy* are flourishing.

But agriculture is more active still. There are many kitchen gardens, in which water melons, the ever-present cucumber, and various other vegetables grow well. Here and there the vine appears on a few of the hillsides, and the area covered by it increases from year to year. Tobacco and sunflowers are also cultivated. A short time ago beet

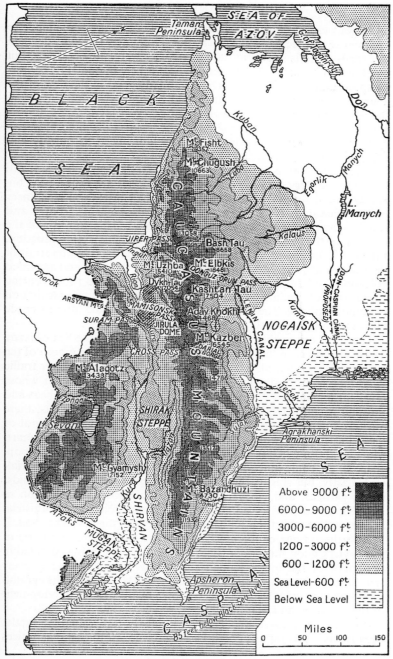

FIG. 45. THE CAUCASUS: PHYSICAL.

329

and soya were successfully introduced, and efforts are being made to acclimatise textile plants like *kenaf*. But the country is mainly devoted to cereals. Rice is grown in only a few very wet valley bottoms, but maize and millet cover large areas. Wheat is here in one of its favourite spots, and production, which was already great in the time of the Tsars, is steadily increasing. It should be noticed that even before the revolution the land was owned not by great landowners, but by well-to-do peasants who made much use of farm machinery; hence, mechanisation of the countryside has seldom been as quickly and completely successful as here.

Energetic farming is the basis of the country's wealth. There is still but little industry. Flour-mills and oil refineries are found near big *kolkhozy* and *sovkhozy*, fish canneries on the coast; farm machinery is manufactured at Armavir, and there are cement-, soap-, and tobacco-factories and tanneries at Krasnodar. This would end the list, but for the need to mention the promising start on oil production. Like the Kerch peninsula, from which it is separated by the strait of the same name, the Taman peninsula has iron deposits and also mud volcanoes and sulphur springs, which last are related to oil-bearing strata. But it is mainly inland to the south-east of Krasnodar that oil is found in plenty. The Maykop field is being worked, and its crude oil is sent by pipeline to the nearby port of Tuapse.

There are some other ports. Right in the north on the Sea of Azov Yeysk exports corn, tallow, and hides. Not far from the mouth of the Kuban is Temryuk, placed so as to avoid the delta. But their traffic is nothing compared with that of Novorossisk (pop. 95,000), whose excellent anchorage formerly saw an enormous trade in wheat and through which petrol is now exported. Apart from the ports, there are few towns. The old Cossack fort at Stavropol at the foot of the Caucasus has become an administrative centre and cattle mart. Maykop (pop. 67,000), Tikhoretsk, Kropotkin, and Armavir (pop. 102,000) are route junctions which have been more or less industrialised. Lastly, but chiefly, there is Krasnodar, which is situated amidst fields, gardens, and vineyards and has increased its population to 271,000, thanks to its administrative, commercial, and industrial activities. But whilst the Kuban district is only slightly urbanised, it is nevertheless one of the most prosperous and progressive parts of the Soviet Union. In former times the district of Adyghia, situated in the south of the lower Kuban valley, was considered very fever-stricken; but it has recently been made more healthy, and its agriculture is making great headway, as is shown by the present development of the tobacco and *kenaf* plantations.

(*b*) *Eastern Ciscaucasia*. This is decidedly less valuable; firstly, because its soil is far less good. Passing from west to east one notices

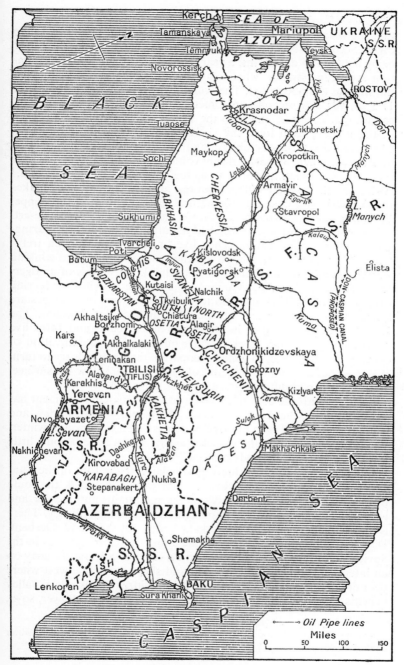

FIG. 46. THE CAUCASUS: DIVISIONS AND TOWNS.

331

that the Black Earth is succeeded by arid sand and finally by saline earth. Secondly, because it is too dry. Not that the rainfall is low' being between 18 and 20 ins. a year, but because there is no precipitation except in summer, when evaporation is intense. Consequently, the streams are poorly fed. The Kuma, which has a mean volume of 17·3 cu. yds. per second and sometimes falls as low as 0·13 cu. yd., cannot reach the sea, and even the Terek, which should be a replica of the Kuban, soon loses the vigour derived from the mountains. More than 300 yds. wide on issuing from the Caucasus, it is only 65 at Kizlyar, where it has a mean volume of only 442 cu. yds. per second and may fall in winter to as low as 130 cu. yds. per second.[1] As a result the country suffers from real aridity. The east wind makes the sky dark with dust, and the natural scenery is that of the steppe, becoming poorer and poorer eastwards until it becomes almost desert.

These steppes and deserts which lie mainly in the north form grazing-grounds for Nogay Tatars. They live 'in *kibitki* of wooden trellis work covered over with felt, or else they shelter in dark and stinking warrens, riddled with tuberculosis like the slum-dwellers of an over-crowded suburb' (Y. M. Goblet). They make a living by rearing camels and ewes. They have no towns, and the very few villages are former Cossack posts and are mainly inhabited by Russians. The Russians who have settled in the valleys of the Kuma and Terek live mainly by fishing and stock-rearing, but also by the cultivation of cereals and vegetables, to which occupation these nomads try to turn. Water is found even in sandy areas from 3 to 6 ft. below the surface, and the parts without it seem capable of irrigation.[2]

Farther south the country is less arid, and Russian settlement has advanced along the rivers, especially the Terek. Wheat, barley, and fruit grow well, and even the vine, if care is taken to bury it in winter. The prosperity of former Cossack *stanitsy*, which have become little towns like Kizlyar, depends on wine.

But conditions improve more particularly at the foot of the Caucasus. Right in the east Derbent (= the gate) commands the route through the Caspian Gate between the mountains and the sea and is a little seaport with an important fish-canning industry. There is much fishing near Makhashkala (pop. 106,000) and Derbent. Dagestan supplies one-quarter of the annual catch of herrings in the Soviet Union. In the neighbourhood Persian agriculturalists carry on an intensive form of tilth with skill and success. Farther west where the rainfall is greater (32 ins.) the Ordzhonikidze (Vladikavkaz) valley benefits also from a fertile soil and has fine crops of sunflower, soya,

[1] Private information from M. Pardé.
[2] There is much talk too of irrigating part of the Nogaisk steppe with water from the Terek.

A Caucasian village beneath the slopes of Mount Kazbek

The River Terek at Ordzhonikidze

The Georgian Military Highway at the Darial Gorge

kenaf, cotton, and fruit. Besides, the town, which was the spring-board for the conquest, is the starting-point of two carriage roads that cross the Caucasus by Cross Pass at the headwaters of the Terek and by Mamison Pass where the Ardon, a feeder of the Terek, has its source. Derbent has various industries and is a little port. Lastly, important mineral resources have been discovered in the local rocks.

The thermal springs of the laccolithic district have long been known. Today more than ever numbers of patients, who are also attracted by the beauty of the views over the mountains, are treated at Esentonki, Kislovodsk (pop. 51,000), and especially at Pyatigorsk (pop. 63,000). Similarly, the silver-lead deposits at Alagir have been known for a long time, but nowadays they are being worked more intensely than before. Not far away zinc and lead mines at Saadon have given rise to a *kombinat*. But above all, in the neighbourhood of the thermal springs at Goryachevodsk a magnificent oil-field has been discovered at Grozny, which began to be worked shortly before 1914 and is after the Baku and Emba districts the most productive in the Union. It is connected by pipeline with Makhashkala on the Caspian on the one hand and on the other with Rostov-on-Don and *via* Maykop with Tuapse. Grozny (pop. 226,000) has large oil refineries, and probably this will lead to industrialisation. Other oil-fields, a good deal smaller, however, have been found between Derbent and Makhashkala.

In short, Ciscaucasia is densely settled by Russians, has fine agricultural and industrial prospects, and derives real importance from the fact emphasised by the part played by Ordzhonikidze, that it commands the routes across the great mountain range which overlooks it.

2. THE CAUCASUS MOUNTAINS

The Caucasus Mountains are 785 miles long, between 60 and 140 miles wide, and cover an area of 55,000 square miles. Like the Alps they seem to have been upfolded at the beginning of the Miocene. Partly eroded and reduced to a peneplain, they were uplifted again in the Pliocene and denuded once more by a rejuvenated erosion. Furthermore, epeirogenic movements have not yet ended, as is shown by frequent earthquakes which sometimes cause catastrophic falls of rock and ice.

The geology of the Caucasus is very varied. Against a crystalline axial zone running from west-north-west to east-south-east and outcropping in the western half of the range between Fisht and the Kazbek lean the Palæozoic and Secondary rocks of the two slopes and even Tertiary deposits on the outside. On the other hand, there occurred at the end of the Tertiary great volcanic eruptions which have left many traces on the slopes of Cross Pass and more generally in the strip between the Elbrus (Elbkis) and Kasbek. These are andesite cones like those of the two peaks, enormous lava-flows cut into escarpments with sharp ridges, cratered peaks, and rocky plateaus containing peaceful lakes.

To make up for this, the structure of the range seems fairly simple. Diagrammatically speaking, an enormous fold has been thrust southwards, has collided with two deeply buried ancient crystalline domes, Kutaisi and Jirula, and has uplifted them with the strength of the thrust. Their resistance has complicated the orography of the southern slopes, in which the Jurassic, Cretaceous, and Miocene beds are much folded and dislocated and on which several layers of sediment have been observed near the road to Georgia. The northern slopes are simpler. There the central belt is separated by longitudinal valleys, monoclinal limestone ranges dipping gently down to Ciscaucasia, but facing south in a majestic escarpment. This, however, cannot be compared with the one which overlooks Transcaucasia. The general asymmetry of the Caucasus is one of its most striking characteristics.

Naturally, this enormous range has undergone since the Pliocene periods of intense glaciation, which was more or less contemporary with that of the Alps. Some glaciers came down to 3000 and even 1200 ft. above sea level and were 50 to 60 miles long. Yet, at any rate outside the central range glaciation seems to have been less intense and less copious than in the Alps. Its traces have been more easily effaced by a fluvial erosion which is now more violent. There are few or no glacial lakes, for they have been silted up; few or no hanging valleys, for the steep slopes have been worn away; and very few typical U-shaped valleys or rock-dams. Contrary to what was believed up to 1868 the Caucasus still has real glaciers; and, whilst they are now distinctly on the decline, their total area is estimated at 776 square miles, and, including some that are mere cirques, they number about 1400.

Of course, the characteristics of the range are not identical throughout. Besides the fact that the rocks vary from place to place, that the folding has not been equally vigorous from the Black Sea to the Caspian, that glacial erosion has acted unevenly in different places, that, in short, the relief is not uniform, there are climatic differences between the northern and southern slopes and even greater differences from one sea coast to the other. Whilst the west has a good rainfall, the east is fairly dry, and this is reflected by the vegetation. In consequence of all this, three divisions of the range are to be recognised: the western, central, and eastern.

(a) *The Western Caucasus.* This runs from the Sea of Azov to the

Elbrus (Elbkis) range, a distance of 250 miles. The ground rises fairly slowly at first, but from the pyramid-like Fisht (9400 ft.) the peaks mount to 9800 and even 13,000 ft., and few of the passes are lower than 6600 or, in the crystalline belt, less than 9800 ft. This central ridge is 'a rampart that has scarcely been breached' (R. Blanchard). Of course the heavy rainfall makes for longer glaciers in the north than in the south because of the shorter slope (from $2\frac{1}{2}$ to $3\frac{1}{2}$ miles); but the topography which they have shaped and which has persisted better here than elsewhere is just what greatly hinders approach to the passes. Furthermore, the crossing of the 'Black Mountains'—the calcareous ranges on the northern slopes—is difficult, for the streams, like the Belaya or the upper Kuban, have sawn narrow gorges which are all the more impenetrable because the damp Pontic climate has engendered an exuberant vegetation of extraordinarily dense forests of oak and beech.

In the sector there is a whole series of little compartments which are almost enclosed, and no valley has succeeded in making itself a main focus of communications. The southern slopes have favoured erosion, but, though there are a number of deep longitudinal valleys, these are separated from each other by ridges difficult to climb and do not reach the sea except by transverse cuts through which it is hard to pass. Besides, owing to the southern aspect, the proximity of a warm sea, and the influence of the mountain ranges on which there is enormous precipitation, the forests are of even greater luxuriance than on the northern slopes and are almost impenetrable. Even along the very narrow coast-strip the forest, the torrents, and the relief hamper communications. Yet the warmth of the climate has lined the coast from Novorossisk to Sochi with popular holiday and health resorts.

(b) *The Central Caucasus.* This sector stretches for a distance of 125 miles from the Elbrus to the Kasbek range. Here the crystalline axis opens out and the zone of folding is most intense. Here, too, more than elsewhere denudation has laid bare the ancient rocks and vulcanism has left its traces. For all these reasons the relief is complex. Instead of one great ridge-line there are clearly two running nearly parallel to each other.

The more northerly has been broken into distinct hill masses by erosion guided probably by transverse down-folds. The Elbrus (19,000 ft.), Koshtan Tau (17,000 ft.), Dykh Tau (16,900 ft.), and the Kasbek (16,500 ft.) are in line along this lofty ridge. The southern ridge is more continuous, but on the average not so high. Uzhba is 15,400 ft. above the sea, Tetmuld 16,500 ft., Juga 16,700 ft., and Aday Kokh 14,400 ft. All the same, this ridge forms the water-parting.

Owing to the recent character of the erosion, these peaks, which rise up over veritable abysses,[1] naturally have immense *névés* and large glaciers. Between Jiper Pass and the Kasbek range there are 700 square miles of glacier. A score of them have areas of more than 7 square miles each, and the Bezinghi glacier is over 11 miles long and has an area of more than 11 square miles. The longest glaciers are generally on the northern slopes, since these are gentler than the southern; and those on the southern slopes are shorter, but reach farther down owing to the steepness of the gradient and the lower snowline. Some fine plateau glaciers also occupy the shoulders of the Elbrus and Kasbek ranges. It may be gathered from all this that the two ridge-lines of the central Caucasus present magnificent and finely carved scenes of glacial topography.

The northern slopes are much the same here as on the west. Again the same flat-topped hills tilt gently northwards to form large plateaus. The streams flow down on parallel courses, widening their valleys into broad vales in the zone of soft shales, but enclosing themselves in real gorges as they pass through hard limestone. Owing to the lower rainfall, however, the vegetation is not so dense as in the western Caucasus. Forest holds its place only on well-watered slopes, but gives way elsewhere to more or less scanty grass, especially in the valleys.

The southern slopes, which are much more complex owing to the obstacle placed in the way of the orogenic thrust by the Georgian domes, consist of several schistous or calcareous anticlinal ranges separated by deep longitudinal valleys in the synclines. The most remarkable are those of the Rion and Ingur Rivers. The many obstacles which erosion must overcome in working its way upstream from Transcaucasia explains why these valleys are very difficult of access, among others those of Upper Svanetia and Dadian Svanetia. As a rule, the surging luxuriance of the vegetation, which is due to precipitation heavier than in the north, does not facilitate travel.

Hence, the central Caucasus is crossed with difficulty. Between Donguz Orun (10,500 ft.) and Mamison Pass, a distance equal to that between Mont Blanc and the St. Gothard, there is no pass lower than 9800 ft., and they all involve crossing over glaciers. In fact, there are only two really practicable passes. First, there is Mamison Pass (9000 ft.) which joins the valleys of the Ardon and Rion and carries the military road to Osetia. Then a little farther east is Cross Pass. The military road to Georgia (or Grusia) from the Terek valley passes through the Darial Gorge and then climbs the highest ridge of 7800 ft., at this pass, coming down to Tiflis, which it thus connects with Ordzhonikidze (see the photograph facing page 333). This road was

---

[1] The vertical interval between the summit of the Elbrus and the bottom of the Badsan valley is more than 13,000 ft.

not completed till 1861. Before it was made, the crossing of the pass
was extremely difficult. The Russians discovered this when they
crossed the pass for the first time in 1769, and the laborious and
dangerous character of the ascent to and descent from the summit
even about 1835 is strikingly described in Lermontov's novel *A Hero
of our own Times*. Furthermore, these passes have up to the present
been of far more military than economic importance. Trade routes
and paths of migration have alike avoided them, and the central
Caucasus has been the refuge of many peoples. 'In spite of the passes
it is a real barrier' (R. Blanchard).

(*c*) *The Eastern Caucasus*. This begins at Darial Gorge, but does
not assume its true characteristics until beyond the Alps of Khevsuria. These mountains, in which the crystalline rocks of the axis
disappear, are formed of soft shales mingled with volcanic rocks.
Erosion has dissected them, cutting valleys here and widening others
there, and carving passes. By all appearances, it is here that a real
Trans-Caucasian railway route will one day pass across the mountains.

But farther east the character of the range changes. It assumes the
appearance of a plateau, and may therefore be considered possibly
to be an old mountain mass which has been peneplained and recently
uplifted. This hypothesis is readily acceptable in view of the fact that
the huge pebbly uplands of Dagestan are an immense limestone
plateau formed of long-radius folds, but have been denuded and
reduced to a condition of gentle undulation. These eastern mountains
have been regarded as a kind of flattened Jura, duller and drier than
the French range. Some recently formed deep narrow valleys are
in contrast with the general uniformity of the surface, a few points
of which rise, however, to 13,000 ft. Similarly, on the slopes, and
especially those on the north, long canyons are seen grooving the
limestone masses, whilst the tributary valleys have scarcely begun
to be formed.

In this sector communication is not hindered by the vegetation.
As the weather becomes drier and drier towards the east, the flora is
definitely xerophilous. There are a few pinewoods and birch or hornbeam groves on the northern slopes; but nearly everywhere else there
is a mountain pasture with Mediterranean species, spiky grass, and
thorn bushes. For all that, crossing the range is scarcely easier. Few
of the passes are lower than 10,000 ft., and Akh Bulag Pass (9300 ft.)
is not entirely free of snow in July.

Beyond Dagestan the mountain mass grows narrower without
being lower (Bazardzhuzi, 14,700 ft.), and the axis is there accompanied by only a few little parallel chains. This 'Caspian Range' has
no glaciers, but is buried under screes. Intense weathering prevails
owing to the dryness of the climate. There are no trees, but only arid

steppes reminiscent of the mountains in Chinese Turkistan. 'The Caucasus begins in Europe and ends in Asia' (R. Blanchard).

The Caucasus Mountains have often been compared with the Pyrenees because of their asymmetry and steep southern slopes, their lofty, deeply trenched eastern mass, their central ice-capped barrier bristling with high peaks, and their western division which gradually narrows and loses height, but gets more and more rain as it goes towards the sea. As in the Pyrenees difficulties of communication break up the country into a series of little communities, and the consequent isolation due to the relief explains the fact that the Caucasus region forms a veritable human patchwork. This isolation has resulted in a long-dated insecurity which is reflected in the form of dwelling and has made its conquest so difficult. Lastly, like the Pyrenees it is an almost impassable barrier, which has forced most migrating nations to go round the ends; and yet it does not separate peoples, for nearly all those found on one slope are represented on the other.

Today the population is very unevenly distributed. In the western Caucasus few good harbours are to be found on the coast strip, but there are some agricultural villages and a few seaside resorts, like Sochi; but as far as human life is concerned, the area is connected with Ciscaucasia or Transcaucasia rather than the mountain range. The interior is nearly empty. A few Abkhazes still live on the southern slopes, but most of them fled away from the Russian conquest; and one can travel dozens of miles without seeing a village. The same is true of the northern slopes, which were deserted eighty years ago by the Cherkesses and are now inhabited by only 20,000 or 30,000 Tatars who are scattered about in little isolated communities. The borders of western Ciscaucasia, which are peopled by Russian settlers, are the only part that is more densely populated.

Owing to its altitude the central Caucasus is also sparsely populated. In its high valleys, which used to be places of refuge, exist communities, like the Svanes, which are backward and have a low standard of living. The zone of important passes is scarcely better endowed, and only the broad, open valleys on the northern slopes are more hospitable, though they are dry. Muslim hillmen and Cossacks live in Kabarda. The Alps of Khevsuria are sparsely peopled. In Dagestan the valleys alone are habitable, and the population is scattered in a number of little villages. Here, indeed, the density is almost great enough to give the impression of over-population.

Finally, the Caspian range, which is Asiatic in both human and physical aspects, is inhabited by Persians, whose infrequent villages are situated higher than any others in the Caucasus. One of them is at an elevation of 8200 ft. On the whole, although the density of population has tended to increase since the advent of Russian-imposed order, it is very low on account of the great exodus from the western districts. There are only a few people to the square mile—four in a very few places, but usually not nearly so many.

This does not mean that the Caucasus is without natural resources. The exploitation of its forests has scarcely begun, and it has some splendid timber, especially in the west, where the high rainfall causes vegetable growth to be gigantic. Even in the centre the forests are very fine. Dagestan alone is almost unwooded. Beech, hornbeam, lime, ash, Russian oak, maple, Norway pine, and various other kinds of pine and fir, not to mention the undergrowth which is extraordinarily luxuriant in the west, represent a real fortune. The treeline rises towards the east and may be as high as 6000 or 8000 ft. on the northern slopes and 8500 ft. on the southern.[1] Park land also covers large areas: 'the sub-alpine zone is distinguished by its pastures with long grass, and the alpine zone which occurs from 7200 to about 10,000 ft. has only short grass; but, thanks mainly to the abundance of meadow-grass and *phleum*, both zones are able to feed a good many animals, and this is all the truer because as a rule they have an adequate rainfall.'

Horse-breeding is for this reason of some importance in Abkhasia and Dagestan, cattle-rearing promises well in the centre and west, and, finally, sheep-farming is the main pastoral occupation in Dagestan, sheep being numerous in many other districts. Only it is a pity that the wool is not of better quality.

Agriculture is particularly important in the foothill country on the northern slopes of the western Caucasus. Here is the green belt between the steppe and the mountains, where the streams and the luxuriant vegetation enraptured writers like Pushkin and Lermontov, maize, wheat, and vegetables are grown, and there are orchards with apple and pear trees. And in many other districts, for instance in the upper valleys or vales in Dagestan, there are fruit-trees and fields of cereals and vegetables. Just as stock-rearing *sovkhozy* and *kolkhozy* have been formed, so an effort is being made to develop agriculture either by irrigation, as in Kabarda, by growing hay to provide better food for the animals, or by introducing *kenaf* cultivation in some favourable valleys. Hunting, of course, yields good returns either in pelts or meat; and numbers of hillmen go in pursuit of the bear, lynx, wild cat, wild boar, roebuck, maral stag, mountain goat, chamois, blackcock, and partridge.

There are a few industries too. Dagestan, which has more people than its agriculture can support, works up wool, leather, and metals, and its native craftsmen produce articles of an unquestionably

[1] These are more or less the limits of permanent tree growth.

artistic quality in the form of weapons, saddles, gold and silver work, and braid. Besides this, there are sawmills, mainly in the Black Mountains in the north-west, and cheese is made in Osetia. This kind of production is encouraged by the Soviet Government, which also inspires diligent search after mineral deposits. In spite of a persistent legend, silver, lead, and copper, which has long been mined, exist only in very small quantities; but, though the graphite which has recently been discovered seems unworkable, the northern slopes of the main range near Nalchik contain molybdenum, tungsten, wolfram, and tin, as well as coal in the Karachay territory. North Dagestan yields mercury and gold, and marble quarries have been opened in Osetia. Lastly, though big waterfalls are rare in the Caucasus, the exploitation of the mountains for hydro-electricity has begun mainly in the eastern sector in Chechenia, but also, among other places, at Stalinir, a little town with a population of 20,000 and the capital of southern Osetia. All this development calls for the construction of a grid, the beginnings of which are appearing here and there. Until conditions are much changed, however, the electric power will mainly serve the neighbouring plains, and the Caucasus will chiefly supply current.

It can also be said that, in spite of the sparse population in the mountains, they are to some extent at least a source of manpower for the plains. Too poor to live at home, a good number of the hill folk look for work in the lowlands. Thus, the half-starved Svanes hire themselves out in summer to the Tatars who dwell in the broad, open valleys on the northern slopes or to the Russians on the borders of Ciscaucasia. Hence, too, many emigrants from Dagestan become workers in Georgian towns and settle there. Others prefer to move down with their flocks into the plains of the lower Kura in winter; but this is only a temporary migration and, strictly speaking, is *transhumance*. In this way the mountains tend to link their life with that of the plains around, with that of rough, but fertile Ciscaucasia and even more with that of Transcaucasia, which is by nature far the richest of the Caucasian lands.

3. TRANSCAUCASIA

The Caucasus is a real climatic barrier; hence, Transcaucasia has, as we have seen, a definitely sub-tropical climate which is quite different from that of Russia. But it does not present the same appearance throughout. On the whole, it seems to be a syncline between the upfolds of the Caucasus and those of Armenia, and its low altitude has been accentuated, in the east at any rate, by great subsidence. But the syncline fills up in the centre and is as if cut in two. The movement caused by the orogenic thrust which built up the Caucasus during the

Pliocene came up against the domes of Kutaisi and Jirula and was deflected southwards; thus, a sort of isthmus of high ground was formed running from north to south and connecting the Caucasus with the Armenian heights. In this way the western depression, or Colchis, was separated from the eastern part of the syncline comprising the valleys of the Shirvan and Talysh. Between them is a region of synclinal domes, which is Georgia.

(a) *Colchis.* This corresponds broadly to the valleys of the Ingur, Rion, and Chorok. As it opens widely towards the west and is influenced by a very wet climate which moderates the temperature ranges, it has an exceptionally vigorous vegetation related by its species to central and western Europe rather than the Mediterranean, but of equatorial luxuriance. The forest contains trees of astonishing size and its undergrowth is wonderfully thick.

This cloak of vegetation does not, however, prevent erosion from being active, and the streams are excessively muddy there. Hence, as soon as the Caucasus is out of sight, the coast assumes a low, muddy appearance, is fringed with an immense line of spits broken only by the deltas of the Rion and Chorok, and is very uninviting with its lagoons and marshes across which a bora blows violently. Behind this is a plain of very recent formation, large areas of which have been swampy up to not long ago and in which the streams are raised on their own sediment to flow between banks of alluvium. For reasons of health the population shuns these low areas and prefers the hillsides and upper valleys, where the density approaches 27 to the square mile. The heart of the country is almost empty, and one sees in it only a few lazy, fever-stricken Mingrelians, whose wretched wooden huts 'perched on four stilts for protection from water and wild animals' (Blanchard) resemble dwellings in wet equatorial forests.

(b) *Georgia.* Farther east the relief stands up strongly. To the south of Batum the Karch Kal Mountains (11,800 ft.), which were returned to Turkey in 1921, are paralleled by the volcanic mountains of Arsyan (9800 ft.). This range is part of the watershed between the Black Sea and Caspian and above its thick forests at a height of about 7400 ft. is dotted with *yaila* which are inhabited by shepherds in summer. After a very appreciable lowering of the ridge the line of heights rises again in the Meskitski, or Mesques, Hills which end by forming a buttress to the Kirula dome. This watershed, which the Trans-Caspian Railway crosses in a long tunnel under Suram Pass (3200 ft.), has sometimes been called, rather incorrectly, 'the plateau of Suram'. It is an orographic as well as a climatic and vegetational boundary.

On going down from Suram Pass or on issuing from the Borzhomi gorges which have been cut by the upper Kura, one enters a country which consists of bosses and wide valleys connected by defiles and whose broken topography is very different from the plain of Colchis. There is also a difference in the appearance of the vegetation. The annual rainfall, which has decreased to 25 ins. at Abbas Tuman near Borzhomi and to 19 ins. at Tiflis, does not permit the growth of luxuriant forests, and, besides, the soil which is full of loose pebbles is very permeable. Hence, there prevails over these expanses a cheerless, yellow-brownish steppe rather like the country in western Ciscaucasia. But it is at any rate often cultivated, and wherever it can be irrigated, its crops are very fine. Consequently, the damper areas are preferred by the population, that is, the river banks and the piedmont strips. On the very first slopes of the Caucasus there again appear forests of fir, spruce, and chestnut with an undergrowth comprising a number of plants of Colchis, namely, cherry-bay, holly, ruscus, Pontic rhododendron, Caucasian wild cherry, and Colchis ivy. At the edge of the woods strings of agricultural villages occur at intervals under incredibly thick-foliaged giant walnut and plane trees, and here and there appear old towns.

(c) *The Valleys of the Shirvan and Talysh.* Eastern Transcaucasia begins a little to the east of the meridian of Tiflis. It is a great plain of subsidence covered over with alluvial soil and is mainly the work of the Kura and its tributary the Araks, or Araxes, whose immense alluvial fan has pushed it northwards, forcing it to flow round in a great bend, so that it reaches the main stream only just before it enters the Caspian. Their united waters have built a delta which forms a salient in a very regular coastline.

This plain is often called Shirvan, but, in fact, Shirvan is the central portion and is by far the largest and most typical part. It is much drier even than Georgia with a mean annual rainfall of 10 ins. at Kirovabad, 9·2 at Baku, and 9 on the lower Araxes, and its appearance is that of a barren steppe. Its slightly clayey light-chestnut soil supports *kargans* (*Salsola verrucosa*), wormwood, and adespogus. The great Shirak steppe between the Kura and Alazan, being a little better watered owing to its more broken relief, is an exception in having a few copses of pistachio-trees (*Pistacia muta*) and on its black earth soil good winter grazing in places. The valleys of the Kura and Araxes have good and relatively well-watered soils. But the delta is waste. On its *solontsy* soil the prevailing vegetation is that of a very poor wormwood steppe which is soon burnt up by the broiling summer, when the mean July temperatures range from 80° F. to 82° F. There, too, only the valleys are cultivated.

Farther south the Mugan steppe is equally marked by drought, having a mean rainfall of 9·2 ins., and its soils are more or less saline.

Apart from the boar-infested reed-brakes which characterise the parts flooded by the shifting of the course of the Araxes, the vegetation is composed of foxtail grass, with artemisia, thorny caper-bush, tamarisk, and various salsolaceæ. This explains why Shirvan is almost uninhabited outside the valleys where there are plantations of willows and poplars. Apart from Caspian fishermen, the whole district and more especially its eastern portion is sparsely peopled by Tatars who spend the winter there with their sheep and camels and return to the mountains in the summer, not without having pretty well plundered the permanent inhabitants.

Fortunately, the plain is much more favourable on its northern and southern borders. In the north the foothills, which have a relatively high rainfall, support forests of oak, beech, chestnut, hornbeam, and yew, and the plain below can be irrigated. Hence, Kakhetia is a fertile area between Alazan and the Caucasus, with populous villages, and as far as the neighbourhood of Shirak the ridges are covered with woods or grass. Farther east at the foot of the Caspian range, the districts of Nukha and Shemakha are inhabited by hardworking Tatars who are good farmers and skilful workmen. In the south the district of Kirovabad is cultivated by settled Tatars who take advantage of the alluvial fans at the foot of the Armenian Hills and of facilities for irrigation; and a moderately numerous population is crowded into the verdant area. Farther east the Talysh valley is almost a replica of Colchis. Heavy rain (27 ins. a year) which falls on the mountains and hills, a mild winter, and a very hot summer give it splendid forests of ironwood, oak, and hornbeam, which are covered with countless climbing plants and haunted by hosts of birds and insects, not to mention the boars, panthers, and tigers which seek shelter in the thickets on their fringes. But at the present day these forests have greatly shrunk before man's advance, and in many places they have been replaced by fields, gardens, and dwellings.

In point of fact, man's influence is effective in Transcaucasia. It is certainly no new thing and has been resumed of late years with renewed vigour. The country is worth while. In spite of its defects, which are not all irremediable, it has valuable resources. No great stress should be laid on fishing, which, however, is of real importance, if not in the Black Sea, at least in the Caspian and on the lower Kura. In the spawning season sterlet, salmon, and sturgeon enter the river from the sea and are caught for their caviar. On the other hand, the variety and importance of the agricultural production must be emphasised, for it cannot but increase owing to the rapid draining of Colchis, an immense task which was completed at the end of the war. On the other hand, irrigation works are being multiplied in Georgia and Shirvan. The dam at Minguichaur on the lower Kura is nearly 200 ft. high, will contain an artificial lake with a water capacity of 17 million cu. yds., and will enable nearly 4000 square miles of steppe to be irrigated. Even now rice covers huge areas especially in the east in Azerbaidzhan, where the Plain of Lenkoran (Talysh) is the main centre of production, but also in the districts of Kutais and Baku. Maize is cultivated on the Black Sea coast, on the heights around Colchis, in the open valleys in Georgia, at the foot of the eastern Caucasus, and in the Talysh valley. Wheat is making headway in Kakhetia, Georgia, and even more in the fertile valleys of the Rion and Kura. The vine grows to some extent everywhere in well-sheltered valleys, particularly in Georgia; but, except in Kakhetia, the wine is generally poor and is usually made into brandy.

Transcaucasia will probably become 'another Florida'; indeed, oranges, citrons, as well as olives are cultivated, especially in Abkhasia and Georgia, and the Soviet Government is increasing the number of fruit farms. This by no means precludes the production of apples and pears in the higher valleys, which are cooler and wetter, or that of peaches, apricots, and cherries in Colchis. The tea plant is now cultivated in the east on the better watered slopes of Azerbaidzhan, where a *sovkhoz* has been established for the purpose. But the Batum district with its mild, wet climate remains the chief producer. It gives a yearly production of more than 2 million lbs. of excellent tea and expects to do even better. The production of vegetables is carried on not only around the towns, but also around the villages at the foot of the Caucasus and Armenian hills and in well-watered valleys. Tomatoes, melons, cucumbers, peas, and lettuce flourish.

Industrial crops are not neglected. Though saffron, madder, and indigo are no longer important and sugar cane is only a curiosity, tobacco is cultivated on a large scale alongside tea above Batum. In Georgia and Abkhasia China-grass covers thousands of acres which were marshy until recently, but are now improved. Its success is as nothing, however, compared with that of cotton, which covers hundreds of thousands of acres in Colchis as well as Georgia, Shirvan, and the Talysh valley. Whilst the area occupied by the crop is ever being increased, the quality of the produce, which was poor for a long time, is improving owing to the growing use of Egyptian varieties.

Stock-rearing holds a place in the life of the country not only because the hill folk of the Caucasus and Armenia move down to the plains in winter, especially in the eastern sector, but also because Transcaucasia itself possesses a large number of beasts. It has more than 1,500,000 sheep, mainly on the steppes of Shirvan, Mugan, Shirak, and even in Georgia, and efforts are being made to improve the wool. There are also more than a million horned cattle, among which are a good number of buffaloes in the damp areas in Colchis and the Talysh valley. Though the meat is not yet much used, the production of milk is the object of growing attention and, in spite of the continued introduction of farm machinery, the animals render yeoman service by working in the fields. Horse-breeding is far less important. On the other hand, bee-keeping in Georgia and in the Dagestan piedmont must be mentioned, as must also be the more important sericulture, which is widespread in the districts of Kirovabad, Baku, and Kakhetia. Though it has been sacrificed to cotton growing in the districts of Shemakha and Nukha, sericulture finds Transcaucasia one of the most favourable parts of the Soviet Union.

On the whole, agricultural and pastoral production is very varied, the quality and diversity of soil and climate enabling temperate crops to be added to others that are almost tropical in character. In spite of the technical progress of recent years, production is far from having reached its peak and will be all the greater since it now has the 'considerable market of a large industrial town in process of development' (Gottmann).

Indeed, Transcaucasia is turning to industry as well as aiming decidedly at the cultivation of tropical crops. Natural resources are not wanting. Besides hot springs there are many quarries, thick beds of clay and a number of brickworks. There are also valuable forests, even outside the Caucasus, and, though their exploitation has scarcely begun, the instance of the Bzyb *kombinat* in Abkhasia shows the results that can be obtained. There is copper in Georgia near Tiflis, and magnificent deposits of manganese at Chiatura in Georgia, whose reserves are almost unequalled in the whole world. Besides, motive power is not wanting. On the northern and southern borders there is potential hydro-electricity, and there is coal at Kutaisi (Tkvibuli) and Tanabcheni (Tkvarcheli).

Lastly, and most important, there are splendid oil-fields. Right at the eastern end of the northern edge of the plain immediately adjacent to the Caucasus the Apsheron peninsula is one of the world's richest oil-producing districts. Mineral oil exists in enormous quantities in the anticlines of Oligocene sandstone and sand surmounted by younger limestones and clays. It is easily extracted, and from early times the natives of Surakhany worshipped the 'everlasting fires'. On the other hand, Transcaucasia has considerable supplies of labour, though it is by no means densely populated. There are normally more than 11·6 persons to the square mile, indeed more than 19 quite often, and sometimes as many as 23, on the perimeter of Colchis, in the favourable valleys of Georgia, and especially in the Kutais district and on the northern and southern fringes of Shirvan.

For a long time, however, almost the only industry in the country was the work of small craftsmen. This was developed particularly in the districts of Nukha and Shemakha, where silk goods were made, and in Georgia, where there were manufactures of wool, silk, various metal goods, and shoes, whilst Akhaltsikhe forged weapons, the province of Baku made carpets, and Mingrelia and Imeretia in the west wove linen. Here and there a few important factories existed in big towns like Baku or Tiflis. But large-scale modern industry scarcely existed outside Baku in 1914 or even 1928. The working of the oilfields had already transformed the district and from the beginning of the present century had made the Russian Empire into the world's second largest producer of oil. But technique, which was quite rudimentary up to the days of the Nobel brothers, remained in 1914 very far behind that of America.

Today a great effort is being made to improve communications. A railway is being built along the Black Sea coast to better the communications between Cis- and Transcaucasia. Many industries have appeared. In Georgia, for instance, the number of workers in large-scale industry has risen from 16,000 in 1927 to 55,000 in 1935. Coal is worked, and a number of waterfalls have been harnessed. The power station of the Rion and the one soon to be completed at Minguichaur are only the most remarkable among them. Though the timber industry at Tiflis and Borzhomi is still small, textile production is in full swing. Proof of this is found in the spinning and weaving of silk at Nukha and of cotton at Kirovabad (formerly Elisavetpol or Ganja), the large cotton-spinning mills at Baku, the great hosiery *kombinat* at Tiflis, and the weaving mills in many places in Georgia. Tanning flourishes in Tiflis and Baku, where more than half a million pairs of shoes are made in a year. Metallurgy is expanding at Chiatura and mechanical engineering at Baku and Tiflis. Paper-making is beginning in Tiflis, chemical industries in Tiflis and Baku, and cement factories, sugar and oil refineries, and canneries are spreading to some extent everywhere.

But the Baku oil industry still heads the list in importance. Reorganised even before 1928, it is ever spreading through the discovery of new wells, like those at Lok Batan. In this 'country of black gold' Balakhlany and Bibi Eibat are the main centres of extraction and Chernogorod the chief centre of refinery. Everywhere there are derricks, wells, pipe-stills, installations for cracking, tanks, pipe-lines, cranes, and engineering shops. Baku is in truth a 'black town', and its industrial area gives an unusual impression of power.

As a matter of fact, the district is exceptional in Transcaucasia. The surge of industry taking place in the country cannot be compared with that of the southern Ukraine, the Urals, and the Kuzbass. With exceptions the growth of towns is relatively slow. But they are growing all the same. Whilst Lenkoran on the Caspian is of little importance, the very moderate port of Poti on the Black Sea exports manganese. Batum (pop. 70,000), the terminus of the Trans-Caucasian Railway as well as of the pipe-line from Baku, exports oil, coal, fruit, tobacco, and silk, and is an intellectual centre, a seaside resort, and capital of Adzharistan. Kutaisi (pop. 114,000) in Colchis is an industrial centre, as is also Borzhomi farther east in Georgia. Mtzkhet, on the other hand, remains merely an old historic city. Shemakha and Nukha in

FIG. 47. THE APSHERON PENINSULA: OIL PRODUCTION.

eastern Transcaucasia must be mentioned and, above all, Kirovabad, whose industry has brought its population up to 98,000.

But only two towns have experienced a development really comparable with that of the big Russian cities. One is Tiflis (or Tbilisi), which is chiefly a nodal town on the routes north-to-south and east-to-west. Its situation is so favourable that after being taken and destroyed a score of times, it has always risen again. Right next to the Russian quarter is the native town which, however, is Armenian and Persian rather than Georgian. Until recently, with its mosques, bazaars, narrow streets, baths, and cookshops where fat-tailed sheep were roasted and wine drawn from goatskin bottles, it presented a mixture and medley which was quite Asiatic. Without wholly losing this character, it has been modernised and by the side of its old quarters, in whose buildings flourishes Oriental and Christian Georgian art, now spread large working-class blocks of flats and many factories. With its population of 635,000 the city, which moreover has become a scientific centre, stands as a symbol of the activity of the new Georgia.

Nevertheless, the first place is due to Baku. This ancient Persian city remains largely Asiatic and, beside the Russian town with its wide streets and low houses, there rises the Iranian city with its many mosques and medieval palaces. But its characteristic appearance is due to the vast size of the factory area. To the oil industry, which is greater and more predominant than ever, there has been added a number of others which have attracted a swarm of workers and have given rise here also to immense working-class quarters. Baku is still a Caspian port trading with Persia and Turkistan. It is a great intellectual centre; and, lastly, it is the capital of Soviet Azerbaidzhan, and its 901,000 inhabitants make it by far the leading town in Transcaucasia and the fourth largest city in the Soviet Union.[1]

Hence, in spite of its defects, Transcaucasia is a prosperous and busy country. So at any rate it appears to one coming from the austere solitudes of the Caucasus as also to one who enters it from the rough Armenian mountains.

4. SOVIET ARMENIA

On passing through Borzhomi to the upper valley of the Kura one comes to a steep slope which forms the borders of Armenia. It is sometimes called the Little Caucasus, a name which stresses its mountainous character, but is most inappropriate, since, except in the east, the hills are a mere 'frontage hiding the Armenian plateau' (Blanchard). They comprise a number of very narrow ranges, namely, the Trialethian and Somkhetian Hills and the Shak Dagh. The Karabagh Hills in the east are the only ones which have any real breadth. But these hills, which are geologically very varied (limestones, marbles, serpentine, ancient eruptive rocks), are all very high. The Karabagh range rises to 8200 ft., Shak Dagh, which is crossed by the Semionovka Pass at a height of 7000 ft., culminates at 7700 ft., and farther west the altitudes vary between 9000 and 13,000. Right in the east, on the other hand, the Talysh Hills, which rise beyond the salient in the northern frontier of Persia and reach a height of 8500 ft., seem to be the advanced guard of the Elburz Mountains in Persia.

Behind this frontage extends the tableland of Armenia with its normally gentle, dull topography. Some parts, however, have undergone uplifting, others subsidence; and vulcanism is one of the

---

[1] It should be noted that the town had a population of only 13,000 in 1860. 'Its growth', says J. Gottmann, 'may be compared with that of Los Angeles.'

essential features of the landscape. In many places crumbling basaltic hills may be seen: here there are andesitic necks, there columnar rock partly eroded away. The Alagotz Hills (13,300 ft.), an enormous shield-shaped mass with a central boss and formed of dislocated Oligocene lavas, is 'a Cantal one hundred miles in circumference, strewn with secondary cones, and grooved by enormous gullies' (Blanchard). In contrast with the mountains which rise up above the tableland there are indeed basins which have been accentuated by subsidence and partially filled with lava. Today these form high plains (that of Akhalkalaki is 7200 ft. above the sea) adorned in some places with lakes. The most remarkable, Lake Sevan, is a fine instance of a lake formed by a volcanic dam. It has an area of 545 square miles.

Naturally, the climate of these highlands is harsh owing as much to drought as to altitude. Except at the western end near Lazistan, where the rainfall and vegetation types are Pontic, the northern edge has very little rain and instead of forest has steppe vegetation. The forest 'island' of Karabagh and the Talysh Hills are the only parts really well wooded and have expanses of hornbeam, oak, beech, and ironwood, with luxuriant undergrowth. The mountain rim allows the interior to have very little rain. The mean annual precipitation at Leninakan is 15 ins., at Yerevan 12·6, and at Novo Bayazet near Lake Sevan 17·8. This fact, together with the altitude (Yerevan being 3300 and Akhalkalaki 7200 ft. above the sea), explains the severity of the temperature. Novo Bayazet, like Akhalkalaki, has a mean January temperature of 20° F. and 126 days on which frost occurs, on 62 of which there is no thaw. Yerevan has experienced temperatures of −31° F. and 104° F. The effects of this uncomfortably continental climate are aggravated by the fairly general permeability of the soil. Whilst some streams like the Araxes are well fed by springs, the majority are small in volume; and besides they are few in number. The vegetation is characterised by the relative absence of woodland and the predominance of feather-grass steppe. The volcanic hills, which are better watered and may have their underlying rock in a permanently frozen condition, support considerably better hill-pastures.

The Armenian tableland is therefore a rough, poor country whose appearance spreads an infinite melancholy. It is mainly grazing-ground over which the flocks of nomadic Kurds and Tatars wander in summer. Its soil, however, is excellent owing to the decomposition of the volcanic elements. Wheat, rye, and barley grow well here and there in the less dry places, but as a general rule cultivation takes shelter in the hollows or in the bottoms of valleys like that of the Araxes. There irrigation permits the cultivation of wheat, maize, rice, tobacco, and above all of cotton around the villages which are built

S.U.—M*

of grey clay and nestle among the foliage of orchards, willows, and poplars. The cultivation of cotton is no Russian innovation here, for it was already being carried on near Yerevan when they took the town in 1827. The Soviet Government has planned to use the water of Lake Sevan to irrigate some 32,000 acres. Already more than 17,000 acres have been reclaimed for cotton by digging ditches for irrigation. Vines too are making headway, as is fruit-growing which yields crops 'worthy of Noah' (Blanchard) around Yerevan. Lastly, stock-rearing is an important occupation not only on the highlands, but also in the valleys. Sheep on the tableland, horned cattle in the valleys, and horses in the Karabagh district are a real form of wealth, and bee-keeping, like sericulture, occupies an important place in the minds of the peasants. Of course, a great effort is being made to modernise agriculture and stock-rearing. *Sovkhozy* are initiating the countryfolk into the secrets of scientific agriculture, in particular of cotton and dairying.

The Armenian economic system is still based on agriculture. Yet the industrial activity of the country is far from negligible. The Armenian craftsman produces gold- and silversmith's work, pottery, textiles, and jewellery which until recently found a market throughout the Russian Empire and which have lost none of their reputation. But large-scale industry has begun here as elsewhere. In 1936 it employed 16,800 workers, and several large hydro-electric plants had been built. In Nakhichevan there is salt, marble, lime, and brick clay. This little republic has opened quarries and makes bricks and cement. The northern edge of Armenia seems to be rich in minerals. The Alaverdy district has rich copper-mines which have given rise to big foundries. Farther east the district of Dashkezan has iron deposits and a metallurgical establishment. There are chemical industries at Alaverdy, Kirovakan, and Yerevan; woodwork at Alaverdy and Yerevan; tanning at Yerevan; textiles at Leninakan, where cotton goods are manufactured, at Stepanakert in the Karabagh district, where silk goods are made, and at Yerevan, where ready-made clothes are produced. Tobacco is prepared at Yerevan, and, finally, the food industry is represented by sugar refinery and meat canning at Leninakan and Yerevan. Although the largest Armenian industry by far is the mining of copper and the associated foundries, and though this makes the Alaverdy district hum with work, there are only two towns of real importance, Leninakan and Yerevan.

Leninakan, which began as a Cossack post at an altitude of 5000 ft. on the road to Kars, developed as a market for agricultural produce and later as a junction of the railway lines to Kars and Yerevan. But the recently formed industries have more than doubled its population since 1926 and given a population of 103,000 to this paradoxical plateau town which is the most Armenian of all Armenian cities. Half-Persian in appearance and nestling in the verdure of a large, deep, well-irrigated valley in which rice, cotton, hemp, castor oil, water melons, and the vine flourish, Yerevan has also been transformed by industry and contains a population of more than 385,000. A centre of learning and Armenian culture, it is the capital of the republic of Armenia, and its well ordered, regular development is a pretty fair symbol of the progress of the whole country, which is barren and rough to the eye, but is nevertheless not without some value and endeavours to make the best of its resources. The city has certainly not reached its peak, for its rubber works were to have been greatly enlarged by the third five-year plan, and an extensive cotton mill was under construction when the war broke out. The republic has a population density of 15 persons to the square mile. This figure, which is more than moderate for a country of bleak uplands, is perhaps significant.

CONCLUSION

Thus our journey ends on the borders of Turkey and Persia, leaving us with an overwhelming impression of size, for the Soviet Union is the only state which spreads continuously over two continents. There is the further impression of an unbelievable variety of resources. In fact, no state other than the Soviet Union can show us Arctic ice-wastes and burning deserts, tundras and almost tropical forests, polar dwarf birches and tea plants, reindeer and camels. The British Empire alone could equal and even surpass the Union in the variety of its climate, vegetation-types, and produce; but the elements which constitute it are scattered over the four quarters of the globe. The Soviet Union is the most compact and most coherent block imaginable.

The only case at all comparable would be the United States. Though the Soviet Union goes much farther north than the American Union, it gets little advantage from its northern parts. Its 'useful area' is scarcely larger, and it does not look out, as America does, on permanently ice-free oceans. Anyhow, it can directly rival the great American republic in the wonderful variety and abundance of its resources. Thirty years ago one would certainly not have dreamed of any such comparison. And what a change there has been too in productive power compared with that of the old Russian Empire.

Owing to historical developments, the isolation with which geographical factors had threatened the state had become a painful reality. Cut off from Europe by the Tatar invasion, the country had properly speaking no Middle Ages, a fact which has had strangely important consequences; and it remained in a sense outside the course of world history, certainly outside the history of Europe. 'The universal education of the human race was unable to affect it' (Massis). Even the conversion of the Russian people to Christianity could not bring them into Christendom or associate them with its enterprises. On the contrary the schism of Photius and the use of the Slavonic liturgy kept it 'outside the great unifying movement which

352

formulated the idea of catholicism and made it in a sense a stranger to the new destinies of mankind' (*ibid.*). Later, the reforms of Peter the Great, which cut off the upper classes from the masses, were not without dangerous social and moral effects. And in spite of certain partial but very brilliant successes, they could not in so short a time place Russia on a level of intellectual and economic equality with central and western Europe. This was only to be expected. But the successors of the imperial genius hardly made up the leeway during the two hundred years that followed his death, and in spite of considerable progress, the Russian Empire in 1914 was still as backward in general education as in economics, sociology, and politics.

And now forty years later it can boast of being in many respects in the van of progress. It is not within our province to study political and social changes and still less to pass judgment on their value. Geography must not venture on such ground. Nor shall we try to decide how far it is true that the Soviet Union is already emerging from its Socialist phase to enter one that is more definitely Communist. But it is impossible to refrain from pointing out the extraordinary metamorphosis which is in progress and has already made considerable headway towards turning this weak and backward country into one of the most powerful in the world, one of the most advanced so far as boldness of technique in the successful launching of artificial Earth satellites and fullness of economic achievement are concerned, and undoubtedly the foremost in respect of its novel and at present unique method of organising labour.

This wonderful transformation was certainly not accomplished without tribulation. The Soviet Union passed through terrible trials and experienced very bitter sufferings. Its material privations are well known, but they were perhaps not the worst. Whether the Union is under a system of State Socialism or State Capitalism, the fact is that the masters of the country were forced, in order to establish their ideal, to organise one of the most oppressive totalitarian régimes the world has ever known. So, at any rate, it appeared to the eyes of many people of the West, people who were nevertheless progressive and were determined enemies of the power of money. It is needless to recall the interference of the State in all spheres of life and business, or to repeat the part played by the police during long years. We know, too, that a terrible want of regard for human life has prevailed and that this has deadened many consciences. 'When wood is chopped, splinters fly,' Lenin was always saying. This Russian proverb is the equivalent of our saying the 'one cannot make omelets without breaking eggs'. But in 1960 it is clear that having paid the price the Soviet Union has overcome the obstacles standing in its way and is certainly taking full advantage of its magnificent natural potentialities.

Let us consider, in fact, its position in world production of various agricultural and industrial commodities. It takes first place in wheat (40 per cent. of world production), rye (50 per cent.), oats (33 per cent.), barley (19 per cent.), potatoes (33 per cent.), sugar (8 per cent.), flax (80 per cent.), hemp (40 per cent.), manganese (40 per cent.), horses, and timber; second place in sheep, platinum (40 per cent.), mineral oil (10 per cent.), gold, cotton (16 per cent.), iron ore (14 per cent.), pig iron and steel (17 per cent.), wool (10 per cent.), coal (22 per cent.), zinc, aluminium (10 per cent.), and phosphates; third place in mineral oil (10 per cent.); fifth place in copper and cement; and seventh place in lead, rayon, etc. 'In 1939 it was', writes P. George, 'the world's leading country in the manufacture of farm machinery, the second in that of industrial equipment and tractors and in the production of gold, the third in the production of electrical power, manufacture of phosphate manures, etc.' Its position is even better now.

As for the world's natural resources which have fallen to the share of the Soviet Union, these seem to comprise about 52 per cent. of the total reserves of iron, 35 per cent. of the mineral oil, 20 per cent. of the coal, 75 per cent. of the peat, 40 per cent. of the hydraulic power, 15 per cent. of the copper, 16 per cent. of the lead and nickel, 80 per cent. of the manganese, 95 per cent. of the platinum, 62 per cent. of the phosphates, not to mention gold, silver, or other rare metals. 'As far as natural resources are concerned', Stalin could say in 1931, 'we are safe.' In the presence of such progress and such potentialities the star of the United States is threatened with eclipse. Twenty years ago Americans boasted of having 38 per cent. of the world's coal, 70 per cent. of the mineral oil, 83 per cent. of the harnessed power, 54 per cent. of the copper, 40 per cent. of the lead, 33 per cent. of the iron ore, 75 per cent. of the maize, 25 per cent. of the wheat, 55 per cent. of the cotton, and 53 per cent. of the timber. Today these percentages have probably been considerably reduced or at any rate materially revised.

The Soviet Union is an agricultural colossus and an industrial giant too. Already it must be regarded as the world's second economic power. But its progress is only just beginning. The exploration of its territory and the exact inventory of its resources are still so far from complete that the list of pleasant surprises is probably not at an end. If the list continues to lengthen, the Union will very possibly one day take first place in the economic world, and this is all the more probable because it has in addition enormous supplies of man-power which continue to increase rapidly. Hence, there is little risk of a labour shortage. On the other hand, its financial power has grown to astonishing proportions. Owing to its increasing facilities for self-sufficiency and its enormous gold production, it has practically no further need of foreign loans, and there is no necessity to emphasise the freedom of movement conferred on the Union by this in regard to its rivals.

Consequently, the Soviet Union has held a high position in the world since 1939 through its vast area, wealth, population, and the number of people who speak Russian. Russian takes third place after Chinese and English among the world's languages. 'Russia is the power best adapted to assimilate Asiatics,' Joseph Chamberlain used to say. Nowadays we say 'The Soviet Union is an Asiatic power,' and the saying becomes more and more true, for, as H. Massis has said, 'Russia is returning to her source' more and more. This, moreover, is what Lenin wanted. 'Let us turn towards Asia,' he used to say; 'we shall overcome the West through the East.' And when he said this, the great revolutionary was departing less perhaps than one might think from the doctrine of Peter the Great, who one day declared: 'We shall need Europe for a few score years, after which we must turn our backs on her.' And there is no need to mention the deep interest the Soviet Union has shown in the affairs of Turkey, Persia, Afghanistan, central Asia, Mongolia, and China; and the influence it enjoys in those countries.

And what great weight it carried in European affairs too! In truth, the Soviet Union is neither Asiatic nor European, but, as has been rightly said, it is one-sixth of the world and Euro-Asiatic. More and more Soviet thinkers believe that the Union should be organised as such and should have a policy harmonising with this idea. Indeed, the Eurasian doctrine existed among the Slavophiles long before the revolution. 'It would be an advantage to Russia', Dostoyevski used to say at the end of his life, 'if she would forget Petersburg for a time and turn her soul towards the east. . . . If we would only devote our-selves to the organisation of our Asiatic territory, we should see a great national renaissance among us.' And this idea found growing belief among the exiles after 1917. 'Do not look upon yourself as sons of Europe', declared Prince Trubetskoy; 'she is not our mother. . . . Our path is clearly marked out towards the east. Russia has been wrong in failing to recognise her Oriental character and to allow her-self to be enticed by Western illusions.' It has become an article of faith in the Soviet Union; nor could it be otherwise. To try to remove all distinction between Russia and her possessions, to industrialise the Asiatic territories to the utmost, and systematically to people the great empty spaces of the east with Russians abolishes in fact as well as in theory the illusory and obsolete Ural-Manych frontier and makes a Eurasia of what was once the Russian Empire. The policy of the five-year plans has necessarily aimed at this grandiose result.

It is true that in 1939 many people—some anxiously, others with hostile joy—thought that the trial of war threatened to be fatal to the Soviet Union. 'The work of the new régime has too many sham sides,' they said; 'it represents a terrible waste of effort, gives statistical triumphs to the country rather than real strength, and is still very brittle.' The frightful conflict of the German War was, on the contrary, to persuade the most incredulous of the strength of the work achieved. Without underrating the great Anglo-American help from which the Soviet Union benefited, this gigantic economic power may be said to have found in its colossal supplies of men, raw materials, and factories the means of becoming a herculean military nation destined to play a leading part in the assembly of the United Nations; and this was another pledge of the eminent position that the Union was destined to hold after the war in Europe and in the world.

'Russia is a world in itself,' said the dying Lenin to his disciples; 'it will be your task to make that world use its full weight in the balance of power.' His successors understood this behest and have fulfilled it. Many Slavophil exiles, in spite of their dislike of the principles of Bolshevism, have finally rallied to the Soviet Government, we know, confident that the new régime would wipe out the shame of the defeats in 1904–5 and 1914–18 and would make Russia again into a first-class power. Their hopes have not been disappointed.

SOME SOVIET PLACE-NAMES THAT HAVE CHANGED

Alexandropol (now Leninakan)
Alexandrovsk, Fort (now Shevchenko)
Alma Ata (formerly Vyerny)
Alupka (formerly Livadia)
Artemovsk (formerly Bakhmut)
Ashkabad (formerly Poltaretsk)
Aulye Ata (now Dzhambul)
Ayaguz (formerly Sergiopol)

Bakhmut (now Artemovsk)
Barnosk (now Marks)
Berdyansk (now Osipenko)
Bobriki (now Stalinogorsk)

Chapayev (formerly Guryev)
Chkalov (formerly Orenburg)

Daugavpils (formerly Dvinsk)
Dmitrovsk (formerly Makeyevka and now so renamed)
Dneprodzherzhinsk (formerly Kamenskoye)
Dnepropetrovsk (formerly Ekaterinoslav)
Dorpat (now Tartu)
Dvinsk (now Daugavpils)
Dzhambul (formerly Aulye Ata)
Dzhushambe (now Stalinabad)

Ekaterinburg (now Sverdlovsk)
Ekaterinodar (now Krasnodar)
Ekaterinoslav (now Dnepropetrovsk)
Ekaterinstadt (later Baronsk, then Marxstadt, and now Marks)
Elisavetpol (now Kirovabad)

Elista (now Stepnoy)
Elizavetgrad (now Zinovievsk)
Engels (formerly Petrovsk)

Fergana (formerly Skobelov)
Frunze (formerly Pishpek)

Gorky (formerly Nidzhni Novgorod)
Guryev (now Chapayev)

Kabakovsk (formerly Nadedzhinsk)
Kalinin (formerly Tver)
Kaliningrad (formerly Koenigsberg)
Kalininsk (formerly Petrozavodsk)
Kamenskoye (now Dneprodzherzhinsk)
Karaklis (now Kirovakan)
Kaunas (formerly Kovno)
Kemerovo (formerly Shcheglovsk)
Khanskaya Stavka (now Urda)
Khibinogorsk (now Kirovsk)
Khojent (now Leninabad)
Kirov (formerly Vyatka)
Kirovabad (formerly Elisavetpol)
Kirovakan (formerly Karaklis)
Kirovo (first Elisavetgrad, then Zinovievsk, then Dzherdzhinski) and now
    Kirovo)
Kirovsk (formerly Khibinogorsk)
Klaypeda (formerly Memel)
Koenigsberg (now Kaliningrad)
Kolchughino (now Leninsk)
Kovno (now Kaunas)
Kozlov (now Michurinsk)
Krasnodar (formerly Ekaterinodar)
Krasnomeisk Gorod (formerly Sarepta; now Solodniki)
Kutaisi (formerly Tkvibuli)
Kuybyshev (formerly Samara)
Kuznetsk (now Stalinsk)
Kzyl Orda (formerly Perovsk)

Leninabad (formerly Khojent)
Leninakan (formerly Alexandropol)
Leningrad (formerly Petrograd)
Leninsk (formerly Kolchughino)
Libau (now Liepaya)
Liepaya (formerly Libau)
Livadia (now Alupka)
Lugansk (now Voroshilovgrad)

Makeyevka (changed to Dmitrovsk, but now renamed Makeyevka)
Makhachkala (formerly Petrovsk)
Mariupol (now Zhdanov)
Marks (first Ekaterinstact, then Baronsk, then Marxstadt, and now Marks)
Memel (now Klaypeda)
Michurinsk (formerly Kozlov)
Mitau (now Yelgava)
Molotov (formerly Perm; renamed Perm in 1957)

Nadedzhinsk (now Kabakorsk)
Nikolayev (now Vyernoleninsk)
Nikolsk (now Voroshilov)
Novonikolayevsk (now Novosibirsk)
Novosibirsk (formerly Novonikolayevsk)

Obdorsk (now Salekhard)
Ordzhonikidze (formerly Vladikavkaz)
Orenburg (now Chkalov)
Osipenko (formerly Berdyansk)

Perm (later Molotov; reverted to Perm in 1957)
Perovsk (now Kzyl Orda)
Petro-Alexandrovsk (now Turtkul)
Petrograd (now Leningrad)
Petrovsk (now Engels)
Petrovsk (now Makhachkala)
Petrozavodsk (now Kalininsk)
Pishpek (now Frunze)
Poltaretsk (now Ashkabad)
Predgornoye (formerly Riddersk)
Pushkin (formerly Tsarskoe Selo)

Reval (now Tallin)
Riddersk (now Predgornoye)

Salekhard (formerly Obdorsk)
Samara (now Kuybyshev)
Sarepta (later Krasnomeisk Gorod, and now Solodniki)
Shcheglovsk (now Kemerovo)
Shevchenko (formerly Fort Alexandrovsk)
Simbirsk (now Ulyanovsk)
Skobelov (now Fergana)
Solodniki (formerly Sarepta)
Stalinabad (formerly Dzhushambe)
Stalingrad (formerly Tsaritsyn)
Stalino (formerly Yuzovka)
Stalinogorsk (once Bobriki)
Stalinsk (formerly Kuznetsk)

Stepnoy (formerly Elista)
Sverdlovsk (formerly Ekaterinburg)
Syktyvkar (formerly Ust Sysolsk)

Tallin (formerly Reval)
Tanabcheni (formerly Tkvarcheli)
Tartu (formerly Dorpat)
Tkvarcheli (now Tanabcheni)
Tkvibuli (now Kutaisi)
Tsaritsyn (now Stalingrad)
Tsarskoe Selo (now Pushkin)
Turtkul (formerly Petro-Alexandrovsk)
Tver (now Kalinin)

Ulan Ude (formerly Verkne Udinsk)
Ulyanovsk (formerly Simbirsk)
Urda (Khanskaya Stavka)
Ust Sysolsk (now Syktyvkar)

Verkne Udinsk (now Ulan Ude)
Vilna (now Vilnyus)
Vilnyus (formerly Vilna)
Vladikavkaz (now Ordzhonikidze)
Voroshilov (formerly Nikolsk)
Voroshilovgrad (formerly Lugansk)
Vyatka (now Kirov)
Vyborg (formerly Viipuri)
Vyernileninsk (formerly Nikolayev)
Vyerny (now Alma Ata)

Yelgava (formerly Mitau)
Yuzovka (now Stalino)

Zhdanov (formerly Mariupol)
Zinovievsk (formerly Elizavetgrad and now Kirovo)

INDEX